T0215520

DIGITAL LOGIC DESIGN

This introductory textbook is a complete teaching tool for turning students into logic designers in one semester, beginning with basic gates and ending with the specification and implementation of simple microprocessors. It shows how to use rigorous mathematical language to accurately define models, specify functionality, describe designs, prove correctness, and analyze cost and delay.

Each chapter first describes new concepts and then gives extensive applications and examples of these new ideas. Assuming no prior knowledge of discrete mathematics, the authors introduce all the necessary background in propositional logic, asymptotics, graphs, hardware, and electronics.

Important features of the presentation are the following:

- All material is presented in full detail, with every claim proved.
- Algorithmic solutions are offered for tasks such as logical simulation, computation of propagation delay, and minimum clock period.
- Connections are drawn from the physical analog world to the digital abstraction.
- The language of graphs is used to describe formulas and circuits.
- Hundreds of examples and exercises enhance understanding.

The extensive Web site http://www.eng.tau.ac.il/~guy/Even-Medina/ includes teaching slides, links to Logisim and a DLX assembly simulator, and other supplements.

Guy Even is a professor in the School of Electrical Engineering at Tel Aviv University, Israel.

Moti Medina is a PhD student in the School of Electrical Engineering at Tel Aviv University, Israel.

DIGITAL LOGIC DESIGN

A Rigorous Approach

GUY EVEN
Tel Aviv University, Israel

MOTI MEDINA
Tel Aviv University, Israel

CAMBRIDGE
UNIVERSITY PRESS

CAMBRIDGE
UNIVERSITY PRESS

University Printing House, Cambridge CB2 8BS, United Kingdom

One Liberty Plaza, 20th Floor, New York, NY 10006, USA

477 Williamstown Road, Port Melbourne, VIC 3207, Australia

314-321, 3rd Floor, Plot 3, Splendor Forum, Jasola District Centre, New Delhi - 110025, India

79 Anson Road, #06-04/06, Singapore 079906

Cambridge University Press is part of the University of Cambridge.

It furthers the University's mission by disseminating knowledge in the pursuit of
education, learning and research at the highest international levels of excellence.

www.cambridge.org
Information on this title: www.cambridge.org/9781108708036

First published 2012
First paperback edition 2019

A catalogue record for this publication is available from the British Library

Library of Congress Cataloging in Publication data
Even, Guy.
Digital logic design : a rigorous approach / Guy Even, Moti Medina.
    pages   cm
Includes bibliographical references and index.
ISBN 978-1-107-02753-4
1. Logic design.   I. Medina, Moti, 1979–   II. Title.
TK7868.L6E94   201
621.39´5–dc23   2012015723

ISBN 978-1-107-02753-4 Hardback
ISBN 978-1-108-70803-6 Paperback

Additional resources for this publication at http://www.eng.tau.ac.il/~guy/Even-Medina/

Contents

PART III: SYNCHRONOUS CIRCUITS

Contents

List of Algorithms

Preface

This book is an introductory textbook on the design and analysis of digital logic circuits. It has been written after 15 years of teaching hardware design courses in the School of Electrical Engineering at Tel Aviv University. The main motivation for writing a new textbook was the desire to teach hardware design rigorously. By rigorously, we mean that mathematical language and exposition are used to define the model, to specify functionality, to describe designs, to prove correctness, and to analyze cost and delay. We believe that students who study formal courses such as algebra and calculus can cope well with a rigorous approach. Moreover, they are likely to benefit from this approach in many ways.

The book covers the material of an introductory course in digital logic design, including an introduction to discrete mathematics. It is self-contained; it begins with basic gates and ends with the specification and implementation of a simple microprocessor. The goal is to turn our students into logic designers within one semester.

The rest of this preface deals with the rationale, structure, and audience of the book. We conclude with a list of the book's highlights, some of which are new to a hardware design text.

HOW TO ACQUIRE INTUITION

It is not fashionable these days to emphasize mathematical rigor. Mathematical rigor is perceived as an alienating form that dries out the passion for learning and understanding. Common teaching tactics avoid rigor (i.e., the holy definition–theorem–proof) and resort to examples. Since intuition is what really matters (and we, of course, agree with that!), in the rare cases when one feels compelled to provide a proof, the following strategy is employed. First, intuition precedes the proof in an attempt to explain in advance what the proof does and why it actually works (is this part actually an apology for what is about to come?). Then, a long proof follows using partially defined terms. All we can say is that this strategy is in complete disregard of the statement "When you have to shoot, shoot. Don't talk" (as stated by Tuco in *The Good, the Bad, and the Ugly*).

Recall the great endeavor of nineteenth-century mathematicians to formalize the calculus of real functions. Weierstrass and others undertook the task of providing a formal abstraction of the presumably well-understood notions of real numbers, real functions, continuous functions, and so on. We still remember our surprise when Weierstrass's function was first described to us: continuous everywhere and differentiable nowhere. The lesson is clear: intuition is gradually acquired and must be based on solid fundamentals.

What does this have to do with digital design? The quest for intuition is confronted by the fact that it is hard to formulate precise statements about objects such as digital circuits. Our approach is to give students a solid, rigorous basis for their intuition. Of course, examples are easy to follow but might give students the false impression that they understand the topic. We have seen many brilliant students in engineering disciplines who find it hard to acquire intuition based only on examples. Such students can easily cope with a rigorous exposition in which delicate issues are not hidden or brushed aside.

LEARN FROM THE SUCCESS OF DATA STRUCTURES AND ALGORITHMS

We believe that successful teaching means that a student can implement the material from the course. After studying data structures, a student should be able to program search trees, sorting, and hashing. We believe that the same goal should be set for a logic design course. Unfortunately, most textbooks describe various circuits, and provide examples for why they work, but do not train engineers who can actually design digital circuits.

The goal of this book is to bring students to a level that will enable them to understand a specification of a combinational or synchronous circuit, to design it, to prove the correctness of their design, and to be able to analyze the efficiency of the design (i.e., delay and cost).

We do not restrict this goal to isolated circuits. We show how a system is built from different circuits working in concert. In fact, we present a simple microprocessor, the design of which combines multiple modules, including an arithmetic logic unit (with an adder, logical operators, and a comparator), a shifter, a file register (with the general-purpose registers), and main memory.

THE KNOWLEDGE HIGHWAY

Our goal is to turn our students into logic designers within one semester. To meet this goal, we follow a bottom-up approach that begins with the basics and ends with a simple microprocessor. We solidify the presentation by using mathematical notations and statements and by defining the abstraction precisely. The effort spent on a formal approach pays off simply because it enables us to teach more material, in more depth, and in a shorter time. It is not surprising that toward the end of the course, students will not only be able to design nontrivial modules but will also be able to identify errors in designs and suggest ways to correct these errors.

OUR TEACHERS

When writing this book, the first author and, by transitivity, the second author were mainly influenced by three people: Shimon Even, Ami Litman, and Wolfgang Paul.

It was Shimon Even who stated (1) never complain or be surprised by the students' lack of knowledge—just teach it! (2) digital design is the same art as algorithm design; the only difference is the model of computation; and (3) identify the methods and be systematic; in other words, turn digital design into a discipline.

It was Ami Litman who demanded (1) always verify that your abstraction makes sense; don't hesitate to refute the model by introducing absurd consequences; (2) introduce a design by a sequence of evolutionary modifications, starting with a simple straightforward yet costly design and ending with an evolved yet efficient design; each modification preserves functionality and hence the final design is correct—describe each modification as a general transformation that can be applied in a wide variety of settings; and (3) focus on large instances—optimization of small instances depends on the technology and is not likely to reveal insights.

Wolfgang Paul's rules are (1) formulate a precise specification and prove that the design satisfies the specification; (2) write the equations that describe the delay and cost—solving these equations asymptotically is nice, but from a practical point of view, it suffices to solve them numerically for the sizes one needs to actually design; and (3) keep in mind that the goal is to design a correct, well-understood system. Avoid fancy optimizations that eventually impede this goal. This rule applies both for teaching and for actual design.

OUR STUDENTS

Our students are electrical engineering undergraduate students in their second or third semester. The students lack background in discrete mathematics, and the first part of the book deals with filling this gap. This is considered the easy part of the course.

Following the logic design course, our students take courses on devices (both analog and digital). Students who choose the computer track also study computer organization and computer architecture and practice digital design in a lab with an FPGA platform. In this lab, they implement the simplified DLX microprocessor described in Part IV of the book. This implementation is from basic gates (e.g., no library modules, such as adders, are used). At the end of the lab, the students program a nontrivial program in assembly language and execute it on their design.

Apart from training the students in logic design, we also teach discrete methods that are used in data structures and algorithms. In particular, we focus on induction and recursion, trees and graphs, and recurrence equations.

STRUCTURE OF THE BOOK

The book consists of four parts: (I) "Preliminaries," (II) "Combinational Circuits," (III) "Synchronous Circuits," and (IV) "A Simplified DLX."

The first part of the book is a short introduction to discrete mathematics. We made an effort to include only topics in discrete math that are actually used in the other parts. This is considered the easy part of the course; however, it is essential for students who lack background in discrete mathematics. In addition, this part helps students get used to working with definitions, mathematical notation, and proofs.

The second part of the book is its heart. It focuses on Boolean functions and on methods for building circuits that compute Boolean functions. We begin by representation by Boolean formulas, for example, sums of products and products of sums. This establishes the connection between Boolean functions and propositional logic. We then define combinational gates and combinational circuits and define two quality measures: cost and propagation delay.

The study of combinational circuits begins with circuits that have a topology of a tree. At this point we introduce lower bounds on the number of gates and the propagation delay of a combinational circuit that implements a Boolean function such as the OR of n bits. Logical simulation is presented in an algorithmic fashion using topological ordering of a directed acyclic graph. The same approach is used for computing the propagation delay of a combinational circuit.

We proceed with a variety of combinational circuits (e.g., decoders, encoders, selectors, shifters, and adders). Designs are presented in a parametric fashion, where the parameter is the length of the input. Whenever possible, designs are recursive and proofs are by induction.

Chapter 10, in Part II, explains the digital abstraction. The purpose of this chapter is to build a bridge between the analog world and the digital world.

Synchronous circuits are studied in the third part of the book. We first introduce the clock signal and edge-triggered D-flip-flops. Only one type of flip-flop is discussed in detail. This discussion explains the different timing parameters of a flip-flop, including an explanation of why so many parameters are required. Other types of flip-flops are considered as finite state machines with two states and are implemented using a D-flip-flop and additional combinational logic. Synchronous circuits are viewed in two ways: (1) memory modules, such as registers, random access memory (RAM), and read-only memory (ROM) and (2) finite state machines, including their analysis and synthesis.

Algorithmic issues related to synchronous circuits include logical simulation and calculation of the minimum clock period. These algorithms are presented via reductions to combinational circuits.

Students who have studied the first three parts of the book should have a good idea of what computer-aided design tools for designing digital circuits do.

The last part of the book deals with the design of a simple microprocessor. Connections are made between the machine language, assembly, high-level programming, and the instruction set architecture (ISA). We present an implementation of the simple microprocessor using the modules from Parts II and III. The design methodology is to present the simplest microprocessor implementation that supports the ISA. We present an unpipelined multicycle microprocessor based on a simple datapath and a small finite state machine.

HOW TO USE THIS BOOK

This book is written as a textbook for an introductory course in digital design for undergraduate students in electrical engineering and computer science. The following material is considered advanced and may be omitted: Section 5.6*, "More on Unique Binary Representation;" Chapter 8, "Computer Stories: Big Endian versus Little Endian;" Section 9.6*, "Minimization Heuristics;" Chapter 10, "The Digital Abstraction;" and Sections 17.3*–17.5*. Advanced material as well as advanced questions and examples are marked with an asterisk.

When we teach this course, we spend roughly five weeks on Part I, five weeks on Part II, and five weeks on Parts III and IV. We suggest starting the course very rigorously and gradually relaxing rigor when repeating a proof technique that was used before.

Logic design, like swimming, cannot be taught without immersion. We therefore include homework assignments in which students practice logic design using a schematic entry tool and a logic simulator. We found the open source Logisim software both easy to use and powerful enough for our purposes.

We also use a DLX assembly simulator so that students can practice assembly programing of constructs in high-level programming (e.g., if-then-else statements, loops, arrays).

HIGHLIGHTS

Here we list the main highlights of the book:

1. *The book is self-contained.* We do not assume that students have any prior knowledge of discrete math, propositional logic, asymptotics, graphs, hardware, electronics, and so on.
2. *A complete teaching tool.* In each chapter, we tried to make a clear separation between (1) conceptual parts containing new materials, (2) applications and examples that are based on this new material, and (3) problems. There are many benefits to this approach for both the teacher and the student. One clear advantage is that the examples can be covered in greater detail during recitations.
3. *"Nothing is hidden."* We adhere to the rule that all the details are complete and every claim is proven.
4. *Methodology as a "ritual."* Each design is presented in four steps: specification, design, correctness proof, and analysis of delay and cost. The specification formally defines what a circuit should do. Without a formal specification, it is impossible to prove correctness. Most designs are described using recursion, and correctness is usually proved using

induction. Finally, analysis of cost and delay is carried out by formulating recurrence equations and solving them.

5. *The recursion–induction pair.* Instead of designing circuits for specific input lengths, we consider the task of designing circuits with a parameter n specifying the length of the inputs. For example, we consider addition of n-bit numbers, n:1-selectors, and so on. These designs are described recursively. The first advantage is that we present a precise and formal definition of the design for any input length. The second advantage is that we prove the correctness of the design for any input length. Naturally, the proof is carried out using induction.

6. *Modeling circuits as graphs.* We use the language of graphs to describe formulas and circuits. Boolean formulas are defined by parse trees. Circuits are defined using directed graphs. This approach enables us to present a clean and precise definition of propagation delay and minimum clock period using longest paths in a directed graph. With small effort, it is possible to extend this approach to the more elaborate setting of nonuniform delays between input and output ports of gates.

7. *Lower bounds.* We prove simple lower bounds on the cost and the delay of a combinational circuit that implements Boolean functions. The ability to formally state that a design is an optimal adder design is remarkably powerful. Our lower bounds are stated in terms of the number of inputs on which an output depends (i.e., the "cone" of an output). These lower bounds are easy to apply to all the Boolean functions that are discussed.

8. *Algorithmic approach.* Tasks such as logical simulation, computation of propagation delay, and minimum clock period are presented as algorithmic problems. Algorithms are presented for solving these problems, and the correctness of these algorithms is proven.

   For example, the algorithmic approach is used to teach timing analysis, as follows: we present an algorithm, prove its correctness, and run it on an example. In this fashion, the topic of timing analysis is described in a precise and concise fashion that does not require lengthy examples. One may ask, why not teach about timing analysis with different delays for different transitions (i.e., the time required for transition of the output from zero to one does not equal the time required for the transition from one to zero)? Indeed, this question pertains to the lasting argument about the usefulness of worst case analysis. We resort to worst case timing analysis simply because it is intractable to decide whether the output of a combinational circuit ever equals one (see Section 9.5).

9. *Relations to analog world.* In Chapters 10 and 17, we connect the physical analog world to the digital abstraction. Two physical phenomena are discussed in detail: noise and metastability. We show how noise is overcome by using different thresholds for inputs and outputs. We show how metastability is mitigated using the timing parameters of a flip-flop (i.e., setup time, hold time, contamination delay, and propagation delay). We explicitly mention issues that cannot be resolved within the digital abstraction (e.g., reset controller).

10. *Zero propagation delay as functional model.* In Chapter 18, on memory modules, we introduce the *zero delay model.* In the zero delay model, transitions of all signals are instantaneous. This means that the flip-flop's output at a certain cycle equals the value of the input sampled during the previous cycle. This simplified discrete timing model is used for specifying and simulating the functionality of circuits with flip-flops. The

advantage of this approach is that it decouples the issues of functionality and timing into two separate issues.

KARNAUGH MAPS

A quick comparison of this book with other books on logic design will reveal that we mention *Karnaugh maps* (Karnaugh, 1953) only very briefly in Section 9.6.6. There is a good reason for this brief mentioning.

Karnaugh maps are a technique for finding the minimum number of products in a sum-of-products representation of a Boolean function. The input to the technique of *Karnaugh maps* is the truth table of the Boolean function. Thus the input to this technique is exponential in the number of variables and therefore cannot be considered efficient. In addition, the maps are actually two-dimensional tables and are convenient to use for at most four variables. Experts, of course, are proud that they can use this technique also for five and even six variables! Given that the technique of *Karnaugh maps* has an exponential running time and is limited to few variables, we do not think it is an important issue in logic design. One should bear in mind that the difference between a reasonable representation and the best representation for a function over six variables is constant. Moreover, with such small functions, even exhaustive search makes sense if one is really interested in finding the "best" representation.

Teachers insisting on teaching heuristics for finding the minimum number of products in a sum-of-products representation of a Boolean function can teach the Quine–McCluskey heuristic (Quine, 1952, 1955; McCluskey, 1956) Our presentation of the Quine–McCluskey heuristic uses a layered graph over the implicants instead of a tabular approach. We hope that this choice favors notions over notation. Unfortunately, the full details of the heuristic require almost 10 pages. We therefore marked this section with an asterisk.

RECURRENCE EQUATIONS

We use recurrences to describe the cost and delay of circuits defined recursively. We do not introduce the "master theorem" for solving recurrences. The reason is that we find this theorem to be too general for the students at this stage (they do learn it later in the algorithms course). Instead, we resort to solving the specific recurrences we encounter later in the book.

REFERENCES

There are many books on discrete mathematics. Two discrete math books that also treat Boolean algebra and logic design are by McEliece et al. (1989) and Mattson (1993).

There are many books on logic design and computer structure. We were mainly influenced by the book of Müeller and Paul (1996) in the choice of combinational circuits and the description of the processor. We use the simplified timing diagrams from the notes of Litman (2003). These notes also helped with the description of the digital abstraction and flip-flops. The book by Ward and Halstead (1990) describes, among other things, the problem of metastability, arbitration, and the abstraction provided by an instruction set architecture. The book by Ercegovac et al. (1998) uses a hardware description language to design circuits. The book by Ercegovac and Lang (2003) deals with computer arithmetic.

Most textbooks do not introduce Boolean formulas via parse trees. In the book by Howson (1997), propositional logic is described by trees.

More material on finite automata (aka finite state machines) appears in the book by Hopcroft et al. (1979). The book by Savage (1997) starts with basic hardware and ends with advanced material in computability.

The DLX processor architecture was designed by Patterson and Hennessy (1994) as an educational architecture that demonstrates the principles of a RISC processor without the elaborate details of a commercial processor. Our simplified DLX architecture is based on it and on the simplified architecture designed in the RESA lab in Wolfgang Paul's group at the University of the Saarland. See also the book by Müeller and Paul (1996) for a concise description of the DLX architecture and its implementation.

BOOK HOME PAGE

The home page of the book is: http://www.eng.tau.ac.il/~guy/Even-Medina/. We plan to maintain this home page so that it contains the following:

- Slides that we use for teaching
- Errata and a simple form for reporting errors
- Links to simulators (logisim and a DLX assembly simulator)
- Supplementary material

Finally, we would like to thank the anonymous reviewers. Reports of mistakes (all of which are solely our fault) would be greatly appreciated.

The photo on the book cover is a closeup from a photo of Y/Surf/Struc* by Marc Fornes that we saw in the exhibition in Centre Pompidou, Paris. We thank Marc Fornes for sending us the photo and for the permission to use it.

Guy Even and Moti Medina
Tel Aviv, March 2012

PART I　PRELIMINARIES

CHAPTER 1

Sets and Functions

This chapter introduces two major notions: sets and functions. We are all familiar with real functions, for example, $f(x) = 2x + 1$ and $g(x) = \sin(x)$. Here the approach is somewhat different. The first difference is that we do not limit the discussion to the set of real numbers; instead, we consider arbitrary sets and are mostly interested in sets that contain only a finite number of elements. The second difference is that we do not define a "rule" for assigning a value for each x; instead, a function is simply a list of pairs (x, y), where y denotes the value of the function when the argument equals x. The definition of functions relies on the definitions of sets and relations over sets. That is why we need to define various operations over sets such as union, intersection, complement, and Cartesian product.

The focus of this book is Boolean functions. Boolean functions are a special family of functions. Their arguments and values are finite sequences of 0 and 1 (also called bits). In this chapter, we show how to represent a Boolean function by a truth table and multiplication tables. Other representations presented later in the book are Boolean formulas and combinational circuits.

1.1 SETS

A *set* is a collection of objects. When we deal with sets, we usually have a *universal set* that contains all the possible objects. In this section, we denote the universal set by U.

The universal set need not be fixed. For example, when we consider real numbers, the universal set is the set of real numbers. Similarly, when we consider natural numbers, the universal set is the set of natural numbers. The universal set need not be comprised only of abstract objects such as numbers. For example, when we consider people, the universal set is the set of all people.

One way to denote a set is by listing the objects that belong to the set and delimiting them by curly brackets. For example, suppose the universe is the set of integers, and consider the set $A = \{1, 5, 12\}$. Then 1 is in A, but 2 is not in A. An object that belongs to a set is called an *element*. We denote the fact that 1 is in A by $1 \in A$ and the fact that 2 is not in A by $2 \notin A$.

Definition 1.1 Consider two sets A and B.

1. We say that A is a *subset* of B if every element in A is also an element in B. We denote that A is a subset of B by $A \subseteq B$.
2. We say that A *equals* B if the two sets consist of exactly the same elements, formally, if $A \subseteq B$ and $B \subseteq A$. We denote that A and B are equal sets by $A = B$.
3. The *union* of A and B is the set C such that every element of C is an element of A or an element of B. We denote the union of A and B by $A \cup B$.
4. The *intersection* of A and B is the set C such that every element of C is an element of A and an element of B. We denote the intersection of A and B by $A \cap B$.
5. The *difference* A and B is the set C such that every element of C is an element of A and not an element of B. We denote the difference of A and B by $A \smallsetminus B$.

The *empty set* is a very important set (as important as the number zero).

Definition 1.2 The empty set is the set that does not contain any element. It is usually denoted by $\varnothing$.

Sets are often specified by a condition or a property. This means that we are interested in all the objects in the universal set that satisfy a certain property. Let P denote a property. We denote the set of all elements that satisfy property P as follows:

$$\{x \in U \mid x \text{ satisfies property } P\}.$$

The preceding notation should be read as follows: the set of all elements x in the universal set U such that x satisfies property P.

Every set we consider is a subset of the universal set. This enables us to define the complement of a set as follows.

Definition 1.3 The *complement* of a set A is the set $U \smallsetminus A$. We denote the complement set of A by $\bar{A}$.

Given a set A, we can consider the set of all its subsets.

Definition 1.4 The *power set* of a set A is the set of all the subsets of A. The power set of A is denoted by $P(A)$ or 2^A.

We can pair elements together to obtain ordered pairs.

Definition 1.5 Two objects (possibly equal) with an order (i.e., the first object and the second object) are called an *ordered pair*. We denote an ordered pair by (x, y). This notation means that x is the first object in the pair and y is the second object in the pair.

Consider two ordered pairs (x, y) and (x', y'). We say that $(x, y) = (x', y')$ if $x = x'$ and $y = y'$.

We usually refer to the first object in an ordered pair as the first *coordinate*. The second object is referred to as the second coordinate.

An important method to build large sets from smaller ones is by the *Cartesian product*.

Definition 1.6 The *Cartesian product* of the sets A and B is the set

$$A \times B \triangleq \{(a, b) \mid a \in A \text{ and } b \in B\}.$$

Every element in a Cartesian product is an ordered pair. Thus the Cartesian product $A \times B$ is simply the set of ordered pairs (a, b) such that the first coordinate is in A and the second coordinate is in B. The Cartesian product $A \times A$ is denoted by A^2.

The definition of ordered pairs is extended to tuples, as follows.

Definition 1.7 A k-tuple is a set of k objects with an order. This means that a k-tuple has k coordinates numbered $\{1, \ldots, k\}$. For each coordinate i, there is an object in the ith coordinate.

An ordered pair is a 2-tuple. A k-tuple is denoted by $(x_1, \ldots, x_k)$, where the element in the ith coordinate is x_i. Tuples are compared in each coordinate, thus $(x_1, \ldots, x_k) = (x_1', \ldots, x_k')$ if and only if $x_i = x_i'$ for every $i \in \{1, \ldots, n\}$.

We also extend the definition of Cartesian products to products of k sets, as follows.

Definition 1.8 The *Cartesian product* of the sets $A_1, A_2, \ldots A_k$ is the set

$$A_1 \times A_2 \times \cdots \times A_k \triangleq \{(a_1, \ldots, a_k) \mid a_i \in A_i \text{ for every } 1 \leq i \leq k\}.$$

The Cartesian product of k copies of A is denoted by A^k.

EXAMPLES

0^*. **Russell's paradox.** A formal axiomatic development of set theory is a branch of logic called *axiomatic set theory*. This branch developed in response to paradoxes in set theory. One of the most famous paradoxes was discovered by Bertrand Russell in 1901.

Suppose we do not restrict ourselves to a subset of a universal set. Consider the set Z defined by

$$Z \triangleq \{x \mid x \notin x\},$$

namely, an object x is in Z if and if only it does not contain itself as an element. *Russell's paradox* is obtained as follows. Is $Z \in Z$? If $Z \in Z$, then because every element $x \in Z$ satisfies $x \notin x$, we conclude that $Z \notin Z$—a contradiction. So we are left with the complementary option that $Z \notin Z$. But if $Z \notin Z$, then Z satisfies the only condition for being a member of Z. Thus $Z \in Z$—again, a contradiction.

1. Examples of sets: (i) $A \triangleq \{1, 2, 4, 8\}$, the universal set is the set of numbers; (ii) $B \triangleq \{\text{pencil, pen, eraser}\}$, the universal set is the set of "the things that we have in our pencil case."

2. Examples of subsets of $A \triangleq \{1, 2, 4, 8\}$ and $B \triangleq \{\text{pencil, pen, eraser}\}$: (i) $\{1, 2, 4, 8\} \subseteq A$; (ii) $\{1, 2, 8\} \subseteq A$; (iii) $\{1, 2, 4\} \subseteq A$; (iv) $\{1, 2\} \subseteq A$; (v) $\{1\} \subseteq A$; (vi) $\varnothing \subseteq A$; (vii) $\{\text{pen}\} \subseteq B$.

3. Examples of equal sets. Let $A \triangleq \{1, 2, 4, 8\}$ and $B \triangleq \{\text{pencil, pen, eraser}\}$: (i) order and repetitions do not affect the set, e.g., $\{1, 1, 1\} = \{1\}$ and $\{1, 2\} = \{2, 1\}$; (ii) $\{2, 4, 8, 1, 1, 2\} = A$; (iii) $\{1, 2, 44, 8\} \neq A$; (iv) $A \neq B$.

4. We claim that $\varnothing \subseteq X$ for every set X. By Item 1 in Definition 1.1, we need to prove that every element in $\varnothing$ is also in X. Because the empty set $\varnothing$ does not contain any element (see Definition 1.2), all the elements in $\varnothing$ are also in X, as required.

5. The empty set is denoted by $\varnothing$. The set $\{\varnothing\}$ contains a single element, which is the empty set. Therefore $\varnothing \in \{\varnothing\}$ but $\varnothing \neq \{\varnothing\}$. Because $\varnothing \subseteq X$ for all set X (see Example 4), $\varnothing \in \{\varnothing\}$ and $\varnothing \subseteq \{\varnothing\}$.

6. Examples of unions: (i) $\{1, 2, 4, 8\} \cup \{1, 2, 4\} = A$; (ii) $\{1, 2\} \cup \{4\} \neq A$; (iii) $A \cup \varnothing = A$; (iv) $A \cup B = \{1, 2, 4, 8, \text{pencil, pen, eraser}\}$.

7. Intersection of sets: (i) $\{1, 2, 4\} \cap A = \{1, 2, 4\}$; (ii) $\{8, 16, 32\} \cap A = \{8\}$; (iii) $\{16, 32\} \cap A = \varnothing$; (iv) $A \cap \varnothing = \varnothing$; (v) $A \cap B = \varnothing$; (vi) for every two sets X and Y, $X \cap Y \subseteq X$.

8. Suppose the universal set is the set of real numbers $\mathbb{R}$. We can define the following sets:

   (i) The set of integers $\mathbb{Z}$ is the set of all reals that are multiples of 1; that is,

   $$\mathbb{Z} \triangleq \{x \in \mathbb{R} \mid \text{x is a multiple of 1}\}$$
   $$= \{0, +1, -1, +2, -2, \ldots\}.$$

   (ii) The set of natural numbers $\mathbb{N}$ is the set of all nonnegative integers; that is,

   $$\mathbb{N} \triangleq \{x \in \mathbb{R} \mid x \in \mathbb{Z} \text{ and } x \geq 0\}$$
   $$= \{0, 1, 2, 3, \ldots\}.$$

   (iii) The set of positive natural numbers $\mathbb{N}^+$ is the set of all positive integers; that is,

   $$\mathbb{N}^+ \triangleq \{x \in \mathbb{R} \mid x \in \mathbb{Z} \text{ and } x > 0\}$$
   $$= \{1, 2, 3, \ldots\}.$$

   (iv) The set of positive real numbers is denoted by $\mathbb{R}^+$; that is,

   $$\mathbb{R}^+ \triangleq \{x \in \mathbb{R} \mid x > 0\}.$$

   (v) The set of nonnegative real numbers is denoted by $\mathbb{R}^{\geq}$; that is,

   $$\mathbb{R}^{\geq} \triangleq \{x \in \mathbb{R} \mid x \geq 0\}.$$

9. If $A \cap B = \varnothing$, then we say that A and B are *disjoint*. We say that the sets $A_1, \ldots, A_k$ are disjoint if $A_1 \cap \cdots \cap A_k = \varnothing$. We say that the sets $A_1, \ldots, A_k$ are *pairwise-disjoint* if, for every $i \neq j$, the sets A_i and A_j are disjoint.

10. Consider the three sets $\{1, 2\}$, $\{2, 3\}$, and $\{1, 3\}$. Their intersection is empty; therefore they are disjoint. However, the intersection of every pair of sets is nonempty; therefore they are not pairwise disjoint.

11. When A and B are disjoint, that is, $A \cap B = \varnothing$, we denote their union by $A \uplus B$: (i) $\{1, 2\} \uplus \{4, 8\} = A$; (ii) $\{1, 2\} \cup A = A$.

12. Difference of sets: (i) $\{1, 2\} \smallsetminus \{2, 4\} = \{1\}$; (ii) $A \smallsetminus \varnothing = A$; (iii) $A \smallsetminus A = \varnothing$; (iv) $A \smallsetminus B = A$.

13. Formal specification of union, intersection, and difference:

    (i) $A \cup B \triangleq \{x \in U \mid x \in A \text{ or } x \in B\}$
    (ii) $A \cap B \triangleq \{x \in U \mid x \in A \text{ and } x \in B\}$
    (iii) $A \smallsetminus B \triangleq \{x \in U \mid x \in A \text{ and } x \notin B\}$

14. We claim that $\bar{A} = \{x \in U \mid x \notin A\}$. Indeed, $x \in \bar{A}$ is shorthand for $x \in U \smallsetminus A$, where U is the universe. Hence $x \in \bar{A}$ if and only if $x \in U$ and $x \notin A$, as required.

15. **Contraposition.** In this example, we discuss a logical equivalence between two statements, called *contraposition*. A rigorous treatment of contraposition appears in Chapter 6. Consider the following two statements (regarding sets A and B):

    - $A \subseteq B$
    - $\bar{B} \subseteq \bar{A}$

    We show that these two statements are equivalent. Assume that $A \subseteq B$. By definition, this means that

    $$\forall x \in U : x \in A \Rightarrow x \in B. \qquad (1.1)$$

    Now we wish to show that $\bar{B} \subseteq \bar{A}$. For the sake of contradiction, assume that there exists an element x for which $x \in \bar{B}$ and $x \notin \bar{A}$. This means that $x \notin B$ and $x \in A$. But this contradicts Eq. 1.1. Hence $\bar{B} \subseteq \bar{A}$, as required.

    Assume that $\bar{B} \subseteq \bar{A}$. By the preceding proof, it follows that $\bar{\bar{A}} \subseteq \bar{\bar{B}}$. Note that $\bar{\bar{A}} = A$ and $\bar{\bar{B}} = B$. Hence $A \subseteq B$, as required.

    In its general form, contraposition states that the statement $P \Rightarrow Q$ is logically equivalent to the statement $\text{NOT}(Q) \Rightarrow \text{NOT}(P)$. The proof of this equivalence is similar to the preceding proof.

16. Operations on sets defined in Definition 1.1 can be depicted using *Venn diagrams*. The idea is to depict each set as a region defined by a closed curve in the plane. For example, a set can be depicted by a disk. Elements in the set are represented by points in the disk, and elements not in the set are represented by points outside the disk. The intersections between regions partition the planes into *cells*, where each cell represents an intersection of sets and complements of sets. In Figure 1.1, we depict the union, intersection, difference, and complement of two sets A and B that are subsets of a universal set U.

17. We claim that $A \smallsetminus B = A \cap \bar{B}$. To prove this, we show containment in both directions. (i) We prove that $A \smallsetminus B \subseteq A \cap \bar{B}$. Let $x \in A \smallsetminus B$. By the definition of subtraction of sets, this means that $x \in A$ and $x \notin B$. By the definition of a complement set, $x \in \bar{B}$. By the definition of intersection, $x \in A \cap \bar{B}$, as required. (ii) We prove that $A \cap \bar{B} \subseteq A \smallsetminus B$. Let $x \in A \cap \bar{B}$. By the definition of intersection of sets, this means that $x \in A$ and $x \in \bar{B}$. By the definition a complement set, $x \in \bar{B}$ implies that $x \notin B$. By the definition of subtraction, $x \in A \smallsetminus B$, as required.

18. Let X denote a set with a finite number of elements. The size of a set X is the number of elements in X. The size of a set is also called its *cardinality*. The size of a set X is denoted by $|X|$: (i) $|A| = 4$; (ii) $|B| = 3$; (iii) $|A \cup B| = 7$; (iv) if X and Y are disjoint finite sets, then $|X \cup Y| = |X| + |Y|$.

19. The power set of $A = \{1, 2, 4, 8\}$ is the set of all subsets of A, namely,

    $$P(A) = \{\varnothing, \{1\}, \{2\}, \{4\}, \{8\},$$
    $$\{1, 2\}, \{1, 4\}, \{1, 8\}, \{2, 4\}, \{2, 8\}, \{4, 8\},$$
    $$\{1, 2, 4\}, \{1, 2, 8\}, \{2, 4, 8\}, \{1, 4, 8\},$$
    $$\{1, 2, 4, 8\}\}.$$

20. Every element of the power set $P(A)$ is a subset of A, and every subset of A is an element of $P(A)$.

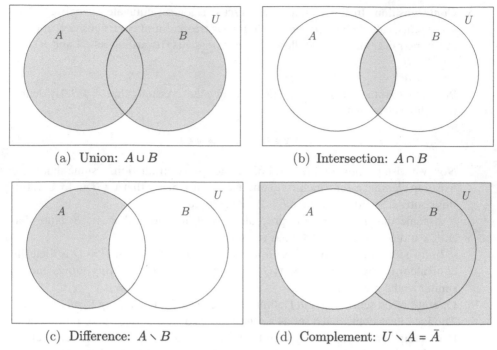

Figure 1.1. Venn diagrams over the sets A and B with respect to the universal set U.

21. Recall that for every set X, the empty set $\varnothing$ is a subset of X (see Example 4). It follows that $\varnothing \in P(X)$ for every set X. In particular, $\varnothing \in P(\varnothing)$.

22. How many subsets does the set A have? By counting the list in Example 19, we see that $|P(A)| = 16$. As we will see later in Problem 2.6, in general, $|P(A)| = 2^{|A|}$. This justifies the notation of the power set by 2^A.

23. Some examples with ordered pairs:

    (i) Consider the set of first names $P \triangleq \{Jacob, Moses, LittleRed, Frank\}$, and the set of last names $M \triangleq \{Jacob, RidingHood, Sinatra\}$. Then,

$$P \times M = \{(Jacob, Jacob), (Jacob, RidingHood), (Jacob, Sinatra),$$

$$(Moses, Jacob), (Moses, RidingHood), (Moses, Sinatra),$$

$$(LittleRed, Jacob), (LittleRed, RidingHood), (LittleRed, Sinatra),$$

$$(Frank, Jacob), (Frank, RidingHood), (Frank, Sinatra)\}.$$

   (ii) Equality of pairs is sensitive to order, namely,

$$(Jacob, RidingHood) \neq (RidingHood, Jacob).$$

   (iii) Obviously, $(Jacob, Jacob) = (Jacob, Jacob)$.

24. For every set X, $\varnothing \times X = \varnothing$.

25. For finite sets X and Y (regardless of their disjointness), $|X \times Y| = |X| \cdot |Y|$.

26. The Euclidean plane is the Cartesian product $\mathbb{R}^2$. Every point in the plane has an x-coordinate and a y-coordinate. Thus a point p is a pair (p_x, p_y). For example, the point $p = (1, 5)$ is the point whose x-coordinate equals 1 and whose y-coordinate equals 5.

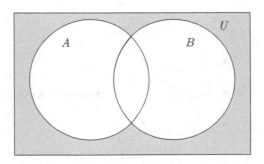

Figure 1.2. Venn diagram demonstrating the identity $U \smallsetminus (A \cup B) = \bar{A} \cap \bar{B}$.

27. A circle C of radius r centered at the origin is the set of ordered pairs defined by $C \triangleq \{(x, y) \mid x^2 + y^2 = r^2\}$.

28. The Cartesian product of n identical sets $\{0, 1\}$ is denoted by $\{0, 1\}^n$, namely,

$$\{0, 1\}^n = \overbrace{\{0, 1\} \times \{0, 1\} \times \cdots \times \{0, 1\}}^{n \text{ times}}.$$

Every element in $\{0, 1\}^n$ is an n-tuple $(b_1, \ldots, b_n)$, where $b_i \in \{0, 1\}$ for every $1 \le i \le n$. We refer to $b_i \in \{0, 1\}$ as a *bit* and to $(b_1, \ldots, b_n)$ as a *binary string*. We write a string without separating the bits by commas, for example, (i) 010 means $(0, 1, 0)$, (ii) $\{0, 1\}^2 = \{00, 01, 10, 11\}$, and (iii) $\{0, 1\}^3 = \{000, 001, 010, 011, 100, 101, 110, 111\}$.

29. De Morgan's law states that $U \smallsetminus (A \cup B) = \bar{A} \cap \bar{B}$. In Figure 1.2, a Venn diagram is used to depict this equality. A formal proof requires using propositional logic and is presented in Section 6.8.

1.2 RELATIONS AND FUNCTIONS

A set of ordered pairs is called a binary relation.

Definition 1.9 A subset $R \subseteq A \times B$ is called a *binary relation*.

A function is a binary relation with an additional property.

Definition 1.10 A binary relation $R \subseteq A \times B$ is a *function* if, for every $a \in A$, there exists a unique element $b \in B$ such that $(a, b) \in R$.

Figure 1.3 depicts a diagram of a binary relation $R \subseteq A \times B$. The sets A and B are depicted by the two oval shapes. The elements of these sets are depicted by solid circles. Pairs in the relation R are depicted by arcs joining the two elements in each pair. The relation depicted in Figure 1.3 is not a function because there are two distinct pairs in which the element $d \in A$ is the first element.

A function $R \subseteq A \times B$ is usually denoted by $R : A \to B$. The set A is called the *domain*, and the set B is called the *range*. Lowercase letters are usually used to denote functions, for example, $f : \mathbb{R} \to \mathbb{R}$ denotes a real function $f(x)$.

One can define new functions from old functions by using *composition*.

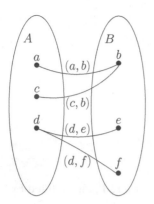

Figure 1.3. A diagram of a binary relation $R \subseteq A \times B$. The relation R equals the set $\{(a,b),(c,b),(d,e),(d,f)\}$.

Definition 1.11 Let $f : A \to B$ and $g : B \to C$ denote two functions. The *composed function* $g \circ f$ is the function $h : A \to C$ defined by $h(a) = g(f(a))$ for every $a \in A$.

Note that two functions can be composed only if the range of the first function is contained in the domain of the second function.

We can also define a function defined over a subset of a domain.

Lemma 1.1 *Let $f : A \to B$ denote a function, and let $A' \subseteq A$. The relation R defined by $R \overset{\Delta}{=} \{(a,b) \in A' \times B \mid f(a) = b\}$ is a function.*

PROOF: All we need to prove is that for every $a \in A'$, there exists a unique $b \in B$ such that (a,b) is in the relation. Indeed, $(a, f(a)) \in R$, and this is the only pair in R whose first coordinate equals a. Namely, if both (a,b) and (a,b') are in the relation, then $f(a) = b$ and $f(a) = b'$, implying that $b = b'$, as required. ∎

Lemma 1.1 justifies the following definition.

Definition 1.12 Let $f : A \to B$ denote a function, and let $A' \subseteq A$. The *restriction* of f to the domain A' is the function $f' : A' \to B$ defined by $f'(x) \overset{\Delta}{=} f(x)$ for every $x \in A'$.

We denote *strict containment*, that is, $A \subseteq B$ and $A \neq B$, by $A \subsetneq B$. Given a function $f : A \to B$, we may want to extend it to a function $g : A' \to B'$, where $A \subsetneq A'$. This means that the relation f is a subset of the relation g.

Definition 1.13 A function g is an extension of a function f if f is a restriction of g.

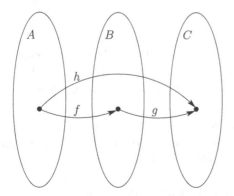

Figure 1.4. The functions $f : A \to B$ and $g : B \to C$ and the composed function $h : A \to C$ defined by $g \circ f$.

Table 1.1. The multiplication table of the
function $f : \{0, 1, 2\}^2 \to \{0, 1, \ldots, 4\}$
defined by $f(a, b) = a \cdot b$

f	0	1	2
0	0	0	0
1	0	1	2
2	0	2	4

Consider a function $f : A \times B \to C$ for finite sets A, B, and C. The *multiplication table* of f is a table with one row per element of A and one column per element of B, namely, a table with $|A|$ rows and $|B|$ columns. For every $(a, b) \in A \times B$, the entry of the table corresponding to (a, b) is filled with $f(a, b)$. For example, consider the function $f : \{0, 1, 2\}^2 \to \{0, 1, \ldots, 4\}$ defined by $f(a, b) = a \cdot b$. The multiplication table of f appears in Table 1.1. Note the term *multiplication table* is used also for functions that have nothing to do with multiplication.

EXAMPLES

---

1. Examples related to relations. Consider a league of n teams $A = \{1, \ldots, n\}$. Each match is between two teams; one team is the hosting team, and the other team is the guest team. Thus a match can be represented by an ordered pair (a, b) in A^2, where a denotes the hosting team and b denotes the guest team. We can consider the set $R \subseteq A^2$ of all matches played in the league. Thus R is the relation of "who played against who" with an indication of the hosting team and the guest team. Note that the matches (a, b) and (b, a) are different due to the different host–guest teams. In addition, the relation R does not include pairs (a, a) since a team cannot play against itself.

2. Let $R \subseteq \mathbb{N} \times \mathbb{N}$ denote the binary relation "smaller than and not equal" over the natural number. That is, $(a, b) \in R$ if and only if $a < b$:

$$R \triangleq \{(0, 1), (0, 2), \ldots, (1, 2), (1, 3), \ldots\}.$$

3. *Examples of relations that are functions and relations that are not functions.* Let us consider the following relations over $\{0, 1, 2\} \times \{0, 1, 2\}$:

$$R_1 \triangleq \{(1, 1)\},$$

$$R_2 \triangleq \{(0, 0), (1, 1), (2, 2)\},$$

$$R_3 \triangleq \{(0, 0), (0, 1), (2, 2)\},$$

$$R_4 \triangleq \{(0, 2), (1, 2), (2, 2)\}.$$

The relation R_1 is not a function since it is not defined for $x \in \{0, 2\}$. The relation R_2 is a function since, for every $x \in \{0, 1, 2\}$, there exists a unique $y \in \{0, 1, 2\}$ such that $(x, y) \in R_2$. In fact, R_2 consists of pairs of the form (x, x). Such a function is called the *identity function*. The relation R_3 is not a function since there are two pairs with $x = 0$. The relation R_4 is a function that consists of pairs of the form $(x, 2)$. Such a function R_4 is called a *constant function* since the value $y = f(x)$ of the function does not depend on the argument x.

4.   *Examples of restriction of a function.* Let us consider the following functions:

$$f(x) = \sin(x),$$

$$salary : People \to \mathbb{N}.$$

The function $f(x)$ is defined for every real number $x \in \mathbb{R}$. The restriction of $f(x)$ to $[0, \pi/2] \subset \mathbb{R}$ is the function $g : [0, \pi/2] \to [0, 1]$ defined by $g(x) = f(x)$, for every $x \in [0, \pi/2]$. Similarly, let us restrict the *salary* function to the set of residents of New York City (which is obviously a subset of the set of people), that is, let $salary' : Residents\ of\ New\ York\ City \to \mathbb{N}$ be defined by $salary'(x) = salary(x)$. This means that $salary'(x)$ is defined only if x is a resident of New York City.

5.   *Examples of extensions of a function.* Let us consider the following functions:

$$f(x) = 1/x; \text{ for every } x \in \mathbb{R} \setminus \{0\}$$

$$g = \{(0, 1), (1, 1), (2, 0)\}.$$

Let us define the extension $h : \mathbb{R} \to \mathbb{R} \cup \{\infty\}$ of f as follows:

$$h(x) \leftarrow \begin{cases} f(x), & \text{if } x \in \mathbb{R} \setminus \{0\} \\ \infty, & \text{if } x = 0. \end{cases}$$

We extended f by adding the pair $(0, \infty)$, that is, the domain of h is $\mathbb{R}$ and the range of h is $\mathbb{R} \cup \{\infty\}$. Let us define the extension $w : \{0, 1, 2, 3\} \to \{0, 1, 2\}$ of g as follows:

$$w(x) \leftarrow \begin{cases} g(x), & \text{if } x \in \{0, 1, 2\} \\ 2, & \text{if } x = 3. \end{cases}$$

We extended g by adding the pair $(3, 2)$. Note that in both cases, we extended the functions by extending both the domain and the range.

6.   Let M denote a set of mothers. Let C denote a set of children. Let $P \subseteq M \times C$ denote the "mother of" relation, namely, $(m, c) \in P$ if and only if m is the mother of c. Similarly, let $Q \subseteq C \times M$ denote the "child of" relation, namely, $(c, m) \in Q$ if and only if c is a child of m. For example,

$$M \triangleq \{1, 2, 3\},$$

$$C \triangleq \{4, 5, 6, 7, 8, 9\},$$

$$P \triangleq \{(1, 4), (2, 5), (2, 6), (3, 7), (3, 8), (3, 9)\},$$

$$Q \triangleq \{(x, y) \mid (y, x) \in P\},$$

$$= \{(4, 1), (5, 2), (6, 2), (7, 3), (8, 3), (9, 3)\}.$$

Note that a mother may have many children while a child has a unique mother. Hence the relation Q is a function while P is not. Note that $Q : C \to M$

is not one-to-one since two children may share the same mother, for example, $Q(5) = Q(6)$.

7. *Examples of compositions of functions.* Let $f(x) = 2x + 4$ and let $g(x) = x^2$; then

$$f(g(x)) = f(x^2)$$

$$= 2(x^2) + 4$$

$$= 2x^2 + 4 \text{ and}$$

$$g(f(x)) = g(2x + 4)$$

$$= (2x + 4)^2$$

$$= (2x)^2 + 2 \cdot 2x \cdot 4 + 4^2$$

$$= 4x^2 + 16x + 16.$$

1.3 BOOLEAN FUNCTIONS

In this section, we focus on functions whose domain and range are binary strings.

Definition 1.14 A *bit* is an element in the set $\{0, 1\}$. An *n-bit binary string* is an element in the set $\{0, 1\}^n$.

Definition 1.15 A function $B : \{0, 1\}^n \to \{0, 1\}^k$ is called a *Boolean function*.

1.3.1 Truth Tables

Bits are related to the logical "true" and "false." According to common convention, a "true" is coded as a 1 and a "false" is coded as a 0. A list of the ordered pairs $(x, f(x))$ is called a *truth table*. This means that there are two columns in a truth table, one for the domain and one for the range. In a truth table of a Boolean function $B : \{0, 1\}^n \to \{0, 1\}^k$, the domain column is usually split, one column per bit.

Table 1.2 depicts the truth tables of four basic Boolean functions: (i) NOT $: \{0, 1\} \to \{0, 1\}$, (ii) AND $: \{0, 1\}^2 \to \{0, 1\}$, (iii) OR $: \{0, 1\}^2 \to \{0, 1\}$, and (iv) XOR $: \{0, 1\}^2 \to \{0, 1\}$.

Table 1.2. Truth tables of four basic Boolean functions

x	NOT(x)	x	y	AND(x, y)	x	y	OR(x, y)	x	y	XOR(x, y)
		0	0	0	0	0	0	0	0	0
0	1	1	0	0	1	0	1	1	0	1
1	0	0	1	0	0	1	1	0	1	1
		1	1	1	1	1	1	1	1	0

Table 1.3. Multiplication tables of three basic Boolean functions

AND	0	1
0	0	0
1	0	1

OR	0	1
0	0	1
1	1	1

XOR	0	1
0	0	1
1	1	0

Table 1.3 depicts the multiplication tables of AND, OR, and XOR.

EXAMPLES

1. The Boolean function $I : \{0, 1\} \to \{0, 1\}$, defined by $I(x) = x$, is called the *identity* function. (We reencounter the identity function in Chapter 6.) Table 1.4 depicts the truth table of the identity function.

2. Consider the Boolean function $\text{OR}\{0, 1\}^2 \to \{0, 1\}$. Define the Boolean function $f : \{0, 1\} \to \{0, 1\}$ by $f(y) = \text{OR}(0, y)$. The function f is the restriction of OR to the domain $\{(0, 0), (1, 0)\}$. Note that $f(y) = y$ for every $y \in \{0, 1\}$, thus f is the identity function.

3. The *parity* function $p : \{0, 1\}^n \to \{0, 1\}$ is defined as follows:

$$p(b_1, \ldots, b_n) \triangleq \begin{cases} 1 & \text{if } \sum_{i=1}^n b_i \text{ is odd} \\ 0 & \text{if } \sum_{i=1}^n b_i \text{ is even.} \end{cases}$$

For example, (i) $p(0, 1, 0, 1, 0) = 0$, (ii) $p(0, 1, 1, 1, 0) = 1$, and (iii) for $n = 2$, the parity function is identical to the XOR function.

4. The *majority* function $m : \{0, 1\}^n \to \{0, 1\}$ is defined as follows:

$$m(b_1, \ldots, b_n) = 1 \quad \text{if and only if} \quad \sum_{i=1}^n b_i > \frac{n}{2}.$$

For example, (i) $m(0, 1, 0, 1, 0) = 0$, (ii) $m(0, 1, 1, 1, 0) = 1$, and (iii) for $n = 2$, the majority function is identical to the AND function.

5. The 3-*bit carry* function $c : \{0, 1\}^3 \to \{0, 1\}$ is defined as follows:

$$c(b_1, b_2, b_3) = 1 \quad \text{if and only if} \quad b_1 + b_2 + b_3 \geq 2.$$

For example, (i) $c(0, 1, 0) = 0$ and (ii) $c(0, 1, 1) = 1$.

6. The truth table of the 3-bit carry function is listed in Table 1.5.

Table 1.4. Truth table
of the identity function
$I : \{0, 1\} \to \{0, 1\}$

x	$I(x)$
0	0
1	1

Table 1.5. The truth table of the 3-bit carry function

b_1	b_2	b_3	$c(b_1, b_2, b_3)$
0	0	0	0
1	0	0	0
0	1	0	0
1	1	0	1
0	0	1	0
1	0	1	1
0	1	1	1
1	1	1	1

1.4 COMMUTATIVE AND ASSOCIATIVE BINARY OPERATIONS

A function whose domain equals the Cartesian product of the range is called a *binary operation*, for example, $f : A \times A \to A$. Common examples of binary operations are arithmetic operations such as addition, subtraction, multiplication, and division. Usually, a binary operation is denoted by a special symbol (e.g., $+, -, \cdot, \div$). Instead of writing $+(a, b)$, we write $a + b$.

Definition 1.16 A binary operation $* : A \times A \to A$ is *commutative* if, for every $a, b \in A$;

$$a * b = b * a.$$

Definition 1.17 A binary operation $* : A \times A \to A$ is *associative* if, for every $a, b, c \in A$;

$$(a * b) * c = a * (b * c).$$

Consider an associative function $f : A \times A \to A$. We can define a function $f_k : A^k \to A$ for any $k \geq 2$ as follows. The function f_2 is simply f. For $k > 2$, we define

$$f_k(x_1, \ldots, x_k) \triangleq f(f_{k-1}(x_1, \ldots, x_k - 1), x_k).$$

In Section 2.2, we refer to such a definition as a recursive definition.

We are so used to this definition that we do not even notice that we use it. For example, $(x_1 + x_2 + \cdots + x_k)$ is defined by (1) first add $y = (x_1 + \cdots + x_{k-1})$ and then (2) add $y + x_k$. This manipulation is often referred to by "placing of parentheses." If f is associative, then the parentheses can be placed arbitrarily without changing the outcome. We return to this issue in Chapter 12.

EXAMPLES

1. The addition operation $+ : \mathbb{R}^2 \to \mathbb{R}$ is commutative and associative.
2. The subtraction operation $- : \mathbb{R}^2 \to \mathbb{R}$ is neither associative nor commutative. For example, (i) $1 - 2 = -1$ but $2 - 1 = 1$; and (ii) $(5 - 3) - 2 = 0$ but $5 - (3 - 2) = 4$.
3. The restriction of a binary operator is not always a binary operator. For example, consider the addition operation $+ : \mathbb{R}^2 \to \mathbb{R}$. Addition is a binary operator over the

Table 1.6. The truth tables of $\text{AND}(\text{AND}(a,b),c)$ and $\text{AND}(a,\text{AND}(b,c))$

a	b	c	$\text{AND}(a,b)$	$\text{AND}(b,c)$	$\text{AND}(\text{AND}(a,b),c)$	$\text{AND}(a,\text{AND}(b,c))$
0	0	0	0	0	0	0
1	0	0	0	0	0	0
0	1	0	0	0	0	0
1	1	0	1	0	0	0
0	0	1	0	0	0	0
1	0	1	0	0	0	0
0	1	1	0	1	0	0
1	1	1	1	1	1	1

       reals. Let $A = \{0,1,2\}$, and consider the restriction of addition to $A \times A$. The range of this restriction is the set $\{0,1,\ldots,4\}$, which does not equal the set A.

4. The multiplication operation $\cdot : \mathbb{R}^2 \to \mathbb{R}$ is commutative and associative.

5. The division operation $\div : (\mathbb{R} \smallsetminus \{0\})^2 \to (\mathbb{R} \smallsetminus \{0\})$ is not associative and not commutative. For example, (i) $1 \div 2 = \frac{1}{2}$ but $2 \div 1 = 2$, hence the operation is not commutative; (ii) let $a,b,c \in \mathbb{R} \smallsetminus \{0\}$ and $c \notin \{-1,+1\}$, then $(a \div b) \div c \neq a \div (b \div c)$ since

$$(a \div b) \div c = \frac{a/b}{c} = \frac{a}{b \cdot c}$$

$$a \div (b \div c) = \frac{a}{b/c} = \frac{a \cdot c}{b}.$$

       Hence division is not associative.

6. Multiplication of real matrices is associative but not commutative, as shown in the following example. Consider the matrices

$$A = \begin{pmatrix} 1 & 0 \\ 0 & 0 \end{pmatrix} \qquad\qquad B = \begin{pmatrix} 0 & 1 \\ 0 & 0 \end{pmatrix}.$$

The products $A \cdot B$ and $B \cdot A$ are:

$$A \cdot B = \begin{pmatrix} 0 & 1 \\ 0 & 0 \end{pmatrix} \qquad\qquad B \cdot A = \begin{pmatrix} 0 & 0 \\ 0 & 0 \end{pmatrix}.$$

Since $A \cdot B \neq B \cdot A$, multiplication of real matrices is not commutative.

7. Prove that the Boolean function AND is associative.

       PROOF: We prove that for every $a,b,c \in \{0,1\}$,

$$\text{AND}(\text{AND}(a,b),c) = \text{AND}(a,\text{AND}(b,c)), \qquad (1.2)$$

by filling the truth values in the truth tables of both sized of Eq. 1.2, that is, $\text{AND}(\text{AND}(a,b),c)$ and $\text{AND}(a,\text{AND}(b,c))$, as depicted in Table 1.6.

     Since the columns of both $\text{AND}(\text{AND}(a,b),c)$ and $\text{AND}(a,\text{AND}(b,c))$ are identical, it implies that the Boolean function AND is associative. ∎

8. We may extend the Boolean function AND to any number of arguments. For example,

$$\text{AND}_3(X,Y,Z) \stackrel{\triangle}{=} (X \text{ AND } Y) \text{ AND } Z.$$

Since the AND function is associative, we have

$$(X \text{ AND } Y) \text{ AND } Z = X \text{ AND } (Y \text{ AND } Z).$$

Thus we often simply write $(X \text{ AND } Y \text{ AND } Z)$ and refer to this as the AND of the three arguments. In a similar fashion, we extend the AND function to any number of arguments, just as we consider addition of multiple numbers.

PROBLEMS

1.1. Prove that for every set A, B, $A = B$ if and only if $A \subseteq B$ and $B \subseteq A$.

1.2. Prove that for every set A, B, $A \setminus B = A \cap \bar{B}$.

1.3. Write the truth table of the parity function for $n = 4$.

1.4. Recall the definition of the 3-bit carry function $c : \{0, 1\}^3 \rightarrow \{0, 1\}$:

$$c(b_1, b_2, b_3) = 1 \quad \text{if and only if} \quad b_1 + b_2 + b_3 \geq 2.$$

The truth table of the 3-bit carry function is listed in Table 1.5.
   (a) Prove that

$$c(b_1, b_2, b_3) = (b_1 \wedge b_2) \vee (b_2 \wedge b_3) \vee (b_1 \wedge b_3),$$

   where $b_1, b_2, b_3 \in \{0, 1\}$.
   (b) Set $b_1 = 1$. Prove that $c(1, b_2, b_3) = b_2 \vee b_3$.
   (c) Set $b_1 = 0$. Prove that $c(0, b_2, b_3) = b_2 \wedge b_3$.

1.5. Prove that (regular) addition is not a binary operation over $A \times A$ if A is finite and contains more than one element.

1.6. Define two binary operators over the set $\{0, 1, 2\}$, one that is commutative and one that is not. Can you state a simple property that a multiplication table of such a function must satisfy so that the function is commutative? Is this property sufficient?

1.7. Define two binary operators over the set $\{0, 1, 2\}$, one that is associative and one that is not.

1.8. Enumerate all the Boolean functions of arity two, that is, all the Boolean functions in the set $\{f : \{0, 1\}^2 \rightarrow \{0, 1\}\}$. Identify the Boolean functions we have seen so far (AND, OR, XOR, implication, equivalence, NAND, NOR).

1.9. Prove that XOR is an associative Boolean function.

1.10. Prove that OR is an associative Boolean function.

1.11. Prove that every binary operator over the set $\{0\}$ is associative and commutative.

1.12. De Morgan's second law states that $\overline{A \cap B} = \bar{A} \cup \bar{B}$. Use Venn diagrams to demonstrate this law.

1.13. Recall Example 15 on page 7. Use Venn diagrams to demonstrate contraposition on sets, that is, for every two sets A, B, show that
   • $A \subseteq B$ implies that $\bar{B} \subseteq \bar{A}$ and
   • $\bar{B} \subseteq \bar{A}$ implies that $A \subseteq B$.

1.14. Recall that for sets A, B,

$$A = B \text{ if and only if } A \subseteq B \text{ and } B \subseteq A.$$

Also recall that a function $g : C \to D$ is a binary relation $g \subseteq C \times D$ such that for every $c \in C$, there exists a unique element $d \in D$ such that $(c, d) \in g$. Conclude that two functions $f, g : C \to D$ are equal if and only if

$$\forall c \in C : f(c) = g(c).$$

1.15. Let $f : A \to B, g : B \to C$ denote two functions. Prove that the composition $h = g \circ f$ is a function.

1.16. Recall the parity function $p : \{0, 1\}^n \to \{0, 1\}$ from Example 3 on page 14. Prove that for $n = 2$, the parity function is identical to the XOR function.

1.17. Recall the majority function $m : \{0, 1\}^n \to \{0, 1\}$ from Example 4 on page 14. Prove that for $n = 2$, the majority function is identical to the AND function.

1.18. Let $f : A \times A \to A$ denote a binary operation. We say that a multiplication table of f is *symmetric* if the entry in the ith row and jth column equals the entry in the jth row and ith column for every i, j.
   (a) Prove or refute: f is commutative if and only if the multiplication table of f is symmetric.
   (b) Prove or refute: f is associative if and only if the multiplication table of f is symmetric.

1.19. Let A denote the set of functions whose range and domain equal B. Recall the definition of composition of functions (see Definition 1.11). Prove or refute each of the following statements:
   (a) Composition $\circ : A \times A \to A$ is a binary operation.
   (b) Composition is commutative (hint: see Example 7 in Section 1.3.1).
   (c) Composition is associative.
   (d) Multiplication of matrices is associative (hint: use your answer to the previous item).

CHAPTER 2

Induction and Recursion

This chapter presents two very powerful techniques for defining infinite sequences (recursion) and proving properties of infinite sequences (induction). The sequences in which we are interested are not only sequences of numbers (e.g., even positive integers) but also sequences of more elaborate objects (e.g., digital circuits).

Suppose we wish to define the even numbers. Typically, one could write $0, 2, 4, \ldots$ This informal description assumes that the reader can guess how the sequence continues and how to generate the next number in the sequence. (The next number is 6!) A more systematic way to describe a sequence $x_0, x_1, x_2, \ldots$ is to build a "device" that when input an element x_n of the sequence, outputs the next element x_{n+1}. In the case of the sequence of even numbers, this device simply adds +2, that is, $x_{n+1} = x_n + 2$. Of course, we need to define the first element x_0 in the sequence to be zero. Once we have defined x_0 and the device for determining x_{n+1} based on x_n, the sequence is well defined. This, in a nutshell, is recursion. In this book, we will use recursion to define sequences of circuits. In the meantime, we establish the topic of recursion on sequences of numbers.

Suppose we wish to prove that each number in the sequence defined recursively by $x_0 = 0$ and $x_{n+1} = x_n + 2$ is divisible by 2. Well, the elements in this sequence are divisible by 2 simply because $x_n = 2n$. Namely, we have a formula for x_n that immediately implies the desired property (i.e., each x_n is divisible by 2). But how do we prove that this formula is correct? Bear in mind that sequences defined recursively can be very complicated. Is there a way to prove that a recursive definition and a formula define the same sequence? The main tool for such proofs is induction.

2.1 INDUCTION

Suppose we wish to prove the formula for the sum of the first n positive integers; that is, we are looking for a fast way to compute the sum $1 + 2 + \cdots + n$. In Section 3.2, we refer to this sum as an *arithmetic series*. We denote the sum by S_n, namely, $S_n \triangleq \sum_{i=1}^{n} i$.

Theorem 2.1

$$S_n = \frac{n \cdot (n+1)}{2}. \tag{2.1}$$

PROOF: One way to prove Eq. 2.1 is by induction. The proof proceeds as follows. First, we check that Eq. 2.1 holds for $n = 0$. This is easy because both sides of the equation equal zero. This part of the proof is called the *induction basis*.

Now we formulate the *induction hypothesis*. It simply states that Eq. 2.1 holds for n, namely,

$$S_n - n \cdot (n+1)/2. \tag{2.2}$$

The final step of the proof is called the *induction step*. Here we need to prove that if Eq. 2.1 holds for n, then it also holds for $n + 1$. Thus we need to prove that

$$S_{n+1} = (n+1) \cdot (n+2)/2. \tag{2.3}$$

Why is this any easier than proving Eq. 2.1? The key point is that we may rely on the induction hypothesis (i.e., Eq. 2.2). Indeed, $S_{n+1} = S_n + (n+1)$. By the induction hypothesis, $S_n = n \cdot (n+1)/2$. Thus $S_{n+1} = n \cdot (n+1)/2 + (n+1)$. To complete the proof, all we need to do is to prove that $n \cdot (n+1)/2 + (n+1) = (n+1)(n+2)/2$, a simple task. ■

A more abstract way of formulating the preceding proof by induction is to denote by P the set of all natural numbers n that satisfy Eq. 2.1. Our goal is to prove that every n satisfies Eq. 2.1, namely, that $P = \mathbb{N}$.

The proof consists of three steps:

1. Induction basis: prove that $0 \in P$.
2. Induction hypothesis: assume that $n \in P$.
3. Induction step: prove that if the induction hypothesis holds, then $n + 1 \in P$.

The following theorem justifies the method of proof by induction. Note that assumption (i) corresponds to the induction basis and assumption (ii) corresponds to the induction step.

Theorem 2.2 *Let $P \subseteq \mathbb{N}$. Assume that (i) $0 \in P$ and (ii) for every $n \in \mathbb{N}$, $n \in P$ implies that $(n+1) \in P$. Then $P = \mathbb{N}$.*

PROOF: Assume, for the sake of contradiction, that $P \subsetneq \mathbb{N}$. Let n denote the smallest element in $\mathbb{N} \setminus P$. Since $0 \in P$, it follows that $n > 0$. By the definition of n, it follows that $(n - 1) \in P$. However, assumption (ii) implies that in this case, $n \in P$, a contradiction, and the theorem follows. ■

We remark that sometimes the induction hypothesis is that $i \in P$ for every $i \leq n$. This form of induction is often called *complete induction*, as formulated in the following theorem.

Theorem 2.3 (*Complete Induction*) *Let $P \subseteq \mathbb{N}$. Assume that (i) $0 \in P$ and (ii) for every $n \in \mathbb{N}$, $\{0, \ldots, n\} \subseteq P$ implies that $(n+1) \in P$. Then $P = \mathbb{N}$.*

Note that sometimes the claims that we wish to prove are valid for $n \geq n_0$, where $n_0 \in \mathbb{N}$. In this case, we apply a variant of Theorem 2.2, as formulated in the following theorem.

Theorem 2.4 *Let $P \subseteq \mathbb{N}$. Assume that (i) $n_0 \in P$ and (ii) $n \in P$ implies that $(n + 1) \in P$ for every $n \in \mathbb{N} \smallsetminus \{0, \ldots, n_0 - 1\}$. Then $\mathbb{N} \smallsetminus \{0, \ldots, n_0 - 1\} \subseteq P$.*

We often wish to prove theorems about structures other than natural numbers. For example, we may want to prove a theorem about sets. Let us consider the following theorem about duality in sets (this is a form of De Morgan's law over sets).

Theorem 2.5 *For every $n \geq 2$ sets $A_1, \ldots, A_n$,*

$$U \smallsetminus (A_1 \cup \cdots \cup A_n) = \bar{A}_1 \cap \cdots \cap \bar{A}_n. \tag{2.4}$$

We now use induction to prove the theorem.

PROOF: Although the theorem is not about natural numbers, we may use induction. Let P denote the set of all natural numbers for which Eq. 2.4 holds. Since Eq. 2.4 is stated only for $n \geq 2$, we wish to prove that $P = \mathbb{N} \smallsetminus \{0, 1\}$.

To prove the induction basis, we need to show that $2 \in P$. This is simply the statement $U \smallsetminus (A_1 \cup A_2) = \bar{A}_1 \cap \bar{A}_2$. This case is discussed in Example 29 on page 9 of Chapter 1. A formal proof of this case is deferred to Section 6.8.

The induction hypothesis states that $n \in P$, namely, that $U \smallsetminus (A_1 \cup \cdots \cup A_n) = \bar{A}_1 \cap \cdots \cap \bar{A}_n$.

Now we wish to prove the induction step, namely, that $(n + 1) \in P$. In other words, we need to prove that $U \smallsetminus (A_1 \cup \cdots \cup A_n \cup A_{n+1}) = \bar{A}_1 \cap \cdots \cap \bar{A}_n \cap \bar{A}_{n+1}$.

Let $B \triangleq A_1 \cup \cdots \cup A_n$. We first prove that $U \smallsetminus (B \cup A_{n+1}) = \bar{B} \cap \bar{A}_{n+1}$. In fact, this holds because $2 \in P$. Now $U \smallsetminus (A_1 \cup \cdots \cup A_n \cup A_{n+1}) = U \smallsetminus (B \cup A_{n+1})$. Since $2 \in P$, we conclude that $U \smallsetminus (B \cup A_{n+1}) = \bar{B} \cap \bar{A}_{n+1}$. Since $\bar{B} = U \smallsetminus (A_1 \cup \cdots \cup A_n)$, by the induction hypothesis (i.e., $n \in P$), $\bar{B} = \bar{A}_1 \cap \cdots \cap \bar{A}_n$. We conclude that

$$U \smallsetminus (A_1 \cup \cdots \cup A_n \cup A_{n+1}) = U \smallsetminus (B \cup A_{n+1})$$

$$= \bar{B} \cap \bar{A}_{n+1}$$

$$= \bar{A}_1 \cap \cdots \cap \bar{A}_n \cap \bar{A}_{n+1},$$

and we complete the proof of the induction step.

The proof of the induction basis, the induction hypothesis, and the proof of the induction step complete the proof of the theorem. ∎

Induction is a very powerful tool for proving theorems. We will use it many times in proofs.

EXAMPLES

---

1. *Pólya's proof that "all horses have the same color."* In this paradox, induction is (mis)-used to prove that all the horses are the same color. It is important to verify

Figure 2.1. A counterexample to the claim that all the (spherical) horses have the same color. To prove that a claim is not correct, all we need is to supply a counterexample.

that you identify the error in the proof (since we obviously know that there are two horses with different colors, as depicted in Figure 2.1).

The proof is by induction on the number of horses, denoted by n. Thus we wish to prove that in every set of n horses, all the horses have the same color. The induction basis, for $n = 1$, is trivial since in a set consisting of a single horse, there is only one color.

The induction hypothesis simply states that in every set of n horses, all horses have the same color. We now prove the induction step, namely, we need to prove that if the claim holds for n, then it also holds for $n + 1$.

Let us number the horses, that is, $\{1, \ldots, n+1\}$. We consider two subsets of horses $A \triangleq \{1, \ldots, n\}$ and $B \triangleq \{2, \ldots, n+1\}$. By the induction hypothesis, the horses in set A have the same color and the horses in set B also have the same color. Since $2 \in A \cap B$, it follows that the horses in $A \cup B$ have the same color. We have proved the induction step, and the theorem follows.

What is wrong with this proof? Note that in the induction step, $A \cap B \neq \varnothing$ only if $n \geq 2$. However, the induction basis was proved only for $n = 1$. Thus we did not prove the induction step for a set of two horses! Obviously a set of two horses may not satisfy the claim, as depicted in the counterexample in Figure 2.1. To summarize, a correct proof would have to extend the basis to $n = 2$, an impossible task.

The take-home advice from this example is to make sure that the induction basis is proved for all the cases. In particular, the induction basis is just as crucial as the induction step.

2.   We prove by induction that $3^n > 2n$ for all $n \in \mathbb{N}^+$.

PROOF: The proof is by induction on n. The induction hypothesis, for $n = 1$, is easy since $3^1 > 2 \cdot 1$.

The induction hypothesis simply states that $3^n > 2n$. We now prove the induction step, namely, we need to prove that if the claim holds for n, then it also holds for $n + 1$. Thus we need to prove that

$$3^{n+1} > 2(n + 1).$$

Indeed,

$$3^{n+1} = 3 \cdot 3^n$$
$$> 3 \cdot (2n)$$
$$> 2(n + 1).$$

The second line follows from the induction hypothesis. The third line follows from the fact that $6n > 2(n + 1)$ for $n \geq 1$. ∎

2.2 RECURSION

Recursion is a method to define a function (or other structures) for large arguments from small arguments. Two main reasons to define functions by recursion are simplicity and amenability to proofs by induction. In this section, we present two simple recursions: the *factorial function* and the *Fibonacci sequence*.

A recursive definition of a function $f : \mathbb{N} \to \mathbb{N}$ has two parts: (i) the base cases and (ii) reduction rules. The base cases define the values of $f(n)$ for small values of n. The reduction rule is applied to values of n that are not small; these rules define $f(n)$ by values of f for smaller values. We now demonstrate two recursive definitions.

The Factorial Function. We define the function $f : \mathbb{N}^+ \to \mathbb{N}^+$ recursively, as follows:

(i) Base case: $f(1) = 1$.
(ii) Reduction rule: $f(n + 1) = f(n) \cdot (n + 1)$.

It is easy to prove by induction that, for $n \geq 1$, $f(n) = 1 \cdot 2 \cdot 3 \cdots \cdot n$. Indeed, the induction basis for $n = 1$ is identical to the base case. The induction step is proved as follows. The reduction rule states that $f(n + 1) = f(n) \cdot (n + 1)$. The induction hypothesis states that $f(n) = 1 \cdot 2 \cdot 3 \cdots n$. Thus $f(n + 1) = 1 \cdot 2 \cdot 3 \cdots n \cdot (n + 1)$, as required.

The function f defined previously is known as the factorial function; one uses $n!$ to denote $f(n)$. The factorial function has many applications in combinatorics. For example, $n!$ equals the number of different ways one can order n different books on a shelf.

The Fibonacci Sequence. We define the function $g : \mathbb{N} \to \mathbb{N}$ recursively, as follows:

(i) Base case: $g(0) = 0$ and $g(1) = 1$
(ii) Reduction rule: $g(n + 2) = g(n + 1) + g(n)$.

Following the reduction rule, we obtain

$$g(2) = g(1) + g(0) = 1 + 0 = 1,$$
$$g(3) = g(2) + g(1) = 1 + 1 = 2,$$
$$g(4) = g(3) + g(2) = 2 + 1 = 3,$$
$$g(5) = g(4) + g(3) = 3 + 2 = 5.$$

Note that the self-reference to g in its definition does not lead to an infinite loop. Indeed, the arguments $(n + 1)$ and n on the right-hand side of the reduction rule are strictly smaller than the argument $(n + 2)$ on the left-hand side. Thus the chain of self-references eventually ends with a base case.

The Fibonacci sequence has many applications. For example, it is used to prove an upper bound on the number of iterations in Euclid's algorithm for computing the greatest common divisor of two integers. The following lemma is proved using complete induction.

Denote the *golden ratio* by $\varphi \triangleq \frac{1+\sqrt{5}}{2}$.

Lemma 2.6 *Let $\{g(n)\}_{n=0}^{\infty}$ be the Fibonacci sequence. Then, for every $n \in \mathbb{N}$,*

$$g(n) \leq \varphi^{n-1} \,. \tag{2.5}$$

PROOF: The proof is by complete induction on n. The induction hypothesis for $n = 0$ and $n = 1$ is easy since for $n = 0$, $0 \leq \left(\frac{1+\sqrt{5}}{2}\right)^{-1}$, and for $n = 1$, $1 \leq 1$, respectively. The induction hypothesis states that Eq. 2.5 holds for all $k \leq n$. We now prove the induction step; namely, we need to prove that if Eq. 2.5 holds for all $k \leq n$, then it also holds for $n + 1$. Thus we need to prove that

$$g(n+1) \leq \varphi^n \,.$$

Indeed,

$$
\begin{aligned}
g(n+1) &= g(n) + g(n-1) \\
&\leq \varphi^{n-1} + \varphi^{n-2} \\
&= \varphi^{n-2} \cdot (\varphi + 1) \\
&= \varphi^n \,.
\end{aligned}
$$

The first line follows from the definition of $g(n+1)$. The second line follows from the induction hypothesis for n and $n-1$. In the third line, we simply arranged the terms. The fourth line follows from the fact that φ is a solution of the quadratic equation $\varphi^2 = \varphi + 1$. We have proved the induction step, and the theorem follows. ∎

2.3 APPLICATION: ONE-TO-ONE AND ONTO FUNCTIONS

Definition 2.1 Let $f : A \rightarrow B$ denote a function from A to B.

1. The function f is *one-to-one* if, for every $a, a' \in A$, if $a \neq a'$ then $f(a) \neq f(a')$.
2. The function f is *onto* if, for every $b \in B$, there exists an $a \in A$ such that $f(a) = b$.
3. The function f is a *bijection* if it is both onto and one-to-one.

A one-to-one function is sometimes called an *injective function* (or an *injection*). A function that is onto is sometimes called a *surjection*.

The following two lemmas show how one-to-one and onto functions can be used to compare cardinalities of sets.

Lemma 2.7 *Let A and B denote two finite sets. If there exists a one-to-one function $f : A \rightarrow B$, then $|A| \leq |B|$.*

PROOF: The proof is by induction on $|A|$. The induction basis for $|A| = 0$ is trivial since $0 \leq |B|$. (A function may have an empty domain! In this case, it is simply an empty relation.)

The induction hypothesis states that the lemma holds if $|A| = n$. We prove the induction step for $|A| = n + 1$ as follows. Pick an element $a \in A$. Define

$$A' \triangleq A \smallsetminus \{a\} \qquad\qquad B' \triangleq B \smallsetminus \{f(a)\}.$$

Let $g \subseteq A' \times B'$ denote the relation $\{(x, f(x)) \mid x \in A'\}$. Since f is a function, so is g. Moreover, since f is one-to-one, g is also one-to-one (see Lemma 2.11 on page 26).

Since $|A'| = n$, by the induction hypothesis, $|A'| \leq |B'|$. But $|A| = |A'| + 1$ and $|B| = |B'| + 1$, hence $|A| \leq |B|$, as required. ■

Recall the contraposition form of a "logical statement" (see Example 15 on page 7). The contrapositive form of Lemma 2.7 is as follows: if $|A| > |B|$, then *every* function $f : A \to B$ is *not* one-to-one. This statement is known as the *pigeonhole principle*, formulated in the following corollary.

Corollary 2.8 (*Pigeonhole Principle*) *Let $f : A \to \{1, \ldots, n\}$ and $|A| > n$; then f is not one-to-one, that is, there are two distinct elements $a_1, a_2 \in A$ such that $f(a_1) = f(a_2)$.*

Lemma 2.9 *Let A and B denote two finite sets. If there exists an onto function $f : A \to B$, then $|A| \geq |B|$.*

PROOF: The proof is by complete induction on $|B|$. The induction basis for $|B| = 0$ is trivial since $|A| \geq 0$. (A function may have an empty range! In this case, it is simply an empty relation.)

The induction hypothesis states that the lemma holds if $|B| \leq n$. We prove the induction step for $|B| = n + 1$ as follows. Pick an element $b \in B$. Let $f^{-1}(b)$ denote the set $\{a \in A \mid f(a) = b\}$. Since f is onto, the set $f^{-1}(b)$ is not empty. Define

$$A' \triangleq A \smallsetminus f^{-1}(b) \qquad\qquad B' \triangleq B \smallsetminus \{b\}.$$

Let $g \subseteq A' \times B'$ denote the relation $\{(x, f(x)) \mid x \in A'\}$. Since f is a function, so is g. Moreover, since f is onto, so is g (see Lemma 2.12 on page 27).

Since $|B'| = |B| - 1$, by the induction hypothesis, $|A'| \geq |B'|$. But $|A| = |A'| + |f^{-1}(b)| \geq |A'| + 1$, hence

$$|A| = |A'| + |f^{-1}(b)| \geq |A'| + 1 \geq |B'| + 1 = |B|,$$

as required. ■

Lemma 2.10 *Assume that A and B are finite sets of equal cardinality (i.e., $|A| = |B|$). If $f : A \to B$ is onto, then f is also one-to-one.*

PROOF: For the sake of contradiction, assume that f is not one-to-one. Thus there exists two distinct elements $a \neq a'$ in A such that $f(a) = f(a')$. Let $b \in B$ be defined by $b \triangleq f(a)$.

As in the proof of Lemma 2.9, define $B' \triangleq B \smallsetminus \{b\}$, $f^{-1}(b) \triangleq \{a \in A : f(a) = b\}$ and $A' \triangleq A \smallsetminus f^{-1}(b)$. Let $g \subseteq A' \times B'$ denote the relation $\{(x, f(x)) \mid x \in A'\}$. Since f is a function, so is g. By Lemma 2.12, g is onto, and by Lemma 2.9, $|A'| \geq |B'|$. Recall that $|f^{-1}(b)| \geq 2$, and therefore $|A'| \leq |A| - 2$.

We now obtain a contradiction, as follows:

$$|B| = |B'| + 1$$
$$\leq |A'| + 1$$
$$\leq |A| - 2 + 1 < |A|.$$

Hence $|B| < |A|$, contradicting the assumption that $|A| = |B|$, and the lemma follows. ■

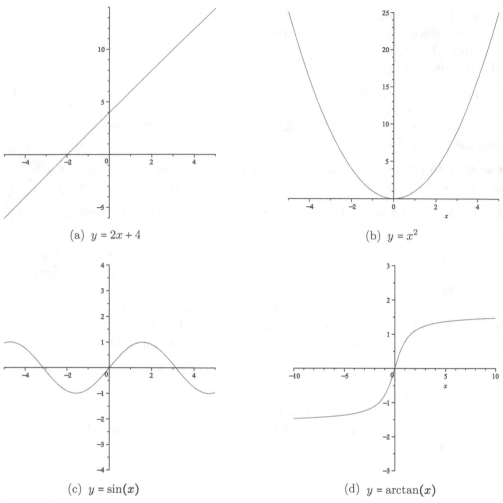

(a) $y = 2x + 4$ (b) $y = x^2$

(c) $y = \sin(x)$ (d) $y = \arctan(x)$

Figure 2.2. Graphs of real functions.

EXAMPLES

1. The functions $y = 2x + 4$, $y = x^2$, $y = \sin(x)$, and $y = \arctan(x)$ are depicted in Figure 2.2.
2. The functions $y = 2x + 4$ and $y = \arctan(x)$ are one-to-one, while $y = x^2$ and $y = \sin(x)$ are not. For example, $4^2 = (-4)^2 = 16$.
3. The functions $y = 2x + 4$ and $y = x^2$ are onto, while $y = \sin(x)$ and $y = \arctan(x)$ are not. For example, the function $y = \sin(x)$ does not attain values that are greater than 1.
4. Prove the following lemma.

   Lemma 2.11 *Let $f : A \to B$ denote a function. Let $A' \subseteq A$ and $B' \triangleq B \setminus \{ f(a') \in B \mid a' \in A \setminus A' \}$. Let $g \subseteq A' \times B'$ denote the relation $\{ (x, f(x)) \mid x \in A' \}$. The relation g is a function. Moreover, if f is one-to-one, then g is also one-to-one.*

PROOF: We need to show that (i) the relation $g \subseteq A' \times B'$ is a function and that (ii) the function $g : A' \to B'$ is one-to-one. The proof is as follows.

We show that for every $a' \in A'$, there exists a unique element $b' \in B'$ such that $(a', b') \in g$. Indeed, $(a', b') \in g$ implies that $b' = f(a')$, hence b' is unique, as required.

Now, we prove that the function $g : A' \to B'$ is one-to-one. We show that for every $a, a' \in A'$, if $a \neq a'$, then $g(a) \neq g(a')$. The proof is by contradiction. Let us assume that there are $a, a' \in A'$ such that $g(a) = g(a')$. Since $g : A' \to B'$ is defined by $g(x) \triangleq f(x)$, it implies that $f(a) = f(a')$, a contradiction to the assumption that f is one-to-one. Hence g is a one-to-one function, as required. ∎

5. Let $f : A \to B$ denote a function. Let $B' \subseteq B$. Let $f^{-1}(B')$ denote the set $\{a \in A \mid f(a) \in B'\}$. Prove the following lemma.

    Lemma 2.12 *Let $f : A \to B$ denote a function. Let $B' \subseteq B$ and $A' \triangleq A \smallsetminus f^{-1}(B \smallsetminus B')$. Let $g \subseteq A' \times B'$ denote the relation $\{(x, f(x)) \mid x \in A'\}$. The relation g is a function. Moreover, if f is onto, then g is also onto.*

    PROOF: We need to show that (i) the relation $g \subseteq A' \times B'$ is a function and that (ii) the function $g : A' \to B'$ is onto. The proof is as follows.

    We show that for every $a' \in A'$, there exists a unique element $b' \in B'$ such that $(a', b') \in g$. Indeed, $b' = f(a')$, and b' is unique, as required.

    Now we prove that the function $g : A' \to B'$ is onto; namely, for every $b' \in B'$, there exists an $a' \in A'$ such that $f(a') = b'$. The proof is as follows. Let $b' \in B'$. Since $B' \subseteq B$, then $b' \in B$. Since $f : A \to B$ is onto, there exists an $a' \in A$ such that $f(a') = b'$. To complete the proof, it suffices to show that $a' \in A'$. Indeed, $a' \notin f^{-1}(B \smallsetminus B')$. It follows that $a' \in A'$, and the lemma follows. ∎

PROBLEMS

2.1.   Prove Theorem 2.3.

2.2.   Prove Theorem 2.4.

2.3.   Prove the following theorem.

   Theorem 2.13 *For every $n \geq 2$ sets $A_1, \ldots, A_n$,*

   $$U \smallsetminus (A_1 \cap \cdots \cap A_n) = \bar{A}_1 \cup \cdots \cup \bar{A}_n.$$

2.4.   Prove that for every finite set A, B, $|A \times B| = |A| \cdot |B|$.

   Hint: Use induction on $|A|$.

2.5.   Prove that $|\{0, 1\}^k| = 2^k$ for every $k \in \mathbb{N}$.

   Hint: Question 2.4.

2.6.   Prove that $|P(A)| = 2^{|A|}$, for every finite set A.

2.7.   Prove the following claim.

   Claim 2.14 *Let A, B be finite sets. Consider the set $F \triangleq \{f \mid f : A \to B\}$ consisting of all the functions whose domain is A and whose range is B. Then, $|F| = |B|^{|A|}$.*

2.8. Does Pólya's proof that "all horses have the same color" hold for $n \geq 3$? Which part fails, the induction basis or the induction step?

2.9. Suppose we wish to prove that $3^n > 2n$ for every $n \in \mathbb{N}$ (including zero). Which part of the proof in Example 2 on page 22 requires $n > 0$? How can you fix the proof so that it applies also to $n = 0$?

2.10. (i) Write a recursive definition of the function 2^n for $n \in \mathbb{N}$. (ii) Prove that your definition is correct.

2.11. (i) Write a recursive definition of the function 2^z for $z \in \mathbb{Z}$. (Hint: recurse over $|z|$ and separate the reduction step to two cases according to the sign of z.) (ii) Prove that your definition is correct.

2.12. Let $f_k(n) = k \cdot n!$, where $k \in \mathbb{N}$, that is, $f_k(n) = k \cdot 1 \cdot 2 \cdot \ldots \cdot n$. Define $f_k(n)$ using a recursive definition. Prove that your definition is correct.

2.13. Let φ denote the "golden ratio" $\frac{1+\sqrt{5}}{2}$. Let $\hat{\varphi}$ denote $\frac{1-\sqrt{5}}{2}$.
  (a) Prove that, for every $n \in \mathbb{N} \setminus \{0, 1\}$,

$$g(n) = \frac{1}{\sqrt{5}} \cdot \left(\varphi^n - \hat{\varphi}^n\right) ,$$

where $\{g(n)\}_{n=0}^{\infty}$ is the Fibonacci sequence.

Hint: note that $\hat{\varphi}$ also satisfies $(\hat{\varphi})^2 = \hat{\varphi} + 1$.
  (b) Prove or refute the following claim. For every $n \in \mathbb{N} \setminus \{0, 1\}$,

$$g(n) \leq (\hat{\varphi})^n .$$

2.14*. Consider the function $f : \mathbb{N}^2 \to \mathbb{N}$ defined by $f(n, k) = \binom{n}{k}$. Recall that the binomial coefficient $\binom{n}{k}$ equals the number of subsets of cardinality k of a set of cardinality n. Redefine $f(n, k)$ using a recursive definition.

2.15. Prove the following lemma.

Lemma 2.15 *Assume that A and B are finite sets of equal cardinality (i.e., $|A| = |B|$). If $f : A \to B$ is one-to-one, then f is also onto.*

2.16. The Tower of Hanoi is a puzzle consisting of three rods and k disks of different sizes. Initially, all the disks are stacked in descending order on the first rod (the largest disk is at the bottom, the smallest on the top). The goal is to transfer the k disks to the third rod using a sequence of moves subject to two rules:
  • In each move, we may move a disk at a top of a stack to the top of another stack.
  • A disk may not be added to a stack if it is larger than the disk currently at the top of the stack.

  Solving this puzzle with one or two disks is trivial. With three disks, we need seven moves. To promote the puzzle, a legend was invented about priests solving a puzzle with $k = 64$ disks, with the danger that once solved, the world will end. Should we really worry about the truthfulness of the legend?

  Let f_k denote the minimum number of moves required to solve the puzzle with k disks. Formulate a closed formula for f_k and prove it by induction.

CHAPTER 3

Sequences and Series

In this chapter, we consider three important types of sequences: arithmetic sequences, geometric sequences, and the harmonic sequence. In an arithmetic sequence, the difference between consecutive elements is constant. In a geometric sequence, the ratio between consecutive elements is constant. The harmonic sequence is simply the sequence $(1, \frac{1}{2}, \frac{1}{3}, \ldots)$.

Given a sequence $(x_0, x_1, \ldots)$, we may wish to define a new sequence that consists of the partial sums

$$y_0 = x_0,$$

$$y_1 = x_0 + x_1,$$

$$y_2 = x_0 + x_1 + x_2, \ldots.$$

The sequence $(y_0, y_1, \ldots)$ of partial sums is a *series*. We consider three types of series: arithmetic series, geometric series, and harmonic series. Our goal is to find explicit formulas for the elements of these series.

3.1 SEQUENCES

Definition 3.1 An infinite *sequence* is a function f whose domain is $\mathbb{N}$ or $\mathbb{N}^+$.

Note that we do not specify the range of a sequence. Any set R may serve as the range of a sequence. Instead of denoting a sequence by a function $f : \mathbb{N} \to \mathbb{R}$, one usually writes $\{f(n)\}_{n=0}^{\infty}$ or $\{f_n\}_{n=0}^{\infty}$. Sometimes sequences are only defined for $n \geq 1$.

A *prefix* of $\mathbb{N}$ is a set $\{i \in \mathbb{N} \mid i \leq n\}$, for some $n \in \mathbb{N}$. One could similarly consider prefixes of $\mathbb{N}^+$.

Definition 3.2 A *finite sequence* is a function f whose domain is a prefix of $\mathbb{N}$ or $\mathbb{N}^+$.

Note that if the domain of a sequence f is $\{i \in \mathbb{N} \mid i < n\}$ or $\{i \in \mathbb{N}^+ \mid i \leq n\}$, then f is simply an n-tuple.

We already saw examples of sequences, for example, the Fibonacci sequence. The factorial function defines the sequence $f_n \triangleq n!$.

29

We now define three important sequences in mathematics:

1. *Arithmetic sequences.* The simplest sequence is the sequence $(0, 1, \ldots)$ defined by $f(n) \triangleq n$ for every $n \in \mathbb{N}$. In general, an arithmetic sequence is specified by two parameters: a_0, the first element in the sequence, and d, the difference between successive elements.

    Definition 3.3 The *arithmetic sequence* $\{a_n\}_{n=0}^\infty$ specified by the parameters a_0 and d is defined by

    $$a_n \triangleq a_0 + n \cdot d.$$

    One can also define the arithmetic sequence $\{a_n\}_{n \in \mathbb{N}}$ by recursion. The first element is simply a_0. The reduction rule is $a_{n+1} = a_n + d$. Claim 3.4 states the equivalence of the two definitions of an arithmetic sequence (see page 36).

2. *Geometric sequences.* The simplest example of a geometric sequence is the sequence of powers of 2: $(1, 2, 4, 8, \ldots)$. In general, a geometric sequence is specified by two parameters: b_0, the first element, and q, the ratio or quotient between successive elements.

    Definition 3.4 The *geometric sequence* $\{b_n\}_{n=0}^\infty$ specified by the parameters b_0 and q is defined by

    $$b_n \triangleq b_0 \cdot q^n.$$

    One can also define the geometric sequence $\{b_n\}_{n \in \mathbb{N}}$ by recursion. The first element is simply b_0. The recursion rule is $b_{n+1} = q \cdot b_n$. Claim 3.5 states the equivalence of these two definitions of a geometric sequence (see page 36).

3. *Harmonic sequence.*

    Definition 3.5 The *harmonic sequence* $\{c_n\}_{n=1}^\infty$ is defined by $c_n \triangleq \frac{1}{n}$ for $n \geq 1$.

    Note that the first index in the harmonic sequence is $n = 1$. The harmonic sequence is simply the sequence $(1, \frac{1}{2}, \frac{1}{3}, \ldots)$.

EXAMPLES

---

1. The digits of π define a sequence $\{d_n\}_{n=0}^\infty$, where d_n is the nth digit of $\pi \approx 3.1415926$; namely, $d_0 = 3$, $d_1 = 1$, $d_2 = 4$, and so no.
2. The sequence of even numbers $\{e_n\}_{n=0}^\infty$ is defined by

    $$e_n \triangleq 2n.$$

    The sequence $\{e_n\}_{n=0}^\infty$ is an arithmetic sequence since $e_{n+1} - e_n = 2$, thus the difference between consecutive elements is constant, as required.
3. The sequence of odd numbers $\{\omega_n\}_{n=0}^\infty$ is defined by

    $$\omega_n \triangleq 2n + 1.$$

    The sequence $\{\omega_n\}_{n=0}^\infty$ is also an arithmetic sequence since $\omega(n+1) - \omega(n) = 2$.
4. If $\{a_n\}_{n=0}^\infty$ is an arithmetic sequence with a difference d, then $\{b_n\}_{n=0}^\infty$ defined by $b_n = a_{2n}$ is also an arithmetic sequence. Indeed, $b_{n+1} - b_n = a_{2n+2} - a_{2n} = 2d$.

5. The sequence of powers of 3, $\{t_n\}_{n=0}^{\infty}$, is defined by

$$t_n \triangleq 3^n .$$

The sequence $\{t_n\}_{n=0}^{\infty}$ is a geometric sequence since $t_{n+1}/t_n = 3$, for every $n \geq 0$.
6. If $\{c_n\}_{n=0}^{\infty}$ is a geometric sequence with a ratio q, then $\{d_n\}_{n=0}^{\infty}$ defined by $d_n = a_{2n}$ is also a geometric sequence. Indeed, $d_{n+1}/d_n = c_{2n+2}/c_{2n} = q^2$.
7. If $q = 1$, then the sequence $\{b_n\}_{n=0}^{\infty}$ defined by $b_n = a_0 \cdot q^n$ is constant. Note that the constant series is both an arithmetic sequence and a geometric sequence.

3.2 SERIES

The sum of a sequence is called a *series*. We are interested in the sum of the first n elements of sequences.

Arithmetic Series. In Section 2.1, we considered the series $\sum_{i=1}^{n} i$. We also proved a formula for this sum. We now consider general arithmetic sequences. Note that the following theorem indeed generalizes Eq. 2.1 since $a_0 = 0$ and $d = 1$ in the sequence $a_n = n$.

Theorem 3.1 *Let*

$$a_n \triangleq a_0 + n \cdot d$$

$$S_n \triangleq \sum_{i=0}^{n} a_i .$$

Then

$$S_n = a_0 \cdot (n+1) + d \cdot \frac{n \cdot (n+1)}{2}. \tag{3.1}$$

PROOF: The proof is by induction on n. The induction hypothesis, for $n = 0$, is easy since $S_0 = a_0$.

The induction hypothesis simply states that Eq 3.1 holds for n. We now prove the induction step; namely, we need to prove that if Eq. 3.1 holds for n, then it also holds for $n + 1$. Thus we need to prove that

$$S_{n+1} = a_0 \cdot (n+2) + d \cdot \frac{(n+1) \cdot (n+2)}{2}. \tag{3.2}$$

Indeed,

$$S_{n+1} \triangleq S_n + a_{n+1}$$

$$= \left(a_0 \cdot (n+1) + d \cdot \frac{n \cdot (n+1)}{2} \right) + (a_0 + (n+1) \cdot d)$$

$$= a_0 \cdot (n+2) + d \cdot \left(\frac{n \cdot (n+1)}{2} + (n+1) \right)$$

$$= a_0 \cdot (n+2) + d \cdot \frac{(n+1) \cdot (n+2)}{2}.$$

The first line follows from the definition of S_{n+1}. The second line follows from the induction hypothesis and the definition of a_{n+1}. In the third and fourth lines, we simply arranged the terms. We have proved the induction step, and the theorem follows. ∎

Geometric Series. We now consider the sum of the first n elements in a geometric sequence.

Theorem 3.2 *Assume that $q \neq 1$. Let*

$$b_n \triangleq b_0 \cdot q^n$$

$$S_n \triangleq \sum_{i=0}^{n} b_i.$$

Then

$$S_n = b_0 \cdot \frac{1 - q^{n+1}}{1 - q}. \tag{3.3}$$

PROOF: The proof is by induction on n. The induction hypothesis, for $n = 0$, is easy since $S_0 = b_0$.

The induction hypothesis simply states that Eq 3.3 holds for n.

We now prove the induction step; namely, we need to prove that if Eq. 3.3 holds for n, then it also holds for $n + 1$. Thus, we need to prove that

$$S_{n+1} = b_0 \cdot \frac{1 - q^{n+2}}{1 - q}. \tag{3.4}$$

Indeed,

$$S_{n+1} \triangleq S_n + b_{n+1}$$

$$= \left(b_0 \cdot \frac{1 - q^{n+1}}{1 - q} \right) + \left(b_0 \cdot q^{n+1} \right)$$

$$= b_0 \cdot \left(\frac{1 - q^{n+1}}{1 - q} + q^{n+1} \right)$$

$$= b_0 \cdot \left(\frac{1 - q^{n+1} + (1 - q) \cdot q^{n+1}}{1 - q} \right)$$

$$= b_0 \cdot \frac{1 - q^{n+2}}{1 - q}.$$

The first line follows from the definition of S_{n+1}. The second line follows from the induction hypothesis and the definition of b_{n+1}. In the third and fourth lines, we simply arranged the terms. We have proved the induction step, and the theorem follows. ∎

Harmonic Series. We now consider the sum of the first n elements in the harmonic sequence. Unfortunately, this sum does not have a nice closed formula. Instead, we will prove a simple lower and upper bound.

Theorem 3.3 *Let*

$$c_n \triangleq \frac{1}{n}, \quad \text{for } n \geq 1, \quad \text{and}$$

$$H_n \triangleq \sum_{i=1}^{n} c_i.$$

Then, for every $k \in \mathbb{N}$,

$$1 + \frac{k}{2} \leq H_{2^k} \leq k + 1. \tag{3.5}$$

The theorem is useful because it tells us that H_n grows logarithmically in n (see Example 2). In particular, H_n tends to infinity as n grows.

PROOF: The proof is by induction on k. The induction basis, for $k = 0$, holds because $2^k = 1$ and $H_1 = 1$. Thus Eq. 3.5 for $k = 0$ simply says that $1 \leq 1 \leq 1$.

The induction hypothesis states that Eq. 3.5 holds for k. In the induction step, we prove that it holds for $k + 1$, as follows.

We first prove the upper bound: since each of the last 2^k elements in $H_{2^{k+1}}$ is less than $1/2^k$,

$$H_{2^{k+1}} \leq H_{2^k} + 2^k \cdot \frac{1}{2^k}$$

$$\leq (k + 1) + 1.$$

The second line follows from the induction hypothesis. Thus the induction step for the upper bound is completed.

We now prove the lower bound: since each of the last 2^k elements in $H_{2^{k+1}}$ is greater than $1/2^{k+1}$,

$$H_{2^{k+1}} > H_{2^k} + 2^k \cdot \frac{1}{2^{k+1}}$$

$$\geq \left(\frac{k}{2} + 1\right) + \frac{1}{2} = \frac{k+1}{2} + 1.$$

The second line follows from the induction hypothesis. Thus the induction step for the lower bound is completed. ■

EXAMPLES

1. Prove that $\sum_{i=0}^{n-1} 2^i = 2^n - 1$.

   PROOF: Let $b_0 = 1$, $q = 2$, and $S_{n-1} = \sum_{i=0}^{n-1} 2^i$. Theorem 3.2 states that

   $$S_{n-1} = b_0 \cdot \frac{1 - q^n}{1 - q} = 1 \cdot \frac{1 - 2^n}{1 - 2} = 2^n - 1,$$

   as required. ■

2. This example bounds the harmonic series for every $n \in \mathbb{N}^+$. For every $n \in \mathbb{N}^+$,

   $$1 + \frac{(\log_2 n) - 1}{2} < H_n < (\log_2 n) + 2. \tag{3.6}$$

PROOF: Observe that for every $n \in \mathbb{N}^+$, there exists $k \in \mathbb{N}$ such that

$$2^k \le n < 2^{k+1} . \tag{3.7}$$

We first prove the upper bound of Eq. 3.6:

$$H_n < H_{2^{k+1}}$$
$$\le (k+1) + 1$$
$$\le (\log_2 n) + 2 .$$

The first line follows since H_n is monotone increasing with n. The second line follows from Eq. 3.5. The last line follows Eq. 3.7, which implies that $k \le \log_2 n$.

We now prove the lower bound of Eq. 3.6:

$$H_n \ge H_{2^k}$$
$$\ge 1 + \frac{k}{2}$$
$$> 1 + \frac{\log_2(n/2)}{2}$$
$$= 1 + \frac{(\log_2 n) - 1}{2} .$$

The first line follows since H_n is monotone increasing with n. The second line follows from Eq. 3.5. The third line follows Eq. 3.7, which implies that $n < 2^{k+1} \Leftrightarrow \frac{n}{2} < 2^k \Leftrightarrow \log_2(n/2) < k$. The last line follows from the fact that $\log_2(n/2) = \log_2(n) - \log_2(2) = \log_2(n) - 1$. ∎

3*. *The Worm Paradox.* This paradox is also called the "worm on the rubber band paradox." The scenario of the paradox is as follows. Consider a worm that crawls along a 1 m rubber band, that is, 100 cm. The velocity of the worm is $1 \frac{cm}{min}$. After every minute, the rubber band is stretched instantaneously by an additional 1 m. Note that since the worm holds the rubber band with its "feet," its location is also changed during this instantaneous stretch. Will the worm reach to the end of the rubber band? Intuitively, it seems that the "slow" worm will not make it—we show that the worm reaches the end of the rubber band in the following series of questions (although we should wish it a long life to reach this goal).

Let $x(t)$ denote the position of the worm in centimeters as a function of the time $t \in [0, \infty)$ in minutes. Let $\ell(t)$ denote the length of the rubber band in centimeters at time t. Let us sample $x(t)$ and $\ell(t)$ at the time instances $n \in \mathbb{N}$ "just before" the stretching occurs.

(a) Express $x(n+1)$ recursively, that is, by using $x(n), \ell(n+1), \ell(n)$, and additional constants.
(b) Express $\ell(n+1)$ recursively, that is, by using $\ell(n)$ and additional constants.
(c) What is $\frac{x(n+1)}{\ell(n+1)}$?
(d) Find an $n_0 \in \mathbb{N}$ such that, for all $n \ge n_0$, the value that H_n attains is greater than 100, that is, $H_n \ge 100$. What does it imply?

The answers to these subquestions are as follows:

(a) The position of the worm $x(n+1)$ is expressed recursively, as follows:

$$x(n+1) = x(n) \cdot \frac{\ell(n+1)}{\ell(n)} + 1 . \tag{3.8}$$

(b) The length of the rubber band $\ell(n+1)$ is expressed recursively as follows:

$$\ell(n+1) = \ell(n) + 100. \qquad (3.9)$$

(c) Plugging in Eqs. 3.8 and 3.9, we get

$$\frac{x(n+1)}{\ell(n+1)} = \frac{x(n) \cdot \frac{\ell(n+1)}{\ell(n)} + 1}{\ell(n+1)}$$

$$= \frac{x(n)}{\ell(n)} + \frac{1}{\ell(n+1)}.$$

Let $a_{n+1} \triangleq \frac{x(n+1)}{\ell(n+1)}$, then we have managed to show that

$$a_{n+1} = a_n + \frac{1}{\ell(n+1)}. \qquad (3.10)$$

Let us work some more on this recursive formula:

$$a_{n+1} = a_n + \frac{1}{\ell(n+1)}$$

$$= \left(a_{n-1} + \frac{1}{\ell(n)}\right) + \frac{1}{\ell(n+1)}$$

$$= \left(a_{n-2} + \frac{1}{\ell(n-1)}\right) + \frac{1}{\ell(n)} + \frac{1}{\ell(n+1)}$$

$$= \ldots = a_{n-k} + \sum_{i=0}^{k} \frac{1}{\ell(n+1-i)}$$

$$= a_0 + \sum_{i=0}^{n} \frac{1}{\ell(n+1-i)} = \sum_{i=0}^{n} \frac{1}{\ell(n+1-i)}.$$

The first line follows from Eq. 3.10. The second and the third line follow by reapplying Eq. 3.10 on a_n and a_{n-1}, respectively. After realizing the general form of the equation in line four, the fifth line follows by plugging $k = n$ and by the fact that $a_0 = \frac{x(0)}{\ell(0)} = \frac{0}{100}$.

The substitution $j = n - k$ gives

$$\sum_{i=0}^{n} \frac{1}{\ell(n+1-i)} = \sum_{j=0}^{n} \frac{1}{\ell(j+1)}. \qquad (3.11)$$

Since $\ell(k+1) = 100 \cdot (k+1)$, Eq. 3.11 implies that

$$a_{n+1} - \sum_{i=0}^{n} \frac{1}{\ell(i+1)}$$

$$= \sum_{i=0}^{n} \frac{1}{100 \cdot (i+1)}$$

$$= \frac{1}{100} \cdot \sum_{i=1}^{n+1} \frac{1}{i} = \frac{1}{100} \cdot H_{n+1}. \qquad (3.12)$$

Observe that $a_n \to \infty$ as $n \to \infty$. Since the worm reaches the end of the rubber band when $a_n \geq 1$, we conclude that the worm reaches the end. How long does it take?

(d) We use Example 2 to find such an n_0. Equation 3.6 implies that $H_n > 1 + \frac{(\log_2 n)-1}{2}$. To find such an n_0, we require that $H_{n_0} > 1 + \frac{(\log_2 n_0)-1}{2} \geq 100$. Let us solve this formula:

$$1 + \frac{(\log_2 n_0) - 1}{2} \geq 100 \Leftrightarrow$$

$$\frac{(\log_2 n_0) - 1}{2} \geq 99 \Leftrightarrow$$

$$(\log_2 n_0) - 1 \geq 198 \Leftrightarrow$$

$$(\log_2 n_0) \geq 199 \Leftrightarrow$$

$$n_0 \geq 2^{199}.$$

We found out that for $n_0 \geq 2^{199}$, the values that H_n attains are greater than 100. Equation 3.6 also implies that $H_n < (\log_2 n) + 2$. It follows that $H_n < 100$ if $n < 2^{98}$. Hence the worm does not reach the end of the rubber band before 2^{98} minutes have passed.

A more careful inspection (using software tools) implies that for $n_0 = 2^{144}$, $H_{n_0} = 100.3904\ldots$. This, amazingly, implies that our beloved worm will eventually arrive to the end of the rubber band after 2^{144} minutes (which is infinity, for all practical purposes).

PROBLEMS

3.1. Consider the following recursive definition of an arithmetic sequence $\{a_n\}_{n=0}^{\infty}$:
- The first element is simply a_0.
- The reduction rule is $a_{n+1} = a_n + d$.

Prove that the recursive definition is equivalent to Definition 3.3, that is, prove the following claim.

Claim 3.4 $\{a_n\}_{n=0}^{\infty}$ *is an arithmetic sequence iff* $\exists d \forall n : a_{n+1} - a_n = d$.

3.2. Consider the following recursive definition of a geometric sequence $\{b_n\}_{n=0}^{\infty}$:
- The first element is simply b_0.
- The reduction rule is $b_{n+1} = q \cdot b_n$.

Prove that the recursive definition is equivalent to Definition 3.4, that is, prove the following claim.

Claim 3.5 $\{b_n\}_{n=0}^{\infty}$ *is a geometric sequence iff* $\exists q \forall n : a_{n+1}/a_n = q$.

3.3. Prove or refute the following claim.

Claim 3.6 *If* $\{b_n\}_{n=0}^{\infty}$ *is a geometric sequence with a quotient q and $b_n > 0$, then the sequence* $\{a_n\}_{n=0}^{\infty}$ *defined by* $a_n \triangleq \log b_n$ *is an arithmetic sequence. Does your answer depend on the basis of the logarithm?*

3.4. Consider the following sequences. For each sequence, prove/refute if it is (i) arithmetic, (ii) geometric, (iii) harmonic, or (iv) none of those:
(a) $a_n \triangleq 5n$.
(b) $b_n \triangleq n^2$.

      (c) $c_n \triangleq 2^n - 1$.

      (d) $d_n \triangleq 1$.

      (e) $e_n \triangleq 7$.

      (f) $f_n \triangleq g_n + h_n$, where $\{g_n\}_n$ and $\{h_n\}_n$ are arithmetic sequences.

      (g) $p_n \triangleq q_n \cdot r_n$, where $\{q_n\}_n$ and $\{r_n\}_n$ are geometric sequences.

3.5. Prove that $\sum_{i=1}^{n} 2^{-i} = 1 - 2^{-n}$.

3.6. Prove or refute: if a sequence $\{a_n\}_{n \in \mathbb{N}}$ is both an arithmetic sequence and a geometric sequence, then it is a constant sequence; namely, there exists a constant c such that $a_n = c$ for every $n \in \mathbb{N}$.

CHAPTER 4

Directed Graphs

A directed graph is simply an abstraction of a network of one-way roads between a set of cities. When one travels in such a network, one may return to the starting point. In this chapter, we are interested in special networks that exclude the possibility of ever returning to the starting point or to any city we have already visited. We refer to a network as *acyclic*.

Suppose we are traveling in an acyclic network of one-way roads. By definition, on each trip, we may visit each city at most once. A very natural question that arises is; what is the maximum number of cities we can visit? In this chapter, we present a simple and efficient algorithm that finds the longest sequence of cities we can visit in the special case of acyclic networks of one-way roads.

Acyclic directed graphs are also an abstraction of assembly instructions of an airplane model. The vertices in this case are not cities but assembly tasks (glue two parts together, paint a part, etc.). An edge from task u to task v is not a one-way road but a dependence indicating that before task v is started, one must complete task u. Given such assembly instructions, we would like to find an ordering of the tasks that obeys the dependencies. A single worker can then assemble the airplane model by completing one task at a time according to this ordering. Such an ordering is a called a *topological ordering*. We present a simple and efficient algorithm for topological ordering.

Finally, we consider a special subclass of acyclic directed graphs called *rooted trees*. Rooted trees play an important role in defining parse trees of Boolean formulas in Chapter 6.

Why are we so interested in directed graphs? Our main motivation for studying directed graphs is that they can be used to model circuits. Instead of one-way roads and assembly instructions, think of wires that connect basic units (gates and flip-flops).

4.1 DEFINITIONS

Definition 4.1 (*Directed Graph*) Let V denote a finite set and $E \subseteq V \times V$. The pair (V, E) is called a *directed graph* and is denoted by $G = (V, E)$. An element $v \in V$ is called a *vertex* or a *node*. An element $(u, v) \in E$ is called an *arc* or a *directed edge*.

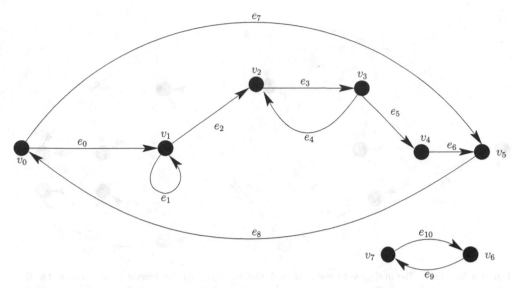

Figure 4.1. A directed graph $G = (V, E)$. The graph has eight vertices, that is, $|V| = 8$. The graph has 11 arcs, that is, $|E| = 11$.

Figure 4.1 depicts a directed graph. The black circles represent the vertices. The arrows represent the arcs. Indeed, an arc is between two nodes. One can think of a directed graph as a road map between cities in which the cities are the nodes and every one-way road is an arc between two cities.

Definition 4.2 (*Path*) A *path* or a *walk* of length ℓ in a directed graph $G = (V, E)$ is a sequence $(v_0, e_0, v_1, e_1, \ldots, v_{\ell-1}, e_{\ell-1}, v_\ell)$ such that (i) $v_i \in V$, for every $0 \leq i \leq \ell$, (ii) $e_i \in E$, for every $0 \leq i < \ell$, and (iii) $e_i = (v_i, v_{i+1})$, for every $0 \leq i < \ell$.

We denote an arc $e = (u, v)$ by $u \xrightarrow{e} v$ or simply $u \longrightarrow v$. A path of length ℓ is often denoted by

$$v_0 \xrightarrow{e_0} v_1 \xrightarrow{e_1} v_2 \cdots v_{\ell-1} \xrightarrow{e_{\ell-1}} v_\ell.$$

Definition 4.3 (*Closed/Simple Path*) The following definitions capture special properties of paths:

1. A path is *closed* if the first and last vertices are equal.
2. A path is *open* if the first and last vertices are distinct.
3. An open path is *simple* if every vertex in the path appears only once in the path.
4. A closed path is *simple* if every interior vertex appears only once in the path. (A vertex is an *interior vertex* if it is not the first or last vertex.)
5. A *self-loop* is a closed path of length 1, for example, $v \xrightarrow{e} v$.

To simplify terminology, we refer to a closed path as a *cycle* and to a simple closed path as a *simple cycle*.

Consider the following paths in the directed graph depicted in Figure 4.1:

1. The path $v_0 \xrightarrow{e_7} v_5 \xrightarrow{e_8} v_0$ is closed.
2. The path $v_2 \xrightarrow{e_3} v_3 \xrightarrow{e_4} v_2 \xrightarrow{e_3} v_3 \xrightarrow{e_5} v_4$ is open.

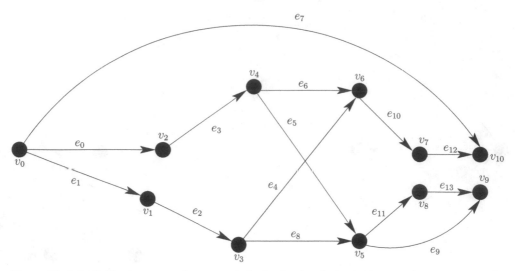

Figure 4.2. A DAG. The in-degree of vertex v_0 is 0, that is, $deg_{in}(v_0) = 0$. Hence v_0 is a source. On the other hand, $deg_{out}(v_0) = 3$. The in-degree of v_9 and v_{10} is 2, while their out-degree is 0, that is, $deg_{out}(v_9) = deg_{out}(v_{10}) = 0$. Hence vertices v_9 and v_{10} are sinks. The in-degree of v_6 is $deg_{in}(v_6) = 2$. The out-degree of v_5 is $deg_{out}(v_5) = 2$.

3. The path $v_7 \xrightarrow{e_{10}} v_6$ is simple.
4. The path $v_0 \xrightarrow{e_0} v_1 \xrightarrow{e_1} v_1 \xrightarrow{e_2} v_2$ is not simple since v_1 appears more than once.
5. The path $v_7 \xrightarrow{e_{10}} v_6 \xrightarrow{e_9} v_7$ is a simple closed path—the interior vertex in this path is v_6.
6. The path $v_1 \xrightarrow{e_1} v_1$ is a self-loop.

Note that $v_0 \longrightarrow v_2$ is not a path.

The special case of directed graphs that lack cycles is used for defining combinational circuits.

Definition 4.4 (*DAG*) A *directed acyclic graph* (DAG) is a directed graph that does not contain any cycles.

Figure 4.2 depicts a DAG. One can check that there are no cycles in the graph depicted in Figure 4.2. Moreover, the graph is depicted in such a way that arcs always "go right." Since there is only one copy of each vertex, we conclude that this graph is a DAG. We say that an arc $u \xrightarrow{e} v$ *enters* v and emanates (or exits) from u.

Definition 4.5 (*In-degree/Out-degree*) The in-degree and out-degree of a vertex v are denoted by $deg_{in}(v)$ and $deg_{out}(v)$, respectively, and defined by

$$deg_{in}(v) \triangleq |\{e \in E \mid e \text{ enters } v\}|$$

$$deg_{out}(v) \triangleq |\{e \in E \mid e \text{ emanates from } v\}|.$$

Definition 4.6 (*Source/Sink*) A vertex is a source if $deg_{in}(v) = 0$. A vertex is a sink if $deg_{out}(v) = 0$.

In circuits, sources correspond to inputs and sinks correspond to outputs.

The following lemma claims that every DAG has at least one sink. The proof idea is to walk in the graph as follows. Let us assume by contradiction that there are no sinks. Pick an arbitrary node as a starting point. Since it is not a sink, it is not a dead end, and there is an arc that emanates from it to another node. We move to the end of this arc and continue our walk from this node. After visiting $|V| + 1$ nodes, we apply the pigeonhole principle (see Corollary 2.8) and conclude that there is a node that we have traversed *twice*, that is, we have revealed a cycle, which contradicts the assumption that the graph is a DAG.

Lemma 4.1 *Every DAG has at least one sink.*

PROOF: Consider a DAG $G = (V, E)$ and assume for the sake of contradiction that no vertex in V is a sink. This means that $deg_{out}(v) > 0$ for every $v \in V$. Pick an arbitrary vertex and denote it by v_0. Since v_0 is not a sink, there is an edge emanating from v_0. Let vertex v_1 be a vertex such that $(v_0, v_1) \in E$. Since G is a DAG, $v_1 \neq v_0$; otherwise, we have revealed a cycle in G. We continue to extend the simple path as follows. Let $v_0 \longrightarrow v_1 \longrightarrow \cdots \longrightarrow v_n$ denote the simple path we have obtained so far. Since v_n is not a sink, there is an edge emanating from v_n. Let vertex v_{n+1} be a vertex such that $(v_n, v_{n+1}) \in E$. Clearly $v_{n+1} \notin \{v_0, \ldots, v_n\}$; otherwise, we have revealed a cycle. Indeed, if $v_{n+1} = v_i$, then $v_i \longrightarrow v_{i+1} \longrightarrow \cdots v_n \longrightarrow v_{n+1} = v_i$ is a cycle, contradicting the assumption that G is acyclic.

Can we really continue this process of extending the path forever? In fact, after building such a path of length $|V|$, we have visited $|V| + 1$ distinct nodes $v_0, \ldots, v_{|V|}$. This is a contradiction since G has only $|V|$ distinct nodes. ∎

We prove the following corollary by a *reduction* of it to Lemma 4.1.

Corollary 4.2 *Every DAG has at least one source.*

PROOF: Given a DAG $G = (V, E)$, consider the *reversed DAG* $G' = (V, E')$, defined by

$$E' \triangleq \{(v, u) \in V \times V \mid (u, v) \in E\}.$$

Indeed, a cycle $v_1 \longrightarrow v_2 \cdots \longrightarrow v_n = v_1$ in G' implies the cycle $v_n \longrightarrow v_{n-1} \cdots \longrightarrow v_1 = v_n$ in G, thus G' is acyclic.

Moreover, a node v is a sink in G' if and only if it is a source in G. By Lemma 4.1, there is a sink v in G'. Hence the vertex v is a source in G, and the corollary follows. ∎

4.2 TOPOLOGICAL ORDERING

In this section we show how one can order the vertices of a DAG so that if u precedes v, then (v, u) is not an arc. This means that if we list the vertices according to this order from left to right, then no arc will point to the left. Our main application of topological ordering is for simulating digital circuits.

Definition 4.7 (*Topological Ordering*) Let $G = (V, E)$ denote a DAG with $|V| = n$. A bijection $\pi : V \rightarrow \{0, \ldots, n-1\}$ is a *topological ordering* if $(u, v) \in E$ implies that $\pi(u) < \pi(v)$.

Note that by contraposition, $\pi(v) < \pi(u)$ implies that $(u, v) \notin E$.

A bijection $\pi : V \to \{0, \ldots, n-1\}$ can be represented by an n-tuple $(v_0, \ldots, v_{n-1})$ in which each vertex appears exactly once. Such an n-tuple is called a *permutation* of the vertices.

Algorithm 4.1 lists a recursive algorithm for sorting the vertices of DAG $G = (V, E)$ in a topological ordering. The algorithm outputs a list of the evaluations of the topological ordering; namely, $\pi(u) = 1, \pi(v) = 2$, and so on. The algorithm uses the following notation:

$$E_v \triangleq \{e \mid e \text{ enters } v \text{ or emanates from } v\}.$$

Algorithm 4.1 $TS(V, E)$—an algorithm for sorting the vertices of a DAG $G = (V, E)$ in Topological Ordering.

---

1. Base case: If $|V| = 1$, then let $v \in V$ and return $(\pi(v) = 0)$.
2. Reduction rule:
   (a) Let $v \in V$ denote a sink.
   (b) Return $(TS(V \smallsetminus \{v\}, E \smallsetminus E_v)$ extended by $(\pi(v) = |V| - 1))$

Algorithm 4.1 and its correctness proof are an example of a *recursion–induction duo*. The algorithm is recursive, and its proof uses induction. In fact, the base case of the recursive algorithm is exactly the induction basis. The reduction rule of the recursive algorithm is used in the proof of the induction step.

Theorem 4.3 *Algorithm* $TS(V, E)$ *computes a topological ordering of a DAG* $G = (V, E)$.

Proof: The proof is by induction on the number of vertices. The induction basis for $|V| = 1$ holds since the algorithm outputs $\pi(v) = 0$, as required.

The induction hypothesis states that if $|V| = n$, then π is a topological ordering.

We now prove the induction step. Assume $|V| = n + 1$. By Lemma 4.1, there is a sink in G. Thus the reduction step succeeds in finding a sink $v \in V$. The directed graph $G' = (V \smallsetminus \{v\}, E \smallsetminus E_v)$ is acyclic and has n vertices. By the induction hypothesis, the recursive call $TS(V \smallsetminus \{v\}, E \smallsetminus E_v)$ computes a topological ordering $\pi : V \smallsetminus \{v\} \to \{0, \ldots, n-1\}$ of G'. This topological ordering is extended by $\pi(v) = n$. Clearly, even after the extension, π is a bijection. To prove that it is a topological ordering, we need to show that $\pi(u') < \pi(v')$ implies that $(v', u') \notin E$. Indeed, if $\pi(v') < n$, then both u' and v' are not the selected sink v. Thus $(v', u') \notin E$ by the induction hypothesis. If $\pi(v') = n$, then $v' = v$ is a sink, and no edge emanates from v', and the theorem follows. ∎

One can think of a DAG as assembly instructions (e.g., how to assemble a couch?). That is, nodes represent actions and arcs between two actions represent dependence between these actions; namely, an arc (u, v) signifies that the action represented by node v cannot begin before the action represented by node u is completed. An example of such an arc in the assembly instructions of a couch is an arc between the action of putting the skeleton together and the action of putting the pillows on the couch. Now, if a single person would like to assemble the couch, she will need to compute a schedule that is a "legal" ordering of the actions. By legal, we mean that she cannot put the pillows on the couch before she has constructed the skeleton of the couch. Such a schedule is a topological sorting of the assembly instructions. In this case, the "time" it will take her to build the couch is, roughly, the number of actions. In Chapter 11, we show how to compute a shortest schedule if the number of workers is large. It is hoped that the more workers there are, the shorter the schedule will become.

EXAMPLES

---

1. Two topological orderings of the vertices of the DAG depicted in Figure 4.2 are

$$(v_0, v_2, v_4, v_7, v_{10}, v_1, v_3, v_6, v_5, v_8, v_9)$$

$$(v_0, v_1, v_3, v_8, v_9, v_2, v_4, v_5, v_6, v_7, v_{10}).$$

   Note that v_6 appears after v_3, since $e_4 = (v_3, v_6)$. Conversely, in one ordering, v_5 precedes v_6, and in the other ordering, v_6 precedes v_5. This is fine because neither $v_5 \longrightarrow v_6$ nor $v_6 \longrightarrow v_5$ are edges.

2. Let us execute Algorithm $TS(V, E)$ on the DAG depicted in Figure 4.2. Since the graph has more than a single node, the algorithm proceeds to the reduction rule. The algorithm picks arbitrarily a sink, that is, v_9. The algorithm removes the edges that enter v_9, that is, e_{13} and e_9. The algorithm sets $\pi(v_9) = |V| = 11$ and makes a recursive call with the DAG $(V \smallsetminus \{v_9\}, E \smallsetminus \{e_{13}, e_9\})$.

   This process continues recursively until the last recursive call, that is, $TS(\{v_0\}, \varnothing)$. Since, in this case, there is only one node, v_0, the algorithm applies the base case and sets $\pi(v_0) = 0$.

   The following is a possible output of the $TS(V, E)$ on the DAG depicted in Figure 4.2:

$$(v_0, v_2, v_1, v_4, v_3, v_6, v_5, v_7, v_8, v_{10}, v_9).$$

4.3 LONGEST PATH IN A DAG

In this section, we show how to compute a longest path in a DAG. Longest paths in DAGs are used to compute the delay of combinational circuits as well as the shortest clock periods of synchronous circuits.

Figure 4.2 depicts a DAG. Note that there might be more than one longest path in a DAG. Indeed, in Figure 4.2, there are four longest paths of length 5. The longest paths are as follows:

1. $v_0 \xrightarrow{e_0} v_2 \xrightarrow{e_3} v_4 \xrightarrow{e_5} v_5 \xrightarrow{e_{11}} v_8 \xrightarrow{e_{13}} v_9,$
2. $v_0 \xrightarrow{e_0} v_2 \xrightarrow{e_3} v_4 \xrightarrow{e_6} v_6 \xrightarrow{e_{10}} v_7 \xrightarrow{e_{12}} v_{10},$
3. $v_0 \xrightarrow{e_1} v_1 \xrightarrow{e_2} v_3 \xrightarrow{e_4} v_6 \xrightarrow{e_{10}} v_7 \xrightarrow{e_{12}} v_{10},$
4. $v_0 \xrightarrow{e_1} v_1 \xrightarrow{e_2} v_3 \xrightarrow{e_8} v_5 \xrightarrow{e_{11}} v_8 \xrightarrow{e_{13}} v_9.$

Note that a longest path in a DAG begins in a source and ends in a sink. We denote the length of a path Γ by $|\Gamma|$.

Definition 4.8 A path Γ that ends in vertex v is a *longest path ending in v* if $|\Gamma'| \leq |\Gamma|$ for every path Γ' that ends in v.

Definition 4.9 A path Γ is a *longest path* if $|\Gamma'| \leq |\Gamma|$ for every path Γ'.

If a directed graph has a cycle, then there does not exist a longest path. Indeed, one could walk around the cycle forever. However, longest paths do exist in DAGs.

Lemma 4.4 *If $G = (V, E)$ is a DAG, then there exists a longest path that ends in v for every v. In addition, there exists a longest path in G.*

PROOF: A path with more than $|V|$ vertices must visit at least one vertex more than once and therefore cannot be simple. A path that is not simple reveals a cycle in G—a contradiction since G is acyclic. Thus the length of every path in G is bounded by $|V|$.

Since there are a finite number of paths of length at most $|V|$ that end in v, it follows that there exists a longest path that ends in v. A similar argument implies that there exists a longest path in G. ■

Lemma 4.4 states that longest paths exist. Our goal in this section is to compute, for every v in a DAG, a longest path that ends in v. We begin with the simpler task of computing the length of a longest path.

The requirements from an algorithm for computing the length of a longest path in a DAG are as follows.

Specification 4.1 *The algorithm longest path is specified as follows:*

input: *A DAG $G = (V, E)$.*
output: *A delay function $d : V \to \mathbb{N}$.*
functionality: *For every vertex $v \in V$, the length of a longest path ending in v equals $d(v)$.*

Note that if a vertex v is a source, then the longest path ending in v has length zero. Indeed, the specification requires in this case that $d(v) = 0$.

The term *delay function* is justified by an application for bounding the delay of a combinational circuit. We later model circuits by DAGs and show that the delay of the output of a gate in the circuit equals $d(v)$ (if all gates have unit delays).

An algorithm for computing lengths of longest paths is listed as Algorithm 4.2. The algorithm uses topological sorting as a subroutine. One could combine the two to obtain a single-pass algorithm; however, the proof of the two-pass algorithm is shorter.

Algorithm 4.2 longest-path-lengths (V, E)—an algorithm for computing the lengths of longest paths in a DAG. Returns a delay function $d(v)$.

---

1. Topological sort: $(v_0, \ldots, v_{n-1}) \leftarrow TS(V, E)$.
2. For $j = 0$ to $(n - 1)$ do
   (a) if v_j is a source, then $d(v_j) \leftarrow 0$
   (b) else

$$d(v_j) = 1 + \max\left\{ d(v_i) \mid i < j \text{ and } (v_i, v_j) \in E \right\}.$$

We now prove the correctness of Algorithm 4.2.

Theorem 4.5 *Algorithm longest-path-lengths(V, E) satisfies Specification 4.1.*

PROOF: The proof is by complete induction on the index j of a vertex in the topological ordering. The induction basis for $j = 0$ holds since v_0 is a source. Thus $d(v_0) = 0$, as required.

The induction hypothesis states that for every $i \leq j$, $d(v_i)$ equals the length of the longest path that ends in v_i.

We now prove the induction step. If v_{j+1} happens to be a source, then $d(v_{j+1}) = 0$, as required. Thus we need to prove the induction step for the case that v_{j+1} is not a source. Consider a longest path Γ that ends in v_{j+1}. Let ℓ denote the length of the path Γ. Clearly $\ell \geq 1$. Denote the vertices and edges in Γ by

$$u_0 \xrightarrow{e_0} u_1 \xrightarrow{e_1} u_2 \cdots u_{\ell-1} \xrightarrow{e_{\ell-1}} u_\ell = v_{j+1}.$$

We need to prove that the algorithm assigns $d(v_{j+1}) = \ell$.
The proof is based on two observations, as follows.

Observation 4.1 *If $v_i \xrightarrow{e} v_{j+1}$ is an arc in E, then $i \leq j$ and $d(v_i) \leq \ell - 1$.*

PROOF OF OBSERVATION 4.1: If $v_i \xrightarrow{e} v_{j+1}$ is an arc in E, then the fact that the vertices are in topological ordering implies that $i \leq j$. To prove the second part, recall that the induction hypothesis says that $d(v_i)$ equals the length of the longest path that ends in v_i. For the sake of contradiction, assume that there exists a path Δ that ends in v_i whose length is longer than $\ell - 1$. Then Γ is not a longest path ending in v_{j+1}. Indeed, consider the path Γ' that begins with Δ and continues with the arc $v_i \xrightarrow{e} v_{j+1}$. The path Γ' is longer than Γ—a contradiction. ∎

Observation 4.2 *The path $\Gamma \setminus \{e_{\ell-1}, u_\ell\}$ is a longest path that ends in $u_{\ell-1}$. In particular, $d(u_{\ell-1}) = \ell - 1$.*

PROOF OF OBSERVATION 4.2: Let i denote the index of $u_{\ell-1}$ in the topological ordering, that is, $u_{\ell-1} = v_i$. By Observation 4.1, $i < j$ and $d(u_{\ell-1}) \leq \ell - 1$. By the induction hypothesis, $d(v_i)$ equals the length of the longest path that ends in $v_i = u_{\ell-1}$. Since $\Gamma \setminus \{e_{\ell-1}, u_\ell\}$ is a path of length $\ell - 1$ that ends in $v_i = u_{\ell-1}$, it follows that $d(u_{\ell-1}) \geq \ell - 1$, and the observation follows. ∎

The algorithm considers the vertex $u_{\ell-1}$ in Line 2. Thus $d(v_{j+1}) \geq 1 + d(u_{\ell-1})$. By Observation 4.2, it follows that $d(v_{j+1}) \geq \ell$. Conversely, by Observation 4.1, every arc that enters v_{j+1} emanates from a vertex v_i with an index $i < j$ and $d(v_i) \leq \ell - 1$. Thus $d(v_{j+1}) \leq \ell$. It follows that $d(v_{j+1}) = \ell$, and the theorem follows. ∎

EXAMPLES

---

1. A *zero length path* that starts at the vertex v is simply the vertex v.
2. *An example of a delay function of DAG.* Let us consider the DAG $G = (V, E)$ depicted in Figure 4.2. Recall that a delay function $d : V \to \mathbb{N}$ satisfies that for every vertex $v \in V$, the length of a longest path ending in v equals $d(v)$. Hence, if we are

interested in computing $d : V \to \mathbb{N}$, we should first find a longest path that ends in v for every $v \in V$, as follows:

(a) v_0: v_0.

(b) v_1: $v_0 \xrightarrow{e_1} v_1$.

(c) v_2: $v_0 \xrightarrow{e_0} v_2$.

(d) v_3: $v_0 \xrightarrow{e_1} v_1 \xrightarrow{e_2} v_3$.

(e) v_4: $v_0 \xrightarrow{e_0} v_2 \xrightarrow{e_3} v_4$.

(f) v_5: $v_0 \xrightarrow{e_0} v_2 \xrightarrow{e_3} v_4 \xrightarrow{e_5} v_5$.

(g) v_6: $v_0 \xrightarrow{e_1} v_1 \xrightarrow{e_2} v_3 \xrightarrow{e_4} v_6$.

(h) v_7: $v_0 \xrightarrow{e_1} v_1 \xrightarrow{e_2} v_3 \xrightarrow{e_4} v_6 \xrightarrow{e_{10}} v_7$.

(i) v_8: $v_0 \xrightarrow{e_0} v_2 \xrightarrow{e_3} v_4 \xrightarrow{e_5} v_5 \xrightarrow{e_{11}} v_8$.

(j) v_9: $v_0 \xrightarrow{e_0} v_2 \xrightarrow{e_3} v_4 \xrightarrow{e_5} v_5 \xrightarrow{e_{11}} v_8 \xrightarrow{e_{13}} v_9$.

(k) v_{10}: $v_0 \xrightarrow{e_1} v_1 \xrightarrow{e_2} v_3 \xrightarrow{e_4} v_6 \xrightarrow{e_{10}} v_7 \xrightarrow{e_{12}} v_{10}$.

Hence the following is the delay function $d : V \to \mathbb{N}$ of the DAG depicted in Figure 4.2:

- $v_0 = 0$.
- $d(v_1) = 1$.
- $d(v_2) = 1$.
- $d(v_3) = 2$.
- $d(v_4) = 2$.
- $d(v_5) = 3$.
- $d(v_6) = 3$.
- $d(v_7) = 4$.
- $d(v_8) = 4$.
- $d(v_9) = 5$.
- $d(v_{10}) = 5$.

Note that although there might be many longest paths, the delay function $d : V \to \mathbb{N}$ is unique.

3. We now execute Algorithm longest-path-lengths(V, E) listed in Algorithm 4.2. The input is the DAG $G = (V, E)$ depicted in Figure 4.2.

The first step in the algorithm is computing a topological sort of the vertices of $G = (V, E)$ by invoking the $TS(V, E)$ algorithm. Recall that in Example 2, on page 43, we have already executed $TS(V, E)$ on the same input. The output of $TS(V, E)$ is:

$$(u_0, \dots, u_{10}) = (v_0, v_2, v_1, v_4, v_3, v_6, v_5, v_7, v_8, v_{10}, v_9) .$$

The second step of the algorithm is to assign a value to $d(u_j)$ for every $j \in \{0, \dots, n-1\}$ in an ordered manner; for example, first we deal with $d(v_0)$ followed by $d(v_2)$.

Hence we first consider $d(v_0)$. Since $d(v_0)$ is a source, we assign it the value 0, that is, $d(v_0) \leftarrow 0$.

We now consider vertex $u_1 = v_2$, that is, we compute $d(v_2)$. The vertex v_2 is not a source, hence we need to calculate

$$d(v_2) = 1 + \max\{d(u_i) \mid i < 1 \text{ and } (u_i, u_1) \in E\}$$

$$= 1 + d(0) = 1 .$$

We then consider v_1, v_4, v_3; the calculation of their delay is similar to that of v_2.

We now consider vertex $u_5 = v_6$, that is, we compute $d(v_6)$. The vertex v_6 is not a source, hence we need to calculate

$$d(v_6) = 1 + \max\{d(u_i) \mid i < 5 \text{ and } (u_i, u_5) \in E\}$$
$$= 1 + \max\{d(v_3), d(v_4)\}$$
$$= 1 + 2 = 3.$$

The rest of the delays are calculated similarly.

4.4 ROOTED TREES

In the following definition, we consider a directed acyclic graph $G = (V, E)$ with a single sink called the root.

Definition 4.10 A DAG $G = (V, E)$ is a *rooted tree* if it satisfies the following conditions:

1. There is a single sink in G.
2. For every vertex in V that is not a sink, the out-degree equals 1.

The single sink in a rooted tree G is called the root, and we denote the root of G by $r(G)$.

Theorem 4.6 *In a rooted tree, there is a unique path from every vertex to the root.*

PROOF: Consider a rooted tree $G = (V, E)$ with a root $r = r(G)$. Assume for the sake of contradiction that there exists a vertex $v \in V$ and two different paths p and q from v to r. First, consider the case that $v \neq r$. Let p^* denote the common prefix of p and q. This means that p^* ends in a vertex u such that p and q exit u via different arcs. Thus the out-degree of u is greater than 1—a contradiction. If $v = r$, then one of these paths from r to r has positive length. This contradicts the fact that r is a sink. Thus we proved that there is at most one path from every vertex to r.

To complete the proof, we show that there exists at least one path. (The proof is similar to the proof of Lemma 4.1.) Clearly the zero length path is a path from r to itself. If $v \neq r$, then follow the arc that exits from v, and continue in this fashion until a sink is reached. Since G is acyclic, a sink is reached after at most $|V| - 1$ arcs. Since the sink is unique, the path reaches the root, as required. ■

Note that the proof of Theorem 4.6 is *constructive*, that is, we show how to find the path from every vertex to the root.

The following claim states that every rooted tree G can be decomposed into rooted trees that are connected to $r(G)$.

Claim 4.7 *Let $G = (V, E)$ denote a* rooted tree. *Let $\{r_i \xrightarrow{e_i} r\}_{i=1}^{k}$ denote the set of arcs that enter the root $r = r(G)$. Define the sets V_i and E_i by*

$$V_i \triangleq \{v \in V : there\ exists\ a\ path\ from\ v\ to\ r_i\ in\ G\}$$

$$E_i \triangleq \{e \in E : the\ arc\ e\ emanates\ from\ a\ vertex\ in\ V_i \smallsetminus \{r_i\}\}.$$

Then

1.   *The sets $V_1, \ldots V_k$ are pairwise disjoint and $V = V_1 \cup \cdots \cup V_k \cup \{r\}$.*
2.   *The graph $G_i \triangleq (V_i, E_i)$ is a rooted tree with $r(G_i) = r_i$, for every $1 \leq i \leq k$.*

PROOF: To prove the first part, we need to show that every vertex in $v \in V \smallsetminus \{r\}$ belongs to exactly one V_i. Fix a vertex $v \in V \smallsetminus \{r\}$. By Theorem 4.6, there is a unique path p from v to r. Let i denote the index such that the path p enters v via the arc $r_i \longrightarrow r$. Hence $v \in V_i$, and v belongs to at least one of the sets $V_1, \ldots, V_k$.

Assume for the sake of contradiction that v belongs to more than one set, namely, $v \in V_i \cap V_j$ for $i \neq j$. Hence there is a path p_i from v to r via r_i and a path p_j from v to r via r_j. The paths p_i and p_j differ in the last arc and are thus different. This contradicts Theorem 4.6. We conclude that every vertex $v \in V \smallsetminus \{r\}$ belongs to exactly one V_i, as required.

To prove the second part, consider a graph $G_i \triangleq (V_i, E_i)$. Since $E_i \subseteq E$, the graph G_i is acyclic. Moreover, the out-degree of every vertex in V_i (with respect to G_i) is at most 1. Since from every vertex in V_i there is a path to r_i, it follows that the out-degree of vertex in $V_i \smallsetminus \{r_i\}$ is at least 1. Finally, r_i is a sink in G_i since E_i does not include edges emanating from r_i. We proved that G_i is a DAG with a single sink, and all the other vertices have an out-degree that equals 1. Hence each G_i is a rooted tree, as required. ■

Note that in the decomposition, we always have $r_i \in V_i$. Indeed, the path with a single node r_i is a zero length path from r_i to r_i. In addition, $r \notin V_i$. Otherwise, we would have a cycle through r and r_i. Thus, for every i, $1 \leq |V_i| \leq |V| - 1$.

We refer to the graphs G_i as *subtrees hanging from the root*. In general, a *subtree H* rooted at v of rooted tree $G = (V, E)$ consists of all the vertices u such that there exists a path in G from u to v. Note that a subtree hanging from the root is simply a subtree that is rooted at a child of the root. We often abbreviate and refer to rooted subtrees simply as subtrees.

The decomposition in Claim 4.7 enables us to design recursive algorithms on rooted trees. Moreover, we can prove the correctness of such a recursive algorithm by induction on the number of vertices in the rooted subtree. Note that the number of vertices in every subtree hanging from the root is strictly smaller than $|V|$.

Figure 4.3 depicts a decomposition in which a rooted tree G is decomposed into two rooted trees G_1 and G_2. We can also obtained larger rooted trees by connecting disjoint rooted trees to a new root.

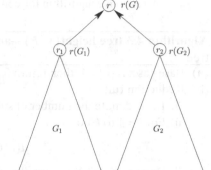

Figure 4.3. A decomposition of a rooted tree G into two rooted trees G_1 and G_2.

Claim 4.8 *If $G_i = (V_i, E_i)$ are disjoint rooted trees, for $1 \leq i \leq k$, then the directed graph $G = (V, E)$ defined subsequently is a rooted tree:*

$$V \triangleq V_1 \cup \cdots \cup V_k \cup \{r\}, \text{ where } \forall i : r \notin V_i \qquad (4.1)$$

$$E \triangleq E_1 \cup \cdots \cup E_k \cup \{r(G_i) \longrightarrow r\}_{i=1}^{k}. \qquad (4.2)$$

PROOF: The out-degree of r is 0, and the out-degree of each r_i is 1. Finally, the out-degree of each vertex $v \in V_i \setminus \{r_i\}$ equals its out-degree in G_i. Thus G is a rooted tree, as required. ∎

Terminology. Given a rooted tree $G = (V, E)$ that contains more than one vertex, we refer to the rooted trees $G_i = (V_i, E_i)$ in Claim 4.7 as the rooted trees *hanging* from $r(G)$. We often refer to sources in a rooted tree as *leaves*. Vertices that are not leaves are called *interior vertices*. The arc that emanates from a vertex in $V \setminus \{r\}$ points to its *parent*. We usually consider rooted trees in which the maximum in-degree equals 2.

The rooted trees hanging from $r(G)$ are ordered. This ordering plays an important role when we use rooted trees as parse trees.

Note that we orient the arcs of a rooted tree from the leaves toward the root. The justification for this orientation is that we use rooted trees for modeling circuits in which the leaves serve as inputs and the root outputs the outcome of the circuit.

EXAMPLES

---

1. Recall that Theorem 4.6 states that if $G = (V, E)$ is a rooted tree, then there is a unique path from every vertex $v \in V$ to the root $r(G)$.

   Hence the following terms are well defined. Let $G = (V, E)$ denote a rooted tree. The *depth* of a vertex $v \in V$ is the length of the path from v to the root. The *height* of a rooted tree $G = (V, E)$ is the maximum depth of a vertex in V.

   Note that a single isolated vertex is a rooted tree. Its height is zero.
2. Consider the special case of computing the longest path in a rooted tree. Clearly Algorithm 4.2 solves this problem. We present a simpler algorithm for rooted trees. One justification for considering this special case are the circuits described in Chapter 12 that have the topology of a tree.

A recursive algorithm for computing tree-height(V, E) is listed in Algorithm 4.3.

Algorithm 4.3 tree height(V, E)—an algorithm for computing the height of a rooted tree.

(a) Base case: if $|V| = 1$, then return 0.
(b) Reduction rule:
    i. Let k denote the number of subtrees hanging from the root $r(G)$.
    ii. For $i = 1$ to k do

$$d(r(G_i)) = \text{tree-height}(V_i, E_i).$$

  iii. Return $d(r(G))$ computed as follows:

$$d(r(G)) = 1 + \max\left\{ d(r(G_i)) \mid i \in \{1, \ldots, k\} \right\}.$$

The correctness of Algorithm 4.3 is formalized in the following claim.

Claim 4.9 *Algorithm tree height(V, E) computes the height of the rooted tree $G = (V, E)$, that is, the length of the longest path ending in $r(G)$.*

PROOF: The proof is by complete induction on the number of vertices. The induction basis for $|V| = 1$ holds since the algorithm outputs 0, as required.

The induction hypothesis states that if $|V| \leq n$, then the output of tree-height(V, E) is the height of the tree $G = (V, E)$. Note that a longest path must end at a sink. Since G is a rooted tree, the only sink is the root r. Hence a longest path ends at the root.

We now prove the induction step. Assume $|V| = n + 1$. By Lemma 4.7, there are k subtrees hanging from the root $r(G)$, denoted by G_i, for $1 \leq i \leq k$. Moreover, Lemma 4.7 implies that $|V_i| < n + 1$ for $1 \leq i \leq k$. Hence the induction hypothesis implies that $d(r(G_i))$, for $1 \leq i \leq k$, equals the height of the tree G_i, for $1 \leq i \leq k$. A longest path ends with an arc $(r(G_i), r(G))$, hence the height of G equals $1 + \max\{d(r(G_i))\}_i$. ∎

3. A topological sorting TREE-TS(V, E) of a rooted tree $G = (V, E)$ can be computed recursively as follows. Sort the vertices in each subtree hanging from the root, and order the root last. (This is a simple depth-first search in the tree.)

PROBLEMS

4.1. The output of Algorithm $TS(V, E)$ when input to the DAG depicted in Figure 4.2 is listed in Example 2 on page 43.

Give another permutation that is a valid output of the algorithm on the same input.

4.2. Prove Corollary 4.2 directly without reducing it to Lemma 4.1.

4.3. Consider a graph $G = (V, E)$ and a subset of vetrices $U \subseteq V$. Let $E_v \triangleq \{e \mid e$ enters v or emanates from $v\}$. The *induced subgraph* $G[U]$ is the graph

$G' = (U, E')$, where the edge set E' is defined by

$$E' \triangleq E \setminus \left(\bigcup_{v \in V \setminus V'} E_v \right).$$

Prove the following claim.

Claim 4.10 *If a graph $G = (V, E)$ is a DAG, then the induced graph $G[U]$ is also a DAG.*

4.4. Consider a DAG $G = (V, E)$. Recall the reversed DAG $G' = (V, E')$ mentioned in Corollary 4.2, that is, given a DAG $G = (V, E)$, the *reversed DAG* $G' = (V, E')$ is defined by

$$E' \triangleq \{(v, u) \in V \times V \mid (u, v) \in E\}.$$

Prove the following claim.

Claim 4.11 *A graph $G = (V, E)$ is a DAG if and only if the graph $G' = (V, E')$ is a DAG.*

4.5. Design an algorithm for topological sorting that recurses by removing a source rather than a sink. Prove the correctness of your algorithm.

4.6. Consider the algorithm described in Example 3.
   (a) Write a detailed recursive algorithm TS-TREE(V, E) that computes a topological sorting of a rooted tree $G = (V, E)$.
   (b) Execute your algorithm on the rooted tree depicted in Figure 6.1 on page 69.
   (c) Prove the correctness of your algorithm by induction.

4.7. Modify Algorithm longest path lengths(V, E) so that it outputs a longest path for each v (rather than its length). Prove the correctness of your algorithm.

4.8. Let $G = (V, E)$ denote a DAG. Let Γ_v denote a path that ends in $v \in V$. Let ℓ denote the length of the path Γ_v. Denote the vertices and edges in Γ_v by

$$u_0 \xrightarrow{e_0} u_1 \xrightarrow{e_1} u_2 \cdots u_{\ell-1} \xrightarrow{e_{\ell-1}} u_\ell = v.$$

Let $\Gamma_v(i)$ denote the prefix of Γ_v of length i, namely,

$$u_0 \xrightarrow{e_0} \cdots \xrightarrow{e_{i-1}} u_i.$$

Prove the following claim.

Claim 4.12 *If Γ_v is a longest path ending in v, then the length of a longest path ending in u_i is i.*

Try to use Claim 4.12 for a different proof of Theorem 4.5.

4.9. Design an algorithm that satisfies the following specification. Prove the correctness of your algorithm.
   Input: A rooted tree $G = (V, E)$ and a vertex $v \in V$.
   Output: A path from v to the root of G.
   Hint: see the proof of Theorem 4.6.

CHAPTER 5

Binary Representation

Perhaps the most natural use of computers is to perform arithmetic operations. Even a simple calculator can add, subtract, multiply, and divide numbers. This leads to the following question: how are numbers stored in a calculator?

You have probably heard the claim that "computers only manipulate zeros and ones." In particular, this claim implies that computers use only zeros and ones to represent numbers. In other words, numbers (as well as everything else) are represented by sequences of zeros and ones.

In this chapter we show how natural numbers (i.e., nonnegative integers) can be represented by sequences of zeros and ones. The representation we use is called *binary representation*. Our main goal in this chapter is to compute the binary representation of a given natural number.

5.1 DIVISION AND MODULO

In this section we consider the outcome of dividing a natural number a by a positive natural number b. If a is *divisible* by b, then we obtain a *quotient* q that is a natural number, namely, $a = q \cdot b$, with $q \in \mathbb{N}$.

However, we also want to consider the case that a is not divisible by b. In this case, division is defined as follows. Consider the two consecutive integer multiples of b that satisfy

$$q \cdot b \le a < (q+1) \cdot b.$$

The *quotient* is defined to be q. The *remainder* is defined to be $r \triangleq a - q \cdot b$. Clearly $0 \le r < b$. Note that the quotient q simply equals $\lfloor \frac{a}{b} \rfloor$.

Notation. Let $(a \bmod b)$ denote the remainder obtained by dividing a by b.

---

1. $3 \bmod 5 = 3$ and $5 \bmod 3 = 2$.
2. $999 \bmod 10 = 9$ and $123 \bmod 10 = 3$.
3. $a \bmod 2$ equals 1 if a is odd, and 0 if a is even. Indeed, if a is even, then $a = 2x$, and then $a - 2 \cdot \lfloor \frac{a}{2} \rfloor = a - 2 \cdot \lfloor \frac{2x}{2} \rfloor = a - 2x = 0$.

    If a is odd, then $a = 2x + 1$, and then $a - 2 \cdot \lfloor \frac{a}{2} \rfloor = a - 2 \cdot \lfloor \frac{2x+1}{2} \rfloor = a - 2 \lfloor x + \frac{1}{2} \rfloor = a - 2x = 1$.
4. $a \bmod b \geq 0$. Indeed, $b \cdot \lfloor \frac{a}{b} \rfloor \leq b \cdot \frac{a}{b} = a$. Therefore $a - b \cdot \lfloor \frac{a}{b} \rfloor \geq a - a = 0$.
5. $a \bmod b \leq b - 1$. Let $q = \lfloor \frac{a}{b} \rfloor$. This means that $b \cdot q \leq a < b \cdot q + b$. Hence $a - b \cdot \lfloor \frac{a}{b} \rfloor = a - b \cdot q < a - (a - b) = b$, which implies that $a \bmod b < b$. Since $a \bmod b$ is an integer, we conclude that $a \bmod b \leq b - 1$.

5.2 BITS AND STRINGS

In decimal numbers, the basic unit of information is a *digit*, that is, a number in the set $\{0, 1, \ldots, 9\}$. In digital computers, the basic unit of information is a *bit*.

Definition 5.1 A bit is an element in the set $\{0, 1\}$.

Since bits are the basic unit of information, we need to represent numbers using bits. How is this done? Numbers are represented in many ways in computers: binary representation, BCD, floating point, two's complement, sign magnitude, and so on. The most basic representation is binary representation. To define binary representation, we first need to define *binary strings*.

Definition 5.2 A binary string is a finite sequence of bits.

There are many ways to denote strings: as a sequence $\{A_i\}_{i=0}^{n-1}$, as a vector $A[0:n-1]$, or simply by $\vec{A}$ if the indexes are known. We often use $A[i]$ to denote A_i.

A basic operation that is applied to strings is called *concatenation*. Given two strings $A[0:n-1]$ and $B[0:m-1]$, the concatenated string is a string $C[0:n+m-1]$ defined by

$$C[i] \triangleq \begin{cases} A[i] & \text{if } 0 \leq i < n \\ B[i-n] & \text{if } n \leq i \leq n+m-1. \end{cases}$$

We denote the operation of concatenating string by $\circ$, for example, $\vec{C} = \vec{A} \circ \vec{B}$.

---

1. Let us consider the string $\{A_i\}_{i=0}^{3}$, where $A_0 = 1$, $A_1 = 1$, $A_2 = 0$, $A_3 = 0$. We often wish to abbreviate and write $A[0:3] = 1100$. This means that when we read the string 1100, we assign the indexes 0 to 3 to this string from left to right.

2. Consider the string $A[0:5] = 100101$. The string $\vec{A}$ has 6 bits, hence $n = 6$. The notation $A[0:5]$ is *zero based*, that is, the first bit in $\vec{A}$ is $A[0]$. Therefore the third bit of $\vec{A}$ is $A[2]$ (which equals 0).

3. We can define strings with arbitrary first and last indexes. For example, $A[3:5] = 110$ means that $\vec{A}$ is a 3-bit string $A_3 A_4 A_5$, where $A_3 = 1$, $A_4 = 1$ and $A_5 = 0$.

4. We can use a formula for the ith bit of a string. For example, let B_i equal 1 if i is odd, and 0 if i is even. This means that $B[0:4] = 01010$.

5. *Examples of concatenation of strings.* Let $A[0:2] = 111$, $B[0:1] = 01$, $C[0:1] = 10$; then

$$\vec{A} \circ \vec{B} = 111 \circ 01 = 11101,$$

$$\vec{A} \circ \vec{C} = 111 \circ 10 = 11110,$$

$$\vec{B} \circ \vec{C} = 01 \circ 10 = 0110,$$

$$\vec{B} \circ \vec{B} = 01 \circ 01 = 0101.$$

5.3 BIT ORDERING

So far, we have used the convention that the indexes of the bits of string increase from left to right. For example, we wrote $A[0:3]$, meaning the sequence (A_0, A_1, A_2, A_3). In particular, the first bit A_0 appears to the left of the second bit A_1, and so on. This convention is natural for text that is written left to right. When we write a number, we place the less significant digit to the right. For example, in the number 123, the digit 3 is less significant than the digit 2, which is less significant than the digit 1. It seems natural to assign the index zero to the units digits. Therefore, if we index the digits so that the index of the units digit is zero, then natural numbers are written in descending index order, for example, (A_3, A_2, A_1, A_0). In this text we continue with the habit of using both ascending indexes and descending indexes. Indeed, bit ordering can be a very confusing issue; in Chapter 8 we discuss further examples of the problems caused by different bit orderings.

Let $i \leq j$. Since we allow bidirectionality, both $A[i:j]$ and $A[j:i]$ denote the same sequence $\{A_k\}_{k=i}^{j}$. However, when we write $A[i:j]$ as a string, the leftmost bit is $A[i]$ and the rightmost bit is $A[j]$. Conversely, when we write $A[j:i]$ as a string, the leftmost bit is $A[j]$ and the rightmost bit is $A[i]$.

We now define the least significant bit and the most significant bit of a string.

Definition 5.3 The *least significant* bit of the string $A[i:j]$ is the bit $A[k]$, where $k \triangleq \min\{i, j\}$. The *most significant* bit of the string $A[i:j]$ is the bit $A[\ell]$, where $\ell \triangleq \max\{i, j\}$.

The abbreviations LSB and MSB are used to abbreviate the least significant bit and the most significant bit, respectively.

EXAMPLES

---

1. . The string $A[3:0]$ and the string $A[0:3]$ denote the same 4-bit string. However, when we write $A[3:0] = 1100$, it means that $A[3] = A[2] = 1$ and $A[1] = A[0] = 0$. When we write $A[0:3] = 1100$, it means that $A[3] = A[2] = 0$ and $A[1] = A[0] = 1$.
2. The least significant bit (LSB) of $A[0:3] = 1100$ is $A[0] = 1$. The most significant bit (MSB) of $\vec{A}$ is $A[3] = 0$.
3. The LSB of $A[3:0] = 1100$ is $A[0] = 0$. The MSB of $\vec{A}$ is $A[3] = 1$.
4. The least significant and most significant bits are determined by the indexes. In our convention, it is not the case that the LSB is always the leftmost bit. Namely, LSB in $A[i:j]$ is the leftmost bit, whereas in $A[j:i]$, the leftmost bit is the MSB.

5.4 BINARY REPRESENTATION

We are now ready to define the natural number represented by a binary string $A[n-1:0]$.

Definition 5.4 The natural number, a, represented in binary representation by the binary string $A[n-1:0]$ is defined by

$$ a \triangleq \sum_{i=0}^{n-1} A[i] \cdot 2^i. $$

In binary representation, each bit has a *weight* associated with it. The weight of the bit $A[i]$ is 2^i.

Notation. Consider a binary string $A[n-1:0]$. We introduce the following notation:

$$ \langle A[n-1:0] \rangle \triangleq \sum_{i=0}^{n-1} A[i] \cdot 2^i. $$

To simplify notation, we often denote strings by capital letters (e.g., A, B, S), and we denote the number represented by a string by a lowercase letter (e.g., a, b, and s).

Leading Zeros. Consider a binary string $A[n-1:0]$. Extending $\vec{A}$ by *leading zeros* means concatenating zeros in indexes higher than $n-1$, namely, (i) extending the length of $A[n-1:0]$ to $A[m-1:0]$, for $m > n$, and (ii) defining $A[i] = 0$, for every $i \in [m-1:n]$.

The following lemma states that extending a binary string by leading zeros does not change the number it represents in binary representation.

Lemma 5.1 *Let $m > n$. If $A[m-1:n]$ is all zeros, then $\langle A[m-1:0] \rangle = \langle A[n-1:0] \rangle$.*

PROOF: We simply follow the definition of $\langle A[m-1:0]\rangle$ and the fact that $A[m-1:n]$ is all zeros to obtain

$$\langle A[m-1:0]\rangle \triangleq \sum_{i=0}^{m-1} A[i]\cdot 2^i$$

$$= \sum_{i=0}^{n-1} A[i]\cdot 2^i + \sum_{i=n}^{m-1} A[i]\cdot 2^i$$

$$= \langle A[n-1:0]\rangle + 0. \quad\blacksquare$$

Representable Ranges. The following lemma bounds the value of a number represented by a k-bit binary string.

Lemma 5.2 *Let $A[k-1:0]$ denote a k-bit binary string. Then $0 \le \langle A[k-1:0]\rangle \le 2^k - 1$.*

PROOF: Since $0 \le A[i] \le 1$ for $0 \le i \le k-1$ and since $\sum_{i=0}^{k-1} 2^i = 2^k - 1$, then

$$0 \le \langle A[k-1:0]\rangle = \sum_{i=0}^{k-1} A[i]\cdot 2^i \le \sum_{i=0}^{k-1} 2^i = 2^k - 1,$$

as required. $\blacksquare$

EXAMPLES

---

1. Consider the strings $A[2:0] \triangleq 000$, $B[3:0] \triangleq 0001$, and $C[3:0] \triangleq 1000$. The natural numbers represented by the binary strings A, B and C are as follows:

    $$\langle A[2:0]\rangle = A[0]\cdot 2^0 + A[1]\cdot 2^1 + A[2]\cdot 2^2 = 0\cdot 2^0 + 0\cdot 2^1 + 0\cdot 2^2 = 0,$$

    $$\langle B[3:0]\rangle = B[0]\cdot 2^0 + B[1]\cdot 2^1 + B[2]\cdot 2^2 + B[3]\cdot 2^3 = 1\cdot 2^0 + 0\cdot 2^1 + 0\cdot 2^2 + 0\cdot 2^3 = 1,$$

    $$\langle C[3:0]\rangle = C[0]\cdot 2^0 + C[1]\cdot 2^1 + C[2]\cdot 2^2 + C[3]\cdot 2^3 = 0\cdot 2^0 + 0\cdot 2^1 + 0\cdot 2^2 + 1\cdot 2^3 = 8.$$

2. For $A[5:0] = 101001$, $\langle A[5:0]\rangle = 1\cdot 2^5 + 0\cdot 2^4 + 1\cdot 2^3 + 0\cdot 2^2 + 0\cdot 2^1 + 1\cdot 2^0 = 41$. Note that the rightmost bit has the "lightest" weight and the leftmost bit is the "heaviest" among the six bits of A. Indeed, the rightmost bit is the LSB, and the leftmost bit is the MSB.

3. For $B[4:0] = 11100$, $\langle B[4:0]\rangle = 0\cdot 2^0 + 0\cdot 2^1 + 1\cdot 2^2 + 1\cdot 2^3 + 1\cdot 2^4 = 28$. Note that if the LSB is 1, then the corresponding natural number is odd, and if the LSB is 0, then the corresponding natural number is even.

4. *Divisibility by powers of* 2. Recall that the natural number represented by the binary string $A[n-1:0]$ is

    $$\langle A[n-1:0]\rangle \triangleq \sum_{i=0}^{n-1} A[i]\cdot 2^i.$$

    We already noticed that if the LSB of A is 0, then $\langle A[n-1:0]\rangle$ is even; furthermore, if both $A[0]$ and $A[1]$ equal 0, then the number $\langle A[n-1:0]\rangle$ is divisible by $4 = 2^2$, for example, 100 represents the number 4, 1100 represents the number 12. We generalize this property in the following lemma.

Lemma 5.3 *Let* $A[n-1:0]$ *be a binary string, and let* $a \triangleq \langle A[n-1:0] \rangle$; *then a is divisible by* 2^k *if* $A[i] = 0$ *for all* $0 \le i \le k-1$.

PROOF: The proof is as follows:

$$\frac{a}{2^k} = \frac{\sum_{i=0}^{n-1} A[i] \cdot 2^i}{2^k}$$

$$= \frac{\sum_{i=k}^{n-1} A[i] \cdot 2^i}{2^k}$$

$$= \frac{\sum_{i=0}^{n-1-k} A[i+k] \cdot 2^{i+k}}{2^k}$$

$$= \frac{2^k \cdot \sum_{i=0}^{n-1-k} A[i+k] \cdot 2^i}{2^k}$$

$$= \sum_{i=0}^{n-1-k} A[i+k] \cdot 2^i,$$

where the first line follows Definition 5.4. The second line follows from the assumption that $A[i] = 0$ for all $0 \le i \le k-1$. The third line follows from changing the indices of the summation. The fourth line follows simply by moving the 2^k term out of the summation.

The lemma follows since summing natural numbers results in a natural number. ∎

5. What is the largest number representable by the following number of bits: (i) 8 bits, (ii) 10 bits, (iii) 16 bits, (iv) 32 bits, and (v) 64 bits?

   Let $A[k-1:0]$ denote a k bit string. Let $a_k \triangleq \langle A[k-1:0] \rangle$; then Lemma 5.2 states that $0 \le a_k \le 2^k - 1$. Hence

   (i) $0 \le a_8 \le 2^8 - 1 = 255$.
   (ii) $0 \le a_{10} \le 2^{10} - 1 = 1023$.
   (iii) $0 \le a_{16} \le 2^{16} - 1 = 65535$.
   (iv) $0 \le a_{32} \le 2^{32} - 1 = 4294967295$.
   (v) $0 \le a_{64} \le 2^{64} - 1 = 18446744073709551615$.

6. Now we can discuss a matter that is close to our hearts, that is, the relation between word length and memory size in a computer. A *central processing unit* (CPU) addresses its memory modules by a fixed-size bit string that is called a *word*. Nowadays it is typical that the CPU's word is 32 and 64 bits.

   Let us define some units of measurement in this context: a *byte* (B) is an 8-bit length word. A *kilo-bit* (Kb) is 2^{10} bits. Hence a *kilo-byte* (KB) is $8 \cdot 2^{10}$ bits. A *mega-bit* (Mb) is $2^{10} \cdot 2^{10} = 2^{20}$ bits. Analogously, a *mega-byte* (MB) is $8 \cdot 2^{20}$ bits. A *giga-bit* (Gb) is $2^{10} \cdot 2^{20} = 2^{30}$ bits. Analogously, a *giga-byte* (GB) is $8 \cdot 2^{30}$ bits. If we consider words of ω bits, then a *giga-word* (GW) is $\omega \cdot 2^{30}$ bits.

   What is the size of single memory module in GW if the CPU's word length is 32 bits?

   Since a_{32} attains values in $\{0, \ldots, 2^{32} - 1\}$, it implies that the CPU can address 2^{32} different values, that is, to address 2^{32} words. That means that if your *personal computer* (PC) has a 32-bit CPU, then there is no need to purchase more than 4 GW of memory. Note that one should check whether the basic data item accessible by the CPU is a word or a byte. Here we assume that the memory is word addressable.

In Part IV we consider the design of such a CPU.

7. Consider $C[6:0] = 0001100$ and $D[3:0] = 1100$. Note that $\langle C \rangle = \langle D \rangle = 12$. Since the leading zeros do not affect the value represented by a string, a natural number has infinitely many binary representations.

8. Consider the string $A[3:0] = 0111$. The extension of $A[3:0]$ by two leading zeros results in the string $A[5:0] = 000111$.

5.5 COMPUTING A BINARY REPRESENTATION

Our goal in this section is to show how to compute a binary representation of a natural number. In addition, we prove that every natural number has a unique binary representation.

An algorithm for computing a binary representation is listed as Algorithm 5.1. The algorithm, called $BR(x, k)$, is specified as follows:

Inputs: $x \in \mathbb{N}$ and $k \in \mathbb{N}^+$, where x is a natural number for which a binary representation is sought and k is the length of the binary string that the algorithm should output.
Output: The algorithm outputs "fail" or a k-bit binary string $A[k - 1:0]$.
Functionality: The relation between the inputs and the output is as follows:

1. If $0 \le x < 2^k$, then the algorithm outputs a k-bit string $A[k - 1:0]$ that satisfies $x = \langle A[k - 1:0] \rangle$.
2. If $x \ge 2^k$, then the algorithm outputs "fail."

The algorithm is recursive. This means that it is described using base cases and reduction rules. The base cases deal with two cases: (i) x is too large, in which case a "fail" is returned, and (ii) $k = 1$, in which case $x \in \{0, 1\}$, and the binary representation of x is simply the bit x.

The reduction rules first compute the most significant bit (MSB) of the binary representation. Next, the algorithm recursively computes the remaining $k - 1$ bits. The output is the MSB concatenated with the remaining $k - 1$ bits.

Algorithm 5.1 BR(x, k)—an algorithm for computing a binary representation of a natural number a using k bits.

---

1. Base cases:
   (a) If $x \ge 2^k$, then return (fail).
   (b) If $k = 1$, then return (x).
2. Reduction rule:
   (a) If $x \ge 2^{k-1}$, then return $(1 \circ BR(x - 2^{k-1}, k - 1))$.
   (b) If $x \le 2^{k-1} - 1$, then return $(0 \circ BR(x, k - 1))$.

The correctness of algorithm $BR(x, k)$ is summarized in the following theorem.

Theorem 5.4 *If $x \in \mathbb{N}$, $k \in \mathbb{N}^+$, and $x < 2^k$, then algorithm $BR(x, k)$ returns a k-bit binary string $A[k - 1 : 0]$ such that $\langle A[k - 1 : 0] \rangle = x$.*

PROOF: The proof is by induction on k. The induction basis for $k = 1$ holds since $x < 2^1$ implies that $x \in \{0, 1\}$. Hence x is represented by the 1-bit string $A[0] = x$.

The induction hypothesis states that for every $x < 2^k$, algorithm $BR(x, k)$ outputs a k-bit binary string $A[k - 1 : 0]$ that $\langle A[k - 1 : 0] \rangle = x$.

We now prove the induction step for $k + 1$. Consider a number x such that $x < 2^{k+1}$. We consider the two cases of the reduction rules:

1. Assume $x \geq 2^k$. In this case, the reduction rule returns $A[k] = 1$ and $A[k - 1 : 0]$ is the output of $BR(x - 2^k, k)$. Since $x < 2^{k+1}$, it follows that $x - 2^k < 2^k$. Hence the induction hypothesis when applied to $BR(x - 2^k, k)$ implies that

$$\langle A[k - 1 : 0] \rangle = x - 2^k. \tag{5.1}$$

    Hence

$$x = 2^k + (x - 2^k)$$
$$= A[k] \cdot 2^k + \langle A[k - 1 : 0] \rangle$$
$$= \langle A[k : 0] \rangle,$$

    where the second line follows from $A[k] = 1$ and Eq. 5.1. The third line follows by the definition of binary representation, and the induction step follows for this case.
2. Assume $x \leq 2^k - 1$. In this case, the reduction rule returns $A[k] = 0$ and $A[k - 1 : 0]$ is the output of $BR(x, k)$. Again, by applying the induction hypothesis to $BR(x, k)$,

$$\langle A[k - 1 : 0] \rangle = x.$$

    Hence

$$x = A[k] \cdot 2^k + \langle A[k - 1 : 0] \rangle$$
$$= \langle A[k : 0] \rangle,$$

    and the induction step follows for this case.

This completes the induction step, and the theorem follows. ∎

One may ask the following question: how can we know for sure that none of the recursive calls returns a "fail"? Is it possible to have $x < 2^k$ in the initial call of $BR(x, k)$ but to have $x' \geq 2^{k'}$ in one of the recursive calls? The proof of Theorem 5.4 indirectly shows that such an overflow cannot happen. We can directly prove that such an overflow cannot happen by induction on k. The induction basis for $k = 1$ is trivial since there are no recursive calls. The induction step is proven as follows. Assume that $x < 2^k$. In the recursive call, if x is "large," then we subtract 2^{k-1} from x to make sure that $x - 2^{k-1} < 2^{k-1}$ in the recursive call. By the induction hypothesis, all recursive calls do not overflow. If $x < 2^{k-1}$, then by the induction hypothesis, the recursive calls do not overflow.

The following corollary states that every positive integer has a binary representation of logarithmic length.

Corollary 5.5 *Every positive integer a has a binary representation by a k-bit binary string if $k \geq \lfloor \log_2(a) \rfloor + 1$.*

PROOF: By Theorem 5.4, if $a < 2^k$, then a can be represented by a k-bit binary string. To complete the proof, it suffices to prove that

$$k \geq \lfloor \log_2(a) \rfloor + 1 \quad \Rightarrow \quad a < 2^k.$$

Indeed, let $k' \triangleq \lfloor \log_2(a) \rfloor$. Then

$$2^{k'} \leq a < 2^{k'+1}.$$

By the assumption on k, we have $k \geq k' + 1$, and therefore $a < 2^{k'+1} < 2^k$, as required. ∎

Theorem 5.6 *The binary representation function $\langle \rangle_k : \{0,1\}^k \to \{0, \ldots, 2^k - 1\}$ defined by*

$$\langle A[k-1:0] \rangle_k \triangleq \sum_{i=0}^{k-1} A[i] \cdot 2^i$$

is a bijection (i.e., one-to-one and onto) from $\{0,1\}^k$ to $\{0, \ldots, 2^k - 1\}$.

PROOF: Lemma 5.2 states that every k-bit string represents a number in $\{0, \ldots, 2^k - 1\}$, thus the range of $\langle \rangle_k$ is indeed in $\{0, \ldots, 2^k - 1\}$. Corollary 5.5 states that every number in the set $\{0, \ldots, 2^k - 1\}$ can be represented by a k-bit string. This implies that the binary representation function $\langle \rangle_k : \{0,1\}^k \to \{0, \ldots, 2^k - 1\}$ is onto.

The cardinality of the domain and the range of the function $\langle \rangle_k$ is 2^k. By Lemma 2.10, the function $\langle \rangle_k$ is also one-to-one, as required. ∎

Corollary 5.7 (*Unique Binary Representation*) *Every number in $\{0, \ldots, 2^k - 1\}$ has a unique binary representation by a k-bit string.*

PROOF: Theorem 5.6 states that $\langle \rangle_k$ is one-to-one and onto. Since $\langle \rangle_k$ is onto, then every $x \in \{0, \ldots, 2^k - 1\}$ has at least one binary representation. Since $\langle \rangle_k$ is one-to-one, then every $x \in \{0, \ldots, 2^k - 1\}$ has at most one binary representation. The corollary follows. ∎

EXAMPLES

---

1. Computing a binary representation. Compute a binary representation by applying Algorithm 5.1 on the following inputs: (i) $(2, 1)$ and (ii) $(7, 3)$.

    (a) Since $2 \geq 2^1$, the algorithm outputs "fail."
    (b) The full execution of the algorithm is as follows.
        i. The input $(7, 3)$ does not match any of the bases, so we proceed to the reduction rules.
        ii. Since $7 \geq 2^{3-1} = 4$, we apply the first reduction rule, that is,

        $$\text{return } (1 \circ BR(7 - 2^{3-1} = 3, 2)).$$

A. The input $(3, 2)$ does not match any of the bases, so we proceed to the reduction rules.

B. Since $3 \geq 2^{2-1} = 2$, we apply the first reduction rule, that is,

$$\text{return } (1 \circ BR(3 - 2^{2-1} = 1, 1)) \,.$$

- The input $(1, 1)$ matches the second base case, hence we return 1.

C. The recursive call returns 11.

iii. The last recursive call returns 111.

Indeed, $\langle 111 \rangle = 7$, as required.

2. We claim that when a natural number is multiplied by 2, its binary representation is "shifted left," while a single zero bit is padded from the right. That property is summarized in the following lemma.

Lemma 5.8 *Let $a \in \mathbb{N}$. Let $A[k-1:0]$ be a k-bit string such that $a = \langle A[k-1:0] \rangle$. Let $B[k:0] \triangleq A[k-1:0] \circ 0$, then*

$$2 \cdot a = \langle B[k:0] \rangle \,.$$

PROOF:

$$\langle B[k:0] \rangle = \sum_{i=0}^{k} B[i] \cdot 2^i$$

$$= \sum_{i=1}^{k} B[i] \cdot 2^i$$

$$= \sum_{i=0}^{k-1} B[i+1] \cdot 2^{i+1}$$

$$= 2 \cdot \sum_{i=0}^{k-1} B[i+1] \cdot 2^i$$

$$= 2 \cdot \sum_{i=0}^{k-1} A[i] \cdot 2^i$$

$$= 2 \cdot \langle A[k-1:0] \rangle$$

$$= 2 \cdot a \,.$$

The first line follows from Definition 5.4 and by the definition of the concatenation operation. The second line follows since the LSB of the $k+1$-bit string $B[k:0]$ is 0. The third line follows by index manipulation. The fourth line follows from the definition of $\vec{B}$. The fifth line follows from, again, Definition 5.4. The last line follows from the assumption that $a = \langle A[k-1:0] \rangle$. The lemma follows. ∎

3. We consider an additional algorithm $BR'(x, k)$ for computing a binary representation. The algorithm is listed as Algorithm 5.2. The algorithm's specification is identical to the $BR(x, k)$ algorithm.

The base cases of this algorithm are identical to the base cases of the $BR(x, k)$ algorithm. The reduction rules of the $BR'(x, k)$ algorithm first compute the LSB of the binary representation. Next the algorithm recursively computes the remaining $k-1$ bits. The output is the LSB concatenated with the remaining $k-1$ bits.

Algorithm 5.2 BR$'$(x, k)—an LSB-to-MSB algorithm for computing a binary representation of a natural number a using k bits.

(a) Base cases:
    i. If $x \geq 2^k$, then return (fail).
    ii. If $k = 1$, then return (x).
(b) Reduction rule:
    i. If x is even, then return $(BR'(x/2, k-1) \circ 0)$.
    ii. If x is odd, then return $(BR'((x-1)/2, k-1) \circ 1)$.

The correctness of algorithm $BR'(x, k)$ is summarized in the following theorem.

Theorem 5.9 *If $x \in \mathbb{N}$, $k \in \mathbb{N}^+$, and $x < 2^k$, then algorithm $BR'(x, k)$ returns a k-bit binary string $A[k-1:0]$ such that $\langle A[k-1:0] \rangle = x$.*

PROOF: The proof is by induction on k. The induction basis for $k = 1$ holds since $x < 2^1$ implies that $x \in \{0, 1\}$. Hence x is represented by the 1-bit string $A[0] = x$.

The induction hypothesis states that for every $x < 2^k$, algorithm $BR'(x, k)$ outputs a k-bit binary string $A[k-1:0]$ that $\langle A[k-1:0] \rangle = x$.

We now prove the induction step for $k+1$. Consider a number x such that $x < 2^{k+1}$. We consider the two cases of the reduction rules:

(a) Assume x is even. In this case, the reduction rule returns $A[0] = 0$ and $A[k:1]$ is the output of $BR'(x/2, k)$. Since x is even, it follows that $x/2 \in \mathbb{N}$. Since $x < 2^{k+1}$, it follows that $x/2 < 2^k$. Hence the induction hypothesis when applied to $BR'(x/2, (k+1) - 1)$ implies that

$$\sum_{i=0}^{k-1} A[i+1] \cdot 2^i = x/2. \tag{5.2}$$

Hence

$$x = 2 \cdot (x/2)$$

$$= 2 \cdot \sum_{i=0}^{k-1} A[i+1] \cdot 2^i$$

$$= \langle A[k:0] \rangle,$$

where the second line follows from Eq. 5.2. The third line follows from Lemma 5.8 and since $A[0] = 0$. The induction step follows for this case.

(b) Assume x is odd. In this case, the reduction rule returns $A[0] = 1$, and $A[k:1]$ is the output of $BR'((x-1)/2, k)$. Since x is odd, it follows that $(x-1)/2 \in \mathbb{N}$. Since $x < 2^{k+1}$, it follows that $(x-1)/2 < 2^k$. Hence the induction hypothesis when applied to $BR'((x-1)/2, (k+1) - 1)$ implies that

$$\sum_{i=0}^{k-1} A[i+1] \cdot 2^i = (x-1)/2. \tag{5.3}$$

Hence

$$x - 1 = 2 \cdot ((x-1)/2)$$

$$= 2 \cdot \sum_{i=0}^{k-1} A[i+1] \cdot 2^i$$

$$= \langle A[k:1] \circ 0 \rangle .$$

Where the second line follows from Eq. 5.3. The third line follows from Lemma 5.8. This implies that $x = \langle A[k:1] \circ 1 \rangle$. The induction step follows for this case.

This completes the induction step, and the theorem follows. ∎

4. *Hexadecimal representation.* In binary representation, the set of digits is $\{0, 1\}$. In decimal representation, the set of digits is $\{0, 1, \ldots, 9\}$. We now present a representation, called hexadecimal representation, in which the set of digits is $\{0, 1, \ldots, 15\}$. Accordingly, the radix is 16. This means that the weight of the ith digit is 16^i.

In hexadecimal representation, a number is represented by a string of digits over the set $\{0, 1, \ldots, 15\}$. One technicality is that the digits above 9 require two letters. This inconvenience is mitigated by using the letters $A, B, \ldots, F$ with the following meaning: $A = 10$, $B = 11$, $C = 12$, $D = 13$, $E = 14$, and $F = 15$.

A *hexadecimal digit* is an element in $\{0, 1, \ldots, 9, A, B, \ldots, F\}$. A *hexadecimal string* is a finite sequence of hexadecimal digits.

Definition 5.5 The natural number, h, represented in hexadecimal representation by the hexadecimal string $H[n-1:0]$ is defined by

$$h \triangleq \sum_{i=0}^{n-1} H[i] \cdot 16^i .$$

Consider the following examples of hexadecimal representation.
(a) $H[2:0] = A02$.

$$h = H[0] \cdot 16^0 + H[1] \cdot 16^1 + H[2] \cdot 16^2 = 2 \cdot 16^0 + 0 \cdot 16^1 + 10 \cdot 16^2$$

$$= 2 + 0 + 2560 = 2562 .$$

(b) $H = FFF$.

$$h = H[0] \cdot 16^0 + H[1] \cdot 16^1 + H[2] \cdot 16^2 = 15 \cdot 16^0 + 15 \cdot 16^1 + 15 \cdot 16^2$$

$$= 15 + 240 + 3840 = 4095 .$$

(c) $H = ABC$.

$$h = H[0] \cdot 16^0 + H[1] \cdot 16^1 + H[2] \cdot 16^2 = 12 \cdot 16^0 + 11 \cdot 16^1 + 10 \cdot 16^2$$

$$= 12 + 176 + 2560 = 2748 .$$

5. *Computing a hexadecimal representation.* Our goal in this example is to show how to compute a hexadecimal representation of a natural number. Recall that in

Section 5.5 and in Example 3, we showed how to compute the binary representation of a given natural number. One could adapt these algorithms to compute the hexadecimal representation. Instead, we show how to "convert" a binary string to a hexadecimal string such that both strings represent the same natural number. The conversion in the other direction is done similarly and is left as an exercise.

The conversion is as follows. Let $X[n - 1 : 0]$ denote an n-bit binary string. For simplicity, assume that $n = 4k$ for some $k \in \mathbb{N}$ (if n is not divisible by 4, simply add leading zeros). Partition $X[n - 1 : 0]$ into k disjoint blocks of 4 bits: $X[3 : 0]$, $X[7 : 4]$, and so on. Let $H_X[k - 1 : 0]$ denote a k-digit hexadecimal string in which $H_X[i]$ equals the number represented by the ith 4-bit block of $X[n - 1 : 0]$. Formally

$$H_X[i] = \langle X[4i + 3 : 4i] \rangle,$$

for every $0 \le i \le k - 1$.

For example,

(a)

$$X[7 : 0] = 0010\ 1010$$

$$H_X[1 : 0] = \quad 2 \quad A.$$

Note that the hexadecimal digit 2 corresponds to the binary string 0010, and that the hexadecimal digit A corresponds to the binary string 1010.

(b)

$$X[15 : 0] = 1^{16}$$

$$H_X[3 : 0] = FFFF.$$

Indeed, the natural number represented by the binary string X is $2^{16} - 1$, and the natural number represented by H_X is $16^4 - 1 = 2^{16} - 1$.

We claim that this conversion has the following property.

Lemma 5.10 *The number represented by* $H_X[k - 1 : 0]$ *is* $\langle X[n - 1 : 0] \rangle$.

PROOF: Let h denote the number represented by $H_X[k - 1 : 0]$, then

$$h = \sum_{i=0}^{k-1} H_X[i] \cdot 16^i$$

$$= \sum_{i=0}^{k-1} \langle X[4i + 3 : 4i] \rangle \cdot 16^i$$

$$= \sum_{i=0}^{k-1} \left(\sum_{\ell=4i}^{4i+3} X[\ell] \cdot 2^{\ell-4i} \right) \cdot 16^i$$

$$= \sum_{i=0}^{k-1} \left(\sum_{\ell=4i}^{4i+3} X[\ell] \cdot 2^{\ell} \cdot 2^{-4i} \right) \cdot 2^{4i}$$

$$= \sum_{i=0}^{n-1} X[i] \cdot 2^i = \langle X[n - 1 : 0] \rangle.$$

where the first equality follows from Definition 5.5. The second equality follows from the definition of H_X. The third equality follows from Definition 5.4. The

fifth equality follows from the definition of H_X. The last equality follows from Definition 5.4, as required. ■

5.6* MORE ON UNIQUE BINARY REPRESENTATION

In the following theorem, we present an alternative proof to Theorem 5.6 that every number has a unique binary representation. This is, of course, false since we can add leading zeros to a string without changing the number it represents. There are two ways to fix this problem. First, we claim that if $0 \leq a < 2^k$, then a has a unique binary representation by a k-bit string. Second, we could claim that if two strings represent the same number, then one string is an extension of the other by leading zeros.

We first prove two lemmas.

Lemma 5.11 *If $a_i \in \{-1, 0, 1\}$ for every $0 \leq i < n$, then*

$$-(2^n - 1) \leq \sum_{i=0}^{n-1} a_i \cdot 2^i \leq 2^n - 1.$$

PROOF: The upper bound follows from $a_i \leq 1$ and by bounding the sum of the geometric series $\sum_{i=1}^{n-1} 2^i$. The lower bound follows from $a_i \geq -1$. Thus

$$\sum_{i=0}^{n-1} a_i \cdot 2^i \geq -\sum_{i=0}^{n-2} 2^i$$

$$= -(2^n - 1). \quad ■$$

Lemma 5.12 *If $a_i \in \{-1, 0, 1\}$ for every $0 \leq i < n$, then*

$$\sum_{i=0}^{n-1} a_i \cdot 2^i = 0 \quad \Longleftrightarrow \quad a_0 = \cdots = a_{n-1} = 0.$$

PROOF: If $a_0 = \cdots = a_{n-1} = 0$, then clearly $\sum_{i=0}^{n-1} a_i \cdot 2^i = 0$. To prove the converse direction, assume that there exists an i such that $a_i \neq 0$. Let

$$i^* \triangleq \max\{i \mid a_i \neq 0\}.$$

Note that i^* is well defined since there the set $\{i \mid a_i \neq 0\}$ is not empty.

Note that since $a_i = 0$, for every $i \geq i^*$, it follows that

$$\sum_{i=0}^{n-1} a_i \cdot 2^i = \sum_{i=0}^{i^*} a_i \cdot 2^i$$

$$= a_{i^*} \cdot 2^{i^*} + \sum_{i=0}^{i^*-1} a_i \cdot 2^i.$$

By Lemma 5.11,

$$-(2^{i^*} - 1) \leq \sum_{i=0}^{i^*-1} a_i \cdot 2^i \leq 2^{i^*} - 1.$$

Now consider two cases:

1. If $a_{i^*} = 1$, then

$$\sum_{i=0}^{n-1} a_i \cdot 2^i = 2^{i^*} + \sum_{i=0}^{i^*-1} a_i \cdot 2^i$$

$$\geq 2^{i^*} - (2^{i^*} - 1) > 0.$$

2. If $a_{i^*} = -1$, then

$$\sum_{i=0}^{n-1} a_i \cdot 2^i = -2^{i^*} + \sum_{i=0}^{i^*-1} a_i \cdot 2^i$$

$$\leq -2^{i^*} + (2^{i^*} - 1) < 0.$$

In both cases, $\sum_{i=0}^{n-1} a_i \cdot 2^i \neq 0$, as required, and the lemma follows. ∎

Theorem 5.13 *Consider two binary strings $A[n-1:0]$ and $B[m-1:0]$, where $m \geq n$. If $\langle \vec{A} \rangle = \langle \vec{B} \rangle$, then $A[n-1:0] = B[n-1:0]$ and $B[m-1:n]$ is all zeros.*

PROOF: The proof is by contradiction. Assume that $\langle \vec{A} \rangle = \langle \vec{B} \rangle$, then

$$0 = \langle \vec{A} \rangle - \langle \vec{B} \rangle \tag{5.4}$$

$$= \left(\sum_{i=0}^{n-1} A_i \cdot 2^i \right) - \left(\sum_{i=0}^{m-1} B_i \cdot 2^i \right)$$

$$= \left(\sum_{i=0}^{n-1} (A_i - B_i) \cdot 2^i \right) + \left(\sum_{i=n}^{m-1} (-B_i) \cdot 2^i \right).$$

Since $(A_i - B_i) \in \{-1, 0, 1\}$ and $(-B_i) \in \{-1, 0\}$, by Lemma 5.12, (1) $A_i - B_i = 0$ for every $0 \leq i < n$ and (2) $B_i = 0$ for every $n \leq i < m$, and the theorem follows. ∎

PROBLEMS

5.1. Let $a, c \in \mathbb{N}$ and let $b, d \in \mathbb{N}^+$. Prove the following inequalities:

(a) $\lceil \frac{a}{b} \rceil \leq \lfloor \frac{a}{b} \rfloor + 1$.

(b) $b \cdot \lceil \frac{a}{b} \rceil \geq a$. Equality holds if and only if a is divisible by b.

(c) $\lceil \frac{a}{b} + \frac{c}{d} \rceil \leq \lceil \frac{a}{b} \rceil + \lceil \frac{c}{d} \rceil$.

(d) $\lceil \frac{a \cdot c}{b} \rceil \leq \lceil \frac{a}{b} \rceil \cdot c$. Hint: prove by induction on c and use item 3.

5.2. What are the numbers represented by the following binary strings?

$$A[1:0] = 10,$$

$$B[2:0] = 110, \ .$$

$$C[3:0] = 1001,$$

$$D[3:0] = 1110.$$

5.3. Compute the binary representation by applying Algorithms 5.1 and 5.2 on the following natural numbers: (i) 3, (ii) 8, and (ii) 15. Show a full execution of the algorithm, including the input you have chosen for every number, for example, $(3, 2)$.

5.4.   Generalize Lemma 5.8 as follows.

Lemma 5.14 *Let* $a \in \mathbb{N}$. *Let* $A[k - 1 : 0]$ *be a* k-*bit string such that* $a = \langle A[k - 1 : 0]\rangle$.

$$\text{Let } B[k + \ell - 1 : 0] \triangleq A[k - 1 : 0] \circ \overbrace{0 \cdots 0}^{\ell \text{ zeros}}, \text{ then}$$

$$2^{\ell} \cdot a = \langle B[k + \ell - 1 : 0]\rangle.$$

5.5.   Prove the other direction of Lemma 5.3, formulated as follows.

Lemma 5.15   *Let* $A[n - 1 : 0]$ *be a binary string, and let* $a \triangleq \langle A[n - 1 : 0]\rangle$; *then* a *is divisible by* 2^k *if and only if* $A[i] = 0$ *for all* $0 \le i \le k - 1$.

5.6.   This question deals with the conversion of a hexadecimal string to a binary string such that both strings represent the same natural number. Let $H[k - 1 : 0]$ denote a k-digit hexadecimal string. Let $X_H[n - 1 : 0]$ denote an n-bit binary string. Answer the following questions:

   (a) Define the conversion, that is, define the binary string X_H as a function of the hexadecimal string H.

   (b) Let h denote the number represented by the hexadecimal string H. Prove that

$$\langle X_H \rangle = h.$$

CHAPTER 6

Propositional Logic

In this chapter, we turn to a topic in mathematical logic called *propositional logic*. Propositional logic is a key tool in logical reasoning and is used to understand and even generate precise proofs. Our attraction to propositional logic is ignited by the ability to represent Boolean functions by *Boolean formulas*. Some Boolean functions can be represented by short Boolean formulas, thus offering a concise and precise way to describe Boolean functions.

6.1 BOOLEAN FORMULAS

Building Blocks. The building blocks of a Boolean formula are constants, variables, and connectives.

1. A *constant* is either 0 or 1. As in the case of bits, we interpret a 1 as "true" and a 0 as "false." The terms *constant* and *bit* are synonyms; the term *bit* is used in Boolean functions and in circuits, while the term *constants* is used in Boolean formulas.
2. A *variable* is an element in a set of variables. We denote the set of variables by U. The set U does not contain constants. Variables are usually denoted by uppercase letters.
3. Connectives are used to build longer formulas from shorter ones. We denote the set of connectives by C. We consider unary, binary, and higher arity connectives.
   (a) There is only one *unary connective* called *negation*. Negation of a variable A is denoted by $\text{NOT}(A)$, $\neg A$, or $\bar{A}$.
   (b) There are several *binary connectives*; the most common are AND (denoted also by $\wedge$ or $\cdot$) and OR (denoted also by $\vee$ or $+$). A binary connective is applied to two formulas. We later show the relation between binary connectives and Boolean functions $B : \{0, 1\}^2 \to \{0, 1\}$.
   (c) A connective has *arity* j if it is applied to j formulas. The arity of negation is 1, the arity of AND is 2, and so on.

To summarize, we use the following notation:

$$U \text{ is the set of variables;}$$
$$C \text{ is the set of connectives.}$$

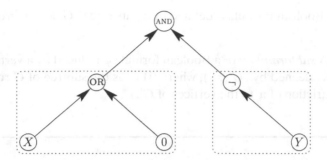

Figure 6.1. A parse tree that corresponds to the Boolean formula $((X \text{ OR } 0) \text{ AND } (\neg Y))$. The rooted trees that are hanging from the root of the parse tree (the AND connective) are bordered by dashed rectangles.

Parse Trees. We use parse trees to define Boolean formulas.

Definition 6.1 A *parse tree* is a pair (G, π), where $G = (V, E)$ is a rooted tree and $\pi : V \to \{0, 1\} \cup U \cup C$ is a labeling function that satisfies the following:

1. A leaf is labeled by a constant or a variable. Formally, if $v \in V$ is a leaf, then $\pi(v) \in \{0, 1\} \cup U$.
2. An interior vertex v is labeled by a connective whose arity equals the in-degree of v. Formally, if $v \in V$ is an interior vertex, then $\pi(v) \in C$ is a connective with arity $deg_{in}(v)$.

We usually use only unary and binary connectives. Thus, unless stated otherwise, a parse tree has an in-degree of at most 2.

In Figure 6.1, a parse tree of a Boolean formula is depicted. The labels of the vertices are written inside the vertices.

Boolean Formulas. A *Boolean formula* is a string containing constants, variables, connectives, and parentheses. Every parse tree defines a Boolean formula. This definition is constructive, and the Boolean formula is obtained by an in-order traversal of the parse tree.

A listing of an in-order traversal that outputs the Boolean formula corresponding to a parse tree is listed as Algorithm 6.1. The algorithm returns a string. In case the parse tree contains a single node v, then the formula is simply $\pi(v)$ (i.e., a constant or a variable). Otherwise, the formula is obtained by applying a reduction rule. There are two cases depending on the in-degree of the root of the parse tree. (i) If the in-degree of the root is 1, then the root must be labeled by a negation. In this case, the output is the string $(\neg \alpha)$, where α is the outcome of a recursive call on the rooted subtree hanging from the root. Note that the parentheses are part of the output. Namely, in line 1, the algorithm returns a constant or a variable not delimited by parentheses. However, in lines 2(a)v and 2(a)iv, the output is delimited by parentheses. (ii) If the in-degree of the root is 2, then the root is labeled by a binary connective. The output in this case is the string $(\alpha \, c \, \beta)$, where the root is labeled by the connective c and α, β are the outcomes of the recursive calls on the rooted trees hanging from the root.

Notation. Let $\mathcal{BF}(U, C)$ denote the set of Boolean formulas over the set of variables U and the set of connectives C. To simplify notation, we abbreviate $\mathcal{BF}(U, C)$ by $\mathcal{BF}$ when the sets of variables and connectives are known.

Consider a Boolean formula φ defined by a parse tree (G, π), where $G = (V, E)$ is a rooted tree.

Definition 6.2 A *subformula* α of a Boolean formula φ induced by a vertex $v \in V$ is the Boolean formula defined by (G', π'), where (i) G' is the subtree of G rooted at v and (ii) π' is the restriction of π to the vertices of G'.

EXAMPLES

---

1. Let us consider the parse tree $G = (V, E)$ in Figure 6.1 and its corresponding Boolean formula:

$$\varphi = ((X \text{ OR } 0) \text{ AND } (\neg Y)).$$

In this example, we list the subformulas of φ.

First, we give "names" to the vertices in V, as follows: (i) the vertex labeled by "X" is v_1, (ii) the vertex labeled by "0" is v_2, (iii) the vertex labeled by "OR" is v_3, (iv) the vertex labeled by "Y" is v_4, (v) the vertex labeled by "$\neg$" is v_5, and (vi) the vertex labeled by "AND" is v_6.

Algorithm 6.1 INORDER(G, π)—an algorithm for generating the Boolean formula corresponding to a parse tree (G, π), where $G = (V, E)$ is a rooted tree with in-degree at most 2 and $\pi : V \to \{0, 1\} \cup U \cup C$ is a labeling function.

---

1. Base case: If $|V| = 1$, then Return $\pi(v)$ *(where $v \in V$ is the only node in V)*.
2. Reduction rule:
   (a) If $deg_{in}(r(G)) = 1$, then

       i. Let $G_1 = (V_1, E_1)$ denote the rooted tree hanging from $r(G)$.
       ii. Let π_1 denote the restriction of π to V_1.
       iii. $\alpha \leftarrow$ INORDER(G_1, π_1).
       iv. Return $(\neg \alpha)$.

   (b) If $deg_{in}(r(G)) = 2$, then

       i. Let $G_1 = (V_1, E_1)$ and $G_2 = (V_2, E_2)$ denote the rooted subtrees hanging from $r(G)$.
       ii. Let π_i denote the restriction of π to V_i.
       iii. $\alpha \leftarrow$ INORDER(G_1, π_1).
       iv. $\beta \leftarrow$ INORDER(G_2, π_2).
       v. Return $(\alpha \ \pi(r(G)) \ \beta)$.

Now, the subformula α_i of φ induced by v_i are

$$\alpha_1 = X, \ \alpha_2 = 0, \ \alpha_3 = (X \text{ OR } 0),$$

$$\alpha_4 = Y, \ \alpha_5 = (\neg Y),$$

$$\alpha_6 = \varphi.$$

Note that every Boolean formula is a subformula of itself.

2. *Inductive definition of $\mathcal{BF}$.* We defined the set of Boolean formulas $\mathcal{BF}$ constructively using parse trees. We now define the set of formulas inductively. We prove that these two definitions are equivalent.

For the sake of simplicity, we focus on the case that the set of connectives is $C = \{\neg, +, \cdot\}$.

We define a *closure* property of a set of strings $\mathcal{F}$ under the set of connectives C as follows.

Definition 6.3 A set of strings $\mathcal{F}$ is *closed* under the set of connectives C if it satisfies the following condition:

If $p, q \in \mathcal{F}$, then
(a) $(\neg p) \in \mathcal{F}$,
(b) $(p \cdot q) \in \mathcal{F}$,
(c) $(p + q) \in \mathcal{F}$.

Definition 6.4 A set of strings $\mathcal{F}$ *contains the atoms* if $\{0, 1\} \subseteq \mathcal{F}$ and $U \subseteq \mathcal{F}$.

Let $C\mathcal{F}$ denote the set of all sets $\mathcal{F}$ that contain the atoms and are closed under the set C. We define the set $\mathcal{BF}'(U, C)$ of formulas as follows.

Definition 6.5

$$\mathcal{BF}'(U, C) \triangleq \bigcap_{\mathcal{F} \in C\mathcal{F}} \mathcal{F}.$$

The following lemma states that both definitions are equivalent.

Lemma 6.1

$$\mathcal{BF} = \mathcal{BF}'.$$

PROOF: We show that (i) $\mathcal{BF} \subseteq \mathcal{BF}'$ and (ii) $\mathcal{BF} \supseteq \mathcal{BF}'$ and conclude the proof. The proof is as follows:

(i) We show that

$$\forall \mathcal{F} \in C\mathcal{F} : \mathcal{BF} \subseteq \mathcal{F}. \tag{6.1}$$

That will conclude part (i) of the proof since Equation 6.1 implies that $\mathcal{BF} \subseteq \bigcap_{\mathcal{F} \in C\mathcal{F}} \mathcal{F} = \mathcal{BF}'$, as required.

Let $\mathcal{F}$ be a set of strings in $C\mathcal{F}$. Let $f \in \mathcal{BF}$ be a formula, and let (G, π) be its parse tree. The proof is by complete induction on the number of vertices n in the rooted tree G. The basis follows since for $n = 1$, the rooted tree corresponds to a constant or a variable and since $\mathcal{F}$ contains the atoms, that is, $f \in \{0, 1\} \cup U \subseteq \mathcal{F}$.

Now we prove the induction step, namely, that if a formula f has a parse tree of $n + 1$ vertices, then $f \in \mathcal{F}$. We observe that the rooted trees $G_1, \ldots, G_k$ hanging from the root $r(G)$ correspond to subformulas $f_1, \ldots, f_k$ of f; furthermore, the number of vertices n_i of G_i satisfies $n_i < n + 1$. For simplicity, let us consider the case of $k = 2$, and the case of $k = 1$ is similar. By the induction hypothesis $f_1, f_2 \in \mathcal{F}$. Since $\mathcal{F}$ is closed under the set of connectives C, in particular, the connective $\pi(r(G))$, then the formula $f = (f_1 \, \pi(r(G)) \, f_2) \in \mathcal{F}$, which concludes the induction step.

(ii) The proof is by contradiction. We assume by contradiction that

$$\mathcal{BF}' \setminus \mathcal{BF} \neq \varnothing , \qquad (6.2)$$

that is, there is a formula $f \in \mathcal{BF}' \setminus \mathcal{BF}$. Let f be the shortest formula in $\mathcal{BF}' \setminus \mathcal{BF}$. Since $\{0, 1\} \cup U \subseteq \mathcal{BF}$, then $\{0, 1\} \cup U \notin \mathcal{BF}' \setminus \mathcal{BF}$, that is, the formula f is not a constant or a variable.

Hence we consider the following four cases:

   i. $f = (\neg g)$,
  ii. $f = (g_1 + g_2)$,
 iii. $f = (g_1 \cdot g_2)$,
 iv. The formula f is none of the above, that is, $f \notin \{(\neg g), (g_1 + g_2), (g_1 \cdot g_2)\}$.

We consider case i (cases ii and iii are proven similarly). We consider two subcases:

   i. If $g \notin \mathcal{BF}'$, then the set $\mathcal{F}' \triangleq \mathcal{BF}' \setminus \{f\}$ is in $\mathcal{CF}$, that is, the closure property holds. Since $\mathcal{BF}' = \bigcap_{\mathcal{F} \in \mathcal{CF}} \mathcal{F}$, it implies that $f \notin \mathcal{BF}'$—a contradiction to the assumption that $f \in \mathcal{BF}' \setminus \mathcal{BF}$.
  ii. Otherwise, if $g \in \mathcal{BF}'$, then $g \in \mathcal{BF}$ (since otherwise we have a contradiction to the assumption that f is the shortest formula in $\mathcal{BF}' \setminus \mathcal{BF}$). Hence $f = (\neg g) \in \mathcal{BF}$, a contradiction to the assumption that $f \in \mathcal{BF}' \setminus \mathcal{BF}$.

We consider case iv and conclude. If $f \notin \{(\neg g), (g_1 + g_2), (g_1 \cdot g_2)\}$, then the set $\mathcal{F}' \triangleq \mathcal{BF}' \setminus \{f\}$ is in $\mathcal{CF}$, that is, the closure property holds. Since $\mathcal{BF}' = \bigcap_{\mathcal{F} \in \mathcal{CF}} \mathcal{F}$, it implies that $f \notin \mathcal{BF}'$, a contradiction to the assumption that $f \in \mathcal{BF}' \setminus \mathcal{BF}$.

In all cases and subcases, we arrived at a contradiction, hence $\mathcal{BF}' \setminus \mathcal{BF} = \varnothing$, that is, $\mathcal{BF}' \subseteq \mathcal{BF}$, and the lemma follows.   ■

3. The binary connective XOR is also denoted by $\oplus$.
4. Some of the connectives have several notations. The following formulas are the same, that is, string equality:

$$(A + B) = (A \vee B) = (A \text{ OR } B) ,$$

$$(A \cdot B) = (A \wedge B) = (A \text{ AND } B) ,$$

$$(\neg B) = (\text{NOT}(B)) = (\bar{B}) ,$$

$$(A \text{ XOR } B) = (A \oplus B) ,$$

$$((A \vee C) \wedge (\neg B)) = ((A + C) \cdot (\bar{B})) .$$

We sometimes omit parentheses from formulas if their parse tree is obvious. When parentheses are omitted, one should use precedence rules as in arithmetic, for example, $a \cdot b + c \cdot d = ((a \cdot b) + (c \cdot d))$.

6.2 TRUTH ASSIGNMENTS

We associate a Boolean function $B_c : \{0,1\}^k \to \{0,1\}$ with each connective $c \in C$ of arity k. In this section, we show how each Boolean formula p over a set U of variables defines a Boolean function $B_p : \{0,1\}^{|U|} \to \{0,1\}$.

To simplify notation, we usually use the same notation for a connective and the Boolean function associated with it. For example, B_{AND} is the Boolean function that corresponds to AND, however, we denote the function B_{AND} simply by AND. The same holds for the other connectives. The Boolean function associated with negation is NOT. We also address the case of constants and variables . The function B_X associated with a variable X is the identity function $I : \{0,1\} \to \{0,1\}$ defined by $I(b) = b$. The function B_σ associated with a constant $\sigma \in \{0,1\}$ is the constant function whose value is always σ.

Consider a Boolean formula p generated by a parse tree (G, π). We now show how to evaluate the truth value of p. First, we need to assign truth values to the variables.

Definition 6.6 An *assignment* is a function $\tau : U \to \{0,1\}$, where U is the set of variables.

Our goal is to extend every assignment $\tau : U \to \{0,1\}$ to a function that assigns truth values to every Boolean formula over the variables in U.

The extension $\hat{\tau} : \mathcal{BF} \to \{0,1\}$ of an assignment $\tau : U \to \{0,1\}$ is defined as follows.

Definition 6.7 Let $p \in \mathcal{BF}$ be a Boolean formula generated by a parse tree (G, π). Then,

$$\hat{\tau}(p) \triangleq \text{EVAL}(G, \pi, \tau),$$

where EVAL is listed as Algorithm 6.2.

EXAMPLES

Recall that we defined $\mathcal{BF}$ inductively in Definition 6.5. We rewrite the EVAL algorithm while considering this inductive definition. The inductive version of the EVAL algorithm with respect to the set of connectives $\mathcal{C} \triangleq \{+, \cdot, \neg\}$ is listed as Algorithm 6.3.

6.3 SATISFIABILITY AND LOGICAL EQUIVALENCE

In the previous section, we fixed a set of variables U and an assignment $\tau : U \to \{0,1\}$. We then extended τ to every Boolean formula $p \in \mathcal{BF}$ over the variables U. In this section, we look at things differently, namely, we fix a Boolean formula p over a set U of variables and consider all possible assignments $\tau : U \to \{0,1\}$.

Definition 6.8 Let p denote a Boolean formula.

1. p is *satisfiable* if there exists an assignment τ such that $\hat{\tau}(p) = 1$.
2. p is a *tautology* if $\hat{\tau}(p) = 1$ for every assignment τ.

Definition 6.9 Two formulas p and q are *logically equivalent* if $\hat{\tau}(p) = \hat{\tau}(q)$ for every assignment τ.

Algorithm 6.2 EVAL(G, π, τ)—an algorithm for evaluating the truth value of the Boolean formula generated by the parse tree (G, π), where (i) $G = (V, E)$ is a rooted tree with in-degree at most 2, (ii) $\pi : V \to \{0, 1\} \cup U \cup C$, and (iii) $\tau : U \to \{0, 1\}$ is an assignment.

1. Base case: If $|V| = 1$, then
   (a) Let $v \in V$ be the only node in V.
   (b) $\pi(v)$ is a constant: if $\pi(v) \in \{0, 1\}$, then return $(\pi(v))$.
   (c) $\pi(v)$ is a variable: if $\pi(v) \in U$, then return $(\tau(\pi(v))$.
2. Reduction rule:
   (a) If $deg_{in}(r(G)) = 1$, then *(in this case $\pi(r(G)) = $ NOT)*
      i. Let $G_1 = (V_1, E_1)$ denote the rooted tree hanging from $r(G)$.
      ii. Let π_1 denote the restriction of π to V_1.
      iii. $\sigma \leftarrow$ EVAL(G_1, π_1, τ).
      iv. Return (NOT(σ)).
   (b) If $deg_{in}(r(G)) = 2$, then
      i. Let $G_1 = (V_1, E_1)$ and $G_2 = (V_2, E_2)$ denote the rooted subtrees hanging from $r(G)$.
      ii. Let π_i denote the restriction of π to V_i.
      iii. $\sigma_1 \leftarrow$ EVAL(G_1, π_1, τ).
      iv. $\sigma_2 \leftarrow$ EVAL(G_2, π_2, τ).
      v. Return ($B_{\pi(r(G))}(\sigma_1, \sigma_2)$).

Algorithm 6.3 EVAL(φ, τ)—An algorithm for evaluating the truth value of the Boolean formula $\varphi \in \mathcal{BF}(U, \{+, \cdot, \neg\})$, where $\tau : U \to \{0, 1\}$ is an assignment.

1. Base cases:
   (a) If $\varphi = 0$, then return 0.
   (b) If $\varphi = 1$, then return 1.
   (c) If $\varphi = (X)$, where $X \in U$, then return $\tau(X)$.
2. Reduction rules:
   (a) If $\varphi = (\neg\psi)$, where $\psi \in \mathcal{BF}$, then
      i. $\sigma \leftarrow$ EVAL(ψ, τ).
      ii. Return (NOT(σ)).
   (b) If $\varphi = (\psi_1 + \psi_2)$, where $\psi_i \in \mathcal{BF}$, then
      i. $\sigma_1 \leftarrow$ EVAL(ψ_1, τ).
      ii. $\sigma_2 \leftarrow$ EVAL(ψ_2, τ).
      iii. Return (OR(σ_1, σ_2)).
   (c) If $\varphi = (\psi_1 \cdot \psi_2)$, where $\psi_i \in \mathcal{BF}$, then
      i. $\sigma_1 \leftarrow$ EVAL(ψ_1, τ).
      ii. $\sigma_2 \leftarrow$ EVAL(ψ_2, τ).
      iii. Return (AND(σ_1, σ_2)).

EXAMPLES

---

1. Let $\varphi \triangleq (X \oplus Y)$. Show that φ is satisfiable.
   Let $\tau(X) = 1$ and $\tau(Y) = 0$, then $\hat{\tau}(\varphi) = 1$. We have shown an assignment τ such that $\hat{\tau}(p) = 1$, hence φ is satisfiable.
2. Let $\varphi \triangleq (X \vee \neg X)$. Show that φ is a tautology.
   We show that $\hat{\tau}(\varphi) = 1$ for every assignment τ. We do that by enumerating all the $2^{|U|}$ assignments and verifying that $\hat{\tau}(\varphi) = 1$ in every one of them. This enumeration is depicted in Table 6.1. We later interpret Boolean formulas as Boolean functions, hence Table 6.1 is the already well-known truth table of that function.
3. Let $\varphi \triangleq (X \oplus Y)$, and let $\psi \triangleq (\bar{X} \cdot Y + X \cdot \bar{Y})$. Show that φ and ψ are logically equivalent.
   We show that $\hat{\tau}(\varphi) = \hat{\tau}(\psi)$ for every assignment τ. We do that by enumerating all the $2^{|U|}$ assignments and verifying that $\hat{\tau}(\varphi) = \hat{\tau}(\psi)$ in every one of them. This enumeration is depicted in Table 6.2.
4. We claim that a Boolean formula φ is satisfiable if and only if the formula $(\neg\varphi)$ is not a tautology. This claim is summarized in the following lemma.

Lemma 6.2 *Let* $\varphi \in \mathcal{BF}$, *then*

$$\varphi \text{ is satisfiable} \Leftrightarrow (\neg\varphi) \text{ is not a tautology.}$$

PROOF: The proof is as follows.

$$\varphi \text{ is satisfiable} \Leftrightarrow \exists \tau : \hat{\tau}(\varphi) = 1$$

$$\Leftrightarrow \exists \tau : \text{NOT}(\hat{\tau}(\varphi)) = 0$$

$$\Leftrightarrow \exists \tau : \hat{\tau}(\neg(\varphi)) = 0$$

$$\Leftrightarrow (\neg\varphi) \text{ is not a tautology.}$$

The first line follows from Definition 6.8. Note that the $\exists$ symbol replaces the words "there exists." The second line follows from the definition of the NOT Boolean function. The third line follows from the definition of the EVAL algorithm (see item 2()ii in Algorithm 6.3). The last line follows, again, by Definition 6.8. ∎

Table 6.1. There is one variable, hence the enumeration consists of two assignments. The first assignment is $\tau(X) = 0$, and the second one is $\tau(X) = 0$. In both rows, $\hat{\tau}(\varphi) = 1$, hence φ is a tautology

$\tau(X)$	$\text{NOT}(\tau(X))$	$\hat{\tau}(X \vee \neg X)$
0	1	1
1	0	1

Table 6.2. There are two variables, hence the enumeration consists of $2^2 = 4$ assignments. The columns that correspond to $\hat{\tau}(\varphi)$ and $\hat{\tau}(\psi)$ are identical, hence φ and ψ are equivalent

$\tau(X)$	$\tau(Y)$	$\text{NOT}(\tau(X))$	$\text{NOT}(\tau(Y))$	$\text{AND}(\text{NOT}(\tau(X)), \tau(Y))$	$\text{AND}(\tau(X), \text{NOT}(\tau(Y)))$	$\hat{\tau}(\varphi)$	$\hat{\tau}(\psi)$
0	0	1	1	0	0	0	0
1	0	0	1	0	1	1	1
0	1	1	0	1	0	1	1
1	1	0	0	0	0	0	0

6.4 INTERPRETING A BOOLEAN FORMULA AS A FUNCTION

As in the previous section, fix a Boolean formula p over a set U of variables. Assume that $U = \{X_1, \ldots, X_n\}$.

Definition 6.10 Given a binary vector $v = (v_1, \ldots, v_n) \in \{0, 1\}^n$, the assignment $\tau_v : \{X_1, \ldots, X_n\} \to \{0, 1\}$ is defined by $\tau_v(X_i) \triangleq v_i$.

The following definition attaches a Boolean function B_φ to each Boolean formula φ. The input to $B_\varphi(v)$ is an assignment represented by a binary vector v. The output of B_φ is the truth value of φ under the assignment τ_v.

Definition 6.11 A Boolean formula p over the variables $U = \{X_1, \ldots, X_n\}$ defines the Boolean function $B_p : \{0, 1\}^n \to \{0, 1\}$ by

$$B_p(v_1, \ldots v_n) \triangleq \hat{\tau}_v(p).$$

Lemma 6.3 *If $\varphi = \alpha_1 \circ \alpha_2$ for a binary connective $\circ$, then*

$$\forall v \in \{0, 1\}^n : \quad B_\varphi(v) = B_\circ(B_{\alpha_1}(v), B_{\alpha_2}(v)).$$

PROOF: The justifications of all the following lines are by the definition of evaluation:

$$B_\varphi(v) = \hat{\tau}_v(\varphi)$$
$$= B_\circ(\hat{\tau}_v(\alpha_1), \hat{\tau}_v(\alpha_2))$$
$$= B_\circ(B_{\alpha_1}(v), B_{\alpha_2}(v)),$$

and the lemma follows. ■

EXAMPLES

---

1. Prove that a Boolean formula p is a tautology if and only if the Boolean function B_p is identically 1, that is, $B_p(v) = 1$, for every $v \in \{0, 1\}^n$.

   PROOF: The proof is as follows.

   $$p \text{ is a tautology} \iff \forall \tau : \hat{\tau}(p) = 1$$
   $$\iff \forall v \in \{0, 1\}^n : \hat{\tau}_v(p) = 1$$
   $$\iff \forall v \in \{0, 1\}^n : B_p(v) = 1,$$

   where the first line follows by Definition 6.8. The second line follows by Definition 6.10. The last line follows by Definition 6.11, as required. ■

Table 6.3. The truth table representation and the multiplication table of the implication connective

X	Y	$X \to Y$
0	0	1
1	0	0
0	1	1
1	1	1

$\to$	0	1
0	1	1
1	0	1

2. Prove that a Boolean formula p is satisfiable if and only if the Boolean function B_p is not identically zero, that is, there exists a vector $v \in \{0,1\}^n$ such that $B_p(v) = 1$.

PROOF: The proof is as follows.

$$p \text{ is a satisfiable} \iff \exists \tau : \hat{\tau}(p) = 1$$
$$\iff \exists v \in \{0,1\}^n : \hat{\tau}_v(p) = 1$$
$$\iff \exists v \in \{0,1\}^n : B_p(v) = 1,$$

where the first line follows by Definition 6.8. The second line follows by Definition 6.10. The last line follows by Definition 6.11, as required. ∎

3. Prove that two Boolean formulas p and q are logically equivalent if and only if the Boolean functions B_p and B_q are identical, that is, $B_p(v) = B_q(v)$, for every $v \in \{0,1\}^n$.

PROOF: The proof is as follows.

$$p \text{ and } q \text{ are logically equivalent} \iff \forall \tau : \hat{\tau}(p) = \hat{\tau}(q)$$
$$\iff \forall v \in \{0,1\}^n : \hat{\tau}_v(p) = \hat{\tau}_v(q)$$
$$\iff \forall v \in \{0,1\}^n : B_p(v) = B_q(v),$$

where the first line follows by Definition 6.9. The second line follows by Definition 6.10. The last line follows by Definition 6.11, as required. ∎

4. *The* implication *connective.* The implication connective is denoted by $\to$. The truth table and multiplication table of $B_\to : \{0,1\}^2 \to \{0,1\}$ is depicted in Table 6.3.

   To simplify notation, we denote the Boolean function $B_\to$ by the connective itself, namely, $B_\to(X, Y)$ is denoted by $X \to Y$. The implication connective is not commutative, namely, $(0 \to 1) \neq (1 \to 0)$. This connective is called *implication* because it models the natural language templates "Y if X" and "if X then Y." For example, let us consider the sentence "if it is raining, then there are clouds." This sentence guarantees clouds if it is raining. If it is not raining, then the sentence trivially holds (regardless of whether there are clouds or not). This explains why $X \to Y$ is always 1 if $X = 0$.

5. *The connectives* NAND *and* NOR. The connective NAND can be considered as an abbreviation of NOT-AND, namely, $(p$ NAND $q)$ means $(\text{NOT}(p$ AND $q))$.

   Similarly, the NOR connective is an abbreviation of NOT-OR, namely, $(p$ NOR $q)$ means $(\text{NOT}(p$ OR $q))$.

Table 6.4. The truth table representation and the multiplication table of the NAND and NOR connectives

X	Y	X NAND Y	X	Y	X NOR Y
0	0	1	0	0	1
1	0	1	1	0	0
0	1	1	0	1	0
1	1	0	1	1	0

NAND	0	1
0	1	1
1	1	0

NOR	0	1
0	1	0
1	0	0

The Boolean functions that correspond to these functions are defined as follows:

$$B_{\text{NAND}}(A, B) \triangleq \text{NOT}(B_{\text{AND}}(A, B))$$

$$B_{\text{NOR}}(A, B) \triangleq \text{NOT}(B_{\text{OR}}(A, B)).$$

To simplify notation, we denote a Boolean function B_c by its connective c. Thus

$$\text{NAND}(A, B) \triangleq \text{NOT}(\text{AND}(A, B))$$

$$\text{NOR}(A, B) \triangleq \text{NOT}(\text{OR}(A, B)).$$

The truth tables and multiplication tables of $B_{\text{NAND}} : \{0, 1\}^2 \to \{0, 1\}$ and $B_{\text{NOR}} : \{0, 1\}^2 \to \{0, 1\}$ are depicted in Table 6.4.

6. *The* equivalence *connective.* The equivalence connective is denoted by $\leftrightarrow$. The equivalence connective can be considered as an abbreviation of two implications, namely,

$$(p \leftrightarrow q) \text{ abbreviates } ((p \to q) \text{ AND } (q \to p)).$$

The Boolean function that corresponds to equivalence is defined as follows:

$$B_{\leftrightarrow}(A, B) \triangleq (A \to B) \text{ AND } (B \to A).$$

As before, we denote $B_{\leftrightarrow}(A, B)$ by $(A \leftrightarrow B)$.

The truth table and multiplication table of $B_{\leftrightarrow} : \{0, 1\}^2 \to \{0, 1\}$ are depicted in Table 6.5.

Note that

$$(A \leftrightarrow B) = \begin{cases} 1 & \text{if } A = B \\ 0 & \text{if } A \neq B. \end{cases}$$

7. Prove that two Boolean formulas p and q are logically equivalent if and only if the formula $(p \leftrightarrow q)$ is a tautology.

Table 6.5. The truth table representation and the multiplication table of the equivalence connective

X	Y	$X \leftrightarrow Y$
0	0	1
1	0	0
0	1	0
1	1	1

$\leftrightarrow$	0	1
0	1	0
1	0	1

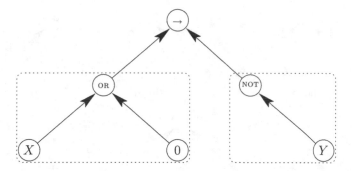

Figure 6.2. A parse tree that corresponds to the Boolean formula $((X \text{ OR } 0) \to (\neg Y))$. The root is labeled by an implication connective. The rooted trees hanging from the root are encapsulated by dashed rectangles.

PROOF: The proof is as follows:

$$p \text{ and } q \text{ are logically equivalent} \Leftrightarrow \forall \tau : \hat{\tau}(p) = \hat{\tau}(q)$$
$$\Leftrightarrow \forall v \in \{0,1\}^n : \hat{\tau}_v(p) = \hat{\tau}_v(q)$$
$$\Leftrightarrow \forall v \in \{0,1\}^n : B_p(v) = B_q(v)$$
$$\Leftrightarrow \forall v \in \{0,1\}^n : B_{\leftrightarrow}(B_p(v), B_q(v)) = 1$$
$$\Leftrightarrow \forall v \in \{0,1\}^n : B_{p \leftrightarrow q}(v) = 1$$
$$\Leftrightarrow \forall v \in \{0,1\}^n : \hat{\tau}_v(p \leftrightarrow q) = 1$$
$$\Leftrightarrow \forall \tau : \hat{\tau}(p \leftrightarrow q) = 1$$
$$\Leftrightarrow (p \leftrightarrow q) \text{ is a tautology,}$$

where the first line follows by Definition 6.9. The second line follows by Definition 6.10. The third line follows by Definition 6.11, as required. The fourth line follows by the definition of the Boolean function that corresponds to the equivalence connective (see Example 6). The fifth line follows from Lemma 6.3. The last line follows from Example 1. ■

8. Since not all connectives are commutative, the order of the hanging rooted trees is important, that is, first subtree and second subtree. Let us set the convention that the hanging trees are ordered from left to right. The arcs that enter a node in a rooted tree are ordered. This order must be kept in the in-order traversal of the parse tree. For example, consider the parse tree depicted in Figure 6.2 and the Boolean formula that corresponds to it. Set $\tau(X) = \tau(Y) = 0$. Hence evaluating the parse tree from right to left will output a 0, while the opposite order will output a 1.

9. A *literal* is a variable or its negation. For example, in the Boolean formula $(X \cdot (Y + \bar{X}))$, there are three literals: $X, \bar{X},$ and Y.

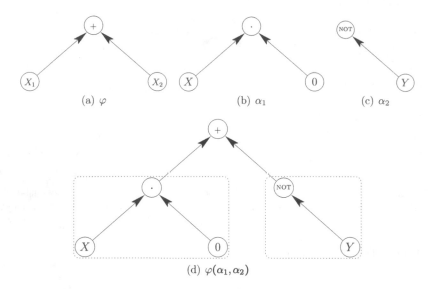

(d) $\varphi(\alpha_1, \alpha_2)$

Figure 6.3. A substitution of $\alpha_1, \alpha_2 \in \mathcal{BF}(\{X, Y\}, \{\cdot, \neg\})$ in $\varphi \in \mathcal{BF}(\{X_1, X_2\}, \{+\})$ yields the Boolean formula $\varphi(\alpha_1, \alpha_2) \in \mathcal{BF}(\{X, Y\}, \{\cdot, +, \neg\})$. The parse trees of $\varphi, \alpha_1, \alpha_2$ are presented in Figures 6.3a, 6.3b, and 6.3c, respectively. The parse tree of $\varphi(\alpha_1, \alpha_2)$ is depicted in Figure 6.3d. Note that α_1, α_2 are encapsulated by dashed rectangles in this "final" parse tree.

6.5 SUBSTITUTION

In this section, we use substitution to compose large formulas from smaller ones. For simplicity, we deal with substitution in formulas over two variables; the generalization to formulas over any number of variables is straightforward. We consider the following setting.

Throughout this section, let

1. $\varphi \in \mathcal{BF}(\{X_1, X_2\}, \mathcal{C})$.
2. $\alpha_1, \alpha_2 \in \mathcal{BF}(U, \mathcal{C})$.
3. (G_φ, π_φ) (respectively $(G_{\alpha_i}, \pi_{\alpha_i})$) denotes the parse tree of φ (respectively α_i).

Definition 6.12 *Substitution* of α_i in φ yields the Boolean formula $\varphi(\alpha_1, \alpha_2) \in \mathcal{BF}(U, \mathcal{C})$ that is generated by the parse tree (G, π) defined as follows. For each leaf of $v \in G_\varphi$ that is labeled by a variable X_i, replace the leaf v by a new copy of $(G_{\alpha_i}, \pi_{\alpha_i})$.

Figure 6.3 depicts a formula obtained by substitution.

Substitution can be obtain by applying a simple find-and-replace, where each instance of variable X_i is replaced by a copy of the formula α_i for $i \in \{1, 2\}$. One can easily generalize substitution to formulas $\varphi \in \mathcal{BF}(\{X_1, \ldots, X_k\}, \mathcal{C})$ for any $k > 2$. In this case, $\varphi(\alpha_1, \ldots, \alpha_k)$ is obtained by replacing every instance of X_i by α_i.

The following lemma allows us to treat a formula φ as a Boolean function B_φ. This enables us to evaluate the truth value after substitution (i.e., $\hat{\tau}(\varphi(\alpha_1, \alpha_2))$) using B_φ and the truth values $\hat{\tau}(\alpha_i)$.

Lemma 6.4 *For every assignment* $\tau : U \to \{0, 1\}$,

$$\hat{\tau}(\varphi(\alpha_1, \alpha_2)) = B_\varphi(\hat{\tau}(\alpha_1), \hat{\tau}(\alpha_2)). \tag{6.3}$$

PROOF: The proof is by complete induction on the size of the parse tree (G_φ, π_φ) of φ. We begin with the induction basis: if G_φ contains a single node, then it is labeled by a constant $\sigma \in \{0, 1\}$ or by a variable X_i.

1. If the root vertex is labeled by constant σ, then $\varphi(\alpha_1, \alpha_2) = \varphi = \sigma$. Since $\hat{\tau}(\sigma) = \sigma$, it follows that $\hat{\tau}(\varphi(\alpha_1, \alpha_2)) = \sigma$.

   Conversely, the Boolean function B_φ is the constant function whose value is always σ. Thus both sides of Eq. 6.3 are equal in this case.

2. If the root vertex is labeled by variable X_i, then $\varphi(\alpha_1, \alpha_2) = \alpha_i$. Hence the left-hand side equals $\hat{\tau}(\varphi(\alpha_1, \alpha_2)) = \hat{\tau}(\alpha_i)$. The Boolean function $B_\varphi(v_1, v_2)$ in this case outputs v_i and ignores the other argument. This implies that $B_\varphi(\hat{\tau}(\alpha_1), \hat{\tau}(\alpha_2)) = \hat{\tau}(\alpha_i)$, as required.

We now prove the induction step. Assume that $\varphi = \varphi_1 \circ \varphi_2$, where $\circ$ is a binary connective. (The case that the root of G_φ is labeled by a negation connective is similar.)

By the induction hypothesis, for $i \in \{1, 2\}$,

$$\hat{\tau}(\varphi_i(\alpha_1, \alpha_2)) = B_{\varphi_i}(\hat{\tau}(\alpha_1), \hat{\tau}(\alpha_2)).$$

Thus we obtain

$$\hat{\tau}(\varphi(\alpha_1, \alpha_2)) = B_\circ(\hat{\tau}(\varphi_1(\alpha_1, \alpha_2)), \hat{\tau}(\varphi_2(\alpha_1, \alpha_2))) \qquad \text{(by Algorithm 6.2)}$$

$$= B_\circ(B_{\varphi_1}(\hat{\tau}(\alpha_1), \hat{\tau}(\alpha_2)), B_{\varphi_2}(\hat{\tau}(\alpha_1), \hat{\tau}(\alpha_2))) \qquad \text{(induction hypothesis)}$$

$$= B_\varphi(\hat{\tau}(\alpha_1), \hat{\tau}(\alpha_2)), \qquad \text{(by Lemma 6.3)}$$

and the lemma follows. ∎

The next corollary shows that substitution preserves logical equivalence. Let $\varphi \in \mathcal{BF}(\{X_1, X_2\}, \mathcal{C})$, $\alpha_1, \alpha_2 \in \mathcal{BF}(U, \mathcal{C})$, and let $\tilde{\varphi} \subset \mathcal{BF}(\{X_1, X_2\}, \tilde{\mathcal{C}})$ and $\tilde{\alpha}_1, \tilde{\alpha}_2 \in \mathcal{BF}(U, \tilde{\mathcal{C}})$.

Corollary 6.5 *If α_i and $\tilde{\alpha}_i$ are logically equivalent, and φ and $\tilde{\varphi}$ are logically equivalent, then $\varphi(\alpha_1, \alpha_2)$ and $\tilde{\varphi}(\tilde{\alpha}_1, \tilde{\alpha}_2)$ are logically equivalent.*

PROOF: To prove the corollary, we need to prove that, for every vector $v \in \{0, 1\}^{|U|}$, the following equality holds:

$$\hat{\tau}_v(\varphi(\alpha_1, \alpha_2)) = \hat{\tau}_v(\tilde{\varphi}(\tilde{\alpha}_1, \tilde{\alpha}_2)).$$

Indeed,

$$\hat{\tau}_v(\varphi(\alpha_1, \alpha_2)) = B_\varphi(\hat{\tau}_v(\alpha_1), \hat{\tau}_v(\alpha_2)) \qquad \text{(by Lemma 6.4)}$$

$$= B_\varphi(\hat{\tau}_v(\tilde{\alpha}_1), \hat{\tau}_v(\tilde{\alpha}_2)) \qquad \text{(since } \alpha_i \text{ and } \tilde{\alpha}_i \text{ are logically equivalent)}$$

$$= B_{\tilde{\varphi}}(\hat{\tau}_v(\tilde{\alpha}_1), \hat{\tau}_v(\tilde{\alpha}_2)) \qquad \text{(by Example 3 on page 77)}$$

$$= \hat{\tau}_v(\tilde{\varphi}(\tilde{\alpha}_1, \tilde{\alpha}_2)), \qquad \text{(by Lemma 6.4)}$$

and the corollary follows. ∎

---

1. Recall that in Figure 6.3, substitution was made using parse trees. Substitution can be applied directly without using a parse tree. Let us consider the Boolean formulas in Figure 6.3:

$$\varphi = (X_1 + X_2)\,,$$
$$\alpha_1 = (X \cdot 0)\,,$$
$$\alpha_2 = (\neg Y)\,.$$

We substitute α_1 for X_1 and α_2 for X_2, as follows. We apply a simple find-and-replace procedure; that is, we replace every symbol X_1 in the string φ with the string $(X \cdot 0)$ and every symbol X_2 in the string φ with the string $(\neg Y)$, as follows:
(a) The original formula: $\varphi = (X_1 + X_2)$.
(b) Replacing X_1 with α_1 results in the formula $((X \cdot 0) + X_2)$.
(c) Replacing X_2 with α_2 results in the formula $((X \cdot 0) + (\neg Y))$.
Indeed, the parse tree of the formula in the last item is the tree depicted in Figure 6.3d.

2. Prove that the following Boolean formulas are logically equivalent:
    * $\beta_1 \overset{\triangle}{=} (A \to B) \to C$
    * $\beta_2 \overset{\triangle}{=} (\bar{A} + B) \to C$.

PROOF: Let

$$\varphi \overset{\triangle}{=} X_1 \to X_2\,,$$
$$\alpha_1 \overset{\triangle}{=} A \to B\,,$$
$$\alpha_2 \overset{\triangle}{=} C\,,$$
$$\tilde{\alpha}_1 \overset{\triangle}{=} \bar{A} + B.$$

We claim that α_1 and $\tilde{\alpha}_1$ are logically equivalent.
    Note that

$$\varphi(\alpha_1, \alpha_2) = \beta_1$$
$$\varphi(\tilde{\alpha}_1, \alpha_2) = \beta_2\,.$$

Corollary 6.5 implies that $\varphi(\alpha_1, \alpha_2)$ and $\varphi(\tilde{\alpha}_1, \alpha_2)$ are logically equivalent, as required. ∎

6.6 COMPLETE SETS OF CONNECTIVES

Every Boolean formula can be interpreted as Boolean function. In this section, we deal with the following question: which sets of connectives enable us to express every Boolean function?

Definition 6.13 A Boolean function $B : \{0,1\}^n \to \{0,1\}$ is *expressible* by $\mathcal{BF}$ $(\{X_1, \ldots, X_n\}, \mathcal{C})$ if there exists a formula $p \in \mathcal{BF}(\{X_1, \ldots, X_n\}, \mathcal{C})$ such that $B = B_p$.

Definition 6.14 A set $\mathcal{C}$ of connectives is *complete* if every Boolean function $B : \{0,1\}^n \to \{0,1\}$ is expressible by $\mathcal{BF}(\{X_1, \ldots, X_n\}, \mathcal{C})$.

The proof of the following theorem is, by induction on n, the arity of the Boolean function $B : \{0,1\}^n \to \{0,1\}$. One of the main observations in the proof is as follows. Fixing one or more of the inputs of a Boolean function $B : \{0,1\}^n \to \{0,1\}$ defines a restricted Boolean function. In particular,

$$B(v_1, \ldots, v_{n-1}, v_n) = \begin{cases} B(v_1, \ldots, v_{n-1}, 0), & \text{if } v_n = 0 \\ B(v_1, \ldots, v_{n-1}, 1), & \text{if } v_n = 1. \end{cases}$$

The induction hypothesis can be used thanks to the ability to split a function over n bits to two functions over $n - 1$ bits.

Theorem 6.6 *The set $\mathcal{C} = \{\neg, \text{AND}, \text{OR}\}$ is a complete set of connectives.*

PROOF: Consider a Boolean function $B : \{0,1\}^n \to \{0,1\}$. We prove by induction on n that there exists a Boolean formula $p \in \mathcal{BF}(\{X_1, \ldots, X_n\}, \mathcal{C})$ such that $B_p = B$.

The induction basis, for $n = 1$, is proved as follows. There are four Boolean functions with the domain $\{0,1\}$. The functions are $B(x) = 0, B(x) = 1$, the identity function $B(X) = x$, and negation $B(X) = \text{NOT}(x)$. The only connective we needed so far is negation, which is in $\mathcal{C}$.

The induction step for $n > 1$ is proved as follows. Define the functions $g, h : \{0,1\}^{n-1} \to \{0,1\}$ as follows:

$$g(v_1, \ldots, v_{n-1}) \triangleq B(v_1, \ldots, v_{n-1}, 0)$$

$$h(v_1, \ldots, v_{n-1}) \triangleq B(v_1, \ldots, v_{n-1}, 1).$$

By the induction hypothesis, there are formulas $q, r \in \mathcal{BF}(\{X_1, \ldots, X_{n-1}\}, \mathcal{C})$ such that $B_q = g$ and $B_r = h$.

Define the formula p by

$$p \triangleq (q \cdot \bar{X}_n) + (r \cdot X_n).$$

The formula p is obtained from the formulas q and r and the connectives NOT, AND, and OR, which all belong to $\mathcal{C}$. Thus $p \in \mathcal{BF}(\{X_1, \ldots, X_n\}, \mathcal{C})$. To complete the proof, we need to show that $B_p = B$.

Recall that $\tau_v(X_n) = v_n$. We consider the following two cases:

1. If $v_n = 1$. We first evaluate the subformula $(q \cdot \bar{X}_n)$ as follows:

$$\hat{\tau}_v(q \cdot \bar{X}_n) = \hat{\tau}_v(q) \cdot \hat{\tau}_v(\bar{X}_n)$$
$$= \hat{\tau}_v(q) \cdot \overline{\hat{\tau}_v(X_n)}$$
$$= \hat{\tau}_v(q) \cdot \bar{1}$$
$$= \hat{\tau}_v(q) \cdot 0$$
$$= 0.$$

We now evaluate the subformula $(r \cdot X_n)$ as follows:

$$\hat{\tau}_v(r \cdot X_n) = \hat{\tau}_v(r) \cdot \tau_v(X_n)$$
$$= \hat{\tau}_v(r) \cdot 1$$
$$= \hat{\tau}_v(r).$$

It follows that the evaluation of p is

$$\hat{\tau}_v(p) = \hat{\tau}_v(q \cdot \bar{X}_n) + \hat{\tau}_v(r \cdot X_n)$$
$$= 0 + \hat{\tau}_v(r)$$
$$= \hat{\tau}_v(r). \tag{6.4}$$

Since $B_r = h$ and B_r is the function induced by r, it follows that

$$h(v_1, \ldots, v_{n-1}) = B_r(v_1, \ldots, v_{n-1}) = \hat{\tau}_v(r).$$

It follows that

$$
\begin{aligned}
B_p(v_1, \ldots, v_{n-1}, 1) &= \hat{\tau}_v(p) && \text{(by definition)} \\
&= \hat{\tau}_v(r) && \text{(By Eq. 6.4)} \\
&= B_r(v_1, \ldots, v_{n-1}) && \text{(by definition)} \\
&= h(v_1, \ldots, v_{n-1}) && \text{(since } B_r = h) \\
&= B(v_1, \ldots, v_{n-1}, 1). && \text{(by definition)}
\end{aligned}
$$

2. If $v_n = 0$. The evaluation of p gives

$$\hat{\tau}_v(p) = \hat{\tau}_v(q \cdot \bar{X}_n) + \hat{\tau}_v(r \cdot X_n)$$
$$= \hat{\tau}_v(q). \tag{6.5}$$

Since $B_q = g$ and B_q is the function induced by q, it follows that

$$g(v_1, \ldots, v_{n-1}) = B_q(v_1, \ldots, v_{n-1}) = \hat{\tau}_v(q).$$

It follows that

$$B_p(v_1, \ldots, v_{n-1}, 0) = \hat{\tau}_v(p) \qquad \text{(by definition)}$$

$$= \hat{\tau}_v(q) \qquad \text{(By Eq. 6.5)}$$

$$= B_q(v_1, \ldots, v_{n-1}) \qquad \text{(by definition)}$$

$$= g(v_1, \ldots, v_{n-1}) \qquad \text{(since } B_q = g)$$

$$= B(v_1, \ldots, v_{n-1}, 0). \qquad \text{(by definition)}$$

In both cases, we proved that $B_p = B$, and the theorem follows. ∎

See Example 2 for an example of the following theorem.

Theorem 6.7 *If the Boolean functions in* {NOT, AND, OR} *are expressible by formulas in* $\mathcal{BF}(\{X_1, X_2\}, \tilde{C})$, *then* $\tilde{C}$ *is a complete set of connectives.*

PROOF: By Theorem 6.6, every Boolean function $B : \{0,1\}^n \to \{0,1\}$ is expressible by a Boolean formula $\beta \in \mathcal{BF}(\{X_1, \ldots, X_n\}, C)$, where $C = \{$NOT, AND, OR$\}$. This means that it suffices to prove that for every Boolean formula $\beta \in \mathcal{BF}(\{X_1, \ldots, X_n\}, C)$, there exists a logically equivalent formula $\tilde{\beta} \in \mathcal{BF}(\{X_1, \ldots, X_n\}, \tilde{C})$.

We prove this statement by induction on the size of the parse tree (G_β, π_β) that generates β. The induction basis in case β is constant or a variable is trivial by setting $\tilde{\beta} = \beta$.

We now prove the induction step for G_β that contains more than one vertex. Let $\circ \in C$ denote the label of the root of G_β. Since $\circ$ is expressible by $\mathcal{BF}(\{X_1, X_2\}, \tilde{C})$, let $\tilde{\varphi}(X_1, X_2)$ denote a formula in $\mathcal{BF}(\{X_1, X_2\}, \tilde{C})$ that is logically equivalent to $(X_1 \circ X_2)$.

Let α_1 and α_2 denote the two subformulas of β, namely, $\beta = (\alpha_1 \circ \alpha_2)$. By the induction hypothesis, there exist formulas $\tilde{\alpha}_1, \tilde{\alpha}_2 \in \mathcal{BF}(\{X_1, \ldots, X_n\}, \tilde{C})$ such that α_i and $\tilde{\alpha}_i$ are logically equivalent.

By Corollary 6.5, the formulas $(\alpha_1 \circ \alpha_2)$ and $\tilde{\varphi}(\tilde{\alpha}_1, \tilde{\alpha}_2)$ are logically equivalent. Set $\tilde{\beta} = \tilde{\varphi}(\tilde{\alpha}_1, \tilde{\alpha}_2)$. Since $\tilde{\beta} \in \mathcal{BF}(\{X_1, \ldots, X_n\}, \tilde{C})$, the theorem follows. ∎

EXAMPLES

---

1. In this example, we clarify some of the notations given in this chapter, in particular $\tau(\varphi), \hat{\tau}(\varphi), \tau_v(\varphi), \hat{\tau}_v(\varphi)$. A formula $\varphi \in \mathcal{BF}(U, C)$ is a string, that is, a sequence of characters. The way we give it a "meaning," that is, semantics, is as follows. First, we consider a truth assignment $\tau : U \to \{0,1\}$ to the variables of the formula φ. Since we are interested in the meaning of the formula, we extend the assignment τ to $\hat{\tau} : \mathcal{BF} \to \{0,1\}$. The extension is based on the EVAL algorithm (see Algorithm 6.2). Note that $\hat{\tau}(X_i) = \tau(X_i)$ for every $X_i \in U$ (otherwise, it would not be a valid extension).

    Every assignment τ can be specified by a binary vector v. We define the assignment τ_v, defined as follows. Given a binary vector $v \in \{0,1\}^n$, define $\tau_v(X_i) \triangleq v_i$. The extension of τ_v to Boolean formulas $\mathcal{BF}$ is done, as before, using the EVAL algorithm. Again, given a vector v, we can evaluate the truth value of φ. Note that there is a one-to-one and onto mapping between the set of assignments over n variables and the set $\{0, 1\}^n$.

2. Let $C = \{\text{AND}, \text{XOR}\}$. We wish to find a formula $\tilde{\beta} \in \mathcal{BF}(\{X, Y, Z\}, C)$ that is logically equivalent to the formula

$$\beta \stackrel{\triangle}{=} (X \cdot Y) + Z.$$

First, we find a formula $\tilde{\varphi} \in \mathcal{BF}(\{X_1, X_2\}, C)$ that is logically equivalent to $(X_1 + X_2)$. It is easy to verify that $\tilde{\varphi}$ defined as follows is logically equivalent to $(X_1 + X_2)$:

$$\tilde{\varphi} \stackrel{\triangle}{=} X_1 \oplus X_2 \oplus (X_1 \cdot X_2).$$

We parse the formula β so that $\beta = \alpha_1 + \alpha_2$, where

$$\alpha_1 \stackrel{\triangle}{=} (X \cdot Y) \qquad\qquad \alpha_2 \stackrel{\triangle}{=} Z.$$

Note that in this example that $\alpha_i \in \mathcal{BF}(\{X, Y, Z\}, C)$, thus we need not "translate" these subformulas.

We apply substitution to define $\tilde{\beta} \stackrel{\triangle}{=} \tilde{\varphi}(\alpha_1, \alpha_2)$, thus

$$\tilde{\beta} \stackrel{\triangle}{=} \tilde{\varphi}(\alpha_1, \alpha_2)$$

$$= \alpha_1 \oplus \alpha_2 \oplus (\alpha_1 \cdot \alpha_2)$$

$$= (X \cdot Y) \oplus Z \oplus ((X \cdot Y) \cdot Z).$$

It is left to verify that indeed, $\tilde{\varphi}(\alpha_1, \alpha_2)$ is logically equivalent to β.

3. The formulas $(X + 0)$ and $(X \cdot 1)$ are logically equivalent to the formula X.

6.7 IMPORTANT TAUTOLOGIES

In this section, we present a short list of important tautologies. Each of these tautologies can be validated by exhaustive testing of all possible assignments. We leave the proofs as an exercise.

Theorem 6.8 *The following Boolean formulas are tautologies:*

1. *Law of excluded middle:* $X + \bar{X}$
2. *Double negation:* $X \leftrightarrow (\neg\neg X)$
3. *Modus ponens:* $(((X \rightarrow Y) \cdot X) \rightarrow Y)$
4. *Contrapositive:* $(X \rightarrow Y) \leftrightarrow (\bar{Y} \rightarrow \bar{X})$
5. *Material implication:* $(X \rightarrow Y) \leftrightarrow (\bar{X} + Y)$.
6. *Distribution:* $X \cdot (Y + Z) \leftrightarrow (X \cdot Y + X \cdot Z)$

The following lemma enables us to create a "new" tautology from an "old" one. Let $\varphi \in \mathcal{BF}(\{X_1, X_2\}, C)$ and $\alpha_1, \alpha_2 \in \mathcal{BF}(U, C)$.

Lemma 6.9 *If a Boolean formula φ is a tautology, then $\varphi(\alpha_1, \alpha_2)$ is a tautology.*

PROOF: To prove that $\varphi(\alpha_1, \alpha_2)$ is a tautology, all we need to prove is that, for every assignment $\tau : U \rightarrow \{0, 1\}$, the following equality holds:

$$\hat{\tau}(\varphi(\alpha_1, \alpha_2)) = 1.$$

Indeed,

$$\hat{\tau}(\varphi(\alpha_1, \alpha_2)) = B_\varphi(\hat{\tau}(\alpha_1), \hat{\tau}(\alpha_2)) \hspace{2cm} \text{(by Lemma 6.4)}$$

$$= 1, \hspace{1cm} \text{(since } \varphi \text{ is a tautology, and Example 1 on page 76)}$$

and the lemma follows. ∎

EXAMPLES

---

1. Prove that the following formulas are tautologies: (i) addition, $\varphi_1 \triangleq (X \rightarrow (X + Y))$, and (ii) simplification, $\varphi_2 \triangleq ((X \cdot Y) \rightarrow X)$.

    PROOF: We prove this claim by truth tables. Table 6.6 depicts the tables of both formulas. Note that the column that represents $\hat{\tau}_v(\varphi_i)$ is all ones. ∎

2. *Proof by contradiction.* Prove that the following formula is a tautology:

    $$\varphi_3 \triangleq ((\neg X \rightarrow 0) \rightarrow X).$$

    PROOF: We prove this claim by truth tables. Table 6.7 depicts the table of the formula. Note that the column that represents $\hat{\tau}_v(\varphi_3)$ is all ones. ∎

3. Prove that the following formula is a tautology:

    $$\varphi_4 \triangleq (((A \wedge \neg B) \rightarrow 0) \rightarrow (A \rightarrow B)).$$

    PROOF: As in the two previous examples, one can prove that φ_4 is a tautology using truth tables. Instead, we prove that φ_4 is a tautology by using substitution, as follows.

Table 6.6. The truth tables of the addition and the simplification tautologies

v_1	v_2	$\hat{\tau}_v(X + Y)$	$\hat{\tau}_v(\varphi_1)$	v_1	v_2	$\hat{\tau}_v(X \cdot Y)$	$\hat{\tau}_v(\varphi_2)$
0	0	0	1	0	0	0	1
1	0	1	1	1	0	0	1
0	1	1	1	0	1	0	1
1	1	1	1	1	1	1	1

Table 6.7. The truth table of the "proof by contradiction" tautology

v_1	$\hat{\tau}_v(\neg X \rightarrow 0)$	$\hat{\tau}_v(\varphi_3)$
0	0	1
1	1	1

Let

$$\psi \triangleq ((X_1 \to 0) \to X_2),$$

$$\alpha_1 \triangleq \neg(A \to B),$$

$$\alpha_2 \triangleq A \to B,$$

$$\tilde{\alpha}_1 \triangleq A \land \neg B.$$

The formulas α_1 and $\tilde{\alpha}_1$ are logically equivalent. Corollary 6.5 implies that $\psi(\alpha_1, \alpha_2)$ is logically equivalent to $\psi(\tilde{\alpha}_1, \alpha_2)$. Note that $\varphi_4 = \psi(\tilde{\alpha}_1, \alpha_2)$, hence it suffices to prove that $\psi(\alpha_1, \alpha_2)$ is a tautology. Note that

$$\psi(\alpha_1, \alpha_2) = ((\neg(A \to B) \to 0) \to (A \to B))$$

$$= \varphi_3(A \to B);$$

indeed, Example 2 and Lemma 6.9 imply that $\varphi_3(A \to B) = \psi(\alpha_1, \alpha_2)$ is a tautology, as required. ∎

We have already applied this tautology, while proving by contradiction that "A implies B." The proof scheme is as follows: (1) add the assumption $\neg B$, (2) derive a contradiction, that is, 0, and (3) hence, by tautology φ_4, the statement "A implies B" is correct.

4. Suppose we are given a (very) long Boolean formula φ with many variables.

    Sometimes, if we are very lucky, we can decide if it is a tautology without working hard. Lemma 6.9 implies that all we need is to recognize whether the formula φ is obtained by a substitution of subformulas instead of the variables in a tautology ψ. This means that a tautology (and formulas in general) can be regarded as a "template" waiting for substitution. In this case, ψ is the template, and φ is an "instance" obtained by applying substitution.

6.8 DE MORGAN'S LAWS

In this section, we show how to simplify a Boolean formula so that negations are only applied to variables. This technique is based on two tautologies called De Morgan's laws.

Theorem 6.10 (*De Morgan s Laws*) *The following two Boolean formulas are tautologies:*

1. $(\neg(X + Y)) \leftrightarrow (\bar{X} \cdot \bar{Y})$
2. $(\neg(X \cdot Y)) \leftrightarrow (\bar{X} + \bar{Y})$

We use De Morgan's laws to compute the dual of Boolean formula. In Algorithm 6.4, a listing of $DM(\varphi)$ is presented. The algorithm is recursive and uses the inductive definition of a Boolean formula (see Definition 6.5).

The idea of a De Morgan dual is that, given a Boolean formula $\varphi \in \mathcal{BF}(U, \{\neg, \lor, \land\})$, the De Morgan dual is obtained by the following simultaneous replacements: replace each instance of a $\wedge$ by a $\vee$, each instance of a $\vee$ by a $\wedge$, a 0 by a 1, a 1 by a 0, a $\bar{X}_i$ by X_i, and an X_i by a $\bar{X}_i$. Note that these replacements can be applied either to the labels in the parse tree of φ or directly to the "characters" of the string φ.

Algorithm 6.4 DM(φ)—an algorithm for evaluating the De Morgan dual of a Boolean formula $\varphi \in \mathcal{BF}(\{X_1, \ldots, X_n\}, \{\neg, \text{OR}, \text{AND}\})$.

---

1. Base cases: (parse tree of size 1 or 2)
   (a) If $\varphi = 0$, then return 1.
   (b) If $\varphi = 1$, then return 0.
   (c) If $\varphi = X_i$, then return $(\neg X_i)$.
   (d) If $\varphi = (\neg 0)$, then return 0.
   (e) If $\varphi = (\neg 1)$, then return 1.
   (f) If $\varphi = (\neg X_i)$, then return X_i.
2. Reduction rules: (parse tree of size at least 3)
   (a) If $\varphi = (\neg \varphi_1)$, then return $(\neg \text{DM}(\varphi_1))$.
   (b) If $\varphi = (\varphi_1 \cdot \varphi_2)$, then return $(\text{DM}(\varphi_1) + \text{DM}(\varphi_2))$.
   (c) If $\varphi = (\varphi_1 + \varphi_2)$, then return $(\text{DM}(\varphi_1) \cdot \text{DM}(\varphi_2))$.

The following theorem states that the De Morgan dual formula is logically equivalent to the negated formula.

Theorem 6.11 *For every Boolean formula φ, $DM(\varphi)$ is logically equivalent to $(\neg\varphi)$.*

PROOF: The proof is by complete induction on the length of φ (i.e., number of vertices in the parse tree of φ). The induction basis, for a parse tree consisting of a single node or two nodes, is immediate because of the base cases. We now proceed to prove the induction step. We consider three cases:

1. $\varphi = (\neg\varphi_1)$. In this case, $\text{DM}(\varphi) = (\neg\text{DM}(\varphi_1))$. By the induction hypothesis, $\text{DM}(\varphi_1)$ is logically equivalent to $\neg\varphi_1$. By substitution (i.e., Corollary 6.5), $\text{DM}(\varphi)$ is logically equivalent to $(\neg(\neg\varphi_1))$. Thus $\text{DM}(\varphi)$ is logically equivalent to $(\neg\varphi)$, as required.
2. $\varphi = \varphi_1 \cdot \varphi_2$. In this case, $\text{DM}(\varphi) = (\text{DM}(\varphi_1) + \text{DM}(\varphi_2))$. By the induction hypothesis, $\text{DM}(\varphi_i)$ is logically equivalent to $\neg\varphi_i$. By substitution (i.e., Corollary 6.5), $\text{DM}(\varphi)$ is logically equivalent to $((\neg\varphi_1) + (\neg\varphi_2))$. By De Morgan's law, Lemma 6.9, and Example 7 on page 78, $((\neg\varphi_1) + (\neg\varphi_2))$ is logically equivalent to $(\neg\varphi)$, as required.
3. $\varphi = \varphi_1 + \varphi_2$. The proof of this case is similar to the previous case. ∎

Corollary 6.12 *For every Boolean formula φ, $DM(DM(\varphi))$ is logically equivalent to φ.*

6.8.1 Negation Normal Form

A formula is in negation normal form if negation is applied only directly to variables.

Definition 6.15 A Boolean formula $\varphi \in \mathcal{BF}(\{X_1, \ldots, X_n\}, \{\neg, \text{OR}, \text{AND}\})$ is in *negation normal form* if the parse tree (G, π) of φ satisfies the following condition. If a vertex in G is labeled by negation (i.e., $\pi(v) = \neg$), then v is a parent of a leaf labeled by a variable.

For example, the formula $(\neg X) \cdot (\neg Y)$ is in negation normal form. However, the formulas $(\neg 0)$, $\neg(A \cdot B)$, and NOT(NOT(X)) are not in negation normal form.

Lemma 6.13 *If φ is in negation normal form, then so is $DM(\varphi)$.*

PROOF: The proof is by induction on the length of φ. The base cases deal with parse trees with one or two vertices. In the induction step, note that the case $\varphi = \neg\varphi_1$ cannot occur. Indeed, $\varphi = \neg\varphi_1$, where the length of φ is at least 3, implies that φ is not in negation normal form—a contradiction. Thus we are left only with the two cases in which $\varphi = \varphi_1 \cdot \varphi_2$ and $\varphi = \varphi_1 + \varphi_2$, the proof of which is straightforward. ■

In this section, we present an algorithm that transforms a Boolean formula into a logically equivalent formula in negation normal form. The algorithm $NNF(\varphi)$ is listed as Algorithm 6.5.

Algorithm 6.5 $NNF(\varphi)$—An algorithm for computing the negation normal form of a Boolean formula $\varphi \in \mathcal{BF}(\{X_1, \ldots, X_n\}, \{\neg, \text{OR}, \text{AND}\})$.

---

1. Base cases: (parse tree of size 1 or 2)
    (a) If $\varphi \in \{0, 1, X_i, (\neg X_i)\}$, then return φ.
    (b) If $\varphi = (\neg 0)$, then return 1.
    (c) If $\varphi = (\neg 1)$, then return 0.
2. Reduction rules: (parse tree of size at least 3)
    (a) If $\varphi = (\neg\varphi_1)$, then return DM(NNF($\varphi_1$)).
    (b) If $\varphi = (\varphi_1 \cdot \varphi_2)$, then return (NNF($\varphi_1$) $\cdot$ NNF(φ_2)).
    (c) If $\varphi = (\varphi_1 + \varphi_2)$, then return (NNF($\varphi_1$) + NNF($\varphi_2$)).

Theorem 6.14 *Let $\varphi \in \mathcal{BF}(\{X_1, \ldots, X_n\}, \{\neg, \text{OR}, \text{AND}\})$. Then $NNF(\varphi)$ is logically equivalent to φ and in negation normal form.*

PROOF: The proof is by induction on the length of φ. The base cases deal with parse trees with one or two vertices. We proceed to prove the induction step. The cases that the root of the parse tree of φ is in $\{\cdot, +\}$ is standard. We focus on the case that $\varphi = (\neg\varphi_1)$. Since φ_1 is shorter than φ, the induction hypothesis implies that $\psi \triangleq NNF(\varphi_1)$ is logically equivalent to φ_1 and in negation normal form. Hence, by Lemma 6.13, DM(ψ) is in negation normal form. By Theorem 6.11, DM(ψ) is logically equivalent to $\neg\psi$. This implies that DM(ψ) is logically equivalent to φ, as required. ■

EXAMPLES

---

1. We show an execution of the DM(φ) algorithm on the input $\varphi = (X \cdot Y)$. The execution is as follows:
    (a) Since φ is not one of the base cases, we proceed to the reduction rules.

(b) Since φ is of the form $(\varphi_1 \cdot \varphi_2)$, we apply the first reduction rule, that is, $\varphi_1 = X$, $\varphi_2 = Y$, and $\text{DM}(\varphi)$ returns $(\text{DM}(X) + \text{DM}(Y))$.

    i. Since X (and Y) matches the third base case, both recursive calls return $(\neg X)$ and $(\neg Y)$, respectively.

(c) Thus $\text{DM}(\varphi)$ returns $((\neg X) + (\neg Y))$.

2. Prove that $\text{DM}(\varphi) \in \mathcal{BF}$.

PROOF: We prove that the string $DM(\varphi)$ is defined by a parse tree (F, π). The proof is by complete induction on the size of the parse tree (G, π) of the Boolean formula φ.

The induction basis for a parse tree G consisting of one or two nodes is immediate because of the four base cases. We now proceed to prove the induction step. We consider three cases:

(a) $\varphi = (\neg\varphi_1)$. In this case, $\text{DM}(\varphi) = (\neg\text{DM}(\varphi_1))$. By the induction hypothesis, $\text{DM}(\varphi_1) \in \mathcal{BF}$. Hence F is simply the parse tree of $\text{DM}(\varphi_1)$ hanging from a new root labeled by the NOT connective.

(b) $\varphi = \varphi_1 \cdot \varphi_2$. In this case, $\text{DM}(\varphi) = (\text{DM}(\varphi_1) + \text{DM}(\varphi_2))$. By the induction hypothesis, $\text{DM}(\varphi_i) \in \mathcal{BF}$. Hence F is simply constructed by the parse trees of $\text{DM}(\varphi_i)$ hanging from a new root labeled by the OR connective.

(c) $\varphi = \varphi_1 + \varphi_2$. The proof of this case is similar to the previous case. ■

3. Recall that De Morgan's law states that for sets A, B,

$$U \smallsetminus (A \cup B) = \bar{A} \cap \bar{B}.$$

We depicted this law using Venn diagrams in Example 29 on p. 9 of Chapter 1. We now prove this law, formally, using propositional logic.

PROOF: We need to show (a) $U \smallsetminus (A \cup B) \subseteq \bar{A} \cap \bar{B}$ and (b) $\bar{A} \cap \bar{B} \subseteq U \smallsetminus (A \cup B)$.
(a) To prove $U \smallsetminus (A \cup B) \subseteq \bar{A} \cap \bar{B}$, we need to show that every $x \in U \smallsetminus (A \cup B)$ is also $x \in \bar{A} \cap \bar{B}$:

$$x \in U \smallsetminus (A \cup B) \Rightarrow x \in U \text{ and } x \notin (A \cup B)$$

$$\Rightarrow x \in U \text{ and not}(x \in A \text{ or } x \in B)$$

$$\Rightarrow x \in U \text{ and } (x \notin A \text{ and } x \notin B)$$

$$\Rightarrow x \in U \text{ and } (x \in \bar{A} \text{ and } x \in \bar{B})$$

$$\Rightarrow x \in U \text{ and } x \in (\bar{A} \cap \bar{B})$$

$$\Rightarrow x \in \bar{A} \cap \bar{B},$$

where the first line follows from the definition of the difference of sets A and B. The second line follows from the definition of the union of sets A and B. Let $X = 1$ iff $x \in A$, and let $Y = 1$ iff $x \in B$; then the third line follows from De Morgan's law applied on the formula $(\neg(X + Y))$. The fifth line follows from the definition of the intersection of sets $\bar{A}$ and $\bar{B}$. The last line follows since $\bar{A} \cap \bar{B} \subseteq U$.
(b) $\bar{A} \cap \bar{B} \subseteq U \smallsetminus (A \cup B)$; that is, we need to show that every $x \in \bar{A} \cap \bar{B}$ is also $x \in U \smallsetminus (A \cup B)$. The same proof holds since each implication holds also in the reverse direction. ■

4. Prove that the following Boolean formulas are logically equivalent:
   - $\beta_2 \triangleq (\bar{A} + B) \rightarrow C$
   - $\beta_3 \triangleq (A \cdot \bar{B}) + C$.

PROOF: Let

$$\varphi \triangleq X_1 \rightarrow X_2 \,,$$

$$\tilde{\varphi} \triangleq \neg X_1 + X_2 \,,$$

$$\alpha_1 \triangleq \bar{A} + B \,,$$

$$\alpha_2 \triangleq C \,,$$

$$\tilde{\alpha}_1 \triangleq \neg(A \cdot \bar{B}) \,.$$

Theorem 6.8 and Example 7 on p. 78 imply that φ and $\tilde{\varphi}$ are logically equivalent. We claim that α_1 and $\tilde{\alpha}_1$ are logically equivalent (exercise).

Note that

$$\varphi(\alpha_1, \alpha_2) = \beta_2 \,,$$

$$\tilde{\varphi}(\tilde{\alpha}_1, \alpha_2) = \neg\neg(A \cdot \bar{B}) + C,$$

$$NNF(\tilde{\varphi}(\tilde{\alpha}_1, \alpha_2)) = NNF(\neg\neg(A \cdot \bar{B})) + C = \beta_3 \,.$$

Corollary 6.5 implies that $\varphi(\alpha_1, \alpha_2)$ and $\tilde{\varphi}(\tilde{\alpha}_1, \alpha_2)$ are logically equivalent. Theorem 6.14 implies that $NNF(\tilde{\varphi}(\tilde{\alpha}_1, \alpha_2))$ is logically equivalent to $\tilde{\varphi}(\tilde{\alpha}_1, \alpha_2)$, hence $\varphi(\alpha_1, \alpha_2)$ is logically equivalent to $NNF(\tilde{\varphi}(\tilde{\alpha}_1, \alpha_2))$, as required. ∎

PROBLEMS

6.1. Recall the closure property of a set of strings as formalized in Definition 6.3. Also recall that a set of strings $\mathcal{F}$ *contains the atoms* if $\{0, 1\} \subseteq \mathcal{F}$ and $U \subseteq \mathcal{F}$ (see Definition 6.4 on page 71). Give an example of a set $\mathcal{F}$ that is closed under the set of connectives $\mathcal{C}$, includes the atoms, but is *not* $\mathcal{BF}(U, \mathcal{C})$.

6.2. Let φ be a formula in $\mathcal{BF}$ and let (G, π) be its parse tree. Let $G_1, \dots, G_k$ be the rooted trees hanging from the root $r(G)$. Assume that $\pi(r(G))$ is an associative connective (but not commutative). Show that $G_1, \dots, G_k$ are parse trees of formulas $\varphi_1, \dots, \varphi_k \in \mathcal{BF}$ such that

$$(\varphi_1 \,\pi(r(G))\, \varphi_2 \,\pi(r(G)) \cdots \pi(r(G))\, \varphi_k) = \varphi \,.$$

6.3. Show that the set of Boolean formulas $\mathcal{BF}(\{X, Y\}, \{+, \cdot, \neg\})$ satisfies the closure property defined in Definition 6.3; that is, show that the set $\mathcal{BF}$ is closed under the set of connectives $\{+, \cdot, \neg\}$. Your proof should not rely on the fact that $\mathcal{BF}' = \mathcal{BF}$.

6.4. Prove that $(A \rightarrow B) \leftrightarrow ((\neg A) \text{ OR } B)$ is a tautology in two ways: (i) show that the truth table of the Boolean function corresponding to the formula is the truth table of the constant function, that is, $\forall A, B \in \{0, 1\} : f(A, B) = 1$, and (ii) show that the truth tables of $(A \rightarrow B)$ and $((\neg A) \text{ OR } B)$ are the same.

6.5. Let $\varphi \triangleq (X + Y \cdot X)$. Show that φ is satisfiable.

6.6. Let $\varphi \triangleq (\overline{\neg X \wedge X})$. Show that φ is a tautology.

6.7. Let φ and α be any Boolean formulas.
   (a) Consider the Boolean formula $\psi \triangleq \varphi + \text{NOT}(\varphi)$. Prove or refute that ψ is a tautology.
   (b) Consider the Boolean formula $\psi \triangleq (\varphi \rightarrow \alpha) \leftrightarrow (\text{NOT}(\varphi) + \alpha)$. Prove or refute that ψ is a tautology.

6.8. Let $\mathcal{C} = \{\text{AND}, \text{OR}\}$. Prove that $\mathcal{C}$ is *not* a complete set of connectives.

6.9. Prove Theorem 6.8.

6.10. Let $\varphi \triangleq (X \cdot (Y + Z))$, and let $\psi \triangleq (X \cdot Y + X \cdot Z)$. Prove that φ and ψ are logically equivalent.

6.11. Let $p, q, r \in \mathcal{BF}$. Prove that if p is logically equivalent to q, and q is logically equivalent to r, then p is logically equivalent to r.

6.12. **Definition 6.16** Let $\varphi \in \mathcal{BF}$; then φ is a *contradiction* if $\hat{\tau}(\varphi) = 0$ for every assignment τ.
   Prove the following claim.

   Lemma 6.15

   $$\varphi \text{ is a contradiction} \Leftrightarrow (\neg \varphi) \text{ is a tautology.}$$

6.13. Let $L'(\varphi)$ denote the number of vertices in the parse tree of φ that are *not* labeled by negation. Example: $L'(A + B + \neg C) = 5$.
   Prove that $L'(DM(\varphi)) = L'(\varphi)$ for every Boolean formula $\varphi \in \mathcal{BF}(U, \{\neg, \vee, \wedge\})$.

6.14. Prove Theorem 6.10.

6.15. Let $\mathcal{C} = \{\neg, \vee, \wedge, \text{XOR}, \text{NXOR}\}$. Add the following two reduction rules to Algorithm $DM(\varphi)$:
   - If $\varphi = (\varphi_1 \text{ XOR } \varphi_2)$, then return $(DM(\varphi_1) \text{ NXOR } DM(\varphi_2))$.
   - If $\varphi = (\varphi_1 \text{ NXOR } \varphi_2)$, then return $(DM(\varphi_1) \text{ XOR } DM(\varphi_2))$.
   Prove that, even after this modification, $DM(\varphi) \leftrightarrow \neg\varphi$ is a tautology.

6.16. Let

$$\varphi_k \triangleq \overbrace{\neg\neg \ldots \neg}^{k \text{ times}} X;$$

that is, in φ_k, the variable X is negated k times. Run algorithm $NNF(\varphi_k)$. What is the outcome? Prove your result. *Hint: distinguish between an even k and an odd k.*

6.17. Let $\varphi \triangleq \bar{A} + B$, and let $\psi \triangleq \neg(A \cdot \bar{B})$. Prove that φ and ψ are logically equivalent in two ways: (i) by using truth tables and (ii) *without* using truth tables. *Hint: apply the NNF algorithm.*

6.18. Let $\varphi \triangleq (A \rightarrow B) \rightarrow C$, and let $\psi \triangleq (A \cdot \bar{B}) + C$. Prove that φ and ψ are logically equivalent in two ways: (i) by using truth tables and (ii) *without* using truth tables. *Hint: apply the NNF algorithm.*

CHAPTER 7

Asymptotics

In this chapter, we study the *rate of growth* of positive sequences. We introduce a formal definition that enables us to say that one sequence does not grow faster than another sequence. Suppose we have two sequences $\{x_i\}_{i=1}^{\infty}$ and $\{y_i\}_{i=1}^{\infty}$. We could say that x_i does not grow faster than y_i if $x_i \leq y_i$ for every i. However, such a restricted definition is rather limited, as suggested by the following examples:

1. The sequence x_i is constant: $x_i = 1000$ for every i, while the sequence y_i is defined by $y_i = i$. Clearly we would like to say that y_i grows faster than x_i even though $y_{100} < x_{100}$.
2. The sequences satisfy $x_i = y_i + 5$ or $x_i = 2 \cdot y_i$ for every i. In this case, we would like to say that the two sequences grow at the same rate even though $x_i > y_i$.

Thus we are looking for a definition that is insensitive to the values of finite prefixes of the sequence. In addition, we are looking for a definition that is insensitive to addition or multiplication by constants. This definition is called the *asymptotic behavior* of a sequence.

7.1 ORDER OF GROWTH RATES

Consider the Fibonacci sequence $\{g(n)\}_{n=0}^{\infty}$. The exact value of $g(n)$, or an analytic equation for $g(n)$, is interesting but sometimes all we need to know is how fast does $g(n)$ grow? Does it grow faster than $f(n) = n$, or $f(n) = n^2$, or $f(n) = 2^n$? The following definition captures the notion of "$g(n)$ does not grow faster than $f(n)$."

Recall that the set of nonnegative real numbers is denoted by $\mathbb{R}^{\geq}$ (see Section 1.1 on page 3).

Definition 7.1 Let $f, g : \mathbb{N} \to \mathbb{R}^{\geq}$ denote two functions.

1. We say that $g(n) = O(f(n))$ if there exist constants $c_1, c_2 \in \mathbb{R}^{\geq}$ such that, for every $n \in \mathbb{N}$,

$$g(n) \leq c_1 \cdot f(n) + c_2.$$

2. We say that $g(n) = \Omega(f(n))$ if there exist constants $c_3 \in \mathbb{R}^+$, $c_4 \in \mathbb{R}^{\geq}$ such that, for every $n \in \mathbb{N}$,

$$g(n) \geq c_3 \cdot f(n) + c_4.$$

3. We say that $g(n) = \Theta(f(n))$ if $g(n) = O(f(n))$ and $g(n) = \Omega(f(n))$.

These definitions should be interpreted as follows:

- If $g(n) = O(f(n))$, then $g(n)$ does not grow faster than $f(n)$.
- If $g(n) = \Omega(f(n))$, then $g(n)$ grows as least as fast as $f(n)$.
- If $g(n) = \Theta(f(n))$, then $g(n)$ grows as fast as $f(n)$.

We read

- $g(n) = O(f(n))$ as "$g(n)$ is big-O of $f(n)$."
- $g(n) = \Omega(f(n))$ as "$g(n)$ is big-Omega of $f(n)$."
- $g(n) = \Theta(f(n))$ as "$g(n)$ is big-Theta of $f(n)$."

EXAMPLES

---

1. $f(n) = O(g(n))$ does *not* imply that $g(n) = O(f(n))$.
2. The notation $f(n) = O(1)$ means that $\exists c \; \forall n : f(n) \leq c$.
3. Let $g(n) \triangleq 2 \cdot n$. We claim that $g(n) = \Theta(n)$.

    PROOF: First we show that $2 \cdot n = O(n)$. We need to show that there exist constants $c_1, c_2 \in \mathbb{R}^{\geq}$ such that, for every $n \in \mathbb{N}$,

    $$2 \cdot n \leq c_1 \cdot n + c_2. \tag{7.1}$$

    That is accomplished by setting $c_1 \leftarrow 2$ and $c_2 \leftarrow 0$.

    Now we show that $2 \cdot n = \Omega(n)$. We need to show that there exist constants $c_3 \in \mathbb{R}^+$, $c_4 \in \mathbb{R}^{\geq}$ such that, for every $n \in \mathbb{N}$,

    $$2 \cdot n \geq c_3 \cdot n + c_4 \tag{7.2}$$

    That is accomplished, again, by setting $c_3 \leftarrow 2$ and $c_4 \leftarrow 0$.

    We have shown that $2 \cdot n = O(n)$ and $2 \cdot n = \Omega(n)$, hence $2 \cdot n = \Theta(n)$, and the claim follows. ∎

4. Let $g(n) \triangleq n^2 + n + 1$. We claim that $g(n) = O(n^2)$.

    PROOF: We need to prove that there exist constants $c_1, c_2 \in \mathbb{R}^{\geq}$ such that, for every $n \in \mathbb{N}$,

    $$n^2 + n + 1 \leq c_1 \cdot n^2 + c_2. \tag{7.3}$$

    Let us find such constant c_1 and c_2. Since $n^2 \geq n$ for every $n \in \mathbb{N}$, then

    $$n^2 + n + 1 \leq n^2 + n^2 + 1$$

    $$= 2 \cdot n^2 + 1.$$

    Hence $c_1 = 2$ and $c_2 = 1$. The claim follows since we found $c_1, c_2 \in \mathbb{R}$ such that Eq. 7.3 holds. ∎

5. Let $g(n) \triangleq n^{\log_2 c}$. We claim that $g(n) = \Theta(c^{\log_2 n})$.

PROOF: We prove the following stronger claim:

$$n^{\log_2 c} = c^{\log_2 n} . \tag{7.4}$$

That will conclude the proof, since for every two functions $f, g : \mathbb{N} \to \mathbb{R}^{\geq}$, if $f = g$, then $f(n) = \Theta(g(n))$ and $g(n) = \Theta(f(n))$ (see Exercise 7.6).

Let us apply the $\log_2$ function on the left-hand side and the right-hand side of Eq. 7.4. We get

$$\log_2(n^{\log_2 c}) \overset{?}{=} \log_2(c^{\log_2 n}) \Leftrightarrow$$

$$\log_2 c \cdot \log_2 n = \log_2 n \cdot \log_2 c, \tag{7.5}$$

where the second line follows from the fact that $\log(a^b) = b \cdot \log(a)$. Since Eq. 7.5 holds with equality, and since the log function is one-to-one, then their arguments are equal as well, that is, $n^{\log_2 c} = c^{\log_2 n}$, as required. ∎

6. Let $g(n) \triangleq \log_3 n$. We claim that $g(n) = \Theta(\log_2 n)$

PROOF: Recall that for every $a, b, c \in \mathbb{R}, a, c \neq 1$,

$$\log_a b = \frac{\log_c b}{\log_c a} . \tag{7.6}$$

Hence $\log_3 n = \frac{\log_2 n}{\log_2 3}$. Since $3/2 < \log_2 3 < 8/5$ is a constant, then $c_1 = 2/3, c_2 = 0, c_3 = 5/8, c_4 = 0$ satisfy the conditions in Definition 7.1. ∎

7. Example 6 shows that when considering the order of growth of log functions with a constant base, that is, $\log_c n$ and $\log_d n$, where c, d are constants, we may omit the base and simply refer to the order of growth of these functions as $O(\log n)$, $\Omega(\log n)$, and $\Theta(\log n)$.

8. Prove that (i) $n = O(n)$ and (ii) $n^2 \neq O(n)$.

PROOF: The first item is trivial since $n \leq 1 \cdot n^2 + 0$ for every $n \in \mathbb{N}$.

To prove that $g(n) \neq O(f(n))$, we need to show that

$$\forall c_1, c_2 \in \mathbb{R}^{\geq} \quad \exists n \in \mathbb{N} : \quad g(n) > c_1 \cdot f(n) + c_2.$$

Hence, to prove item (ii), we set $g(n) = n^2$ and $f(n) = n$. Let $c_1, c_2 \in \mathbb{R}^{\geq}$; it suffices to find an $n \in \mathbb{N}$ such that

$$n^2 > \max\{c_1, 1\} \cdot n + c_2. \tag{7.7}$$

Indeed, $n = \lceil \max\{c_1, 1\} + c_2 \rceil$ satisfies the preceding inequality. ∎

9. Let us consider the following alternative definition of order of growth.

Definition 7.2 Let $f, g : \mathbb{N} \to \mathbb{R}^{\geq}$ denote two functions.

(a) We say that $g(n) = O(f(n))$ if there exist constants $c \in \mathbb{R}^{\geq}$ and $N \in \mathbb{N}$ such that $n \in \mathbb{N}$,

$$\forall n > N : g(n) \leq c \cdot f(n) .$$

(b) We say that $g(n) = \Omega(f(n))$ if there exist constants $d \in \mathbb{R}^{\geq}$ and $N \in \mathbb{N}$ such that

$$\forall n > N : g(n) \geq d \cdot f(n) .$$

(c) We say that $g(n) = \Theta(f(n))$ if $g(n) = O(f(n))$ and $g(n) = \Omega(f(n))$.

Prove that Definitions 7.1 and 7.2 are equivalent if $f(n) \geq 1, g(n) \geq 1$ for every n.

PROOF: We show equivalence with respect to Item (a). A similar proof shows the equivalence of item (b) of both definitions. Item (c) is the same in both definitions.

We need to show that for every $f, g : \mathbb{N} \to \mathbb{R}^2$; (i) if $g(n) = O(f(n))$ by Definition 7.1, then $g(n) = O(f(n))$ by Definition 7.2, and (ii) if $g(n) = O(f(n))$ by Definition 7.2, then $g(n) = O(f(n))$ by Definition 7.1.

Let $f, g : \mathbb{N} \to \mathbb{R}^2$ such that $g(n) = O(f(n))$ by Definition 7.1 Hence there exist constants $c_1, c_2 \in \mathbb{R}^2$ such that, for every $n \in \mathbb{N}$,

$$g(n) \leq c_1 \cdot f(n) + c_2.$$

Since $f(n) \geq 1$, then

$$g(n) \leq c_1 \cdot f(n) + c_2 \cdot f(n)$$

$$= (c_1 + c_2) \cdot f(n).$$

Hence $g(n) = O(f(n))$ by Definition 7.2 with $c \triangleq (c_1 + c_2)$ and $N \triangleq 0$.

We now prove the second direction: let $f, g : \mathbb{N} \to \mathbb{R}^2$ such that $g(n) = O(f(n))$ by Definition 7.2. Hence there exist constants $c \in \mathbb{R}^2$ and $N \in \mathbb{N}$ such that

$$\forall n > N : g(n) \leq c \cdot f(n).$$

Let $c_1 \triangleq c$ and $c_2 \triangleq \max_{0 \leq n \leq N} \{g(n)\}$; then

$$\forall n \in \mathbb{N} : g(n) \leq c_1 \cdot f(n) + c_2.$$

We showed that both directions hold, as required. ∎

10. Consider two functions $f, g : \mathbb{N} \to \mathbb{R}^2$. Let

$$h(n) \triangleq \begin{cases} g(n) & \text{if } n \leq n_1 \\ f(n) & \text{if } n > n_1. \end{cases}$$

Prove that $h(n) = \Theta(f(n))$.

PROOF: The lemma follows from Definition 7.2 by plugging $c \triangleq 1$, $d \triangleq 1$, and $N \triangleq n_1$. ∎

11. Exercise 10 implies that we can consider the order of growth of functions whose domain is $\mathbb{N} \smallsetminus \{n_0, n_0 + 1, \ldots, n_1\}$. We simply extend the function arbitrarily in the range $\{n_0, n_0 + 1, \ldots, n_1\}$ and apply Definition 7.2.

12. Prove that $\log_2 n + \log_2(\log_2 n) = \Theta(\log n)$.

PROOF: We prove that $\log_2 n + \log_2(\log_2 n) = O(\log n)$ using Definition 7.2. The other direction is similar. Since $\log_2 n + \log_2(\log_2 n) \leq 2 \cdot \log_2 n$ for every $n > 2$, it follows that $\log_2 n + \log_2(\log_2 n) = O(\log n)$, as required. ∎

13. Recall that in Lemma 2.6, we proved that the Fibonacci sequence $g(n)$ is bounded by φ^{n-1}. This implies that $g(n) = O(\varphi^n)$.

7.2 RECURRENCE EQUATIONS

In this section, we deal with the problem of solving or bounding the rate of growth of functions $f : \mathbb{N}^+ \to \mathbb{R}$ that are defined recursively. We consider the typical cases that we will encounter later.

Recurrence 1. Consider the recurrence

$$f(n) \triangleq \begin{cases} 1 & \text{if } n = 1 \\ n + f\left(\left\lfloor \frac{n}{2} \right\rfloor\right) & \text{if } n > 1. \end{cases} \tag{7.8}$$

Lemma 7.1 *The rate of growth of the function $f(n)$ defined in Eq. 7.8 is $\Theta(n)$.*

PROOF: Clearly $f(n) > 0$ for every n; therefore, by the definition of $f(n)$, we obtain

$$f(n) = n + f\left(\left\lfloor \frac{n}{2} \right\rfloor\right) > n.$$

Thus we proved that $f(n) = \Omega(n)$.

Prove that $f(n) = O(n)$ is divided into two parts. First, we deal with powers of 2 to get an intuition of the constant we need. In the second part, we use this intuition to prove the bounds.

We claim that $f(2^k) = 2^{k+1} - 1$. The proof is by induction on $k \in \mathbb{N}$. The induction basis for $k = 0$ holds by the definition of $f(1)$. The induction step is proved as follows:

$$f(2^{k+1}) = 2^{k+1} + f(2^k) \qquad \qquad \text{(by definition)}$$

$$= 2^{k+1} + 2^{k+1} - 1 \qquad \text{(induction hypothesis)}$$

$$= 2^{k+2} - 1.$$

This part gives us the intuition that $f(n) < 2n$.

We now claim that $f(n) < 2n$. The proof is by complete induction on n. The induction basis for $n = 1$ is immediate. The induction step is proved as follows:

$$f(n) = n + f\left(\left\lfloor \frac{n}{2} \right\rfloor\right)$$

$$< n + 2 \cdot \left(\frac{n}{2}\right) = 2n. \qquad \blacksquare$$

In the following lemma, we show that under reasonable conditions, it suffices to consider powers of 2 when bounding the rate of growth.

Lemma 7.2 *Assume that*

1. *The functions $f(n)$ and $g(n)$ are both monotonically nondecreasing.*
2. *The constant ρ satisfies, for every $k \in \mathbb{N}$,*

$$\rho \geq \frac{g(2^{k+1})}{g(2^k)}.$$

If $f(2^k) = O(g(2^k))$, then $f(n) = O(g(n))$.

PROOF: Since $f(2^k) = O(g(2^k))$, let c denote a constant such that for every $k > K$, it holds that $f(2^k) \le c \cdot g(2^k)$. We claim that for every $n > 2^K$,

$$f(n) \le \rho \cdot c \cdot g(n).$$

Indeed, let $2^k \le n < 2^{k+1}$. Then

$$f(n) \le f(2^{k+1}) \qquad\qquad \text{(since } f \text{ is monotone)}$$

$$\le c \cdot g(2^{k+1})$$

$$= \frac{g(2^{k+1})}{g(2^k)} \cdot c \cdot g(2^k)$$

$$\le \rho \cdot c \cdot g(n). \qquad\qquad \text{(by definition of } \rho \text{ and since } g \text{ is monotone)}$$

Thus we obtain that $f(n) = O(g(n))$, as required. ∎

There is an analogous lemma that states that $f(n) = \Omega(g(n))$ can be proved if $\frac{g(2^{k+1})}{g(2^k)} \ge \rho$, for a constant ρ. The lemma is as follows.

Lemma 7.3 *Assume that*

1. *The functions $f(n)$ and $g(n)$ are both monotonically nondecreasing.*
2. *The constant ρ satisfies, for every $k \in \mathbb{N}$,*

$$\rho \le \frac{g(2^{k+1})}{g(2^k)}.$$

If $f(2^k) = \Omega(g(2^k))$, then $f(n) = \Omega(g(n))$.

We leave the proof of Lemma 7.3 as an exercise.

Recurrence 2. Consider the recurrence

$$f(n) \triangleq \begin{cases} 1 & \text{if } n = 1 \\ n + 2 \cdot f(\lfloor \frac{n}{2} \rfloor) & \text{if } n > 1. \end{cases} \qquad (7.9)$$

Lemma 7.4 *The rate of growth of the function $f(n)$ defined in Eq. 7.9 is $\Theta(n \log n)$.*

PROOF: The proof proceeds as follows. We deal with powers of 2 and then apply Lemma 7.2 and Lemma 7.3.

We claim that $f(2^k) = 2^k \cdot (k + 1)$. The proof is by induction on $k \in \mathbb{N}$. The induction basis for $k = 0$ holds by the definition of $f(1)$. The induction step is proved as follows:

$$f(2^{k+1}) = 2^{k+1} + 2 \cdot f(2^k) \qquad\qquad \text{(by definition)}$$

$$= 2^{k+1} + 2 \cdot 2^k \cdot (k + 1) \qquad\qquad \text{(induction hypothesis)}$$

$$= 2^{k+1} \cdot (k + 2).$$

We have proved that for $n = 2^k$, where $k \in \mathbb{N}$, recurrence 7.9 satisfies that $f(n) = n \cdot (\log(n) + 1) = \Theta(n \log n)$.

To complete the proof, we need to apply Lemma 7.2 and Lemma 7.3. First, the functions $f(n)$ and $g(n) = n \cdot (\log(n) + 1)$ are both monotonically nondecreasing. Second, to apply Lemma 7.2 and Lemma 7.3, we also need to prove that $\rho_1 \leq \frac{2^{k+1} \cdot (k+2)}{2^k \cdot (k+1)} \leq \rho_2$ such that $\rho_1, \rho_2 = O(1)$ for every $k \in \mathbb{N}$. Indeed,

$$
\begin{aligned}
\frac{2^{k+1} \cdot (k+2)}{2^k \cdot (k+1)} &= \frac{2 \cdot (k+2)}{(k+1)} \\
&= \frac{2 \cdot (k+1) + 2}{(k+1)} \\
&= 2 + \frac{2}{(k+1)} \leq 4, \text{ for every } k \in \mathbb{N}.
\end{aligned}
$$

Obviously, $2 + \frac{2}{(k+1)} \geq 2$ for every $k \in \mathbb{N}$. The lemma follows. ∎

Recurrence 3. Consider the recurrence

$$
f(n) \triangleq \begin{cases} 1 & \text{if } n = 1 \\ n + 3 \cdot f(\lfloor \frac{n}{2} \rfloor) & \text{if } n > 1. \end{cases} \tag{7.10}
$$

Lemma 7.5 *The rate of growth of the function $f(n)$ defined in Eq. 7.10 is $\Theta(n^{\log_2 3})$.*

PROOF: The proof proceeds as follows. We deal with powers of 2 and then apply Lemma 7.2 and Lemma 7.3.

We claim that $f(2^k) = 3 \cdot 3^k - 2 \cdot 2^k$. The proof is by induction on $k \in \mathbb{N}$. The induction basis for $k = 0$ holds by the definition of $f(1)$. The induction step is proved as follows:

$$
\begin{aligned}
f(2^{k+1}) &= 2^{k+1} + 3 \cdot f(2^k) & \text{(by definition)} \\
&= 2^{k+1} + 3 \cdot (3 \cdot 3^k - 2 \cdot 2^k) & \text{(induction hypothesis)} \\
&= 3 \cdot 3^{k+1} - 2 \cdot 2^{k+1}.
\end{aligned}
$$

We have proved that for $n = 2^k$, where $k \in \mathbb{N}$, Recurrence 7.10 satisfies $f(n) = 3 \cdot 3^{\log_2 n} - 2 \cdot n = \Theta(n^{\log_2 3})$.

To complete the proof, we need to apply Lemma 7.2 and Lemma 7.3. First, the functions $f(n)$ and $g(n) = n^{\log_2 3}$ are both monotonically nondecreasing. Second, to apply Lemmas 7.2 and Lemma 7.3, we also need to find constants ρ_1, ρ_2 such that $\rho_1 \leq \frac{g(2^{k+1})}{g(2^k)} \leq \rho_2$ for every $k \in \mathbb{N}$. Indeed,

$$
\begin{aligned}
\frac{2^{(k+1) \cdot \log_2 3}}{2^{k \cdot \log_2 3}} &= \frac{3^{k+1}}{3^k} \\
&= 3.
\end{aligned}
$$

The lemma follows. ∎

EXAMPLES

---

1. Consider the recurrence

$$f(n) \triangleq \begin{cases} c & \text{if } n = 1 \\ a \cdot n + b + f(\lfloor \frac{n}{2} \rfloor) & \text{if } n > 1, \end{cases} \tag{7.11}$$

where a, b, c are constants.

Lemma 7.6 *The rate of growth of the function $f(n)$ defined in Eq. 7.11 is $\Theta(n)$.*

PROOF: The proof proceeds as follows. We deal with powers of 2 and then apply Lemma 7.2 and Lemma 7.3.

We claim that $f(2^k) = 2a \cdot 2^k + b \cdot k + c - 2a$. The proof is by induction on $k \in \mathbb{N}$. The induction basis for $k = 0$ holds by the definition of $f(1)$. The induction step is proved as follows:

$$f(2^{k+1}) = a \cdot 2^{k+1} + b + f(2^k) \qquad \text{(by definition)}$$

$$= a \cdot 2^{k+1} + b + (2a \cdot 2^k + b \cdot k + c - 2a) \qquad \text{(induction hypothesis)}$$

$$= 2a \cdot 2^{k+1} + b \cdot (k + 1) + c - 2a.$$

We have proved that for $n = 2^k$, where $k \in \mathbb{N}$, Recurrence 7.11 satisfies $f(n) = 2a \cdot n + b \cdot \log_2 n + c - 2a = \Theta(n)$.

To complete the proof, we need to apply Lemma 7.2 and Lemma 7.3. First, the functions $f(n)$ and $g(n) = n$ are both monotonically nondecreasing. Second, to apply Lemma 7.2 and Lemma 7.3, we also need to prove that there exist constants ρ_1, ρ_2 such that $\rho_1 \leq \frac{g(2^{k+1})}{g(2^k)} \leq \rho_2$ for every $k \in \mathbb{N}$. Indeed,

$$\frac{2^{(k+1)}}{2^k} = \frac{2^{k+1}}{2^k}$$

$$= 2.$$

The lemma follows. ∎

2. Consider the recurrence

$$f(n) \triangleq \begin{cases} c & \text{if } n = 1 \\ a \cdot n + b + 2 \cdot f(\lfloor \frac{n}{2} \rfloor) & \text{if } n > 1, \end{cases} \tag{7.12}$$

where $a, b, c = O(1)$.

Lemma 7.7 *The rate of growth of the function $f(n)$ defined in Eq. 7.12 is $\Theta(n \log n)$.*

PROOF: The proof proceeds as follows. We deal with powers of 2 and then apply Lemma 7.2 and Lemma 7.3.

We claim that $f(2^k) = a \cdot k2^k + (b + c) \cdot 2^k - b$. The proof is by induction on $k \in \mathbb{N}$. The induction basis for $k = 0$ holds by the definition of $f(1)$. The induction step is proved as follows:

$$f(2^{k+1}) = a \cdot 2^{k+1} + b + 2 \cdot f(2^k) \qquad \text{(by definition)}$$

$$= a \cdot 2^{k+1} + b + 2 \cdot (a \cdot k2^k + (b+c) \cdot 2^k - b) \quad \text{(induction hypothesis)}$$

$$= a \cdot (k+1)2^{k+1} + (b+c) \cdot 2^{k+1} - b.$$

We have proved that for $n = 2^k$, where $k \in \mathbb{N}$, Recurrence 7.11 satisfies that $f(n) = a \cdot n \log_2 n + (b+c) \cdot n - b = \Theta(n \cdot [\log(n) + 1])) = \Theta(n \log n)$.

To complete the proof, we need to apply Lemma 7.2 and Lemma 7.3. First, the functions $f(n)$ and $g(n) = n \cdot (\log(n) + 1)$ are both monotonically nondecreasing. Second, to apply Lemma 7.2 and Lemma 7.3, we also need to prove that there exist constants ρ_1, ρ_2 such that $\rho_1 \le \frac{g(2^{k+1})}{g(2^k)} \le \rho_2$ for every $k \in \mathbb{N}$. Indeed,

$$\frac{2^{k+1} \cdot (k+2)}{2^k \cdot (k+1)} = \frac{2 \cdot (k+2)}{(k+1)}$$

$$= \frac{2 \cdot (k+1) + 2}{(k+1)}$$

$$= 2 + \frac{2}{(k+1)} \le 4, \text{ for every } k \in \mathbb{N}.$$

Obviously, $2 + \frac{2}{(k+1)} \ge 2$ for every $k \in \mathbb{N}$. The lemma follows. ∎

3. Consider the recurrence

$$F(k) \triangleq \begin{cases} 1 & \text{if } k = 0 \\ 2^k + 2 \cdot F(k-1) & \text{if } k > 0. \end{cases} \qquad (7.13)$$

Lemma 7.8 $F(k) = (k+1) \cdot 2^k$.

PROOF: One may repeat the same technique as in the last examples. Instead, we reduce the recurrence to one that we already solved. Define $f(n) \triangleq F(\lceil \log_2 n \rceil)$. Observe that $f(2^x) \triangleq F(x)$. The function f satisfies the recurrence

$$f(2^k) = 2^k + 2 \cdot f(2^k/2).$$

Hence, for powers of 2, the function f satisfies the recurrence in Eq. 7.9. In Lemma 7.4, we proved that $f(2^k) = (k+1) \cdot 2^k$. Therefore $F(k) = f(2^k) = (k+1) \cdot 2^k$, and the lemma follows. ∎

PROBLEMS

7.1. Prove that $n^3 + 2 \cdot n^2 = O(n^3)$.

7.2. Recall the harmonic series $H_n \triangleq \sum_{i=1}^n \frac{1}{i}$. Prove that $H_n = \Theta(\log n)$.

7.3. Prove that the Fibonacci sequence $g(n)$ is $\Theta(\varphi^n)$.
Hint: recall Question 2.13 on page 28.

7.4. Prove that Definitions 7.1 and 7.2 are equivalent definitions for $g(n) = \Omega(f(n))$ if $f(n) \geq 1$.

7.5. Consider the following alternative definition of $g(n) = \Theta(f(n))$.

> **Definition 7.3** Let $f, g : \mathbb{N} \to \mathbb{R}$ denote two functions. We say that $g(n) = \Theta(f(n))$ if there exist constants $c_1, c_2, c_4 \in \mathbb{R}^2, c_3 \in \mathbb{R}^+$ such that, for every $n \in \mathbb{N}$,
>
> $$c_3 \cdot f(n) + c_4 \leq g(n) \leq c_1 \cdot f(n) + c_2 \, .$$

Prove that this definition and item 3 in Definition 7.1 are equivalent.

7.6. Prove that for every two functions $f, g : \mathbb{N} \to \mathbb{R}$, if $f = g$, then $f(n) = \Theta(g(n))$ and $g(n) = \Theta(f(n))$.

7.7. Prove that $\log n + \log \log n = \Omega(\log n)$.

7.8. Prove Lemma 7.3.

7.9. Solve the following recurrences.

    (a)

$$f(n) \triangleq \begin{cases} 1 & \text{if } n = 1 \\ \log_2 n + f(\lfloor \frac{n}{2} \rfloor) & \text{if } n > 1. \end{cases}$$

    (b*)

$$f(n) \triangleq \begin{cases} d & \text{if } n = 1 \\ an + b + c \cdot f(\lfloor \frac{n}{c} \rfloor) & \text{if } n > 1, \end{cases}$$

    where $a, b, c, d = O(1)$, and $c > 2$.

    (c)

$$f(n) \triangleq \begin{cases} 1 & \text{if } n = 1 \\ 1 + f(\lfloor \frac{n}{2} \rfloor) & \text{if } n > 1. \end{cases}$$

    (d)

$$f(n) \triangleq \begin{cases} 1 & \text{if } n = 1 \\ n + f(\lfloor \frac{n}{2} \rfloor) + f(\lceil \frac{n}{2} \rceil) & \text{if } n > 1. \end{cases}$$

CHAPTER 8

Computer Stories: Big Endian versus
Little Endian[1]

A long-standing source of confusion is the order of bits in binary strings. This issue is very important when strings of bits are serially communicated or stored in memories. Consider the following two scenarios.

In the first setting, Alice wishes to send to Bob a binary string $a[n-1:0]$. The channel that Alice and Bob use for communication is a serial channel. This means that Alice can only send one bit at a time. Now Alice has two natural choices:

- She can send $a[n-1]$ first and $a[0]$ last; namely, she can send the bits in descending index order. This order is often referred to as *most significant bit first* or just MSB first.
- She can send $a[0]$ first and $a[n-1]$ last; namely, she can send the bits in ascending index order. This order is often referred to as *least significant bit first* or just LSB first.

In the second setting, computer words are stored in memory. A memory is a vector of storage places. We denote this vector by $M[0], M[1], \ldots$. Suppose that each storage place is capable of storing a byte (i.e., 8 bits). The typical word size in modern computers is 32 bits (and even 64 bits). This means that a word is stored in four memory slots. The question is, how do we store a word $a[31:0]$ in four memory slots?

Obviously, it is a good idea to store the word in four consecutive slots, say, $M[i:i+3]$. There are two natural options. In the first option, storage is as follows:

$$M[i] \leftarrow a[31:24],$$
$$M[i+1] \leftarrow a[23:16],$$
$$M[i+2] \leftarrow a[15:8],$$
$$M[i+3] \leftarrow a[7:0].$$

This option is referred to as *Big Endian*.

---

[1] Danny Cohen (1981) coined the terms *Big Endian* and *Little Endian* in the treatise "On Holy Wars and a Plea for Peace."

In the second option, storage is as follows:

$$M[i] \leftarrow a[0:7],$$

$$M[i+1] \leftarrow a[8:15],$$

$$M[i+2] \leftarrow a[16:23],$$

$$M[i+3] \leftarrow a[24:31].$$

This option is referred to as *Little Endian*. Note that for the sake of aesthetics, we used increasing bit indexes in the second option.

Each of these options has certain advantages and disadvantages. For example, if an architecture supports multiple word lengths, then it is convenient to have the most significant bit (MSB) stored in a fixed position relative to the address of the word (in our example, we can see that in Big Endian, the MSB is stored in $M[i]$ regardless of the number of bytes in $\bar{a}$). Conversely, if multiple word lengths are supported and we wish to add a half word (i.e., a two-byte string) with a word (i.e., a four-byte string), then Little Endian may simplify the task of aligning the two words (i.e., making sure that bits of the same weight are placed in identical offsets).

It is of no surprise that both conventions are used in commercial products. Architectures from the X86 family (such as Intel processors) use Little Endian byte ordering, while Motorola 68000 CPUs follow the Big Endian convention. Interestingly, the Power PC supports both! Nevertheless, operating systems also follow different conventions: Microsoft operating systems follow Little Endian, and Apple operating systems follow Big Endian. So a MAC with a Power PC CPU that runs an Apple operating system runs in Big Endian mode.

This confusion spreads beyond hardware to software (e.g., Java uses Big Endian) and to file formats (e.g., GIF uses Little Endian and JPEG uses Big Endian).

What does this story have to do with us? You might have noticed that we use both ascending indexes and descending indexes (e.g., $u[n-1:0]$ vs. $a[0:n-1]$) to denote the same string. These two conventions are simply an instance of the Big Endian versus Little Endian controversy.

Following Jonathan Swift (at the risk of not obeying Danny Cohen's plea), we use both ascending and descending bit orders according to the task we are considering. When considering strings that represent integers in binary representation, descending indexes are used (i.e., the leftmost bit is the MSB). However, in many parts of this book, ascending indexes are used; the reason is to simplify handling of indexes in the text. We can only hope that this simplification does not lead to confusion.

PART II COMBINATIONAL CIRCUITS

CHAPTER 9

Representations of Boolean Functions
by Formulas

In Chapter 6, we used Boolean formulas to represent Boolean functions. The idea was to write a Boolean formula over a set of n variables and then assign 0–1 values to each variable. This assignment induces a truth value to the formula, and thus we have a Boolean function over n bits. In fact, any Boolean function can be represented by a Boolean formula if the set of connectives is complete. In Section 6.6, we proved that the set $\{\neg, \text{AND}, \text{OR}\}$ is a complete set of connectives.

In this chapter, we consider special representations of functions that are often called *normal forms*. Boolean formulas in a normal form are restricted forms of formulas.

Given a Boolean function, one may want to find a shortest representation of the function by a Boolean formula. This question is not well defined because one needs to specify how a Boolean function is represented. Suppose the function is described by its truth table. In this case, the truth table has 2^n entries, where n denotes the number of bits in the domain of the function. Obviously, we can only read or write truth tables for rather small values of n. If $n \geq 100$, then all the atoms in the universe would not suffice!

Nevertheless, we present a method by Quine and McCluskey to find a shortest representation of a function by a Boolean formula in a normal form called a sum of products. This method is input the truth table of the function and outputs a shortest Boolean formula in sum of products form. We describe this algorithm using a graph defined over the implicants.

9.1 SUM OF PRODUCTS

The first normal form we consider is called the *disjunctive normal form* (DNF) or *sum of products* (SOP).

We recall the definition of a literal.

Definition 9.1 A variable or a negation of a variable is called a *literal*.

Recall that the AND connective is associative. Thus we may apply it to multiple arguments without writing parentheses. To simplify notation, we use the · notation for the AND connective so that

$$X \cdot Y \cdot Z \tag{9.1}$$

simply means (X AND Y AND Z). We often refer to such an AND as a *product*.

Definition 9.2 A formula that is the AND of literals is called a *product term*.

We say that a variable X *appears* in a product term p if either X or $\bar{X}$ is an argument of the AND in p. Of course, a variable might appear more than once in a term. For example, X appears three times in the product term ($X \cdot Y \cdot \bar{X} \cdot X$). Recall that $X \cdot \bar{X}$ is always false and that $X \cdot X$ is equivalent to X. Similarly, $\bar{X} \cdot \bar{X}$ is equivalent to $\bar{X}$. Thus any product in which a variable appears more than once can be simplified either to the constant zero or to a product term in which every variable appears at most once.

Definition 9.3 A product term p is *simple* if every variable appears at most once in p.

Notation. With each product term p, we associate the set of variables that appear in p. The set of variables that appear in p is denoted by $vars(p)$. Let $vars^+(p)$ denote the set of variables that appear in p that appear without negation. Let $vars^-(p)$ denote the set of variables that appear in p that appear with negation. Let $literals(p)$ denote the set of literals that appear in p.

For example, let $p = X_1 \cdot \bar{X}_2 \cdot X_3$, then $vars(p) = \{X_1, X_2, X_3\}$, $vars^+(p) = \{X_1, X_3\}$, and $vars^-(p) = \{X_2\}$, and $literals(p) = \{X_1, \bar{X}_2, X_3\}$.

Definition 9.4 A simple product term p is a *minterm* with respect to a set U of variables if $vars(p) = U$.

A minterm is a simple product term, and therefore every variable in U appears exactly once in p.

Lemma 9.1 *A minterm p attains the truth value 1 for exactly one truth assignment.*

PROOF: Consider the assignment $\tau : U \to \{0, 1\}$ defined by

$$\tau(X_i) \triangleq \begin{cases} 1 & \text{if } X_i \in vars^+(p) \\ 0 & \text{if } X_i \in vars^-(p). \end{cases}$$

By definition, for every literal ℓ in p, we have $\hat{\tau}(\ell) = 1$. Therefore $\hat{\tau}(p) = 1$.

To complete the proof, we need to show that this is the only assignment that satisfies the minterm p. Namely, if an assignment γ satisfies $\hat{\gamma}(p) = 1$, then $\gamma = \tau$.

Suppose that $\hat{\gamma}(p) = 1$. This implies that $\hat{\gamma}(\ell) = 1$ for every literal ℓ in p. If $\ell = X_i$, then this implies that $\gamma(X_i) = 1$. If $\ell = \bar{X}_i$, then this implies that $\gamma(X_i) = 0$. Therefore $X_i \in vars^+(p)$ implies $\gamma(X_i) = 1$. Similarly, $X_i \in vars^-(p)$ implies $\gamma(X_i) = 0$. We conclude that $\gamma = \tau$, as required. ∎

Recall that the OR connective is also associative. We use the + to denote the OR connective. The OR of multiple arguments is written as a sum. For example,

$$X + Y + Z \tag{9.2}$$

simply means $(X$ OR Y OR $Z)$. We often refer to such an OR as a *sum*. Substitution allows us to replace each occurrence of a variable by a product. This leads us to the terminology *sum of products*.

Definition 9.5 For a $v \in \{0,1\}^n$, define the minterm p_v to be $p_v \triangleq (\ell_1^v \cdot \ell_2^v \cdots \ell_n^v)$, where

$$\ell_i^v \triangleq \begin{cases} X_i & \text{if } v_i = 1 \\ \bar{X}_i & \text{if } v_i = 0. \end{cases}$$

Definition 9.6 Let $f^{-1}(1)$ denote the set

$$f^{-1}(1) \triangleq \{v \in \{0,1\}^n \mid f(v) = 1\}.$$

Definition 9.7 The set of minterms of f is defined by

$$M(f) \triangleq \{p_v \mid v \in f^{-1}(1)\}.$$

Theorem 9.2 *Every Boolean function $f : \{0,1\}^n \to \{0,1\}$ that is not a constant zero is represented by the sum of the minterms in $M(f)$.*

PROOF: Every minterm $p \in M(f)$ equals p_v for a vector $v \in f^{-1}(1)$. We associate the ith argument v_i of $f(v)$ with the Boolean variable X_i. Let $f^{-1}(1) = \{v^1, \ldots, v^k\}$. We claim the formula

$$\varphi \triangleq p_{v^1} + p_{v^2} + \cdots + p_{v^k}$$

represents the function f, namely, $B_\varphi = f$.

To prove that $B_\varphi = f$, we consider two cases:

1. If $f(v) = 1$, then $v = v^i$ for some $1 \leq i \leq k$. The minterm p_{v^i} is satisfied by the assignment τ_v, namely, $\hat{\tau}_v(p_{v^i}) = 1$. This implies that $\hat{\tau}_v(\varphi) = 1$. Therefore $B_\varphi(v) = 1$.
2. If $f(v) = 0$, then every minterm p_{v^i} is not satisfied by τ_v, namely, $\hat{\tau}_v(p_{v^i}) = 0$ for every $1 \leq i \leq k$. This implies that $\hat{\tau}_v(\varphi) = 0$, and therefore $B_\varphi(v) = 0$.

We proved that $f(v) = B_\varphi(v)$ for every $v \in \{0,1\}^n$, and the theorem follows. ∎

Definition 9.8 A Boolean formula is called a *sum of products* if it is a constant or an OR of product terms.

Consider the constant Boolean function $f : \{0,1\}^n \to \{0,1\}$ that is defined by $f(v) = 1$, for every v. The sum of minterms that represents f is the sum of all the possible minterms over n variables. This sum contains 2^n minterms. Conversely, f can be represented by the constant 1. The question of finding the shortest sum of products that represents a given Boolean formula is discussed in more detail later in this chapter.

EXAMPLES

---

1. The following formulas are product terms:
    (a) $p_1 = X \cdot Y$.
    (b) $p_2 = \bar{A}$ AND B AND C.
    (c) $p_3 = L$.
    (d) $p_4 = G \wedge (\neg H) \wedge G$.

The variables A, B, and C appear in p_2. The product term in p_4 is not simple since the variable G appears twice. Conversely, the product term in p_1 is simple since both X and Y appear once. Moreover,

- $vars(p_1) = \{X, Y\}$,
- $vars(p_2) = \{A, B, C\}$,
- $vars(p_3) = \{L\}$,
- $vars(p_4) = \{G, H\}$,
- $vars^+(p_1) = \{X, Y\}$,
- $vars^+(p_2) = \{B, C\}$,
- $vars^+(p_3) = \{L\}$,
- $vars^+(p_4) = \{G\}$,
- $vars^-(p_1) = \varnothing$,
- $vars^-(p_2) = \{A\}$,
- $vars^-(p_3) = \varnothing$,
- $vars^-(p_4) = \{H\}$.

2. The following formulas are *not* product terms:
   (a) $X + Y$.
   (b) A OR B AND C.

3. Each of the following formulas is a SOP:
   (a) $\varphi_1 = X \cdot Y + X \cdot Y$.
   (b) $\varphi_2 = (\bar{A}$ AND B AND $C)$ OR $(A$ AND $\bar{B}$ AND $C)$ OR $\bar{D}$.
   (c) $\varphi_3 = L$.

4. Each of the following formulas is *not* a SOP:
   (a) $(X + Y) \cdot Z$.
   (b) $(A$ OR $B)$ AND $(C$ OR $D)$.

5. Represent the following Boolean functions as an SOP formula: (i) $f(a, b) = \max\{a, b\}$ and (ii) $g(a, b) = \min\{a, b\}$.

   Recall Theorem 9.2. The proof of Theorem 9.2 is *constructive*, that is, it algorithmically builds the sum of minterms.

   (i) First, we need to find $f^{-1}(1)$. Let us write down the truth table of f, depicted in Table 4. Now, the task of finding $f^{-1}(1)$ is quite easy—all we need to do is look for the rows in which f attains the value 1. Hence $f^{-1}(1) = \{(0, 1), (1, 0), (1, 1)\}$.

   Finally, we construct the sum of minterms formula φ_f. The minterm that corresponds to the vector $v^1 = (0, 1)$ is $p_{v^1} = \bar{X}_1 \cdot X_2$. The minterm that corresponds to the vector $v^2 = (1, 0)$ is $p_{v^2} = X_1 \cdot \bar{X}_2$. The minterm that corresponds to the vector $v^3 = (1, 1)$ is $p_{v^2} = X_1 \cdot X_2$. Hence

   $$\varphi_f = (\bar{X}_1 \cdot X_2) + (X_1 \cdot \bar{X}_2) + (X_1 \cdot X_2).$$

Table 9.1. The truth table of the max Boolean function

a	b	$\max\{a, b\}$
0	0	0
1	0	1
0	1	1
1	1	1

We observe that the truth table of φ_f is equivalent to the OR Boolean function, that is, this method of constructing a sum of minterms not necessarily produces the shortest representation.

(ii) The set $g^{-1}(1)$ contains only one ordered pair, that is, $(1, 1)$. Hence the SOP formula for g is $\varphi_g = X_1 \cdot X_2$, and g is simply the AND function.

9.2 PRODUCT OF SUMS

The second normal form we consider is called the *conjunctive normal form* (CNF) or *product of sums* (POS).

Definition 9.9 A formula that is the OR of literals is called a *sum term*.

As in the case of product terms, we say that a variable X appears in a sum term p if X or $\bar{X}$ is one of the arguments of the OR in p. A sum term is simple if every variable appears at most once in it.

We use the notation $vars(p)$ also for a sum term p. As in the case of a product term, it means the set of variables that appear in p. The notations $vars^+(p)$ and $vars^-(p)$ are used as well.

Definition 9.10 A simple sum term p is a *maxterm* with respect to a set U of variables if $vars(p) = U$.

As in the case of a minterm, each variable appears at most once in a maxterm since it is a simple sum term.

Recall that $DM(\varphi)$ is the De Morgan dual of the formula φ.

Observation 9.1 *(1) If p is a minterm, then the formula $DM(p)$ is a maxterm. (2) If p is a maxterm, then the formula $DM(p)$ is a minterm.*

PROOF: An AND becomes an OR, an OR becomes an AND, and the De Morgan dual of a literal is a literal. ∎

Lemma 9.3 *A maxterm p attains the truth value 0 for exactly one truth assignment.*

PROOF: Consider a maxterm p. Let $q = DM(p)$. By Observation 9.1, q is a minterm. By Lemma 9.1, $\hat{\tau}(q) = 1$ for exactly one assignment τ. By Theorem 6.11, q is logically equivalent to $\neg p$. This implies that $\hat{\tau}(q) \neq \hat{\tau}(p)$ for every assignment τ. Hence $\hat{\tau}(p) = 0$ for exactly one assignment τ, and the lemma follows. ∎

Theorem 9.4 *Every Boolean function $f : \{0, 1\}^n \to \{0, 1\}$ that is not a constant 1 can be represented by a product of maxterms.*

PROOF: Define $g(v) \triangleq \text{NOT}(f(v))$. Since f is not a constant 1, the function g is not constant 0. By Theorem 9.2, g can be represented by a sum-of-minterms p. Since $f(v) = \text{NOT}(g(v))$, it follows that f is represented by $DM(p)$. By Example 5i on Page 114, $DM(p)$ is a product-of-sums formula.

To complete the proof, we need to show that each sum in $DM(p)$ is a maxterm. Indeed, each sum in $DM(p)$ is the De Morgan dual of a minterm in p. By Observation 9.1, it follows that each sum in $DM(p)$ is a maxterm, as required. ∎

Definition 9.11 A Boolean formula is called a *product-of-sums* if it is a constant or an AND of sum terms.

The following observation extends Observation 9.1

Observation 9.2 *(1) If p is a sum of products, then the formula $DM(p)$ is a product of sums. (2) If p is a product of sums, then the formula $DM(p)$ is a sum of products.*

EXAMPLES

---

1. The following formulas are sum terms:
   (a) $p_1 = X + Y$.
   (b) $p_2 = \bar{A}$ OR B OR C.
   (c) $p_3 = L$.
   (d) $p_4 = G \vee (\neg H) \vee G$.
   The variables A, B, and C appear in p_2. The sum term in p_4 is not simple, since the the variable G appears twice. Conversely, the sum term in p_1 is simple since both X and Y appear once. Moreover,
   * $vars(p_1) = \{X, Y\}$,
   * $vars(p_2) = \{A, B, C\}$,
   * $vars(p_3) = \{L\}$,
   * $vars(p_4) = \{G, H\}$,
   * $vars^+(p_1) = \{X, Y\}$,
   * $vars^+(p_2) = \{B, C\}$,
   * $vars^+(p_3) = \{L\}$,
   * $vars^+(p_4) = \{G\}$,
   * $vars^-(p_1) = \varnothing$,
   * $vars^-(p_2) = \{A\}$,
   * $vars^-(p_3) = \varnothing$,
   * $vars^-(p_4) = \{H\}$.
2. The following formulas are *not* sum terms:
   (a) $X \cdot Y$.
   (b) A AND B OR C.
3. Each of the following formulas is a product-of-sums:
   (a) $\varphi_1 = (X + Y) \cdot (X + Y)$.
   (b) $\varphi_2 = (\bar{A}$ OR B OR $C)$ AND $(A$ OR $\bar{B}$ OR $C)$ AND $\bar{D}$.
   (c) $\varphi_3 = L$.
4. Each of the following formulas is *not* a product-of-sums:
   (a) $(X \cdot Y) + Z$.
   (b) $(A$ AND $B)$ OR $(C$ AND $D)$.
5. Represent the following Boolean functions as a POS formula: (i) $f(a, b) = \min\{a, b\}$ and (ii) $h(a, b) = \max\{a, b\}$.
   Recall Theorem 9.4. The proof of Theorem 9.4 is, also, *constructive*, that is, it algorithmically builds the product of maxterms. Note that the proof of Theorem 9.4 uses Theorem 9.2 as a subroutine.
   (i) First, let f denote the negation of the Boolean formula g, that is, $f(v) =$ NOT$(g(v))$.

Table 9.2. The truth table of the
NOT(max) Boolean function

a	b	NOT(min$\{a, b\}$)
0	0	1
1	0	1
0	1	1
1	1	0

Second, we need to find $f^{-1}(1)$. Let us write down the truth table of f, depicted in Table 9.2. Now, the task of finding $f^{-1}(1)$ is quite easy; all we need to do is to look for the rows in which f attains the value 1. Hence $f^{-1}(1) = \{(0, 0), (0, 1), (1, 0)\}$.

Third, we construct the sum of minterms formula φ_f. The minterm that corresponds to the vector $v^1 = (0, 0)$ is $p_{v^1} = \bar{X}_1 \cdot \bar{X}_2$. The minterm that corresponds to the vector $v^1 = (0, 1)$ is $p_{v^1} = \bar{X}_1 \cdot X_2$. The minterm that corresponds to the vector $v^2 = (1, 0)$ is $p_{v^2} = X_1 \cdot \bar{X}_2$. Hence

$$\varphi_f = (\bar{X}_1 \cdot \bar{X}_2) + (\bar{X}_1 \cdot X_2) + (X_1 \cdot \bar{X}_2).$$

Finally, the required POS ψ_f formula is $\psi_f = DM(\varphi_f)$, that is,

$$\psi_g = (X_1 + X_2) \cdot (X_1 + \bar{X}_2) \cdot (\bar{X}_1 + X_2).$$

We observe that the truth table of ψ_f is equivalent to the AND Boolean function, that is, this method of constructing a sum of maxterms does not necessarily produce the shortest representation.

(ii) Let f denote the negation of the Boolean formula h, that is, $f(v) = \text{NOT}(h(v))$. The set $f^{-1}(1)$ contains only one ordered pair, that is, $(0, 0)$. Hence the POS formula for g is $\varphi_g = X_1 + X_2$, and H is simply the OR function.

9.3 THE FINITE FIELD $GF(2)$

In this section, we consider the set $\{0, 1\}$ with the Boolean functions XOR, AND. We regard this triple as a special structure called the Galois field of two elements. This structure is often denoted by $GF(2)$.

Definition 9.12 The *Galois field $GF(2)$* is defined as follows:

1. Elements: the elements of $GF(2)$ are $\{0, 1\}$. The 0 is called the additive unity, and 1 is called the multiplicative unity.
2. Operations:
    (a) Addition, which is simply the XOR function
    (b) Multiplication, which is simply the AND function

In the context of $GF(2)$, we denote multiplication by $\cdot$ and addition by $\oplus$.

We are used to infinite fields like the rationals (or reals) with regular addition and multiplication. In these fields, $1 + 1 \neq 0$. However, in $GF(2)$, $1 \oplus 1 = 0$.

Observation 9.3 $X \oplus X = 0$, *for every* $X \in \{0, 1\}$.

A minus sign in a field means the additive inverse.

Definition 9.13 The element $-X$ stands for the element Y such that $X \oplus Y = 0$.

Observation 9.4 *In $GF(2)$, the additive inverse of X is X itself, namely, $-X = X$, for every $X \in \{0, 1\}$.*

Thus we need not write minus signs, and adding an X is equivalent to subtracting an X.

The distributive law holds in $GF(2)$, namely; as follows:

Observation 9.5 $(X \oplus Y) \cdot Z = X \cdot Z \oplus Y \cdot Z$ *for every $X, Y, Z \in \{0, 1\}$.*

PROOF: Consider two cases: 1. if $Z = 0$, then both sides equal 0; 2. if $Z = 1$, then $(X \oplus Y) \cdot Z = X \oplus Y$, and $X \cdot Z \oplus Y \cdot Z = X \oplus Y$, as required. ∎

Let X^k denote the product

$$X^k \triangleq \overbrace{X \cdots \cdots X}^{k \text{ times}}.$$

We define $X^0 = 1$ for every $X \in \{0, 1\}$. The following observation proves that multiplication is *idempotent*.

Observation 9.6 $X^k = X$ *for every $k \in \mathbb{N}^+$ and $X \in \{0, 1\}$.*

PROOF: By induction on k, the induction basis for $k = 1$ is immediate. The induction basis is proved as follows:

$$X^{k+1} = X^k \cdot X$$
$$= X \cdot X$$
$$= X.$$

The first line follows by associativity, the second line follows by the induction hypothesis, and the last line holds since X AND $X = X$. ∎

The structure of a field allows us to solve systems of equations. In fact, *Gauss elimination* works over any field. The definition of a vector space over $GF(2)$ is just like the definition of vector spaces over the reals. Definitions such as linear dependence, dimension of vector spaces, and even determinants apply also to vector spaces over $GF(2)$.

EXAMPLES

---

1. Consider the equation

$$X_1 \oplus X_2 = 0. \tag{9.3}$$

    If we add X_2 to both sides of Eq. 9.3, we obtain

$$X_1 \oplus X_2 \oplus X_2 = X_2.$$

    But $X_2 \oplus X_2 = 0$. Thus we conclude that

$$X_1 \oplus X_2 = 0 \quad \Leftrightarrow \quad X_1 = X_2.$$

2.   Conversely, if we add $(-X_2)$ to both sides of Eq. 9.3, we obtain

$$X_1 \oplus X_2 \oplus (-X_2) = -X_2.$$

Since $X_2 \oplus (-X_2) = 0$, we obtain

$$X_1 = -X_2.$$

Finally, since $-X_2 = X_2$, we conclude that

$$X_1 \oplus X_2 = 0 \quad \Leftrightarrow \quad X_1 = X_2.$$

3.   We show how to solve a simple systems of equalities over $GF(2)$ using Gauss elimination. Consider the following system of equations:

$$\begin{array}{ccccccc}
X_1 & \oplus & X_2 & \oplus & X_3 & = 0, \\
X_1 & & & \oplus & X_3 & = 0, \\
& & X_2 & \oplus & X_3 & = 1.
\end{array}$$

This system of equations corresponds to the following matrix, where columns 1–3 correspond to X_1–X_3 and column 4 corresponds to their sum:

$$A = \begin{pmatrix} 1 & 1 & 1 & 0 \\ 1 & 0 & 1 & 0 \\ 0 & 1 & 1 & 1 \end{pmatrix}.$$

Let r_i denote the ith row. We now apply a sequence of row operations, as follows. The first operation, $r_1 \leftarrow r_1 \oplus r_2$, results in matrix A_1, as follows:

$$A_1 = \begin{pmatrix} 0 & 1 & 0 & 0 \\ 1 & 0 & 1 & 0 \\ 0 & 1 & 1 & 1 \end{pmatrix}.$$

The second operation, $r_3 \leftarrow r_1 \oplus r_3$, results in matrix A_2, as follows:

$$A_2 = \begin{pmatrix} 0 & 1 & 0 & 0 \\ 1 & 0 & 1 & 0 \\ 0 & 0 & 1 & 1 \end{pmatrix}.$$

The third operation, $r_2 \leftarrow r_2 \oplus r_3$, results in matrix A_3, as follows:

$$A_3 = \begin{pmatrix} 0 & 1 & 0 & 0 \\ 1 & 0 & 0 & 1 \\ 0 & 0 & 1 & 1 \end{pmatrix}.$$

Every row of A_3 has a single nonzero entry in the columns corresponding to variables. Hence A_3 corresponds to the following system of equations:

$$X_2 = 0,$$

$$X_1 = 1,$$

$$X_3 = 1.$$

Note that the solution of this system over reals $\mathbb{R}$ with the well-known addition $+$ and multiplication $\times$ is quite different, for example,

$$X_1 = -1\,,$$

$$X_2 = 0\,,$$

$$X_3 = 1\,.$$

9.3.1 Polynomials Over $GF(2)$

Definition 9.14 A *monomial* in $GF(2)$ over the variables in the set U is a finite product of the elements in $U \cup \{0, 1\}$.

For example, X_1, $X_1 \cdot X_3$, $X_1 \cdot X_2 \cdot X_3 \cdot X_1$, are all monomials in $GF(2)$. If a variable appears more than once in a product, then by commutativity, we may write an exponent to signify the number of times the variables appear in the product. Thus the products $X_1 \cdot X_2 \cdot X_3 \cdot X_1$ and $X_1^2 \cdot X_2 \cdot X_3$ are equal.

By Observation 9.6, positive exponents can be reduced to 1. For example, $X_1^2 \cdot X_2 \cdot X_3$ equals $X_1 \cdot X_2 \cdot X_3$. Moreover, if the constant 1 appears in a product, then we may remove it (since $X \cdot 1 = X$). If the constant 0 appears in a product, then we may remove the product entirely (since $X \cdot 0 = 0$ and since $x \oplus 0 = x$). We conclude with the following observation.

Observation 9.7 *Every monomial p in $GF(2)$ over the variables in U can be reduced to a product of variables in p.*

Definition 9.15 A *polynomial* in $GF(2)$ over the variables in the set U is a finite sum of monomials.

We denote the set of all polynomials in $GF(2)$ over the variables in U by $GF(2)[U]$. Just as multivariate polynomials over the reals can be added and multiplied, so can polynomials in $GF(2)[U]$.

Clearly every polynomial $p \in GF(2)[U]$ is a Boolean function $f_p : \{0, 1\}^{|U|} \to \{0, 1\}$. The converse is also true.

Theorem 9.5 *Every Boolean function $f : \{0, 1\}^n \to \{0, 1\}$ can be represented by a polynomial in $GF(2)[U]$, where $U = \{X_1, \ldots, X_n\}$.*

PROOF: Without loss of generality, f is not a constant zero (if it is, then the polynomial 0 represents it).

We associate the ith argument v_i of $f(v)$ with the variable $X_i \in U$. Consider the set

$$f^{-1}(1) \triangleq \{v \in \{0, 1\}^n \mid f(v) = 1\}.$$

Since f is not constant 0, the set $f^{-1}(1)$ is not empty. For each $v \in f^{-1}(1)$, we define the product $p_v \triangleq (\ell_1^v \cdot \ell_2^v \cdots \ell_n^v)$ as follows:

$$\ell_i^v \triangleq \begin{cases} X_i & \text{if } v_i = 1 \\ (1 \oplus X_i) & \text{if } v_i = 0. \end{cases}$$

Denote the elements of $f^{-1}(1)$ by $\{v^1, \ldots, v^k\}$.

The polynomial $p \in GF(2)[U]$ is defined as follows:

$$p \stackrel{\triangle}{=} p_{v^1} \oplus p_{v^2} \oplus \cdots \oplus p_{v^k}.$$

We claim the the polynomial p represents the function f, namely, $p = f$.
To prove that $p = f$, we consider two cases:

1. If $f(v) = 1$, then $v = v^i$ for some $1 \leq i \leq k$. The product $p_{v^i}(v^i) = 1$ and $\forall j \neq i : p_{v^j}(v^i) = 0$. This implies that $p(v^i) = 1$.
2. If $f(v) = 0$, then $\forall i : p_{v^i} = 0$. This implies that $p(v) = 0$.

We proved that $f(v) = p(v)$ for every $v \in \{0,1\}^n$; moreover, p is a polynomial in $GF(2)[U]$. Indeed, by the distributive law (see Observation 9.5), p is a finite sum of monomials in U, and the theorem follows. ■

Corollary 9.6 *The set of connectives* {XOR, AND} *is complete.*

9.4 SATISFIABILITY

The problem of satisfiability of Boolean formulas is defined as follows:

Input: A Boolean formula φ.
Output: The output should equal "yes" if φ is satisfiable. If φ is not satisfiable, then the output should equal "no."

Note that the problem of satisfiability is quite different if the input is a truth table of a Boolean function. In this case, we simply need to check if there is an entry in which the function attains the value 1.

9.5 RELATION TO *P* VERSUS *NP*

The main open problem in Computer Science since 1971 has been whether $P = NP$. We will not define the classes P and NP, but we will phrase an equivalent question in this section.

Consider a Boolean formula φ. Given a truth assignment τ, it is easy to check if $\hat{\tau}(\varphi) = 1$. We showed how this can be done in Algorithm EVAL on page 74 . In fact, the running time of the EVAL algorithm is linear in the length of φ.

Conversely, can we find a satisfying truth assignment by ourselves (rather than checking if τ is a satisfying assignment)? Clearly we could try all possible truth assignments. However, if n variables appear in φ, then the number of truth assignments is 2^n.

We are ready to formulate a question that is equivalent to the question $P = NP$.

Satisfiability in Polynomial Time. Does there exist a constant $c > 0$ and an algorithm *Alg* such that

1. Given a Boolean formula φ, algorithm *Alg* decides correctly whether φ is satisfiable?
2. The running time of *Alg* is $O(|\varphi|^c)$, where $|\varphi|$ denotes the length of φ?

Note that the naive algorithm that tries all possible truth assignments has a running time that is at least 2^n, where n is the number of variables in φ. By a simple reduction that introduces new variables without changing the satisfiability, it can be assumed that $|\varphi| < 5n$. But 2^n grows faster than any polynomial in n, namely, for every constant c, $2^n = \Omega(n^{c+1})$. Therefore the naive algorithm does not meet the requirement of deciding satisfiability in polynomial time.

This seemingly simple question turns out to be a very deep problem about what can be easily computed versus what can be easily proved. It is related to the question of whether there is a real gap between checking that a proof is correct and finding a proof.

9.6* MINIMIZATION HEURISTICS

In this section, we consider the problem of finding a shortest representation of a Boolean function. This problem captures also the problem of satisfiability, hence do not expect us to present an algorithm whose running time is polynomial in the number of variables. We refer to an algorithm with an exponential running time as a *heuristic* to make sure that the reader understands that such an algorithm cannot be used in practice for functions with many variables.

We consider the following minimization problem:

Input: A truth table of a Boolean function $f : \{0,1\}^n \to \{0,1\}$.
Output: An SOP Boolean formula ψ such that the Boolean function B_ψ defined by ψ satisfies $f = B_\psi$.
Goal: Find a shortest SOP ψ such that $B_\psi = f$.

If f is a constant function, then the minimization problem is easy. So we assume that f is not a constant function. By Theorem 9.2, f can be represented as a sum of minterms. Let φ_f denote the sum of minterms that represents f. Thus our goal is to find a shortest SOP formula ψ that is logically equivalent to φ_f.

We remark that there might be more than one shortest SOP formula that is logically equivalent to φ_f. For example, let $f : \{0,1\}^3 \to \{0,1\}$, defined by the truth table depicted in Table 9.3. In this case,

$$\varphi_f = \bar{X} \cdot \bar{Y} \cdot \bar{Z} + \bar{X} \cdot Y \cdot \bar{Z} + X \cdot \bar{Y} \cdot Z + \bar{X} \cdot Y \cdot Z + X \cdot Y \cdot Z.$$

Table 9.3. The truth table of $f\colon \{0,1\}^3 \to \{0,1\}$

X	Y	Z	$f(X,Y,Z)$
0	0	0	1
1	0	0	0
0	1	0	1
1	1	0	0
0	0	1	0
1	0	1	1
0	1	1	1
1	1	1	1

There are two shortest SOP formulas φ_1, φ_2 are logically equivalent to φ_f, as follows:

$$\varphi_1 = \bar{X} \cdot \bar{Z} + X \cdot Z + \bar{X} \cdot Y$$

$$\varphi_2 = \bar{X} \cdot \bar{Z} + X \cdot Z + Y \cdot Z.$$

9.6.1 Basic Terminology and Properties

Throughout this section, f denotes a Boolean function and φ_f is a Boolean formula that represents f (i.e., φ_f is the sum of the minterms of f). We assume that the Boolean function f is not a constant function. Therefore φ_f is satisfiable and not a tautology.

Definition 9.16 A satisfiable product term p is an *implicant* of f if $(p \to \varphi_f)$ is a tautology.

We denote the set of implicants of f by $\mathcal{I}(f)$. Note that an implicant must be satisfiable, and hence an implicant cannot contain both a variable and its negation as literals.

Claim 9.7 *Every minterm $p_v \in M(f)$ is a implicant of f, hence $M(f) \subseteq \mathcal{I}(f)$.*

PROOF: We need to prove that for every assignment τ, if $\hat{\tau}(p_v) = 1$, then $\hat{\tau}(\varphi_f) = 1$. By Lemma 9.1, the minterm p_v is satisfied by a unique assignment. In fact, this satisfying assignment is τ_v (i.e., $\tau_v(X_i) \triangleq v_i$). By definition, $v \in f^{-1}(1)$, therefore $f(v) = 1$ and $\hat{\tau}(\varphi_f) = 1$, as required. ■

Claim 9.8 *The sum (OR) of the implicants of f is logically equivalent to φ_f.*

PROOF: Let $\sigma(f)$ denote the sum of implicants of f. We need to prove that $\sigma(f) \leftrightarrow \varphi_f$ is a tautology. We first prove that $\varphi_f \to \sigma(f)$ is a tautology. By Claim 9.7, $M(f) \subseteq \mathcal{I}(f)$. This implies that $\varphi_f \to \sigma(f)$ is a tautology, as required.

We now prove that $\sigma(f) \to \varphi_f$ is a tautology. Let τ be an assignment such that $\hat{\tau}(\sigma(f)) = 1$; then there exists an implicant $p \in \mathcal{I}(f)$ such that $\hat{\tau}(p) = 1$. Therefore $(p \to \varphi_f)$ is a tautology. Hence $\hat{\tau}(\varphi_f) = 1$, as required. ■

The following claim shows that $\mathcal{I}(f)$ is closed under subsets in the sense that removing part of the literals from an implicant keeps it an implicant.

Claim 9.9 *Let $p \in \mathcal{I}(f)$. If q is a satisfiable product and* literals$(p) \subseteq$ literals(q), *then $q \in \mathcal{I}(f)$.*

PROOF: We show that $(q \to \varphi_f)$ is a tautology. Let τ be an assignment such that $\hat{\tau}(q) = 1$. We need to show that $\hat{\tau}(\varphi_f) = 1$. Since $\hat{\tau}(q) = 1$, then $\hat{\tau}(p) = 1$. Since p is an implicant, then by Definition 9.16, it follows that $\hat{\tau}(\varphi_f) = 1$, as required. ■

Claim 9.10 *For every two satisfiable products p, q, the following holds:*

$$(p \to q) \text{ is a tautology} \iff (\text{literals}(q) \subseteq \text{literals}(p)).$$

PROOF: We prove the following two directions:

1. $(p \to q)$ is a tautology $\Rightarrow$ (*literals*$(q) \subseteq$ *literals*(p)).
2. (*literals*$(q) \subseteq$ *literals*(p)) $\Rightarrow$ $(p \to q)$ is a tautology.

The First direction. We assume that $(p \to q)$ is a tautology. Assume, for the sake of contradiction, that $(literals(q) \nsubseteq literals(p))$, that is, there exists a literal ℓ such that $\ell \in literals(q)$ and $\ell \notin literals(p)$. Let τ be an assignment that satisfies

$$\hat{\tau}(b) = \begin{cases} 0, & \text{if } b = \ell \\ 1, & \text{if } b \in (literals(p) \cup literals(q)) \setminus \{\ell\} \,. \end{cases}$$

Since both $\hat{\tau}(p) = 1$ and $\hat{\tau}(q) = 0$, it follows that $\hat{\tau}(p \to q) = 0$—a contradiction to the assumption that $(p \to q)$ is a tautology. Hence $literals(q) \subseteq literals(p)$.

The Second Direction. We assume that $literals(q) \subseteq literals(p)$. Let τ be an assignment such that $\hat{\tau}(p) = 1$. Since $literals(q) \subseteq literals(p)$, it follows that $\hat{\tau}(q) = 1$. Hence $(q \to p)$ is a tautology, as required. ∎

A prime implicant is an implicant that is minimal with respect to containment.

Definition 9.17 An implicant $p \in \mathcal{I}(f)$ is a *prime implicant* of f if the following holds:

$$\forall q \in \mathcal{I}(f) : literals(q) \subseteq literals(p) \Rightarrow (literals(q) = literals(p)).$$

We denote the set of prime implicants of f by $\mathcal{I}'(f)$.

Definition 9.18 Let $p, q \in \mathcal{I}(f)$. We say that p is an *immediate predecessor* of q if (i) $literals(q) \subseteq literals(p)$ and (ii) $literals(p) \setminus literals(q)$ contains a single literal.

9.6.2 The Implicants' Graph

One usually defines a partial order over the implicants of a Boolean function by containment of the set of literals. We represent this partial order by a directed graph, which we call the *implicants' graph*.

Definition 9.19 The implicants' graph $G_f = (V, E)$ of a Boolean function f is a directed graph, defined as follows:

1. $V \overset{\Delta}{=} \mathcal{I}(f)$.
2. $E \overset{\Delta}{=} \{(p, q) \in V \times V \mid p \text{ is an immediate predecessor of } q\}$.

Claim 9.11 *The implicants' graph is acyclic.*

PROOF: If $(p, q) \in E$, then $|literals(p)| - |literals(q)| = 1$. Therefore, if p belongs to a cycle, then $|literals(p)| < |literals(p)|$—a contradiction. ∎

Lemma 9.12 *An implicant $p \in \mathcal{I}(f)$ is a prime implicant iff it is a sink in G_f.*

PROOF: Assume, for the sake of contradiction, that $p \in \mathcal{I}'(f)$ is not a sink. Let (p, r) denote an arc emanating from p in G_f. Since r is an implicant such that $literals(r)$ is a proper subset of $literals(p)$, it follows that p is not a prime implicant—a contradiction.

If $p \in \mathcal{I}(f)$ is a not prime implicant, then there exists an implicant $q \in \mathcal{I}(f)$ such that $literals(q)$ is a proper subset of $literals(p)$. Let r denote a product obtained from p by removing one of the literals in $literals(p) \setminus literals(q)$. By Claim 9.9, since $literals(q) \subseteq literals(r)$, it follows that r is an implicant in $\mathcal{I}(f)$. By definition, p is an immediate predecessor of r; therefore $(p, r) \in E$, and p is not a sink, as required. ∎

Claim 9.13 *If $p \in \mathcal{I}(f) \setminus \mathcal{I}'(f)$, then the following two statements hold: (i) there exists an implicant $q \in \mathcal{I}(f)$ such that p is an immediate predecessor of q and (ii) there exists a prime implicant $q \in \mathcal{I}'(f)$ such that* literals$(q) \subset$ literals(p).

PROOF OF ITEM (i): Lemma 9.12 implies that p is not a sink in G_f. Hence there exists a $q \in V$ such that $(p, q) \in E$, that is, there exists an implicant $q \in \mathcal{I}(f)$ such that p is an immediate predecessor of q, as required. ∎

PROOF OF ITEM (ii): Since p is not a sink in G_f, and since G_f is acyclic, it follows that there is a path that emanates from p that reaches a sink q:

$$p = a_0 \longrightarrow a_1 \longrightarrow \ldots \longrightarrow a_k = q.$$

Definition 9.19 implies that

$$literals(p) \supset literals(a_1) \supset \ldots \supset literals(q).$$

Lemma 9.12 implies that q is a prime implicant. Therefore there exists a prime implicant $q \in \mathcal{I}'(f)$ such that $literals(q) \subset literals(p)$, as required. ∎

9.6.3 Essential Prime Implicants

We now define a covering relation between minterms and prime implicants. Recall that $M(f)$ denotes the set of minterms of f and $\mathcal{I}'(f)$ denotes the set of prime implicants of f.

Definition 9.20 The *covering relation* $C_f \subseteq M(f) \times \mathcal{I}'(f)$ is the set

$$C_f \triangleq \{(r, p) \in M(f) \times \mathcal{I}'(f) \mid r \to p \text{ is a tautology}\}.$$

Observation 9.8 *Let $(r, p) \in M(f) \times \mathcal{I}'(f)$. Then $(r, p) \in C_f$ iff there exists a path from r to p in the implicants' graph G_f.*

PROOF: By Claim 9.10, $r \to p$ is a tautology iff $literals(p) \subseteq literals(r)$ and this is equivalent to the existence of path from r to p in G_f. ∎

We say that a prime implicant p *covers* r if $(r, p) \in C_f$.

Definition 9.21 A prime implicant $p \in \mathcal{I}'(f)$ is an *essential prime implicant* if there exists minterm r such that p is the only prime implicant that covers r.

We denote the set of essential prime implicants of f by $\mathcal{I}^e(f)$.

Observation 9.9 *A prime implicant $p \in \mathcal{I}'(f)$ is an essential prime implicant iff there exists a minterm r such that every path in G_f from r to a prime implicant ends in p.*

PROOF: If a product p is an essential prime implicant, then there exists a minterm r that is covered only by p. By Observation 9.8, any path from r to a prime implicant ends in a prime implicant that covers r. Since p is the only prime implicant that covers r, we conclude that every maximal path from r ends in p.

If every maximal path that begins in r ends in p, then by Observation 9.8, p is the only prime implicant that covers r. This implies that p is an essential prime implicant. ∎

Claim 9.14 *A prime implicant $p \in \mathcal{I}'(f)$ is an* essential *prime implicant iff there exists a truth assignment τ such that (i) $\hat{\tau}(p) = 1$, and (ii) $\hat{\tau}(q) = 0$, for every $q \in \mathcal{I}'(f) \smallsetminus \{p\}$.*

PROOF: We assume that $p \in \mathcal{I}^e(f)$. We need to find an assignment that satisfies the two conditions. Let r be a minterm that is covered only by p. By Lemma 9.1, there exists a unique assignment that satisfies r. Denote this assignment by τ. Clearly $\hat{\tau}(p) = 1$.

Consider a prime implicant $q \neq p$. Since q does not cover r, it follows that $r \rightarrow q$ is not a tautology. Since τ is the only assignment that satisfies r, it follows that $\hat{\tau}(q) = 0$.

To prove the other direction, we need to find a minterm that is covered only by p. Suppose the assignment τ satisfies the two conditions. Let r denote the minterm that is satisfied by τ. We prove the following: (i) $r \in M(f)$, (ii) $(r, p) \in C_f$, and (iii) for every $q \in \mathcal{I}'(f) \smallsetminus \{p\}, (r, q) \notin C_f$.

PROOF OF (i): Let v denote the binary vector defined by $v_i = \tau(X_i)$. Since $\hat{\tau}(p) = 1$, it follows that $f(v) = 1$. The minterm r corresponds to v (i.e., $r = p_v$), and therefore $r \in M(f)$.

PROOF OF (ii): Since r is a minterm, it is satisfied only by τ. Since $\hat{\tau}(p) = 1$, it follows that $r \rightarrow p$ is a tautology, hence $(r, p) \in C_f$.

PROOF OF (iii): Since $\hat{\tau}(q) = 0$, it follows that $r \rightarrow q$ is not a tautology, as required. ∎

9.6.4 Optimality Conditions

The following claim provides an SOP representation of f using only prime implicants. This is the first step toward finding a shortest SOP representation.

Claim 9.15 *The sum (i.e., OR) of the prime implicants of f is logically equivalent to φ_f.*

PROOF: Let us denote the sum of implicants of f by $\sigma(f)$. Let us denote the sum of prime implicants of f by $\sigma'(f)$. Claim 9.8 states that $\sigma(f)$ is logically equivalent to φ_f. Thus we need to prove that $\sigma(f) \leftrightarrow \sigma'(f)$ is a tautology.

First we show that $\sigma'(f) \rightarrow \sigma(f)$ is a tautology. Let τ be an assignment such that $\hat{\tau}(\sigma'(f)) = 1$. Since $\mathcal{I}'(f) \subseteq \mathcal{I}(f)$, it follows that $\hat{\tau}(\sigma(f)) = 1$.

Now we show that $\sigma(f) \rightarrow \sigma'(f)$ is a tautology. Let τ be an assignment such that $\hat{\tau}(\sigma(f)) = 1$; then there exists an implicant p such that $\hat{\tau}(p) = 1$. If $p \in \mathcal{I}'(f)$, then we are done. If $p \in \mathcal{I}(f) \smallsetminus \mathcal{I}'(f)$, then by Claim 9.13, there exists a prime implicant q such that *literals*(q) is a proper subset of *literals*(p). Claim 9.10 implies that the Boolean formula $(p \rightarrow q)$ is a tautology, hence $\hat{\tau}(q) = 1$. It follows that $\hat{\tau}(\sigma'(f)) = 1$, as required. ∎

Suppose that f is represented by an SOP that contains an implicant that is not prime. Can this SOP be shortened? The following claim shows that we can substitute a nonprime implicant by a prime implicant (that covers the non-prime implicant) to make the SOP shorter.

Claim 9.16 *Let $p \in \mathcal{I}(f) \smallsetminus \mathcal{I}'(f)$. Let $\varphi \in \mathcal{BF}$, such that $(\varphi \vee p)$ is equivalent to φ_f. Then there exists $q \in \mathcal{I}'(f)$ such that (i)* literals(q) *is a proper subset of* literals(p) *and (ii) $(\varphi \vee q)$ is equivalent to φ_f.*

PROOF: By Claim 9.13, there exists a prime implicant q such that *literals*(q) is a proper subset of *literals*(p). We claim that $(\varphi \vee p)$ and $(\varphi \vee q)$ are logically equivalent.

Let τ be an assignment such that $\hat{\tau}(\varphi \vee p) = 1$. We need to show that $\hat{\tau}(\varphi \vee q) = 1$. If $\hat{\tau}(\varphi) = 1$, then clearly $\hat{\tau}(\varphi \vee q) = 1$. If $\hat{\tau}(p) = 1$ then, by Claim 9.10, $(p \to q)$ is a tautology, hence $\hat{\tau}(q) = 1$. Therefore $\hat{\tau}(\varphi \vee q) = 1$, as required.

Let τ be an assignment such that $\hat{\tau}(\varphi \vee q) = 1$. We need to show that $\hat{\tau}(\varphi \vee p) = 1$. If $\hat{\tau}(\varphi) = 1$, then $\hat{\tau}(\varphi \vee p) = 1$. Otherwise, $\hat{\tau}(\varphi) = 0$ and $\hat{\tau}(q) = 1$. Since $q \in \mathcal{I}(f)$, the Boolean formula $(q \to \varphi_f)$ is a tautology. Since φ_f and $(\varphi \vee p)$ are equivalent, it follows that $\hat{\tau}(p) = 1$, as required. ∎

Corollary 9.17 *If ψ is a shortest SOP formula that is logically equivalent to φ_f, then every product term in ψ is a prime implicant of f.*

PROOF: Let us assume in contrary that there exists a product term $p \in \mathcal{I}(f) \smallsetminus \mathcal{I}'(f)$ in ψ. Since ψ is a SOP formula, then $\psi = (\varphi \vee p)$ for some $\varphi \in \mathcal{BF}$. Claim 9.16 implies that there exists a shorter $q \in \mathcal{I}'(f)$ such that $(\varphi \vee q)$ is equivalent to φ_f. This contradicts the assumption that ψ is a shortest SOP formula that is equivalent to φ_f. Hence every product term in ψ is a prime implicant of f, as required. ∎

Claim 9.18 *Suppose that (i) ψ is the sum of a subset of the prime implicants of f and (ii) ψ is logically equivalent to φ_f. Then every essential prime implicant $p \in \mathcal{I}'(f)$ appears as a product term in ψ.*

PROOF: Let $\mathcal{E} \subseteq \mathcal{I}'(f)$ denote the subset of the prime implicants of f such that ψ is the sum of products in $\mathcal{E}$. Assume, for the sake of contradiction, that $p \in \mathcal{I}^e(f) \smallsetminus \mathcal{E}$.

Claim 9.14 implies that there is a truth assignment τ such that $\hat{\tau}(p) = 1$, and $\hat{\tau}(q) = 0$, for every $q \in \mathcal{I}'(f) \smallsetminus \{p\}$.

Since $\mathcal{E} \subseteq \mathcal{I}'(f) \smallsetminus \{p\}$, it follows that $\hat{\tau}(\psi) = 0$. Conversely, $\hat{\tau}(\varphi_f) = 1$, since p is an implicant of f. Thus φ_f and ψ are not logically equivalent—a contradiction. ∎

We remark that there exist Boolean functions f such that f is not logically equivalent to the sum of the essential prime implicants of f. For example, consider the function f represented by the Boolean formula $\varphi_f(X, Y, Z) = \bar{X} \cdot Z + Y \cdot Z + X \cdot Y + X \cdot \bar{Z} + \bar{Y} \cdot \bar{Z}$. Since $\mathcal{I}^e(f) = \varnothing$, it follows that f is not logically equivalent to the sum of its essential prime implicants, as required.

Claim 9.18 suggests the following heuristic for finding a shortest SOP ψ that represents f.

1.   Compute $\mathcal{I}'(f)$ and $\mathcal{I}^e(f)$.
2.   Add every product in $\mathcal{I}^e(f)$ to ψ.

3. Find a shortest subset $A \subseteq \mathcal{I}'(f) \setminus \mathcal{I}^e(f)$ such that adding the products in A to ψ makes ψ logically equivalent to φ_f.

In the sequel, we discuss how to compute $\mathcal{I}'(f)$ and $\mathcal{I}^e(f)$. For Boolean functions with very small domains, the last task of finding A is achieved through exhaustive search.

9.6.5 The Quine–McCluskey Heuristic

In this section, we present an algorithm for computing the prime implicants and the essential prime implicants of formula φ. The algorithm simply constructs the implicants' graph of f. The specification of the algorithm is as follows.

Input: A truth table T_f of a nonconstant Boolean function $f : \{0,1\}^n \to \{0,1\}$.
Output: The sets $\mathcal{I}'(f)$ and $\mathcal{I}^e(f)$, where $\mathcal{I}'(f)$ and $\mathcal{I}^e(f)$ are the sets of prime implicants and essential prime implicants of f, respectively.

The algorithm uses the following terminology.

Definition 9.22 The *symmetric difference* of two sets A, B is the set $(A \setminus B) \cup (B \setminus A)$.

We denote the symmetric difference by $A \bigtriangleup B$.

Definition 9.23 Let p and q denote two satisfiable product terms.

1. The product term $p \cap q$ is the product of the literals in $literals(p) \cap literals(q)$.
2. If $vars(p) = vars(q)$, then the *distance* between p and q is defined by

$$dist(p,q) \triangleq \left| \{ i : \{X_i, \bar{X}_i\} \subseteq literals(p) \bigtriangleup literals(q) \} \right|.$$

If $vars(p) \neq vars(q)$, then define $dist(p,q) \triangleq \infty$.

The Quine–McCluskey algorithm for computing the prime implicants of a Boolean function is listed as Algorithm 9.1. The input is a truth table T_f of Boolean function $f : \{0,1\}^n \to \{0,1\}$. The algorithm constructs a layered directed graph G whose

---

Algorithm 9.1 QM(T_f)—an algorithm for computing the prime implicants of f: $\{0,1\}^n \to \{0,1\}$ given its truth table T_f.

---

1. Construct the implicants' graph G_f over implicants of f, as follows:
    (a) $I_n \leftarrow \{p \mid p \text{ is a minterm of } f\}$.
    (b) For $k = n$ downto 2, do:
        i. $I_{k-1} \leftarrow \emptyset$.
        ii. For each pair of implicants $p, q \in I_k$ such that $dist(p,q) = 1$, do

            A. $I_{k-1} \leftarrow I_{k-1} \cup \{p \cap q\}$.
            B. add the arcs: $p \longrightarrow (p \cap q)$ and $q \longrightarrow (p \cap q)$ to G.

2. Return $\{p \mid p \text{ is a sink in } G\}$.

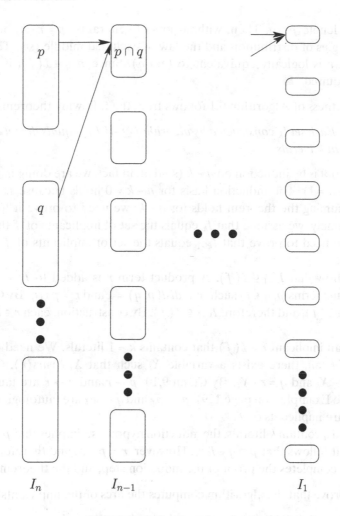

Figure 9.1. The implicants' graph.

vertex set is the set of implicants of f. The graph has n layers, where layer I_k consists of the implicants that contain k literals. Layer I_n consists of all the minterms of f. There are arcs from layer I_k to layer I_{k-1}. Once I_k is constructed, the algorithm constructs layer I_{k-1} and the arcs from I_k to I_{k-1}, as follows. For each pair of implicants $p, q \in I_k$ such that $dist(p, q) = 1$, the algorithm adds the implicant $p \cap q$ to I_{k-1}. Note that the product $p \cap q$ may have been already added to I_{k-1}. In this case, the union operator does *not* modify I_{k-1}. It also adds arcs from p and q to the new implicant $p \cap q$, as depicted in Figure 9.1. Finally, the algorithm returns the set of sinks in the graph G.

The following claim justifies the addition of $p \cap q$ to I_{k-1} in line (1(b)iiA) of the algorithm.

Claim 9.19 *If $p, q \in \mathcal{I}(f)$ and* $dist(p, q) = 1$, *then $p \cap q \in \mathcal{I}(f)$.*

PROOF: Let r denote $p \cap q$. Then, without loss of generality, $p = r \cdot X_i$ and $q = r \cdot \bar{X}_i$. By the tautologies of distribution and the law of excluded middle (see Theorem 6.8), it follows that r is logically equivalent to $(p + q)$. Since $p, q \in \mathcal{I}(f)$, it follows that $r \in \mathcal{I}(f)$, as required. ∎

The correctness of Algorithm 9.1 follows from the following theorem.

Theorem 9.20 *Each set I_k constructed by algorithm $QM(T_f)$ equals the set of implicants of f that contain k literals.*

PROOF: The proof is by induction on $n - k$ (so that, in fact, we are doing induction from $k = n$ down to $k = 1$). The induction basis for $n - k = 0$ holds because I_n is the set of minterms. Assuming the theorem holds for $n - k$, we need to prove it for $n - k + 1 = n - (k - 1)$. Namely, we assume that I_k equals the set of implicants of f that contain k literals, and we need to prove that I_{k-1} equals the set of implicants of f that contain $(k - 1)$ literals.

We first show that $I_{k-1} \subseteq \mathcal{I}(f)$. A product term r is added to I_{k-1} only if there exist two product terms $p, q \in I_k$ such that $dist(p, q) = 1$ and $r = p \cap q$. By Claim 9.19, it follows that $r \in \mathcal{I}(f)$, and therefore $I_{k-1} \subseteq \mathcal{I}(f)$. By construction, each $r \in I_{k-1}$ contains $k - 1$ literals.

Consider an implicant $r \in \mathcal{I}(f)$ that contains $k - 1$ literals. We need to show that $r \in I_{k-1}$. Since $k < n$, there exists a variable X_i such that $X_i \notin vars(r)$. Consider the products $p \triangleq r \cdot X_i$ and $q \triangleq r \cdot \bar{X}_i$. By Claim 9.10, $p \to r$ and $q \to r$ are tautologies. By transitivity (see Example 1 on page 129), $p \to \varphi_f$ and $q \to \varphi_f$ are tautologies. Therefore, both p and q are implicants of f.

Since p and q contain k literals, the induction hypothesis implies that $p, q \in I_k$. Since $dist(p, q) = 1$, it follows that $p \cap q \in I_{k-1}$. However, $r = p \cap q$, and therefore $r \in I_{k-1}$, as required. This completes the proof of the induction step, and the theorem follows. ∎

We now prove that the algorithm computes the arcs of the implicants' graph.

Claim 9.21 *Algorithm $QM(T_f)$ constructs the implicants' graph G_f.*

PROOF: By Theorem 9.20, Algorithm $QM(T_f)$ constructs all the implicants, so we only need to prove that all the arcs are computed as well. If the arc $(p, p \cap q)$ is computed by the algorithm, then $(p, p \cap q) \in E$. Indeed, by Theorem 9.20, p and $p \cap q$ are implicants, and p is an immediate predecessor of $p \cap q$.

Conversely, if $(p, r) \in E$, then $p = r \cdot X_i$ or $p = r \cdot \bar{X}_i$. Assume that $p = r \cdot X_i$ (the other case is proved similarly). Let $p' \triangleq r \cdot \bar{X}_i$. Since r is an implicant, by Claim 9.9, p' is also an implicant. Since p and p' belong to the same layer, the algorithm will consider the pair p, p', add the vertex $r = p \cap p'$, and add the arcs (p, r) and (p', r), as required. ∎

Algorithm $QM(T_f)$ computes the implicants' graph. By Observation 9.9, the essential prime implicants can be computed as follows:

1. For each minterm r, compute the set of sinks in G_f that are reachable from r.
2. If this set contains a single sink p, then add p to $\mathcal{I}^e(f)$.
3. After all minterms have been scanned, return $\mathcal{I}^e(f)$.

9.6.6 Karnaugh Maps

A tabular method to obtain the prime implicants and the essential prime implicants is called *Karnaugh maps*. This method works reasonably well for Boolean functions $f : \{0, 1\}^n \to \{0, 1\}$ where $n \leq 4$. The idea is as follows:

1. Write the multiplication table of f. It is useful to order the columns and rows in a *Gray code* order.
2. Identify $a \times b$ "generalized" maximal rectangles of all ones in the table where both a and b are powers of 2.
3. Each such maximal rectangle corresponds to a prime implicant.
4. If a 1 is covered only by one such rectangle, then this rectangle corresponds to an essential prime implicant.

See Example 3 for a demonstration of this method.

EXAMPLES

---

1. Prove the following lemma.

   Lemma 9.22 *Let τ be an assignment. Let $\varphi_1 \triangleq (x \to y)$, $\varphi_2 \triangleq (y \to z)$, and $\varphi_3 \triangleq (x \to z)$; then*

   $$(\hat{\tau}(\varphi_1) = 1) \ and \ (\hat{\tau}(\varphi_2) = 1) \Rightarrow (\hat{\tau}(\varphi_3) = 1),$$

   where x, y, z are Boolean formulas over the same set of variables and connectives.

   PROOF: Let us assume in contrary that $\hat{\tau}(\varphi_3) = 0$. It follows that $\hat{\tau}(x) = 1$ and $\hat{\tau}(z) = 0$. Since $\hat{\tau}(\varphi_2) = 1$, then $\hat{\tau}(y) = 0$. Since $\hat{\tau}(x) = 1$ and $\hat{\tau}(y) = 0$, it follows that $\hat{\tau}(\varphi_1) = 0$, a contradiction to the assumption that $\hat{\tau}(\varphi_1) = 0$. ∎

   Note that Lemma 9.22 implies that

   $$((x \to y) \land (y \to z)) \to z$$

   is a tautology.

2. *Quine–McCluskey heuristic example.* Let $f_1 : \{0, 1\}^3 \to \{0, 1\}$, defined by the truth table depicted in Table 9.4.

   Table 9.4. The truth table of $f_1: \{0, 1\}^3 \to \{0, 1\}$

X	Y	Z	$f_1(X, Y, Z)$
0	0	0	1
1	0	0	1
0	1	0	0
1	1	0	1
0	0	1	1
1	0	1	0
0	1	1	1
1	1	1	1

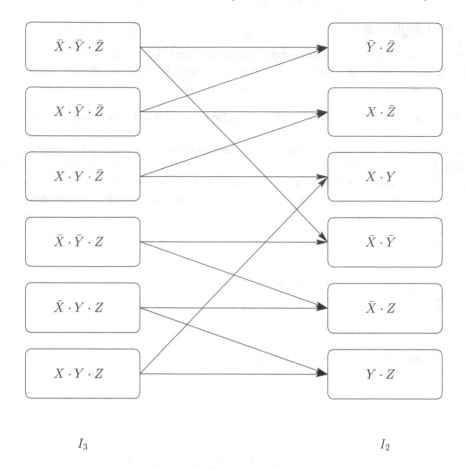

$$I_3 \qquad\qquad\qquad\qquad\qquad\qquad\qquad\qquad I_2$$

Figure 9.2. The implicants' graph G_{f_1}.

In this case, f_1 can be represented as a SOP of minterms, as follows:

$$\varphi_{f_1} = \bar{X} \cdot \bar{Y} \cdot \bar{Z} + X \cdot \bar{Y} \cdot \bar{Z} + X \cdot Y \cdot \bar{Z} + \bar{X} \cdot \bar{Y} \cdot Z + \bar{X} \cdot Y \cdot Z + X \cdot Y \cdot Z.$$

Figure 9.2 depicts the implicants' graph G_{f_1} that the Quine–McCluskey heuristic calculates during its execution. Since all minterms are covered by more than one sink, then $\mathcal{I}^e(f) = \varnothing$.

Now, we should find a shortest subset $A \subseteq \mathcal{I}'(f)$ such that adding the products in A to ψ makes ψ logically equivalent to φ_f. For example:

$$\psi_{f_1}(X, Y, Z) = X \cdot \bar{Z} + \bar{X} \cdot \bar{Y} + Y \cdot Z.$$

Note that since $\mathcal{I}^e(f) = \varnothing$, the Boolean functions f_1 is not logically equivalent to the sum of its essential prime implicants.

3. *Karnaugh maps example.* In the following example, we demonstrate the method as well as the terms: *Gray code* order, generalized maximal rectangles, and the correspondence between a rectangle and an implicant.

Table 9.5. The truth table of $f_2 \colon \{0, 1\}^3 \to \{0, 1\}$

X	Y	Z	$f_2(X, Y, Z)$
0	0	0	1
1	0	0	1
0	1	0	1
1	1	0	1
0	0	1	0
1	0	1	1
0	1	1	1
1	1	1	0

Table 9.6. The Karnaugh map of $f_2 \colon \{0, 1\}^3 \to \{0, 1\}$

$\frac{YZ}{X}$	00	01	11	10
0	1	0	1	1
1	1	1	0	1

Let $f_2 \colon \{0, 1\}^3 \to \{0, 1\}$, defined by the truth table depicted in Table 9.5. In this case, f_2 can be represented as a SOP of minterms, as follows:

$$\varphi_{f_2} = \bar{X} \cdot \bar{Y} \cdot \bar{Z} + X \cdot \bar{Y} \cdot \bar{Z} + \bar{X} \cdot Y \cdot \bar{Z} + X \cdot Y \cdot \bar{Z} + X \cdot \bar{Y} \cdot Z + \bar{X} \cdot Y \cdot Z.$$

The *Karnaugh map* of f_2 is depicted in Table 9.6. The columns correspond to the variables Y and Z. The rows correspond to the variable X.

Note that the columns' labels are ordered by a *Gray code*, that is, two consecutive labels differ by a single bit (if $n = 4$, then the rows' labels are coded in the same way).

We now identify the prime implicants of f_2. There are three prime implicants. These implicants are depicted in Table 9.7. The implicants are depicted as maximal generalized gray rectangles. Note that the dimensions of these rectangles are powers of 2, and furthermore, they are maximal, that is, one cannot extend the rectangle in a way that its dimensions are powers of 2 and that it covers only values of 1.

The minimized SOP formula ψ_{f_2} is as follows:

$$\psi_{f_2} = \bar{Z} + \bar{X} \cdot \bar{Y} + X \cdot \bar{Y}.$$

Table 9.7. The prime implicants of f_2. Note that the leftmost implicant is, in fact, a 2×2 rectangle. In this case, all prime implicants are essential

$\frac{YZ}{X}$	00	01	11	10		$\frac{YZ}{X}$	00	01	11	10		$\frac{YZ}{X}$	00	01	11	10
0	1	0	1	1		0	1	0	1	1		0	1	0	1	1
1	1	1	0	1		1	1	1	0	1		1	1	1	0	1

PROBLEMS

9.1. Prove that every nonconstant Boolean function has a unique representation as a sum of (distinct) minterms.

9.2. Represent the following Boolean functions as SOP: (i) the parity function p: $\{0, 1\}^3 \rightarrow \{0, 1\}$ (see Example 3 on page 14) and (ii) the majority function m: $\{0, 1\}^3 \rightarrow \{0, 1\}$ (see Example 4 on page 14).

9.3. Represent the following Boolean functions as POS: (i) the parity function p: $\{0, 1\}^3 \rightarrow \{0, 1\}$ (see Example 3 on page 14) and (ii) the majority function m: $\{0, 1\}^3 \rightarrow \{0, 1\}$ (see Example 4 on page 14).

9.4. Represent the following Boolean functions as polynomials in $GF(2)[\{X, Y, Z\}]$: (i) The parity function $p: \{0, 1\}^3 \rightarrow \{0, 1\}$ (see Example 3 on page 14) and (ii) the majority function $m: \{0, 1\}^3 \rightarrow \{0, 1\}$ (see Example 4 on page 14).

9.5. Let $p \in \mathcal{I}'(f)$. Let τ be an assignment such that $\hat{\tau}(p) = 1$. Prove that there exists a minterm r such that $\hat{\tau}(r) = 1$.

9.6. Minimize the following Boolean formulas using (i) the Quine–McCluskey heuristic, (ii) Karnaugh maps, and (iii) a software tool:
(a) $\varphi_1 = \bar{X} \cdot \bar{Y} \cdot \bar{Z} + \bar{X} \cdot Y \cdot Z + \bar{X} \cdot Y \cdot \bar{Z} + X \cdot \bar{Y} \cdot \bar{Z} + X \cdot \bar{Y} \cdot Z + X \cdot Y \cdot \bar{Z}$.
(b) $\varphi_2 = \bar{X} \cdot \bar{Y} \cdot \bar{Z} + \bar{X} \cdot \bar{Y} \cdot Z + X \cdot \bar{Y} \cdot Z + X \cdot Y \cdot \bar{Z}$.

In (i) draw the implicants' graph and mark the essential implicants' vertices in it.

9.7. What is the maximum height of a parse tree of a CNF or DNF formula?

9.8. Let (G, π) denote the parse tree of a Boolean formula φ. Define sufficient and necessary conditions for T so that φ is a DNF formula. Repeat this task for a CNF formula.

CHAPTER 10

The Digital Abstraction

The term a *digital circuit* refers to a device that works in a binary world. In the binary world, the only values are zeros and ones. In other words, the inputs of a digital circuit are zeros and ones, and the outputs of a digital circuit are zeros and ones. Digital circuits are usually implemented by *electronic devices* and operate in the *real* world. In the real world, there are no zeros and ones; instead, what matters is the voltages of inputs and outputs. Since voltages refer to energy, they are continuous (unless quantum physics is used). So we have a gap between the continuous real world and the two-valued binary world. One should not regard this gap as absurd. Digital circuits are only an *abstraction* of electronic devices. In this chapter, we explain this abstraction, called the *digital abstraction*.

In the digital abstraction, one interprets voltage values as binary values. The advantages of the digital model cannot be overstated; this model enables one to focus on the digital behavior of a circuit, to ignore analog and transient phenomena, and to easily build larger, more complex circuits out of small circuits. The digital model together with a simple set of rules, called *design rules*, enable logic designers to design complex digital circuits consisting of millions of gates that operate as expected.

10.1 TRANSISTORS

The basic building blocks of digital electronic circuits are *transistors*. The hierarchy starts with transistors, from which gates are built. Gates are then used for building bigger circuits. The most common technology used in digital electronics these days is called Complementary Metal-Oxide-Semiconductor (CMOS). In CMOS, there are only two types of transistors: N-type and P-type. From these two types of transistors all digital designs can be built.

Each transistor has three connections to the outer world, called the *gate*, *source*, and *drain*. Figure 10.1 depicts diagrams describing these transistors. Although inaccurate, we will refer, for the sake of simplicity, to the gate and source as inputs and to the drain as an output. An overly simple specification of an N-type transistor in CMOS technology is as follows.

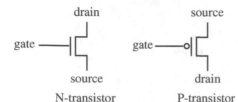

Figure 10.1. Schematic symbols of an N-transistor and a P-transistor

Notation. Let V_g denote the voltage of the gate of a transistor. Let R_{sd} denote the resistance between the source and a drain of a transistor. We use $R_{sd}^N(V_g)$ to denote the resistance R_{sd} in an N-type transistor as a function of the voltage V_g. Similarly, $R_{sd}^P(V_g)$ denotes the resistance R_{sd} in a P-type transistor as a function of V_g. Let $V_{low} < V_{high}$ denote two threshold voltages (the values of V_{low} and V_{high} depend on the technology). The resistance R_{sd} behaves in an ideal setting as follows:

$$R_{sd}^N(V_g) \triangleq \begin{cases} \infty & \text{if } V_g < V_{low}, \\ 0 & \text{if } V_g > V_{high}, \end{cases}$$

$$R_{sd}^P(V_g) \triangleq \begin{cases} 0 & \text{if } V_g < V_{low}, \\ \infty & \text{if } V_g > V_{high}. \end{cases}$$

In reality, zero resistance means a very small resistance, and infinite resistance means a very high resistance.

The voltages in an electronic circuit change when the circuit is engaged in some computation. Nevertheless, we distinguish between the changes (or transitions) that are supposed to be very fast and the periods between transitions that are called the *steady state*. For example, consider two players X and Y passing a ball to each other. We regard the travel from one player to the other as a transition. We regard the state of the ball as steady if the ball is held by one of the players. Thus we say that the ball alternates between the states X and Y.

Let us focus on the steady state of an N-type transistor. If the voltage of the gate is high ($V_g > V_{high}$), then there is no resistance between the source and the drain. Such a small resistance causes the voltage of the drain to equal the voltage of the source. If the voltage of the gate is low ($V_g < V_{low}$), then there is a very high resistance between the source and the drain. Such a high resistance means that the voltage of the drain is unchanged by the transistor. It could be changed by another transistor, if the drains of the two transistors are connected. A P-type transistor behaves in a dual manner: the resistance between drain and the source is low if the gate voltage is below V_{low}. If the voltage of the gate is above V_{high}, then the source-to-drain resistance is very high.

Note that this description of transistor behavior implies that transistors are highly nonlinear. (Recall that a linear function $f(x)$ satisfies $f(a \cdot x) = a \cdot f(x)$.) See Figure 10.2 for a graph of R_{sd} as a function of V_g in N- and P-type transistors.

Specifically, $R_{sd}(V_g)$ is not a linear function of V_g, namely,

$$V_g > V_{high} \Rightarrow R_{sd}^N(1.1 \cdot V_g) \approx R_{sd}(V_g) \approx 0$$

$$V_g < V_{low} \Rightarrow R_{sd}^P(0.9 \cdot V_g) \approx R_{sd}(V_g) \approx 0.$$

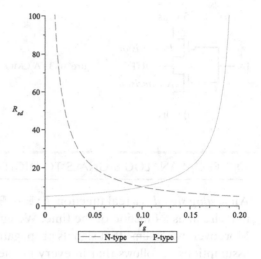

Figure 10.2. A qualitative graph of R_{sd} as a function of V_g in N- and P-type transistors. The y-axis is the resistance between the source and the drain R_{sd}. The x-axis is the voltage of the gate V_g. The dashed line depicts $R_{sd}^N(v_g)$. The solid line depicts $R_{sd}^P(v_g)$.

However, for $V = 0.5 \cdot (V_{low} + V_{high})$, we have

$$V_g > V \Rightarrow \frac{R_{sd}^P(1.1 \cdot V)}{R_{sd}^P(V)} \gg 1.1$$

$$V_g < V \Rightarrow \frac{R_{sd}^N(1.1 \cdot V)}{R_{sd}^N(V)} \ll 1/1.1.$$

The absolute value of the derivative $\partial R_{sd}/\partial V_g$ for $V_g \approx V$ is often referred to as the *gain* of a transistor.

10.2 A CMOS INVERTER

Figure 10.3 depicts a CMOS inverter. If the input voltage is above V_{high}, then the source-to-drain resistance in the P-transistor is very high and the source-to-drain resistance in the N-transistor is very low. Since the source of the N-transistor is connected to low voltage (i.e., ground), the output of the inverter is low.

If the input voltage is below V_{low}, then the source-to-drain resistance in the N-transistor is very high and the source-to-drain resistance in the P-transistor is very low. Since the source of the P-transistor is connected to high voltage, the output of the inverter is high.

We conclude that the voltage of the output is low when the input is high, and vice versa, and the device is indeed an inverter.

It is hoped that the qualitative description of a CMOS inverter conveys some intuition about how gates are built from transistors. A quantitative analysis of such an inverter requires precise modeling of the functionality of the transistors to derive the input–output voltage relation. One usually performs such an analysis by computer programs (e.g., SPICE). Quantitative analysis is relatively complex and inadequate for designing large systems like computers. (This would be like having to deal with the chemistry of ink when using a pen.)

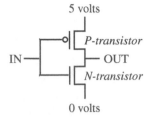

Figure 10.3. A CMOS inverter.

10.3 FROM ANALOG SIGNALS TO DIGITAL SIGNALS

An *analog signal* is a real function $f : \mathbb{R} \to \mathbb{R}$ that describes the voltage of a given point in a circuit as a function of the time. We ignore the resistance and capacities of wires. Moreover, we assume that signals propagate through wires immediately.[1] Under these assumptions, it follows that in every moment, the voltages measured along different points of a wire are identical. Since a signal describes the voltage (i.e., derivative of energy as a function of electric charge), we also assume that a signal is a continuous function.

A *digital signal* is a function $g : \mathbb{R} \to \{0, 1, \text{nonlogical}\}$. The value of a digital signal describes the *logical value* carried along a wire as a function of time. To be precise, there are two logical values: 0 and 1. The nonlogical value simply means that the signal is neither zero or one.

How does one interpret an analog signal as a digital signal? The simplest interpretation is to set a threshold V'. Given an analog signal $f(t)$, the digital signal $dig(f(t))$ can be defined as follows:

$$dig(f(t)) \triangleq \begin{cases} 0 & \text{if } f(t) < V' \\ 1 & \text{if } f(t) > V'. \end{cases} \tag{10.1}$$

According to this definition, a digital interpretation of an analog signal is always 0 or 1, and the digital interpretation is never nonlogical.

There are several problems with the definition in Eq. 10.1. One problem with this definition is that all the components should comply with *exactly* the same threshold V'. In reality, devices are not completely identical; the actual thresholds of different devices vary according to a tolerance specified by the manufacturer. This means that instead of a fixed threshold, we should consider a range of thresholds.

Another problem with the definition in Eq. 10.1 is caused by perturbations of $f(t)$ around the threshold t. Such perturbations can be caused by *noise* or oscillations of $f(t)$ before it stabilizes. We will elaborate more on noise later and now explain why oscillations can occur. Consider a spring connected to the ceiling with a weight w hanging from it. We expect the spring to reach a length ℓ that is proportional to the weight w. Assume that all we wish to know is whether the length ℓ is greater than a threshold ℓ_t. Sounds simple! But what if ℓ is rather close to ℓ_t? In practice, the length only tends to the length ℓ as time progresses; the actual length of the spring oscillates

---

[1]   This is a reasonable assumption if wires are short.

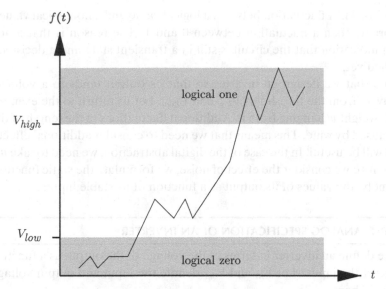

Figure 10.4. A digital interpretation of an analog signal in the zero-noise model.

around ℓ with a diminishing amplitude. Hence the length of the spring fluctuates below and above ℓ_t many times before we can decide. This effect may force us to wait for a long time before we can decide if $\ell < \ell_t$. If we return to the definition of $dig(f(t))$, it may well happen that $f(t)$ oscillates around the threshold V'. This renders the digital interpretation defined in Eq. 10.1 useless.

Returning to the example of weighing weights, assume that we have two types of objects: light and heavy. The weight of a light (respectively, heavy) object is at most (respectively, at least) w_0 (respectively, w_1). The bigger the gap $w_1 - w_0$, the easier it becomes to determine if an object is light or heavy (especially in the presence of noise or oscillations).

Now we have two reasons to introduce two threshold values instead of one, namely, different threshold values for different devices and the desire to have a gap between values interpreted as logical zero and logical one. We denote these thresholds by V_{low} and V_{high} and require that $V_{low} < V_{high}$. An interpretation of an analog signal is depicted in Figure 10.4. Consider an analog signal $f(t)$. The digital signal $dig(f(t))$ is defined as follows:

$$dig(f(t)) \triangleq \begin{cases} 0 & \text{if } f(t) < V_{low}, \\ 1 & \text{if } f(t) > V_{high}, \\ \text{non-logical} & \text{otherwise.} \end{cases} \quad (10.2)$$

We often refer to the logical value of an analog signal f. This is simply a shorthand way of referring to the value of the digital signal $dig(f)$.

It is important to note that fluctuations of $f(t)$ are still possible around the threshold values. However, if the two thresholds are sufficiently far away from each other, fluctuations of f do not cause fluctuations of $dig(f(t))$ between 0 and 1. Instead, we will have at worst fluctuations of $dig(f(t))$ between a nonlogical value and a logical value (i.e., 0 or 1). A fluctuation between a logical value and a nonlogical value is much more favorable than a fluctuation between 0 and 1. The reason is that a nonlogical value is an indication that the circuit is still in a transient state and a decision has not been reached yet.

Assume that we design an inverter so that its output tends to a voltage that is bounded away from the thresholds V_{low} and V_{high}. Let us return to the example of the spring with weight w hanging from it. Additional fluctuations in the length of the spring might be caused by wind. This means that we need to consider additional effects so that our model will be useful. In the case of the digital abstraction, we need to take *noise* into account. Before we consider the effect of noise, we formulate the static functionality of a gate, namely, the values of its output as a function of its stable inputs.

EXAMPLE: ANALOG SPECIFICATION OF AN INVERTER

Can we define an inverter in terms of the voltage of the output as a function of the voltage of the input? Let V_{in} and V_{out} denote the input and output voltages of an inverter. Then,

$$V_{out} = \begin{cases} < V_{low} & \text{if } V_{in} > V_{high} \\ > V_{high} & \text{if } V_{in} < V_{low}. \end{cases} \tag{10.3}$$

What should V_{out} be if $V_{low} < V_{in} < V_{high}$? Formally, such an input voltage is not legal in the steady state, so we should not be worried about it. However, to avoid a wrong digital interpretation of V_{out}, it could help if $dig(V_{out})$ is nonlogical if $dig(V_{in})$ is nonlogical.

10.4 TRANSFER FUNCTIONS OF GATES

The voltage at an output of a gate depends on the voltages of the inputs of the gate. This dependence is called the *transfer function* (or the *voltage-transfer characteristic*; VTC). Consider, for example, an inverter with an input x and an output y. To make things complicated, the value of the signal $y(t)$ at time t is not only a function of the signal x at time t since $y(t)$ depends on the history. Namely, $y(t_0)$ is a function of $x(t)$ over the interval $(-\infty, t_0]$.

Partial differential equations are used to model gates, and the solution of these equations is unfortunately a rather complicated task. A good approximation of transfer functions is obtained by solving differential equations—still a complicated task that can be computed quickly only for a few transistors. So how are chips that contain millions of transistors designed if the models are too complex to be solved?

The way this very intricate problem is handled is by restricting designs. In particular, only a small set of building blocks is used. The building blocks are analyzed intensively, their properties are summarized, and designers rely on these properties for their designs.

One of the most important steps in characterizing the behavior of a gate is computing its *static transfer function*. Returning to the example of the inverter, a "proper" inverter has a unique output value for each input value. Namely, if the input $x(t)$ is stable for a sufficiently long period of time and equals x_0, then the output $y(t)$ stabilizes on a value y_0 that is a function of x_0.

Before we define what a static transfer function is, we point out that there are devices that do not have static transfer functions. We need to distinguish between two cases: (a) Stability is not reached: this case occurs, for example, with devices called oscillators. Note that oscillating devices must consume energy even when the input is stable. We point out that in CMOS technology it is easy to design circuits that do not consume energy if the input is logical, so such oscillations are avoided. (b) Stability is reached: in this case, if there is more than one stable output value, it means that the device has more than one equilibrium point. Such a device can be used to store information about the "history." It is important to note that devices with multiple equilibriums are very useful as storage devices (i.e., they can "remember" a small amount of information). Nevertheless, devices with multiple equilibriums are not "good" candidates for gates, and it is easy to avoid such devices in CMOS technology.

EXAMPLE

A device with many equilibriums. Consider a pot that is initially filled with water. At time t, the pot is held in angle $x(t)$. A zero angle means that the pot is held upright. An angle of 180° means that the pot is upside down. Now, we are told that $x(t) = 0°$ for $t \geq 100$. Can we say how much water is contained in the pot at time $t = 200$? The answer, of course, depends on the history during the interval $t \in [0, 100)$, namely, whether the pot was tilted.

We formalize the definition of a static transfer function of a gate G with one input x and one output y in the following definition. We begin with a naive definition.

Definition 10.1 Consider a device G with one input x and one output y. The device G is a *gate* if its functionality is specified by a function $f : \mathbb{R} \rightarrow \mathbb{R}$ as follows: there exists a $\Delta > 0$ such that, for every x_0 and every t_0, if $x(t) = x_0$ for every $t \in [t_0 - \Delta, t_0]$, then $y(t_0) = f(x_0)$.

Such a function $f(x)$ is called the *static transfer function* of G.

Since circuits operate over a bounded range of voltages, static transfer functions are usually only defined over bounded domains and ranges (say, $[0, 5]$ volts).

To make the definition useful, one should allow perturbations of $x(t)$ during the interval $[t_0 - \Delta, t_0]$. Static transfer functions model physical devices and hence are continuous. This implies the following definition.

Definition 10.2 A function $f(x)$ is the static transfer function of a gate G if the following holds. For every $\epsilon > 0$ there exists a $\delta > 0$ and a $\Delta > 0$ such that

$$\forall t \in [t_1, t_2] : |x(t) - x_0| \leq \delta \quad \Rightarrow \quad \forall t \in [t_1 + \Delta, t_2] : |y(t) - f(x_0)| \leq \epsilon.$$

Note that in the preceding definition, Δ does not depend on x_0 (although it may depend on ϵ). Typically, we are interested on the values of Δ only for logical values of $x(t)$ (i.e., $x(t) \leq V_{low}$ and $x(t) \geq V_{high}$). Once the value of ϵ is fixed, this constant Δ is called the *propagation delay* of the gate G and is one of the most important characteristics of a gate.

It is easy to extend Definition 10.2 to gates with n inputs and m outputs. Thus the input is a vector $x(t) \in \mathbb{R}^n$ and the output is a vector $y(t) \in \mathbb{R}^m$. First, the static transfer function should be a function $f : \mathbb{R}^n \to \mathbb{R}^m$. For a vector $z \in \mathbb{R}^k$, let

$$\|z\| \triangleq \sqrt{z_1^2 + \cdots + z_k^2}.$$

Now require, for every $\epsilon > 0$, there exists a $\delta > 0$ and a $\Delta > 0$ such that

$$\forall t \in [t_1, t_2] : \|x(t) - x_0\| \le \delta \quad \Rightarrow \quad \forall t \in [t_1 + \Delta, t_2] : \|y(t) - f(x_0)\| \le \epsilon.$$

Finally, we can now define an inverter in the zero-noise model. Observe that according to this definition, a device is an inverter if its static transfer function satisfies a certain property. We already stated this property in Eq. 10.3.

Definition 10.3 (*Inverter in Zero-Noise Model*) A gate G with a single input x and a single output y is an inverter if its static transfer function $f(z)$ satisfies the following two conditions:

1. If $z < V_{low}$, then $f(z) > V_{high}$
2. If $z > V_{high}$, then $f(z) < V_{low}$.

The implication of this definition is that if the logical value of the input x is zero (respectively, one) during an interval $[t_1, t_2]$ of length at least Δ, then the logical value of the output y is one (respectively, zero) during the interval $[t_1 + \Delta, t_2]$.

We are now ready to strengthen the digital abstraction so that it will be useful also in the presence of bounded noise.

10.5 THE BOUNDED-NOISE MODEL

Consider a wire from point A to point B. Let $A(t)$ denote the analog signal measured at point A. Similarly, let $B(t)$ denote the analog signal measured at point B. We would like to assume that wires have zero resistance and zero capacitance and that signals propagate through a wire with zero delay. This assumption means that the signals $A(t)$ and $B(t)$ should be equal at all times. Unfortunately, this is not the case; the main reason for this discrepancy is *noise*.

There are many sources of noise. The main source of noise is heat that causes electrons to move randomly. These random movements do not cancel out perfectly, and random currents are created. These random currents create perturbations in the voltage. The difference between the signals $B(t)$ and $A(t)$ is a *noise signal*.

Consider, for example, the setting of *additive noise*: A is an output of an inverter and B is an input of another inverter. We consider the signal $A(t)$ to be a reference signal. The signal $B(t)$ is the sum $A(t) + n_B(t)$, where $n_B(t)$ is the noise signal.

The *bounded-noise model* assumes that the noise signal along every wire has a bounded absolute value. We will use a slightly simplified model in which there is a constant $\epsilon > 0$ such that the absolute value of all noise signals is bounded by ϵ. We refer to this model as the *uniformly bounded noise model*. The justification for assuming that noise is bounded is probabilistic. Noise is a random variable whose distribution has a

Figure 10.5. Two inverters connected in series.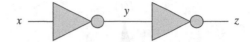

rapidly diminishing tail. This means that if the bound is sufficiently large, then the probability of the noise exceeding this bound during the lifetime of a circuit is negligibly small.

10.6 THE DIGITAL ABSTRACTION IN THE PRESENCE OF NOISE

Consider two inverters connected in series. Namely, the output of one gate feeds the input of the second gate (see Figure 10.5).

Assume that the input x has a value that satisfies (a) $x > V_{high}$, so the logical value of x is one, and (b) $y = V_{low} - \epsilon'$, for a very small $\epsilon' > 0$. This might not be possible with every inverter, but Definition 10.3 does not rule out such an inverter. (Consider a transfer function with $f(V_{high}) = V_{low}$ and x slightly higher than V_{high}.) Since the logical value of y is zero, it follows that the second inverter, if not faulty, should output a value z that is greater than V_{high}. In other words, we expect the logical value of z to be 1. At this point, we consider the effect of adding noise.

Let us denote the noise added to the wire y by n_y. This means that the input of the second inverter equals $y(t) + n_y(t)$. Now, if $n_y(t) > \epsilon'$, then the second inverter is fed a nonlogical value! This means that we can no longer deduce that the logical value of z is one. We conclude that we must use a more resilient model; in particular, the functionality of circuits should not be affected by noise. Of course, we can only hope to be able to cope with bounded noise, namely, noise whose absolute value does not exceed a certain value ϵ.

10.6.1 Input and Output Signals

Definition 10.4 An *input signal* is a signal that is fed to a circuit or to a gate. An *output signal* is a signal that is output by a gate or a circuit.

For example, in Figure 10.5, the signal y is both the output signal of the left inverter and an input signal of the right inverter. If noise is not present and there is no delay, then the signal output by the left inverter always equals the signal input to the right inverter.

10.6.2 Redefining the Digital Interpretation of Analog Signals

The way we deal with noise is that we interpret input signals and output signals differently. An input signal is a signal measured at an input of a gate. Similarly, an output signal is a signal measured at an output of a gate. Instead of two thresholds, V_{low} and V_{high}, we define the following four thresholds:

- $V_{in,low}$—an upper bound on a voltage of an input signal interpreted as a logical zero
- $V_{out,low}$—an upper bound on a voltage of an output signal interpreted as a logical zero
- $V_{in,high}$—a lower bound on a voltage of an input signal interpreted as a logical one
- $V_{out,high}$—a lower bound on a voltage of an output signal interpreted as a logical one

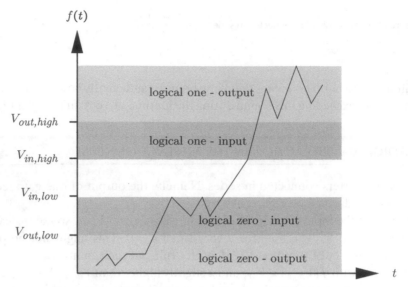

Figure 10.6. A digital interpretation of an input and output signals.

These four thresholds satisfy the following equation:

$$V_{out,low} < V_{in,low} < V_{in,high} < V_{out,high}. \tag{10.4}$$

Figure 10.6 depicts these four thresholds. Note that the interpretation of input signals is less strict than the interpretation of output signals. The actual values of these four thresholds depend on the transfer functions of the devices we wish to use.

Consider an input signal $f(t)$. The digital signal $dig_{in}(f(t))$ is defined as follows:

$$dig_{in}(f(t)) \triangleq \begin{cases} 0 & \text{if } f(t) < V_{in,low}, \\ 1 & \text{if } f(t) > V_{in,high}, \\ \text{non-logical} & \text{otherwise.} \end{cases} \tag{10.5}$$

Consider an output signal $g(t)$. The digital signal $dig_{out}(g(t))$ is defined analogously:

$$dig_{out}(g(t)) \triangleq \begin{cases} 0 & \text{if } g(t) < V_{out,low}, \\ 1 & \text{if } g(t) > V_{out,high}, \\ \text{non-logical} & \text{otherwise.} \end{cases} \tag{10.6}$$

Definition 10.5 The differences $V_{in,low} - V_{out,low}$ and $V_{out,high} - V_{in,high}$ are called *noise margins*.

Consider the following setting. The signal $g(t)$ is the output of gate G_1. On its way to an input of G_2, the signal $g(t)$ accumulates noise so that the input signal to G_2 is the signal $f(t) \triangleq g(t) + n(t)$. Our goal is to show that if the absolute value of the noise is less than the noise margins, then the noise does not corrupt the signal.

Claim 10.1 *Assume that* $f(t) = g(t) + n(t)$. *Assume that* $|n(t)|$ *is less than the noise margins. If* $\text{dig}_{out}(g)(t) \in \{0, 1\}$, *then* $\text{dig}_{in}(f)(t) = \text{dig}_{out}(g)(t)$.

PROOF: Assume that $dig_{out}(g)(t) = 0$. Therefore $g(t) < V_{out,low}$. Hence

$$f(t) = g(t) + n(t)$$

$$< V_{out,low} + (V_{in,low} - V_{out,low}) = V_{in,low}.$$

Therefore $dig_{in}(f)(t) = 0$, as required. The proof of the case $dig_{out}(g)(t) = 1$ is analogous. ∎

We can now fix the definition of an inverter so that bounded noise added to outputs does not affect the logical interpretation of signals.

Definition 10.6 (*Inverter in the Bounded-Noise Model*) A gate G with a single input x and a single output y is an inverter if its static transfer function $f(z)$ satisfies the following the following two conditions:

1. If $z < V_{in,low}$, then $f(z) > V_{out,high}$
2. If $z > V_{in,high}$, then $f(z) < V_{out,low}$.

10.7 STABLE SIGNALS

In this section, we define terminology that will be used later. To simplify notation, we define these terms in the zero-noise model. We leave it to the curious reader to extend the definitions and notation to the bounded-noise model.

An analog signal $f(t)$ is said to be *logical at time* t if $dig(f(t)) \in \{0, 1\}$. An analog signal $f(t)$ is said to be *stable* during the interval $[t_1, t_2]$ if $f(t)$ is logical for every $t \in [t_1, t_2]$. Continuity of $f(t)$ and the fact that $V_{low} < V_{high}$ imply the following claim.

Claim 10.2 *If an analog signal* $f(t)$ *is stable during the interval* $[t_1, t_2]$, *then one of the following holds:*

1. $dig(f(t)) = 0$, *for every* $t \in [t_1, t_2]$
2. $dig(f(t)) = 1$, *for every* $t \in [t_1, t_2]$.

From this point, we will deal with digital signals and use the same terminology. Namely, a digital signal $x(t)$ is *logical* at time t if $x(t) \in \{0, 1\}$. A digital signal is *stable* during an interval $[t_1, t_2]$ if $x(t)$ is logical for every $t \in [t_1, t_2]$.

10.8 SUMMARY

In this chapter, we presented the digital abstraction of analog devices. For this purpose, we defined analog signals and their digital counterpart, called digital signals. In the digital abstraction, analog signals are interpreted either as zero, one, or nonlogical.

We discussed noise and showed that to make the model useful, one should set stricter requirements from output signals than from input signals. Our discussion is based on the bounded-noise model, in which there is an upper bound on the absolute value of noise.

We defined gates using transfer functions and static transfer functions. This functions describe the analog behavior of devices. We also defined the propagation delay of a device as the amount of time that input signals must be stable to guarantee stability of the output of a gate.

PROBLEMS

10.1. Define the static transfer function of a NAND-gate and a NOR-gate in the zero-noise model.

10.2. Define the static transfer function of a NAND-gate and a NOR-gate in the bounded-noise model.

10.3. Consider the following piecewise linear function:

$$f(x) = \begin{cases} 5 & \text{if } x \leq \frac{5}{3}, \\ 0 & \text{if } x \geq \frac{10}{3}, \\ -3x + 10 & \text{if } \frac{5}{3} < x < \frac{10}{3}. \end{cases}$$

Show that if $f(x)$ is the transfer function of a device C, then one can define threshold values $V_{out,low} < V_{in,low} < V_{in,high} < V_{out,high}$ so that C is an inverter according to Definition 10.6.

10.4. Consider the function $f(x) = 1 - x$ over the interval $[0, 1]$. Suppose that $f(x)$ is a the transfer function of a device C. Can you define threshold values $V_{out,low} < V_{in,low} < V_{in,high} < V_{out,high}$ so that C is an inverter according to Definition 10.6?

Hint: prove that $V_{out,high} \leq 1 - V_{in,low}$ *and that* $V_{out,low} \geq 1 - V_{in,high}$. *Derive a contradiction from these two inequalities.*

10.5. Can you justify or explain the saying that "computers use only zeros and ones"?

10.6. Can you explain the following anomaly? The design of an adder is a simple task. However, the design and analysis of a single electronic device (e.g., a single gate) is a complex task.

CHAPTER 11

Foundations of Combinational Circuits

In this chapter, we define and study combinational circuits. The underlying graph of a combinational circuit is more general than the underlying graph of a Boolean formula. In a formula, the underlying graph is a rooted tree. However, in a combinational circuit, the underlying graph is a directed acyclic graph.

We focus on the representation of Boolean functions by combinational circuits, a representation that is different from tables and formulas. Our goal is to prove two theorems: (i) every Boolean function can be implemented by a combinational circuit and (ii) every combinational circuit implements a Boolean function.

We introduce an efficient algorithm for simulating a combinational circuit. Simulation means that we can determine the value of the outputs if we are given the values of the inputs. In addition, we analyze the time that elapses until the outputs of a combinational circuit stabilize.

We measure the quality of a combinational circuit using two criteria: cost and delay. Cost refers to the number of gates in a circuit. Delay refers to the speed of the circuit. Obviously, we prefer cheap and fast circuits over costly and slow circuits.

11.1 COMBINATIONAL GATES: AN ANALOG APPROACH

By Definition 10.1, a gate is a device whose static functionality is specified by a static transfer function. This means that the output is a function of the inputs, provided that the input values do not change for a sufficiently long amount of time.

Our goal now is to define *combinational* gates. According to Definition 10.1, a gate is a deterministic memoryless device. A combinational gate must satisfy an additional property. Namely, if the inputs are logically stable, then the output is logical. Hence, not only is the output a function of the present value of the inputs, the output is logical if the inputs are stable. We now formalize the definition of a combinational gate.

First, we extend the definition of the digital interpretation of an analog signal to real vectors. Let $\vec{y} \in \mathbb{R}^n$, where $\vec{y} = (y_1, y_2, \cdots, y_n)$. The function $dig_n : \mathbb{R}^n \to \{0, 1, \text{non-logical}\}^n$ is defined by

$$dig_n(y_1, y_2, \cdots, y_n) \triangleq (dig(y_1), dig(y_2), \cdots, dig((y_n))).$$

145

To simplify notation, we denote dig_n simply by dig, when the length n of the vector is clear.

We now define a combinational gate. Consider a gate g with n inputs (denoted by $\vec{x}$) and k outputs (denoted by $\vec{y}$). When we write $dig(\vec{x}(t)) \in \{0,1\}^n$, we mean that every component of $\vec{x}(t)$ is logical.

Definition 11.1 The gate g is a *combinational gate* if there exists a $\Delta > 0$ such that, for all $\vec{x}(t) \in \mathbb{R}^n$,

$$\forall t \in [t_1, t_2]: dig_{in}(\vec{x}(t)) \in \{0,1\}^n \Rightarrow \forall t \in [t_1 + \Delta, t_2]: dig_{out}(\vec{y}(t)) \in \{0,1\}^k. \quad (11.1)$$

The preceding definition says that in a combinational gate, a stable input during $\lfloor t_1, t_2 \rfloor$ leads to a stable output during $[t_1 + \Delta, t_2]$. Note that this definition is stricter than the definition of a gate in two ways. First, we require that the static transfer function $f : \mathbb{R}^n \to \mathbb{R}^k$ satisfies

$$\forall \vec{x} : dig_{in}(\vec{x}) \in \{0,1\}^n \Rightarrow dig_{out}(f(\vec{x})) \in \{0,1\}^k. \quad (11.2)$$

Second, we allow the input $\vec{x}(t)$ to fluctuate as much as it wishes, as long as it is logically stable (i.e., each component must have the same logical value during the interval $[t_1, t_2]$ but its analog value may fluctuate within the intervals $[0, V_{in,low}]$ and $[V_{in,high}, +\infty]$).

Consider a combinational gate g and let $f : \mathbb{R}^n \to \mathbb{R}^k$ denote its static transfer function. The function f induces a Boolean function $B_f : \{0,1\}^n \to \{0,1\}^k$, as follows. Given a Boolean vector $(b_1, \cdots, b_n) \in \{0,1\}^n$, define x_i as follows:

$$x_i \triangleq \begin{cases} V_{low} - \varepsilon & \text{if } b_i = 0 \\ V_{high} + \varepsilon & \text{if } b_i = 1. \end{cases}$$

The Boolean function B_f is defined by

$$B_f(\vec{b}) \triangleq dig_{out}(f(\vec{x})).$$

Since g is a combinational gate, it follows that every component of $dig_{out}(f(\vec{x}))$ is logical and hence B_f is a Boolean function, as required.

After defining the Boolean function B_f, we can rephrase Eq. 11.2 as follows (note that this formulation ignores timing):

$$dig(\vec{x}) \in \{0,1\}^n \Rightarrow dig(f(\vec{x})) = B_f(dig(\vec{x})).$$

Claim 11.1 *In a combinational gate, the relation between the logical values of the inputs and the logical values of the outputs is specified by a Boolean function.*

PROOF: Since $dig_{out}(f(\vec{x})) \in \{0,1\}^k$ if $dig_{in}\vec{x} \in \{0,1\}^n$, we conclude that $dig_{out}(f(\vec{x}))$ does not depend on the real values of $\vec{x}$ but only on their digital interpretation. Moreover, $dig_{out}(f(\vec{x}))$ must be stable. This means that transitions from 0 to 1 (or vice versa) are not possible. Indeed, during each such transition, the digital interpretation must be nonlogical. ∎

Recall that the propagation delay is an upper bound on the amount of time that elapses from the moment that the inputs (nearly) stop changing until the moment that the output (nearly) equals the value of the static transfer function. Hence one must allow some time until the logical values of the outputs of a combinational gate properly reflect the value of the Boolean function. We say that a combinational gate is *consistent* if this relation holds.

Consider a combinational gate g with inputs $\vec{x}(t)$ and outputs $\vec{y}(t)$. Let f denote the static transfer function of g.

Definition 11.2 Gate g is *consistent* at time t if $dig(\vec{x}(t)) \in \{0, 1\}^n$ and $dig(\vec{y}(t)) = B_f(dig(\vec{x}(t)))$.

11.2 BACK TO THE DIGITAL WORLD

In the previous section, we defined combinational gates using analog signals and their digital interpretation. This approach is useful when one wishes to determine if an analog device can be used as a digital combinational gate. Here simplify matters and deal only with digital signals.

To simplify notation, we consider a combinational gate g with two inputs, denoted by x_1, x_2, and a single output, denoted by y. Instead of using analog signals, we refer only to digital signals. Namely, we denote the digital signal at terminal x_1 by $x_1(t)$. The same notation is used for the other terminals.

Our goals are to (i) specify the functionality of combinational gate g by a Boolean function, (ii) define when a combinational gate g is consistent, and (iii) define the propagation delay of g.

We use a looser definition of the propagation delay. Recall that we decided to refer only to digital signals. Hence we are not sensitive to the analog value of the signals. This means that a (logically) stable signal is considered to have a fixed value, and the analog values of inputs may change as long as they remain with the same logical value.

In the looser definition of propagation delay, we only ask about the time that elapses from the moment the inputs are stable until the gate is consistent.

Definition 11.3 A combinational gate g is *consistent* with a Boolean function B at time t if the input values are logical at time t and

$$y(t) = B(x_1(t), x_2(t)).$$

Note that $y(t)$ must be also logical since $x_1(t), x_2(t) \in \{0, 1\}$ and B is a Boolean function.

Let $B : \{0, 1\}^2 \to \{0, 1\}$ denote the Boolean function induced by the static transfer function of the combinational gate g. The following definition defines propagation delay t_{pd} of a combinational gate.

Definition 11.4 The *propagation delay* of a combinational gate g is t_{pd} if the following holds. If the inputs are stable during the interval $[t_1, t_2]$, then the gate is consistent with the function B during the interval $[t_1 + t_{pd}, t_2]$.

Note that the definition is interesting only if $t_2 > t_1 + t_{pd}$. In practice, this means that the periods of steady state must be longer than the propagation delays. Otherwise, the combinational gate may not reach consistency.

The propagation delay is an upper bound on the amount of time that elapses until a combinational gate becomes consistent (provided that its inputs are stable). The actual amount of time that passes until a combinational gate is consistent is very hard to compute, and in fact, it is random. It depends on $x(t)$ during the interval $(-\infty, t)$ (i.e., how fast does the input change?), noise, and manufacturing variance. This is why upper bounds are used for propagation delays rather than the actual times.

Suppose that a combinational gate g implements a Boolean function $B : \{0, 1\}^n \to \{0, 1\}$ with propagation delay t_{pd}. Assume that $t' \geq t_{pd}$. Then g also implements the Boolean function $B(x)$ with propagation delay t'. It is legitimate to use upper bounds on the actual propagation delay, and pessimistic assumptions should not render a circuit incorrect. Timing analysis of circuits composed of many gates depends on the upper bounds we use; the tighter the bounds, the more accurate the timing analysis is.

Assume that the combinational gate g is consistent at time t_2 and that at least one input is not stable in the interval (t_2, t_3). We cannot assume that the output of g remains stable after t_2. However, in practice, an output may remain stable for a short while after an input becomes instable. We formalize this as follows.

Definition 11.5 The *contamination delay* of a combinational device is a lower bound on the amount of time that the output of a consistent gate remains stable after its inputs stop being stable.

Throughout this course, unless stated otherwise, we will make the most "pessimistic" assumption about the contamination delay. Namely, we do not rely on an output remaining stable after an input becomes instable. Formally, we will assume that the contamination delay is zero.

Figure 11.1 depicts the propagation delay and the contamination delay. The outputs become stable at most t_{pd} time units after the inputs become stable. The outputs remain stable at least t_{cont} time units after the inputs become instable.

11.2.1 Example

In this example, we discuss timing analysis and inferring output values based on partial inputs. Consider an AND-gate with inputs $x_1(t)$ and $x_2(t)$ and an output $y(t)$. Suppose that the propagation delay of the gate is $t_{pd} = 2$ seconds. (All time units are in seconds in this example, so units will not be mentioned anymore in this example.)

- Assume that the inputs equal 1 during the interval $[100, 109]$. Since $t_{pd} = 2$, it follows that $y(t) = 1$ during the interval $[102, 109]$. It may very well happen that $y(t) = 1$ before $t = 102$, however, we are not certain that this happens. During the interval $[100, 102)$,

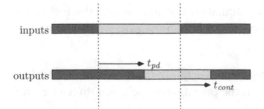

Figure 11.1. The propagation delay and contamination delay of a combinational gate. The x-axis corresponds to time. The dark segments signify that the signal is not guaranteed to be logical; the light segments signify that the signal is guaranteed to be stable.

we are uncertain about the value of $y(t)$; it may be 0, 1, or nonlogical, and it may fluctuate arbitrarily between these values.

• Assume that $x_1(t) = 1$ during the interval $(109, 115]$, $x_2(t) = $ nonlogical during the interval $(109, 110)$ and $x_2(t) = 0$ during the interval $[110, 115]$.

During the interval $(109, 110)$ we know nothing about the value of the output $y(t)$ since $x_2(t)$ is nonlogical. The inputs are stable again starting $t = 110$. Since $t_{pd} = 2$, we are only sure about the value of $y(t)$ during the interval $[112, 115]$ (during the interval $[112, 115]$, $y(t) = 0$). We are uncertain about the value of $y(t)$ during the interval $(109, 112)$.

• Assume that $x_2(t)$ remains stable during the interval $[110, 120]$, $x_1(t)$ becomes non-logical during the interval $(115, 116)$, and $x_1(t)$ equals 1 again during the interval $[116, 120]$.

Since $x_2(t)$ is stable during the interval $[110, 120]$, we conclude that it equals 0 during this interval. The truth table of an AND-gate implies that if one input is zero, then the output is zero. Can we conclude that $y(t) = 0$ during the interval $[110, 120]$?

There are some technologies in which we could draw such a conclusion. However, our formalism does not imply this at all! As soon as $x_1(t)$ becomes nonlogical (after $t = 115$), we cannot conclude anything about the value of $y(t)$. We remain uncertain for 2 seconds after both inputs stabilize. Both inputs stabilize at $t = 116$. Therefore we can only conclude that $y(t) = 0$ during the interval $[118, 120]$.

The inability to determine the value of $y(t)$ during the interval $(115, 118)$ is a short-coming of our formalism. For example, in a CMOS NAND-gate, one can determine that the output is zero if one of the outputs is one (even if the other input is nonlogical). The problem with using such deductions is that timing depends on the values of the signals. On one hand, this improves the estimates computed by timing analysis. One the other hand, timing analysis becomes a very hard computational problem. In particular, instead of a task that can be computed in linear time, it becomes an NP-hard task (i.e., a task that is unlikely to be solvable in polynomial time).

11.3 COMBINATIONAL GATES

A combinational gate, as defined in Definition 11.4, is a device that implements a Boolean function. From this point on, we refer to a combinational gate, in short, as a gate.

The inputs and outputs of a gate are often referred to as *terminals*, *ports*, or even *pins*. The *fan-in* of a gate g is the number of input terminals of g (i.e., the number of bits in the domain of the Boolean function that specifies the functionality of g). The fan-in of the basic gates that we will be using as building blocks for combinational circuits is constant (i.e., we usually consider at most two input ports). The basic gates that we consider are inverter (NOT-gate), OR-gate, NOR-gate, AND-gate, NAND-gate, XOR-gate, NXOR-gate, and multiplexer (MUX). All this gates have a single output. To avoid confusion, note that the fan-out of a gate is not the number of output ports. (The definition of fan-out appears later.)

Given a gate g, we denote the fan-in (i.e., number of input ports) of g by IN(g) and the number of output ports of g by OUT(g). The input ports of a gate g are denoted by

Input Gate   Output Gate

Figure 11.2. An input gate and an output gate.

the set $\{in(g)_i\}_{i=1}^{\text{IN}(g)}$. The output ports of a gate g are denoted by the set $\{out(g)_i\}_{i=1}^{\text{OUT}(g)}$. Let

$$terminals(g) \triangleq \{in(g)_i\}_{i=1}^{\text{IN}(g)} \cup \{out(g)_i\}_{i=1}^{\text{OUT}(g)}.$$

We introduce two special gates used for external inputs and outputs.

Definition 11.6 (*Input and Output Gates*) An *input gate* is a gate with zero inputs and a single output. An *output gate* is a gate with one input and zero outputs.

Figure 11.2 depicts an input gate and an output gate. Inputs from the "external world" are fed to a circuit via input gates. Similarly, outputs to the "external world" are fed by the circuit via output gates. The second coordinate x_i of an input-gate (IN, x_i) is simply the name of the signal along the wire that emanates from it. Similarly, the second coordinate y_i of an output-gate (OUT, y_i) is simply the name of the signal along the wire that enters it. We usually name the inputs x_i and the outputs y_j, but they could be assigned arbitrary names. (Of course, it is a good practice to use meaningful names.)

11.4 WIRES AND NETS

A wire is a connection between two terminals (e.g., an output of one gate and an input of another gate). In the zero-noise model, the signals at both ends of a wire are identical.

Very often we need to connect several terminals (i.e., inputs and outputs of gates) together. We could, of course, use any set of edges (i.e., wires) that connects these terminals together. Instead of specifying how the terminals are physically connected together, we use nets.

Definition 11.7 A *net* is a subset of terminals that are connected by wires. The *fan-out* of a net N is the number of input terminals that are contained in N.

For example, let us consider the leftmost drawing in Figure 11.3. All the gates in this drawing are inverters, that is, NOT-gates. A NOT-gate has a single input port and a single output port, that is, IN(NOT) = OUT(NOT) = 1. There is a single net in this drawing. This net consists of five terminals: a single output port and four input ports. Hence the fan-out of this net is 4.

How to Draw Multiterminal Nets? We say that a net is multiterminal if it contains more than two terminals. The issue of drawing a multiterminal net is a bit confusing. Figure 11.3 depicts three different drawings of the same net. All three nets contain an output terminal of an inverter and four input terminals of inverters. However, the nets are drawn differently. Recall that the definition of a net is simply a subset of terminals. We may draw a net in any way that we find convenient or aesthetic. The interpretation of the drawing is that terminals that are connected by lines or curves constitute a net.

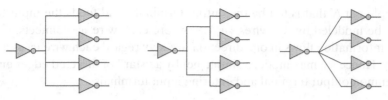

Figure 11.3. Three equivalent nets.

The Digital Signal in a Net. Consider a net N. We would like to define the digital signal $N(t)$ for the whole net. The problem is that owing to noise (and other reasons), the analog signals at different terminals of the net might not equal each other. This might cause the digital interpretations of analog signals at different terminals of the net to be different, too. We solve this problem by defining $N(t)$ as logical only if there is a consensus among all the digital interpretations of the analog signals at all the terminals of the net. Namely, $N(t)$ is zero (respectively, one) if the digital values of all the analog signals in the net are zero (respectively, one). If there is no consensus, then $N(t)$ is nonlogical. Recall that in the bounded-noise model, different thresholds are used to interpret the digital values of the analog signals measured in input and output terminals.

Direction in Nets. We direct a net from the output terminals to the input terminals as follows. We say that a net N *feeds* an input terminal t if the input terminal t is in N. We say that a net N is *fed* by an output terminal t if t is in N. Figure 11.4 depicts an output terminal that feeds a net and an input terminal that is fed by a net. The notion of feeding and being fed implies a direction according to which information flows, namely, information is supplied by output terminals and is consumed by input terminals.

From a physical point of view, direction of signals along nets is obtained in "pure" CMOS gates as follows. Output terminals are connected (via low resistance) to the ground or to the power (but not both!). Input terminals, conversely, are connected only to capacitors. To avoid conflicts between output terminals, we use only simple nets, defined next.

Simple Nets. The following definition captures the type of nets we would like to use. We call these nets *simple*.

Definition 11.8 A net N is *simple* if (i) N is fed by exactly one output terminal and (ii) N feeds at least one input terminal.

Figure 11.4. A terminal that is fed by a net and a terminal that feeds a net.

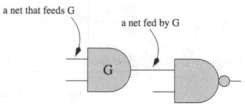

a net that feeds G

a net fed by G

G

A simple net N that is fed by the output terminal t and feeds the input terminals $\{t_i\}_{i \in I}$ can be modeled by the wires $\{w_i\}_{i \in I}$, where each wire w_i connects t and t_i. In fact, since information flows in one direction, we may regard each wire w_i as a directed edge $t \to t_i$. Hence we may model a simple net by a "star" of directed edges emanating from a common output terminal and entering input terminals.

11.5 COMBINATIONAL CIRCUITS

Let Γ denote a library of combinational gates that contains standard combinational gates such as an inverter, OR-gate, AND-gate, and so on. The library Γ contains a sub-library IO that contains two special types of gates: input gates (IN, x_i) and output gates (OUT, y_j).

Terminals in a Circuit. Suppose we want to design a circuit that contains two AND gates, three inputs, x_1, x_2, x_3, and two outputs, y_1, y_2, where $y_1 = $ AND(x_1, x_2) and $y_2 = $ AND(x_2, x_3). One way to describe the circuit is to draw a schematic as depicted in Figure 11.5. We would like to describe the circuit formally (a schematic is perhaps easy to read, but hard to argue about a circuit defined by a schematic).

First, we count the number of gates. We have, in total, $2 + 3 + 2 = 7$ gates (including the input and output gates). We define a set $V \triangleq \{v_i\}_{i=1}^{7}$ of nodes. Now, we need to assign a gate type to each node. We do this by defining a function $\pi : V \to \Gamma$. The function π is simply

$$\pi(v_1) = (\text{IN}, x_1), \pi(v_2) = (\text{IN}, x_2), \pi(v_3) = (\text{IN}, x_3),$$

$$\pi(v_4) = \pi(v_5) = \text{AND}, \tag{11.3}$$

$$\pi(v_6) = (\text{OUT}, y_1), \pi(v_7) = (\text{OUT}, y_2).$$

Both v_4 and v_5 are assigned AND-gates. An AND-gate has two input ports, called $in(\text{AND})_1$ and $in(\text{AND})_2$, and one output terminal, called $out(\text{AND})$. How can we distinguish between the input ports of v_4 and the input ports of v_5? We do this by giving family names to terminals. For example, the first input port of v_4 is called $(v_4, in(\text{AND})_1)$. This is a bit cumbersome but unambiguous.

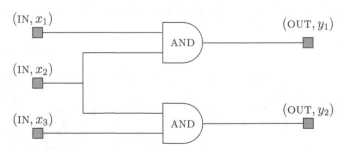

Figure 11.5. A combinational circuit.

In the case of input and output gates, we abbreviate and write (IN, x_i), instead of $out((\text{IN}, x_i))$. Similarly, we write (OUT, y_j), instead of $in((\text{OUT}, y_j))$.

We now generalize this example. Consider a set of nodes V and a function $\pi : V \to \Gamma$ assigns a gate type to each node.

Definition 11.9 The set of *terminals* of V with respect to π is defined as follows:

$$terminals(V, \pi) \triangleq \{(v, t) : v \in V, t \in terminals(\pi(v))\}.$$

Netlist. A netlist is a way to describe how gates are connected to each other.

Definition 11.10 A *netlist* is a tuple $H = (V, N, \pi)$, where V is a set of nodes, $\pi : V \to \Gamma$ assigns a gate type to each node, and N is a set of nets over $terminals(V, \pi)$. We require that the nets in N are pairwise disjoint.

We continue with the foregoing example. The netlist in this example is as follows. The set of nodes is $V \triangleq \{v_i\}_{i=1}^{7}$, and the function π is defined in Eq. 11.3. The set N of nets consists of the following nets:

$$\{(v_1, (\text{IN}, x_1)), (v_4, in(\text{AND})_1)\},$$

$$\{(v_2, (\text{IN}, x_2)), (v_4, in(\text{AND})_2), (v_5, in(\text{AND})_1)\},$$

$$\{(v_3, (\text{IN}, x_3)), (v_5, in(\text{AND})_2)\},$$

$$\{(v_4, out(\text{AND})), (v_6, (\text{OUT}, y_1))\},$$

$$\{(v_5, out(\text{AND})), (v_7, (\text{OUT}, y_2))\}.$$

The requirement that the nets are disjoint implies that each terminal may belong to at most net in N. We often use the term *circuit* for a netlist. In fact, a netlist is a formal way to describe a circuit.

In our foregoing example, the netlist tells us how to construct the circuit depicted in Figure 11.5. First, place seven gates according to the set V and the labeling function π. Now, all that remains to do is to solder the wires between the gates. Indeed, the soldering rules are dictated by the nets in N. We connect a wire between the input gate (IN, x_1) and the first input port of the AND-gate that corresponds to v_4, and so on.

A netlist with multiterminal nets is also called a *hypergraph*. We prefer to work with directed graphs. Indeed, this can be done if all nets are simple, as follows.

Graph Representation of a Netlist with Simple Nets. A netlist $H = (V, N, \pi)$ in which all nets are simple can be represented by a directed graph $DG(H) = (V, \tilde{N})$. Consider a net $n = \{t, t_1, \ldots, t_k\}$ in N with an output terminal t and input terminals $t_1, \ldots, t_k$. Suppose that t is a terminal of node v and t_i is a terminal of node v_i. This net n is represented in $\tilde{N}$ by the set of directed edges $\{(v, v_i)\}_{i=1}^{k}$.

Note that in our foregoing example, all the nets are simple. Hence the set $\tilde{N}$ in this example is as follows:

$$\tilde{N} = \{(v_1, v_4), (v_2, v_4), (v_2, v_5), (v_3, v_5), (v_4, v_6), (v_5, v_7)\}.$$

Note that the directed graph $DG(H)$ may have directed edges of the form (v, v); such edges are called *self-loops*. In addition, the directed graph $DG(H)$ may have

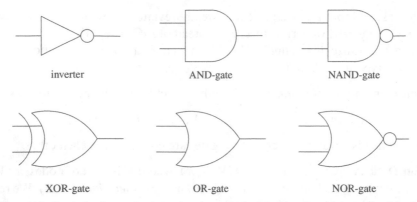

Figure 11.6. Symbols of common gates. Inputs are on the left side, outputs are on the right side.

parallel edges, that is, more than one edge may emanate from a node u and enter the same node v. For example, let us consider two combinational gates with multiple inputs and outputs. Connecting the outputs of one to the inputs of the other, by using simple nets, yields a directed graph with parallel edges between the corresponding nodes. Self-loops can be obtained by gates that their output is connected to their input. Such a circuit is *not* a combinational circuit, defined as follows.

Definition of Combinational Circuits.

Definition 11.11 A netlist $H = (V, N, \pi)$ is a *combinational circuit* if it satisfies the following conditions:

1. Every net in N is simple.
2. Every terminal in *terminals*(V, π) belongs to exactly one net in N.
3. The directed graph $DG(H)$ is acyclic.

One can easily check if a netlist $H = (V, N, \pi)$ is a combinational circuit. We need to check that the nets are simple, are pairwise disjoint, and contain all the terminals exactly once. In addition, we need to check that $DG(H)$ is acyclic. To check that the graph G is acyclic, one can try to sort the vertices in topological order. This procedure succeeds if and only if the graph is acyclic.

In many cases, a gate implements a commutative Boolean function (e.g., an AND-gate). In such cases, we may connect to either input terminals without modifying the functionality.

In a depiction of a combinational circuit, one often omits the orientation of the directed edges. The reason is that the orientation is implied—an edge emanates from an output terminal and enters an input terminal. In addition, one uses special symbols for different gate types. Thus, instead of writing the label $\pi(v)$ in the vertex v, one sometimes depicts the vertex by a symbol that represents $\pi(v)$. Figure 11.6 depicts the symbols used to depict common gates. In Figure 11.6, the input ports are on the left side and the output terminal is on the right side.

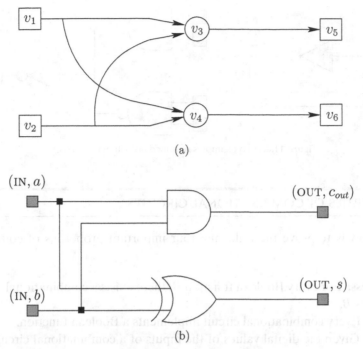

Figure 11.7. A half-adder combinational circuit and its matching DAG.

EXAMPLE

In Figure 11.7, a combinational circuit $C = (V, N, \pi)$ is depicted. This circuit is called a half-adder. Figure 11.7a depicts the graph G. Figure 11.7b depicts the graph G with the labels. Note that the labels are depicts using special symbols for each vertex. Edge directions are omitted in Figure 11.7b since they are implied.

The set of the combinational gates in this example is $\Gamma = \{$AND, XOR$\}$. The labeling function $\pi : V \to \Gamma$ is as follows:

$$\pi(v_1) = (\text{IN}, a),$$

$$\pi(v_2) = (\text{IN}, b),$$

$$\pi(v_3) = \text{AND},$$

$$\pi(v_4) = \text{XOR},$$

$$\pi(v_5) = (\text{OUT}, c_{out}),$$

$$\pi(v_6) = (\text{OUT}, s).$$

EXAMPLE

Consider the circuits depicted in Figure 11.8. Can you explain why these are not valid combinational circuits?

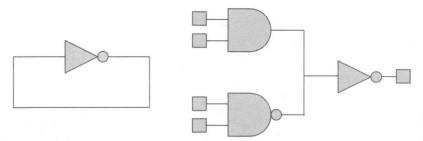

Figure 11.8. Two examples of noncombinational circuits.

11.6 PROPERTIES OF COMBINATIONAL CIRCUITS

Our goal now is to prove the following four important properties of combinational circuits.

Completeness: For every Boolean function B, there exists a combinational circuit that implements B.

Soundness: Every combinational circuit implements a Boolean function.

Simulation: Given the digital values of the inputs of a combinational circuit, one can simulate the circuit efficiently (the running time is linear in the size of the circuit). Namely, one can compute the digital values of the outputs of the circuit that are output by the circuit once the circuit becomes consistent.

Delay analysis: Given the propagation delays of all the gates in a combinational circuit, one can compute in linear time an upper bound on the propagation delay of the circuit.

The proof that these properties hold proceeds as follows. First, we present an algorithm for simulation and delay analysis. The correctness of this algorithm implies the property of soundness. We then prove completeness by presenting a simple algorithm that constructs a combinational circuit that implements a given Boolean formula.

11.7 SIMULATION AND DELAY ANALYSIS

In this section, we prove that combinational circuits are sound and can be simulated efficiently. In fact, soundness is proved by a simulation, namely, we prove that, in a combinational circuit, the stable signal along every wire is a Boolean function of the inputs of the circuit.

Assumption. To simplify the presentation, we assume that every combinational gate has a single output terminal and implements a commutative Boolean function. Moreover, we assume that the fan-in of combinational gates is one or two.

Consider a combinational circuit $C = (G, N, \pi)$. We identify a vertex v with its output terminal and denote the digital signal at the output terminal of v simply by $v(t)$. For an output gate v, we denote the digital signal at the input terminal of v also by $v(t)$. We assume that C has k input gates named (IN, x_i), for $1 \le i \le k$. To simplify notation, we use $\vec{x}(t)$ to denote the vector $x_1(t), \ldots, x_k(t)$.

Theorem 11.2 (*Simulation Theorem of Combinational Circuits*) *Assume that the digital signals $\{x_i(t)\}_{i=1}^k$ are stable during the interval $[t_1, t_2]$. Then, for every vertex $v \in V$, there exist*

1. *A Boolean function $f_v : \{0,1\}^k \to \{0,1\}$*
2. *A propagation delay $t_{pd}(v)$*

such that $v(t) = f_v(\vec{x}(t))$ for every $t \in [t_1 + t_{pd}(v), t_2]$.

Note the difference between $t_{pd}(v)$ and $t_{pd}(\pi(v))$. The propagation delay $t_{pd}(\pi(v))$ refers to the delay of a single gate of type $\pi(v)$. This delay is measured with respect to the input of the gate. Conversely, the propagation delay $t_{pd}(v)$ refers to the delay of the output of v with respect to the input gates of the circuit C.

We prove the simulation theorem by presenting algorithm $\text{SIM}(C, \vec{x})$ (a listing appears as Algorithm 11.1). The algorithm computes the value of $f_v(\vec{x})$ and the propagation delays $t_{pd}(v)$. We prove later that for all $v \in V$, $v(t) = f_v(\vec{x})$ during the interval $[t_1 + t_{pd}(v), t_2]$. The algorithm first sorts the vertices in topological order. We rename the vertices so that v_i is the vertex given the ith position in the topological ordering. Without

---

Algorithm 11.1 $\text{SIM}(C, \vec{x})$—An algorithm for simulating the combinational circuit $C = (V, N, \pi)$ with respect an input vector $\vec{x}$.

$(v_1, v_2, \ldots, v_n) \leftarrow TS(DG(C))$ {topological sorting of $DG(C)$}

For $i = 1$ to n do

switch $deg_{in}(v_i)$

case $deg_{in}(v_i) = 0$: $\{\pi(v_i) = (\text{IN}, x_j)\}$

- Let x_j denote the name of v_i before topological sorting.
- Set $f_{v_i}(\vec{x}) \triangleq x_j$ and $t_{pd}(v_i) \triangleq 0$.

case $deg_{in}(v_i) = 1$:

If $\{\pi(v_i) = \text{NOT}\}$, then

- Let $v_j \longrightarrow v_i$ denote the arc that enters v_i.
- Set $f_{v_i}(\vec{x}) = \text{NOT}(f_{v_j}(\vec{x}))$ and $t_{pd}(v_i) = t_{pd}(v_j) + t_{pd}(\text{NOT})$.

If $\{\pi(v_i) = (\text{OUT}, y)\}$, then

- Let $v_j \longrightarrow v_i$ denote the arc that enters v_i.
- Set $f_{v_i}(\vec{x}) = f_{v_j}(\vec{x})$ and $t_{pd}(v_i) = t_{pd}(v_j)$.

case $deg_{in}(v_i) = 2$:

- Let $v_j \longrightarrow v_i$ and $v_k \longrightarrow v_i$ denote the arcs that enter v_i.
- Set $f_{v_i}(\vec{x}) = B_{\pi(v_i)}(f_{v_j}(\vec{x}), f_{v_k}(\vec{x}))$, and $t_{pd}(v_i) = \max\{t_{pd}(v_j), t_{pd}(v_k)\} + t_{pd}(\pi(v_i))$.

---

loss of generality, the sources appear first in the topological ordering so that $v_i = x_i$ for $1 \le i \le k$. The algorithm scans the vertices in this order. Source vertices are the easiest. Each source vertex v_i equals x_i. So f_{v_i} simply equals x_i, and the propagation delay of an input gate is zero. Suppose that the in-degree of the next vertex v_i is one. In this case, v_i is either an output gate or an inverter. If v_i is an output gate, then let v_j denote the gate that feeds v_i. Clearly $f_{v_i} = f_{v_j}$ and $t_{pd}(v_i) = t_{pd}(v_j)$. If v_i is an inverter, then it outputs the negation of its input. The propagation delay of the v_i is the propagation delay of the vertex that feeds the inverter plus the propagation delay of the inverter itself. Finally, a vertex v_i whose in-degree equals two is treated as follows. We apply the local Boolean function $f_{\pi(v_i)}$ to the values of its inputs. The propagation delay equals the maximum propagation delay of the gates that fed v_i plus the propagation delay of $\pi(v_i)$.

PROOF OF THEOREM 11.2: We prove that Algorithm SIM$(C, \vec{x})$ computes correct functionalities f_{v_i} and propagation delays $t_{pd}(v_i)$. By correct, we mean that

$$\forall i \in [1..n] \; \forall \vec{x} \in \{0,1\}^k \; \forall t \in [t_1 + t_{pd}(v_i), t_2] \; : \; v_i(t) = f_{v_i}(\vec{x}). \tag{11.4}$$

The proof is by complete induction on i, the index of a vertex after topological sorting takes place. We assume that topological ordering orders the sources first, namely, $v_i = x_i$, for $1 \le i \le k$. In Lemma 11.3, this assumption is justified.

Induction Basis. Recall that the first k nets are the input signals, hence $v_i(t) = x_i(t)$, if $i \le k$. The algorithm sets $f_{v_i}(\vec{x}(t)) = x_i(t)$ and the propagation delay $t_{pd}(v_i)$ is zero.
The induction basis follows for $i \le k$.

Induction Step. We assume that Eq. 11.4 holds for every j, provided that $j < i$, and prove it for i. Since $i > k$, the vertex v_i is not a source. By our assumption, its in-degree is either one or two.

If $deg_{in}(v_i) = 1$, then $\pi(v_i) = $ NOT. Let v_j the vertex such that (v_j, v_i) is the arc that enters v_i. Since the vertices are topologically sorted, it follows that $j < i$. Hence we may apply the induction hypothesis to v_j. The induction hypothesis states that $v_j(t) = f_{v_j}(\vec{x}(t))$ during the interval $[t_1 + t_{pd}(v_j), t_2]$. Thus the input to v_i is stable during the interval $[t_1 + t_{pd}(v_j), t_2]$. Since v_j is a combinational gate, this implies that its output is consistent with $B_{\pi(v_i)}$ during the interval $[t_1 + t_{pd}(v_j) + t_{pd}(\text{NOT}), t_2]$. Thus $v_i(t) = \text{NOT}(v_j(t))$ during this interval, and Eq. 11.4 holds for i.

If $deg_{in}(v_i) = 2$, then let v_j and v_k denote the two vertices such that (v_j, v_i) and (v_k, v_i) are the arcs that enter v_i. Since the vertices are topologically sorted, it follows that $j, k < i$. Hence we may apply the induction hypothesis to v_j and v_k. The induction hypothesis states that $v_j(t) = f_{v_j}(\vec{x}(t))$ during the interval $[t_1 + t_{pd}(v_j), t_2]$. Similarly, $v_k(t) = f_{v_k}(\vec{x}(t))$ during the interval $[t_1 + t_{pd}(v_k), t_2]$. Thus both inputs to v_i are stable during the interval $[t_1 + \max\{t_{pd}(v_j), t_{pd}(v_k)\}, t_2]$. Since v_j is a combinational gate, this implies that its output is consistent with $B_{\pi(v_i)}$ during the interval $[t_1 + \max\{t_{pd}(v_j), t_{pd}(v_k)\} + t_{pd}(\pi(v_i)), t_2]$. Thus $v_i(t) = B_{\pi(v_i)}(v_j(t), v_k(t))$ during this interval. We conclude that Eq. 11.4 holds for i, and the induction step follows. ∎

Recall that a DAG may have more than one topological ordering. The following lemma shows that Algorithm SIM$(C, \vec{x})$ outputs the same results independent of the topological ordering computed in the first line.

Lemma 11.3 *The output of* $SIM(C, \vec{x})$ *does not depend on the topological ordering computed by* $TS(G)$.

PROOF: Consider two topological orderings. The first one, $(v_1, \ldots, v_n)$, is specific in the sense that $v_i = x_i$ for $i \leq k$. Namely, the input gates appear first. The second ordering $(u_1, \ldots, u_n)$ is arbitrary. We consider two executions of Algorithm $SIM(C, \vec{x})$: In the first execution, Algorithm TS computed the topological ordering $(v_1, \ldots, v_n)$. In the second execution, Algorithm TS computed the topological ordering $(u_1, \ldots, u_n)$. It suffices to prove that in both executions, $SIM(C, \vec{x})$ computes the same functionalities and propagation delays. The proof is by complete induction on i, the index of a vertex in the second ordering $(u_1, \ldots, u_n)$.

The induction basis for $i = 1$ holds because u_1 is a source and therefore an input gate. This means that $u_i = v_j$ for some $j \leq k$. Therefore, in the second execution, $f_{u_1}(\vec{x}) = x_j$ and $t_{pd}(u_1) = 0$. It follows that the second execution agrees with the first execution, as required.

The induction step is proved as follows:

1. If u_i is a source, then the proof is identical to the proof of the induction basis.
2. If $deg_{in}(u_i) = 1$, then let $u_j \longrightarrow u_i$ denote the incoming edge. Since the vertices are sorted in topological order, $j < i$. The induction hypothesis implies that both execution agree on the functionality and propagation delay of u_j. It follows that they also agree on the functionality of u_i.
3. If $deg_{in}(u_i) = 2$, then let $u_j \longrightarrow u_i$ and $u_k \longrightarrow u_i$ denote the incoming edges. Since the vertices are sorted in topological order, $j, k < i$. The induction hypothesis implies that both execution agree on the functionality and propagation delay of u_j and u_k. It follows that they also agree on the functionality of u_i. ■

An important interpretation of Theorem 11.2 is that it enables us to regard a combinational circuit as a macrogate. This macrogate computes a Boolean function $B: \{0,1\}^k \to \{0,1\}^\ell$, where k denotes the number of input gates and ℓ denotes the number of output gates. All instances of the same combinational circuit implement the same Boolean function and have the same propagation delay.

Corollary 11.4 (*Soundness*) *Every combinational circuit implements a Boolean function.*

PROOF: Consider a combinational circuit C with k input gates and ℓ output gates. Let x_i denote the ith input gate, and let y_i denote the ith output gate. Let $t_{pd}(C) \triangleq \max_{v \in V}\{t_{pd}(v)\}$. By Theorem 11.2, $y_i(t) = f_{y_i}(\vec{x})$ during the interval $[t_1 + t_{pd}(C), t_2]$. Thus C implements the Boolean function $f: \{0,1\}^k \to \{0,1\}^\ell$, defined by

$$f(\vec{x}) \triangleq (f_{y_1}(\vec{x}), \ldots, f_{y_\ell}(\vec{x})). \quad ■$$

Remarks

1. The computation of the values $f_{v_i}(\vec{x})$ by Algorithm $SIM(C, \vec{x})$ is actually identical to the evaluation of the truth value of a Boolean formula (see Algorithm 6.2 $EVAL(G, \pi, \tau)$). One could rewrite algorithm $EVAL(G, \pi, \tau)$ so that instead of employing recursion, it runs as follows: scan the vertices according to a topological order, and evaluate the output of each vertex v as the Boolean function $B_{\pi(v)}$ applied to the values that enter v.

2. The computation of the propagation delays is, in fact, a computation of longest paths in DAGs with nonunit delays. Assume that each vertex v has a delay $\delta(v) \geq 0$. (In our case, sources and sinks have zero delay, but we can deal with the general case just the same.) The delay of a path p is defined by $d(p) \triangleq \sum_{v \in p} \delta(v)$. Algorithm 11.2 computes the longest delay of paths in a DAG. It is a straightforward generalization of Algorithm 4.2. Note that the computation of the propagation delays by Algorithm $SIM(C, \bar{x})$ follows the same method.

Algorithm 11.2 weighted-longest-path-lengths(V, E, δ)—an algorithm for computing the longest delays of paths in a DAG. Returns a delay function $d(v)$.

(a) topological sort: $(v_0, \ldots, v_{n-1}) \leftarrow TS(V, E)$.
(b) For $j = 0$ to $(n - 1)$ do
    i. If v_j is a source then $d(v_j) \leftarrow \delta(v_j)$.
    ii. Else

$$d(v_j) = \delta(v_j) + \max\left\{ d(v_i) \mid i < j \text{ and } (v_i, v_j) \in E \right\}.$$

---

3. The running time of the Algorithm $SIM(C, \bar{x})$ is linear in the number of gates in C. Indeed, we perform a constant amount of work per vertex.
4. We do not rule out the usage of constants as inputs. In this case, we add the possibility for input gates labeled $(\text{IN}, 0)$ and $(\text{IN}, 1)$. Such an input gate feeds a constant to the circuit. Algorithm 11.1 needs to be modified to handle constant inputs. Namely, the case that v_i is a source has to be split to a constant input and a variable input.

11.8 COMPLETENESS

Theorems 6.6 and 9.2 state that the set $\{\neg, \text{OR}, \text{AND}\}$ of logical connectives is complete. Therefore every Boolean function $B : \{0, 1\}^n \to \{0, 1\}$ can be represented by a Boolean formula φ. To complete the proof of completeness, we need to show that every Boolean formula can be implemented by a combinational circuit.

The case that B is a constant Boolean function is handled quite easily. Simply construct a combinational gate with one input gate that feeds one output gate. Let the input gate output a constant, and we are done. Thus we focus on the case that B is not a constant Boolean function. In this case, by Theorem 9.2, the Boolean formula φ is a sum of minterms and therefore lacks constants. Thus we focus on the construction of a combinational circuit C_φ that implements the function B_φ, where φ is a Boolean formula in which the constants $\{0, 1\}$ do not appear.

Note that the key difference between a formula and a Boolean circuit is that multiple leaves may be labeled by the same variable in a parse tree. For example, in the parse tree depicted in Figure 11.9, there are two leaves that are labeled by X_1.

Our proof uses an operation of merging (or coalescing) of vertices in a directed graph defined as follows.

Definition 11.12 Let $G = (V, E)$ denote a directed graph, and let $X \subseteq V$ denote a nonempty set of vertices. The graph $G_X = (V', E')$ obtained by *merging* the vertices

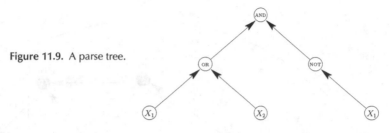

Figure 11.9. A parse tree.

in X is defined as follows (the new merged vertex is denoted by x, so we assume that $x \notin V$):

$$V' \triangleq (V \setminus X) \cup \{x\}$$

$$E' \triangleq (E \setminus \{e \mid e \text{ enters or emanates from a vertex in } X\})$$
$$\cup \{(u, x) \mid \exists v \in X : (u, v) \in E\} \cup \{(x, u) \mid \exists v \in X : (v, u) \in E\}.$$

EXAMPLE

Consider the DAG $G = (V, E)$ depicted in Figure 11.10.

In this example, the graph $G_X = (V', E')$ obtained by merging the vertices in $X = \{v_3, v_4, v_5, v_6\}$. The edges that enter or emanate from a vertex in X are in the set

$$\{e_2, e_3, e_4, e_5, e_6, e_8, e_9, e_{10}, e_{11}\}.$$

The new edges are in the set $\{e_2', e_3', e_9', e_{10}', e_{11}'\}$. In this example, the set X is not a set of sources. In general, merging of an arbitrary set of vertices may lead to a cyclic graph, for example, $G_{\{v_2, v_7\}}$ is cyclic since it contains the cycle $x \to v_4 \to v_6 \to x$.

Claim 11.5 *If $G = (V, E)$ is a DAG and X is a subset of sources, then the graph G_X is also a DAG.*

PROOF: Since X contains only sources, the vertex x in G_X is also a source. Therefore a cycle in G_X does not contain x. Conversely, any path p in G_X that does not traverse x is also a path in G. Since G is acyclic, such a path p cannot be closed. ∎

Consider a Boolean formula φ that is generated by a parse tree (G, π), where $G = (V, E)$. We construct the combinational circuit C_φ as follows.

Definition 11.13 The combinational circuit $C_\varphi = (V', N', \pi')$ is defined as follows. Construct the directed graph $G' = (V', E')$ as follows:

1. For each $1 \leq i \leq n$, merge all sources in G labeled X_i into one new source vertex u_i and define $\pi'(u_i) \triangleq (\text{IN}, x_i)$.
2. Add a new vertex y labeled $\pi'(y) \triangleq (\text{OUT}, y)$ and an arc form the root of G to y, that is, add the arc $r(G) \longrightarrow y$.

The nets in N are defined as follows. For each node u, define the net N_u by

$$N_u \triangleq \{u\} \cup \{v : (u, v) \in E'\}.$$

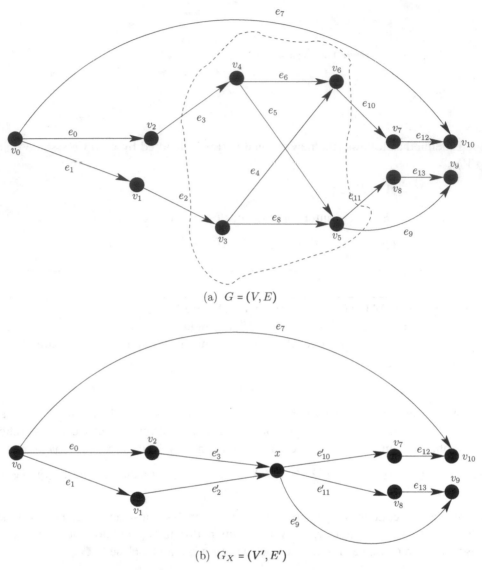

Figure 11.10. The merging operation on DAGs. The set X is bordered by a dashed line.

We chose an imprecise definition of the net N_u to avoid cumbersome notation. Note that N_u is a subset of nodes instead of terminals. One could replace u by the unique output port of u. However, defining the input terminals in N_u requires some work. Note that there can be two edges entering v in E'. Which input terminal is fed by which edge? Luckily, it does not matter as long as the node is assigned a commutative Boolean function. One should just make sure that the two edges are connected to distinct input terminals. Thus the definition of N_u can be fixed by employing a one-to-one correspondence between incoming edges and input ports for each node.

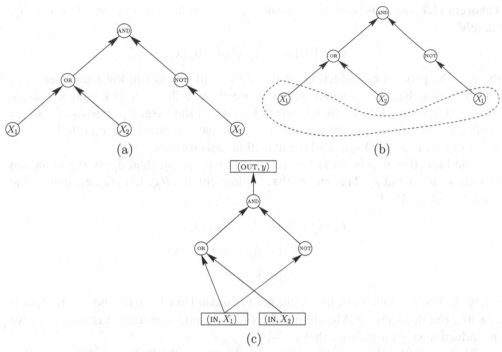

Figure 11.11. The combinational circuit C_φ: (a) the parse tree of φ, (G, π), (b) the dashed line borders the sources labeled by X_1, and (c) these sources are merged to a single source vertex. The source labeled by x_2 is merged to a single source as well. The labels of these merged sources are (IN, x_1) and (IN, x_2). An additional vertex (OUT, y) is added and connected by an arc to $r(G)$.

EXAMPLE

Consider the parse tree depicted in Figure 11.11a. In this example, the Boolean formula is $\varphi = ((X_1 \vee X_2) \cdot \wedge \neg X_1)$. The combinational circuit C_φ is derived from the parse tree (G, π) depicted in Figure 11.11a, as follows. We merge the bordered sources that are labeled by X_1. The source labeled by X_2 is also merged. The labels of these merged sources are (IN, X_1) and (IN, X_2), respectively. An additional vertex is added (OUT, y). That vertex is connected by an arc to $r(G)$. Note that the labeling function π is augmented so that it is defined over all the vertices of C_φ.

Claim 11.6 C_φ *is a combinational circuit.*

PROOF: By Claim 11.5, the merging of the sources labeled X_i keeps the graph acyclic. The root $G(r)$ is a sink in G; therefore connecting it to the new sink y does not introduce a cycle. Note also that all terminals belong to exactly one net and that the nets are all simple. ∎

To complete the proof of completeness, we need to show that C_φ implements the same Boolean function B_φ that is represented by φ. Note that the signal that enters the output gate y is output by $r(G)$.

Theorem 11.7 *The combinational circuit C_φ implements the Boolean function B_φ, namely,*

$$\forall \vec{x} \in \{0,1\}^n \; : \; f_{r(G)}(\vec{x}) = B_\varphi(\vec{x}).$$

PROOF: The proof is by induction on the number of vertices in the parse tree of φ. The induction basis for a single vertex proceeds as follows. If G contains a single vertex $r(G)$, then it labeled by a variable, say, X_i. In this case, C_φ consists of a single input gate labeled (IN, x_i) connected to the output gate labeled (OUT, y). It follows that $f_{r(G)}(\vec{x}) = x_i$. But $B_\varphi(\vec{x}) = x_i$, and the induction basis follows.

The induction step is proved as follows. If $\varphi - \varphi_1 \circ \varphi_2$, then apply the induction hypothesis to φ_1 and φ_2. This means that C_{φ_i} implements B_{φ_i}. Let (G_i, π_i) denote the parse tree of φ_i. Then

$$B_\varphi(\vec{x}) = B_\circ(B_{\varphi_1}(\vec{x}), B_{\varphi_2}(\vec{x}))$$
$$= B_\circ(f_{r(G_1)}(\vec{x}), f_{r(G_2)}(\vec{x})$$
$$= f_{r(G)}(\vec{x}),$$

where the first line follows from Lemma 6.3, the second line from the induction hypothesis, and the third line by Algorithm $\text{SIM}(C, \vec{x})$. A similar argument is used to prove the induction step for the case that $\varphi = \neg\varphi_1$.

We remark that there is one subtle point that we omitted. One needs to show that the simulations $\text{SIM}(C_\varphi, \vec{x})$ and $\text{SIM}(C_{\varphi_i}, \vec{x})$ agree on the value of $f_{r(G_i)}(\vec{x})$. This can be shown as follows. By Lemma 11.3, we may assume that in the execution of $\text{SIM}(C_\varphi, \vec{x})$, the topological ordering puts all the vertices of G_{φ_i} first. Thus both executions agree while scanning the vertices of G_{φ_i}. ∎

11.9 COST AND PROPAGATION DELAY

In this section, we define the cost and propagation delay of a combinational circuit. Throughout this section, let $C = (V, N, \pi)$ denote a combinational circuit.

Let $c : \Gamma \to \mathbb{R}^{\geq 0}$ denote a cost function. Usually, input gates and output gates have zero cost.

Definition 11.14 The cost of C is defined by

$$c(C) \triangleq \sum_{v \in V} c(\pi(v)).$$

Recall that the propagation delays $t_{pd}(v)$ are computed by Algorithm $\text{SIM}(C, \vec{x})$.

Definition 11.15 The propagation delay of C is defined by

$$t_{pd}(C) \triangleq \max_{v \in V} t_{pd}(v).$$

We often refer to the propagation delay of a combinational circuit as its *depth* or simply its *delay*.

Table 11.1. Costs and delays of gates

Gate	Motorola		Venus	
	cost	delay	cost	delay
INV	1	1	1	1
AND, OR	2	2	2	1
NAND, NOR	2	1	2	1
XOR, NXOR	4	2	6	2
MUX	3	2	3	2

Definition 11.16 The propagation delay of a path p in G is defined as

$$t_{pd}(p) \triangleq \sum_{v \in p} t_{pd}(\pi(v)).$$

The following claim states that Algorithm $\text{SIM}(C, \bar{x})$ computes the largest delay of a path in G.

Claim 11.8

$$t_{pd}(C) = \max \{t_{pd}(p) \mid p \text{ is a path in } G\}.$$

PROOF: Follows the proof of Theorem 4.5. ∎

Definition 11.17 Let $C = (V, N, \pi)$ denote a combinational circuit. A path p in C is *critical* if $t_{pd}(p) = t_{pd}(C)$.

We focus on critical paths that are maximal (i.e., cannot be further augmented). This means that maximal critical paths begin in an input gate and end in an output gate.

11.10 EXAMPLE: RELATIVE GATE COSTS AND DELAY

Müller and Paul compiled a table of costs and delays of gates (Mueller and Paul 1996). These figures were obtained by considering ASIC libraries of two technologies and normalizing them with respect to the cost and delay of an inverter. They referred to these technologies as Motorola and Venus. Table 11.1 summarizes the normalized costs and delays in these technologies according to Müller and Paul.

11.11 SEMANTICS AND SYNTAX

The term *semantics* (in our context) refers to the function that a circuit implements. Synonyms for semantics of a circuit are *functionality* or even the *behavior* of the circuit. In general, the semantics of a circuit is a formal description that relates the outputs of the circuit to the inputs of the circuit (including timing). In the case of combinational circuits, the simulation theorem implies that semantics are described by Boolean functions. Note that in noncombinational circuits, the output depends not only on the current inputs, so semantics cannot be described simply by a Boolean function.

The term *syntax* refers to a formal set of rules that govern how "grammatically correct" circuits are constructed from smaller circuits (just as sentences are built by combining words). In the syntactic definition of combinational circuits, the functionality (or gate type) of each gate is not important. The only part that matters is that the rules for connecting gates together are followed. Following syntax in itself does not guarantee that the resulting circuit is useful. Following syntax is, in fact, a restriction that we are willing to accept so that we can enjoy the benefits of well-defined functionality, simple simulation, and simple timing analysis. The restriction of following syntax rules is a reasonable choice since every Boolean function can be implemented by a syntactically correct combinational circuit.

In this chapter, we defined *design rules* for building combinational circuits. These design rules define syntactically correct circuits. Our main result is that syntactically correct circuits, called combinational circuits, can implement any Boolean function. We are now left with the following design task: given a Boolean function B, design a combinational circuit C that implements B such that the delay and cost of C is as small as possible.

11.12 SUMMARY

Combinational circuits are formally defined in this chapter. We started by considering the basic building blocks: gates and wires. Gates are simply implementations of Boolean functions. The digital abstraction enables a simple definition of what it means to implement a Boolean function B. Given a propagation delay t_{pd} and stable inputs whose digital value is $\vec{x}$, the digital values of the outputs of a gate equal $B(\vec{x})$ after t_{pd} time elapses.

Wires are used to connect terminals together. Bunches of wires are used to connect multiple terminals to each other and are called *nets*. Simple nets are nets in which the direction in which information flows is well defined: from a single output terminal of a gate to input terminals of gates.

The formal definition of combinational circuits turns out to be most useful. It is a syntactic definition that only depends on the topology of the circuit, namely, how the terminals of the gates are connected. One can check in linear time whether a given circuit is indeed a combinational circuit. Even though the definition ignores functionality, one can compute in linear time the digital signals of every wire in the circuit. Moreover, one can also compute in linear time the propagation delay of every net with respect to the circuit inputs.

Two quality measures are defined for every combinational circuit: cost and propagation delay. The cost of a combinational circuit is the sum of the costs of the gates in the circuit. The propagation delay of a combinational is the maximum delay of a path in the circuit.

PROBLEMS

11.1. Does every collection of combinational gates and wires constitute a combinational circuit?

11.2. Which of these tasks is easy?
(a) Check if a circuit is combinational.
(b) Simulate a combinational circuit.
(c) Estimate the propagation delay of a combinational circuit for an arbitrary input.

11.3. Describe a combinational circuit with n gates that has at least $2^{n/2-1}$ paths. Can you describe a circuit with 2^n different paths?

11.4. In Claim 11.8 the propagation delay of a combinational circuit is claimed to equal the maximum delay of a path in the circuit. The number of paths can be exponential in n. Does this mean that we cannot compute the propagation delay of a combinational circuit in linear time?

11.5. Suggest criteria for comparing functionally equivalent combinational circuits. For example, suppose C_1 and C_2 are 32-bit adders. Which circuit should we use as an adder?

11.6*. For a Boolean function f, let $c^*(f)$ denote the minimum cost of a combinational circuit that implements f.

Prove that for every n, there exists a Boolean function $f : \{0, 1\}^n \to \{0, 1\}$ such that $c^*(f) \geq \frac{2^n}{4n}$.

Can you extend your proof to show this lower bound for most Boolean functions? (Assume that a combinational circuit uses only gates with two inputs and that the cost of all gates is one.)

CHAPTER 12

Trees

Consider the problem of designing a circuit that computes the OR of n bits. A natural approach for solving this problem is to partition the bits into pairs, compute the OR of each pair, and continue recursively until we are left with one bit—the result. The underlying graph, or topology, of the combinational circuit we obtain is a rooted tree. Is this the best design? In this chapter, we prove that indeed, this is the case.

We consider this question in a more general setting. First, we define a class of functions for which the preceding problem can be easily formulated. This is the class of associative Boolean functions. Second, we define a combinational circuit with a topology of a rooted tree, all gates of which are identical.

We prove two lower bounds: one for cost and one for delay. These lower bounds do not assume that topology of the circuits is a rooted tree. The lower bounds prove that rooted trees have optimal cost and that balanced rooted trees have optimal delay.

12.1 ASSOCIATIVE BOOLEAN FUNCTIONS

Definition 12.1 A Boolean function $f : \{0, 1\}^2 \to \{0, 1\}$ is *associative* if

$$f(f(\sigma_1, \sigma_2), \sigma_3) = f(\sigma_1, f(\sigma_2, \sigma_3))$$

for every $\sigma_1, \sigma_2, \sigma_3 \in \{0, 1\}$.

A Boolean function defined over the domain $\{0, 1\}^2$ is often denoted by a dyadic operator, say, $*$. Namely, $f(\sigma_1, \sigma_2)$ is denoted by $\sigma_1 * \sigma_2$. Associativity of a Boolean function $*$ is then formulated by

$$\forall \sigma_1, \sigma_2, \sigma_3 \in \{0, 1\} : (\sigma_1 * \sigma_2) * \sigma_3 = \sigma_1 * (\sigma_2 * \sigma_3).$$

This implies that one may omit parentheses from expressions involving an associative Boolean function and simply write $\sigma_1 * \sigma_2 * \sigma_3$. Thus we obtain a function defined over $\{0, 1\}^n$ from a dyadic Boolean function. We formalize this composition of functions as follows:

Definition 12.2 Let $f : \{0, 1\}^2 \to \{0, 1\}$ denote a Boolean function. The function $f_n : \{0, 1\}^n \to \{0, 1\}$, for $n \geq 1$, is defined recursively as follows:

1. If $n = 1$, then $f_1(x) = x$.
2. If $n = 2$, then $f_2 = f$.
3. If $n > 2$, then f_n is defined based on f_{n-1} as follows:

$$f_n(x_1, x_2, \ldots x_n) \triangleq f(f_{n-1}(x_1, \ldots, x_{n-1}), x_n).$$

If $f(x_1, x_2)$ is an associative Boolean function, then one could define f_n in many equivalent ways, as summarized in the following claim.

Claim 12.1 *If $f : \{0, 1\}^2 \to \{0, 1\}$ is an associative Boolean function, then*

$$f_n(x_1, x_2, \ldots x_n) = f(f_{n-k}(x_1, \ldots, x_{n-k}), f_k(x_{n-k+1}, \ldots, x_n))$$

for every $n \geq 2$ and $k \in [1, n - 1]$.

PROOF: The proof is by double induction on n and k. The induction basis for $n = 2$ is proved as follows. Since $n = 2$ and $k \in [1, n-1]$, it follows that $k = 1$. Therefore the claim simply states that

$$f_2(x_1, x_2) = f(f_1(x_1), f_1(x_2)).$$

But $f_1(x_i) = x_i$, and the induction basis holds.

The induction step is proved as follows. Let $n \geq 3$. Assume the claim holds for all $n' < n$. We wish to prove the claim for n. We now apply induction on k. The induction basis for $k = 1$ holds because this is the definition of f_n. We now prove the induction step for $k + 1 < n$. Let

$$F_{i,j} \triangleq f_{j-i+1}(x_i, \ldots, x_j).$$

In this notation, the induction hypothesis states that for every $n' < n$ and every $k' \leq k$,

$$F_{1,n'} = f(F_{1,n'-k'}, F_{n'-k'+1,n'}).$$

In the induction step, we need to prove that

$$F_{1,n} = f(F_{1,n-(k+1)}, F_{n-(k+1)+1,n}).$$

But

$$\begin{aligned}
f(F_{1,n-(k+1)}, F_{n-(k+1)+1,n}) &= f(F_{1,n-(k+1)}, f(F_{n-(k+1)+1,n-1}, x_n)) \\
&= f(f(F_{1,n-(k+1)}, F_{n-(k+1)+1,n-1}), x_n) \\
&= f(F_{1,n-1}, x_n) \\
&= F_{1,n}.
\end{aligned}$$

The first line follows from $F_{n-(k+1)+1,n} = f(F_{n-(k+1)+1,n-1}, x_n))$. The justification for this is the definition of f_{k+1}. The second line follows by applying associativity of f. The third line follows by the induction hypothesis for $n' = n - 1$ and $k' = k$. The last line follows from the definition of f_n. ∎

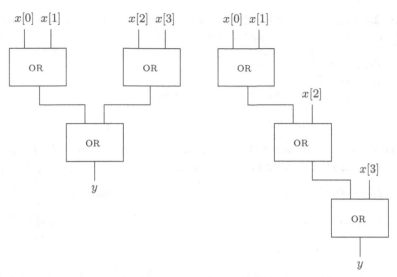

Figure 12.1. Two implementations of an OR-tree(n) with $n = 4$ inputs.

12.2 TREES OF ASSOCIATIVE BOOLEAN GATES

In this section, we deal with combinational circuits that have a topology of a tree. All the gates in the circuits we consider are instances of the same gate, which implements an associative Boolean function. To simplify the presentation, we consider only the Boolean function OR_n. The discussion for the other three nontrivial associative functions is analogous.

Definition 12.3 A combinational circuit $C = (G, \pi)$ that satisfies the following conditions is called an OR-tree(n).

1. *Topology.* The graph G is a rooted tree with n sources.
2. Each vertex v in G that is not a source or a sink is labeled $\pi(v) = OR$.

Figure 12.1 depicts two OR-tree(n) for $n = 4$. The following claim states that these trees implement the same Boolean function.

Claim 12.2 *Every OR-tree(n) implements the Boolean function OR_n.*

PROOF: The proof is by complete induction on n. For the purpose of the proof, we define $OR_1(x) \triangleq x$. The induction basis for $n = 1$ and $n = 2$ is trivial. The proof of the induction step relies on Claim 4.7, which decomposes a rooted tree. Let $C = (G, \pi)$ denote an OR-tree(n) for $n > 2$. The root $r(G)$ is an output gate. Let v denote the child of $r(G)$. Since C is an OR-tree, $\pi(v) = OR$. Consider the two rooted trees G_1 and G_2 hanging from v. Let $C_i = (G_i, \pi_i)$ denote the subcircuit that corresponds to G_i. Note that the root of G_i is an OR-gate, so we attach its output to a new root that is labeled as an output gate. The labeling π_i keeps all the labels assigned by π to the leaves and the internal nodes. Hence leaves are labeled as input gates, and internal nodes (except for the new roots) are labeled as OR-gates. Let n_i denote the number of leaves in G_i. Note that $n_i > 0$ and

$n_1 + n_2 = n$, therefore $n_1 < n$. The induction hypothesis states that C_i implements the function OR_{n_i}. This implies that the output y of C equals

$$y = OR(OR_{n_1}(x_1, \ldots, x_{n_1}), OR_{n_2}(x_{n_1+1}, \ldots, x_n)).$$

By Claim 12.1, $y = OR_n(x_1, \ldots, x_n)$, as required. ∎

12.2.1 Cost Analysis

You may have noticed that both OR-trees depicted in Figure 12.1 contain three OR-gates. However, their delay is different. The following claim summarizes the fact that all OR-trees have the same cost. Recall that we use the convention that input gates and output gates have zero cost.

Claim 12.3 *The cost of every* OR-*tree*(n) *is* $(n-1) \cdot c(OR)$.

PROOF: The proof is by complete induction on n. The induction basis for $n = 2$ follows because OR-tree(2) contains a single OR-gate. (What about the case $n = 1$?)

We now prove the induction step. The proof is similar to the proof of the induction step in Claim 12.2. Let $C = (G, \pi)$ denote an OR-tree(n) for $n > 2$. Let $C_i = (G_i, \pi_i)$ denote the subcircuit generated by (i) the subtree G_i hanging from child v of the root of G and (ii) the labeling π_i. We attach a new root to G_i that is labeled as an output gate. Let n_i denote the number of leaves in G_i. Note that $n_1 + n_2 = n$. The induction hypothesis states that $c(C_1) = (n_1 - 1) \cdot c(OR)$ and $c(C_2) = (n_2 - 1) \cdot c(OR)$. We conclude that

$$c(C) = c(v) + c(C_1) + c(C_2)$$
$$= (1 + n_1 - 1 + n_2 - 1) \cdot c(OR)$$
$$= (n - 1) \cdot c(OR),$$

and the claim follows. ∎

In fact, Claim 12.3 is a restatement of the well-known relationship between the number of leaves and interior nodes of in-degree two in rooted binary trees.

Lemma 12.4 *Let* $G = (V, E)$ *denote a rooted tree in which the in-degree of each vertex is at most two. Then*

$$|\{v \in V \mid \deg_{in}(v) = 2\}| = |\{v \in V \mid \deg_{in}(v) = 0\}| - 1.$$

PROOF: The proof is almost identical to the proof of Claim 12.3. The only difference is in the induction when the root of the subtree has an in-degree that equals one. In this case, we apply the induction hypothesis to the subtree hanging from this root. ∎

12.2.2 Delay Analysis

The delay of an OR-tree(n) is simply the number of OR-gates along the longest path from an input to an output times the delay of an OR-gate. In terms of rooted trees, depth is defined as follows.

Definition 12.4 The *depth* of a rooted tree T is the maximum number of vertices with in-degree greater than one in a path in T. We denote the depth of T by *depth(T)*.

We emphasize that this definition of depth is nonstandard. It ignores input gates, output gates, and gates with in-degree one. Input and output gates have zero delay. However, inverters have positive delay. The fact that we ignore inverters in this definition does not affect the lower bound on the delay because they only increase the delay.

Binary Rooted Trees. In this section, we focus on binary trees, defined as follows.

Definition 12.5 A rooted tree is a binary tree if the maximum in-degree is two.

We refer to a rooted tree as a *minimum depth tree* if its depth is minimum among all the rooted trees with the same number of leaves.

Consider the set of all rooted binary trees that have n leaves. By Lemma 12.4, each tree in this set has $n-1$ nodes whose in-degree equals two. Thus we focus on minimizing the depth of the tree without worrying about the cost. The natural candidates to minimize delay are "balanced" trees (we formalize the term balanced trees in Definition 12.8). We will show that if n that is a power of 2, then there is a unique minimum depth tree, namely, the perfect binary tree with $\log_2 n$ levels. Conversely, if n is not a power of 2, we show that there is more than one minimum depth tree, as demonstrated in the following example.

Example 12.1 Consider the two trees that are depicted in Figure 12.2, each with six inputs. One tree is obtained from two binary trees with three leaves each. The second tree is obtained from one binary tree with four leaves and one with two leaves. Although both these trees have six leaves, they are quite different. Conversely, their depth is the same. Are these minimum depth trees?

Our goal is to prove that the depth of every rooted binary tree with n leaves is at least $\lceil \log_2 n \rceil$. Moreover, we wish to show that this bound can be obtained rather easily.

Claim 12.5 *If T_n is a rooted binary tree with n leaves, then the depth of T_n is at least* $\lceil \log_2 n \rceil$.

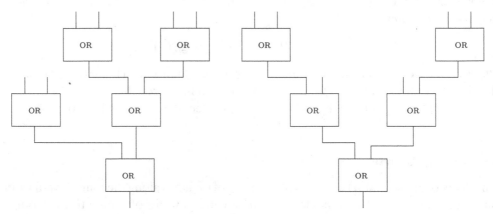

Figure 12.2. Two trees with six inputs.

PROOF: Since the depth is an integer, it suffices to prove that it is at least $\log_2 n$. We now modify the tree so that all vertices have in-degree 0 or 2. This modification proceeds by merging, one by one, vertices with in-degree one with their child. Note that this modification does not increase the depth.

We now assume that all vertices in T_n have in-degree 0 or 2. We prove that the depth of T_n is at least $\log_2 n$. Since $T_n \in \mathbb{N}$, it follows that $T_n \geq \lceil \log_2 n \rceil$, as required.

The proof is by complete induction on n. The induction basis follows since the depth of T_1 is $0 \geq \log_2 1 = 0$. We now prove the induction step.

Let T_n denote a binary rooted tree for $n > 2$. Let T_{n_1}, T_{n_2} denote the subtrees hanging from the root of T_n. Let $n_1 + n_2 = n$ denote the number of leaves in T_n. The induction hypothesis states that $depth(T_{n_1}) \geq \log_2 n_1$ and $depth(T_{n_2}) \geq \log_2 n_2$. We conclude that

$$depth(T_n) = 1 + \max\{depth(T_{n_1}), depth(T_{n_2})\}$$
$$\geq 1 + \max\{\log_2 n_1, \log_2 n_2\}$$
$$\geq 1 + \log_2(n/2)$$
$$= \log_2 n,$$

where the first line follows from Definition 12.4. The second line follows from the induction hypothesis. The third line follows from the assumption that $n_1 + n_2 = n$ and the fact that the $\log_2$ function is monotone increasing, and the claim follows. ∎

Perfect Binary Trees. The distance of a vertex v to the root r in a rooted tree is the length of the path from v to r. Note that the length of a path equals the number of edges along it, hence it includes traversed nodes with in-degree one.

Definition 12.6 A rooted binary tree is *perfect* if (i) the in-degree of every nonleaf is two and (ii) all leaves have the same distance to the root.

Note that the depth of a perfect tree equals the distance from the leaves to the root.

Claim 12.6 *The number of leaves in a perfect tree is 2^k, where k is the distance of the leaves to the root.*

PROOF: By induction on the distance from the leaves to the root, the induction basis is trivial for $k = 0$ since the tree consists only of the root. The induction step is proved as follows. Consider a perfect tree T rooted at r such that the distance from the leaves to r equals $k + 1$. Let r_1 and r_2 denote the children of r. The subtrees T_i rooted at r_i, for $i = 1, 2$, are also perfect, and the distance of a leaf of T_i to the root r_i is k. By the induction hypothesis, each subtree has 2^k leaves, and hence the tree T has $2^k + 2^k = 2^{k+1}$ leaves, as required. ∎

Claim 12.7 *Let n denote the number of leaves in a perfect tree. Then the distance from every leaf to the root is $\log_2 n$.*

PROOF: Let k denote the distance of the leaves to the root. By Claim 12.6, the tree has 2^k leaves. Therefore $n = 2^k$, and the claim follows. ∎

Minimum Depth Trees. Let T_n^* denote a minimum depth tree with n leaves. We now show that for every n, the depth of T_n^* is $\lceil \log_2 n \rceil$. In fact, if n is not a power of 2, then there are many such trees.

We start with a simple rule for determining how to split the leaves between the subtrees hanging from the root.

Definition 12.7 Two positive integers a, b are a *balanced partition* of n if

1. $a + b = n$
2. $\max\{\lceil \log_2 a \rceil, \lceil \log_2 b \rceil\} \le \lceil \log_2 n \rceil - 1$.

Claim 12.8 *If $n = 2^k - r$, where $0 \le r < 2^{k-1}$, then the set of balanced partitions is*

$$P \triangleq \{(a, b) \mid 2^{k-1} - r \le a \le 2^{k-1} \text{ and } b = n - a\}.$$

PROOF: First, we observe that if $n = 2^k - r$, where $0 \le r < 2^{k-1}$, then

$$\lceil \log_2 n \rceil = k. \tag{12.1}$$

Let $(a, b) \in P$. By the definition of P, it follows that $a + b = n$, as required. Moreover,

$$b = n - a$$
$$\le 2^k - r - 2^{k-1} + r$$
$$= 2^{k-1},$$

where the first line follows from the definition of P. The second line follows since $n = 2^k - r$ and $2^{k-1} - r \le a$.

We now prove that $\max\{\lceil \log_2 a \rceil, \lceil \log_2 b \rceil\} \le \lceil \log_2 n \rceil - 1$:

$$\max\{\lceil \log_2 a \rceil, \lceil \log_2 b \rceil\} \le \left\lceil \log_2 \left(2^{k-1}\right) \right\rceil$$
$$= \log_2 \left(2^{k-1}\right)$$
$$= k - 1$$
$$= \lceil \log_2(n) \rceil - 1,$$

where the first line follows since $a, b \le 2^{k-1}$ and since $\log_2$ is a monotone increasing function. The last line follows from Eq. 12.1. Hence (a, b) is a balanced partition, as required.

To prove the other direction, one must prove that if (a, b) is a balanced partition, then $(a, b) \in P$. Indeed, if (a, b) is a balanced partition, then $\max\{a, b\} \le 2^{k-1}$. Hence $a = n - b \ge (2^k - r) - 2^{k-1} = 2^{k-1} - r$, as required. ∎

The following algorithm deals with the construction of minimum depth trees. The algorithm partitions $n = a + b$ using any balanced partition described in Claim 12.8. Note that if n is not a power of 2, then there are multiple balanced partitions. In such a case, the algorithm has more than one valid output. Note also that the in-degree of every vertex in the tree output by the algorithm is either 2 or 0.

Claim 12.9 *The depth of a binary tree T_n^* constructed by Algorithm Balanced Tree(n) equals $\lceil \log_2 n \rceil$.*

PROOF: The proof is by complete induction on n. The induction basis for $n = 1$ holds since the depth of T_1^* is 0.

Algorithm 12.1 Balanced Tree(n)—a recursive algorithm for constructing a binary tree T_n^* with $n \geq 1$ leaves.

---

1. The case that $n = 1$ is trivial (an isolated root).
2. If $n \geq 2$, then let a, b be balanced partition of n.
3. Compute trees T_a^* and T_b^*. Connect their roots to a new root to obtain T_n^*.

We now prove the induction step. Let $a + b = n$ be a balanced partition of n that the algorithm has chosen in step 2. By Definition 12.4, $depth(T_n^*) = 1 + \max\{depth(T_a^*), depth(T_b^*)\}$. Hence

$$depth(T_n^*) = 1 + \max\{depth(T_a^*), depth(T_b^*)\}$$

$$= 1 + \max\{\lceil \log_2 a \rceil, \lceil \log_2 b \rceil\}$$

$$\leq 1 + \lceil \log_2 n \rceil - 1$$

$$= \lceil \log_2 n \rceil,$$

where the second line follows from the induction hypothesis. The third line follows since $a + b = n$ is a balanced partition.

Claim 12.5 implies that $depth(T_n^*) \geq \lceil \log_2 n \rceil$. We conclude that $depth(T_n^*) = \lceil \log_2 n \rceil$, as required. ∎

The conclusion from Claims 12.5 and 12.9 is summarized in the following corollary.

Corollary 12.10 *The propagation delay of a minimum depth OR-tree(n) is $\lceil \log_2 n \rceil \cdot t_{pd}(\text{OR})$.*

PROOF: A balanced OR-tree(n) is constructed from T_n^* as follows. Label all leaves as input gates and all other vertices in T_n^* as OR-gates. Add a new root, labeled as an output gate, and connect the new root to the root of T_n^*. ∎

Definition 12.8 A rooted binary tree T_n is a *balanced tree* if it is a valid output of Algorithm Balanced Tree(n).

12.3 OPTIMALITY OF TREES

In this section, we deal with the following questions: what is the best choice of a topology for a combinational circuit that implements the Boolean function OR_n? Is a tree indeed the best topology? Perhaps one could do better if another implementation is used? (Say, using other gates or connecting an input x_i to more than one gate.)

We attach two measures to every design: cost and delay. In this section, we prove lower bounds on the cost and delay of every circuit that implements the Boolean function OR_n. These lower bounds imply that a balanced OR-tree is an optimal combinational circuit both in terms of cost and in terms of delay.

12.3.1 Definitions

In this section, we present the definition of a cone of a Boolean function.

Definition 12.9 (*Restricted Boolean Functions*) Let $f : \{0,1\}^n \to \{0,1\}$ denote a Boolean function. Let $\sigma \in \{0,1\}$. The Boolean function $g : \{0,1\}^{n-1} \to \{0,1\}$ defined by

$$g(w_0, \ldots, w_{n-2}) \triangleq f(w_0, \ldots, w_{i-1}, \sigma, w_i, \ldots, w_{n-2})$$

is called the *restriction* of f with $x_i = \sigma$. We denote it by $f_{\restriction x_i = \sigma}$.

EXAMPLE

Consider the Boolean function $f(\vec{x}) = \text{XOR}_n(x_1, \ldots, x_n)$. The restriction of f with $x_n = 1$ is the Boolean function

$$f_{\restriction x_n = 1}(x_1, \ldots, x_{n-1}) \triangleq \text{XOR}_n(x_1, \ldots, x_{n-1}, 1)$$

$$= \text{INV}(\text{XOR}_{n-1}(x_1, \ldots, x_{n-1})).$$

Definition 12.10 A Boolean function $f : \{0,1\}^n \to \{0,1\}$ *depends* on its ith input if

$$f_{\restriction x_i = 0} \neq f_{\restriction x_i = 1}.$$

EXAMPLE

Consider the Boolean function $f(\vec{x}) = \text{XOR}_2(x_1, x_2)$. The function f depends on the ith input for $i = 2$. Indeed, $f_{\restriction x_2 = 1}(x_1) = \text{NOT}(x_1)$ and $f_{\restriction x_2 = 0}(x_1) = x_1$.

Definition 12.11 (*Cone of a Boolean Function*) The *cone* of a Boolean function $f : \{0,1\}^n \to \{0,1\}$ is defined by

$$cone(f) \triangleq \{i : f_{\restriction x_i = 0} \neq f_{\restriction x_i = 1}\}.$$

EXAMPLE

The cone of the Boolean function $f(\vec{x}) = \text{XOR}_2(x_1, x_2)$ equals $\{1,2\}$ because XOR depends on both inputs.

Definition 12.12 Let $flip_i : \{0,1\}^n \to \{0,1\}^n$ be the Boolean function defined by $flip_i(\vec{x}) \triangleq \vec{y}$, where

$$y_j \triangleq \begin{cases} x_j & \text{if } j \neq i \\ \text{NOT}(x_j) & \text{if } i = j. \end{cases}$$

EXAMPLE

Let $x[1:5] = 11111$. Then $flip_3(x) = 11011$.

Claim 12.11 *Let* $f : \{0,1\}^n \to \{0,1\}$ *denote a Boolean function. Then*

$$i \in \text{cone}(f) \iff \exists \vec{v} \in \{0,1\}^n : f(\vec{v}) \neq f(flip_i(\vec{v})).$$

PROOF: By definition, $i \in cone(i)$ iff $f_{|x_i=0} \neq f_{|x_i=1}$. This is equivalent to $f(v) \neq f(flip_i(\vec{v}))$, for a vector $\vec{v} \in \{0,1\}^n$. ∎

Claim 12.12 *The Boolean function* OR_n *depends on all its inputs, namely,*

$$|\text{cone}(\text{OR}_n)| = n.$$

PROOF: For every i, $\text{OR}(0^n) = 0$, but $\text{OR}(flip_i(0^n)) = 1$. ∎

EXAMPLE

Consider the following Boolean function:

$$f(\vec{x}) = \begin{cases} 0 & \text{if } \sum_i x_i < 3 \\ 1 & \text{otherwise.} \end{cases}$$

Suppose that one reveals the input bits one by one. As soon as three ones are revealed, one can determine the value of $f(\vec{x})$. Nevertheless, the function $f(\vec{x})$ depends on all its inputs (why?), and hence $cone(f) = \{1, \ldots, n\}$.

The following trivial claim deals with the case that $cone(f) = \varnothing$.

Claim 12.13 $cone(f) = \varnothing \iff f$ *is a constant Boolean function.*

PROOF: If f is constant, then $f(v) = f(flip_i(\vec{v}))$ for every i and every $\vec{v}$. To prove the other direction, we prove that if f is not constant, then there exists an index i and a vector $\vec{v}$ such that $f(\vec{v}) \neq f(flip_i(\vec{v}))$, thus implying that $i \in cone(f)$.

To prove this, we consider the undirected graph $G = (V, E)$, where $V = \{0,1\}^n$ (the range of f). The edge set E consists of all the pairs $(\vec{u}, \vec{v})$ such that $\vec{u}$ and $\vec{v}$ disagree in a single bit. Namely, there exists an index i such that $\vec{v} = flip_i(\vec{u})$. Thus all we need to prove is that, if f is not constant, then there exists an edge $(\vec{u}, \vec{v}) \in E$ such that $f(\vec{u}) \neq f(\vec{v})$.

It is easy to see that G is connected, that is, between every two vertices $\vec{u}$ and $\vec{v}$, there is a path. To obtain a path from $\vec{u}$ to $\vec{v}$, simply flip, one by one, the bits on which $\vec{u}$ and $\vec{v}$ disagree.

Now, if f is not constant, then there exist vectors $\vec{u}$ and $\vec{v}$ such that $f(\vec{u}) \neq f(\vec{v})$. If $(\vec{u}, \vec{v}) \in E$, then we are done. But what do we do if $(\vec{u}, \vec{v}) \notin E$? We may assume that $\vec{u}$ and $\vec{v}$ are a pair of closest vertices in G such that $f(\vec{u}) \neq f(\vec{v})$. Now, consider a shortest path p in G from $\vec{u}$ to $\vec{v}$. Let $(\vec{u}, \vec{w}) \in E$ denote the first edge along p. Clearly $f(\vec{u}) = f(\vec{w})$; otherwise, the pair $\vec{u}$ and $\vec{w}$ are closer than $\vec{u}$ and $\vec{v}$—a contradiction. Hence $f(\vec{v}) \neq f(\vec{w})$. But $\vec{v}$ and $\vec{w}$ are closer to each other than $\vec{v}$ and $\vec{u}$—a contradiction. ∎

12.3.2 Lower Bound on Cost

The following claim shows that if a combinational circuit $C = (G, \pi)$ implements a Boolean function $B : \{0, 1\}^n \to \{0, 1\}$, then there must be a path in G from every input labeled x_i, where $i \in cone(B)$ to the output gate of C.

Claim 12.14 *Let $C = (G, \pi)$ denote a combinational circuit that implements a Boolean function $B : \{0, 1\}^n \to \{0, 1\}$. If $i \in cone(B)$, then G must contain an input gate feeds the ith input. Moreover, denote this input gate by x_i, and let $y \in G$ denote the output gate of C. Then there is a path in G from x_i to y.*

PROOF: Assume, for the sake of contradiction, that G does not contain an input gate that feeds the ith input. Hence x_i does not appear in the topological ordering of the vertices of G.

Since $i \in cone(B)$, there exists a vector $v \in \{0, 1\}^n$ such that $B(\vec{v}) \neq B(flip_i(\vec{v}))$. Consider the executions of $SIM(C, \vec{v})$ and $SIM(C, flip_i(\vec{v}))$. We claim that both executions agree on the value f_y that is attached to the input of y. Namely, $f_y(\vec{v}) = f_y(flip_i(\vec{v}))$. This can be proved by induction on the position (or index) of y in the topological ordering.

By Theorem 11.2, $B(\vec{v}) = f_y(\vec{v})$ and $B(flip_i(\vec{v})) = f_y(flip_i(\vec{v}))$—a contradiction. Thus G contains an input gate that feeds the ith input.

To complete the claim, consider a maximal path p in G that starts in x_i. By maximal, we mean that p is not a proper subpath of another path. Note that since G is acyclic, there is a maximal path. This means that the endpoint of p must be a sink. However, G contains a single sink, that is, the output gate y. Thus there is a path from x_i to y, as required, and the claim follows. ∎

In the following theorem, we assume that the cost of every nontrivial gate is at least one. (Input and output gates are considered trivial and have zero cost.)

Theorem 12.15 (*Linear Cost Lower Bound Theorem*) *Let C denote a combinational circuit that implements a Boolean function $f : \{0, 1\}^n \to \{0, 1\}$. If the fan-in of every gate in C is at most 2, then*

$$c(C) \geq |cone(f)| - 1.$$

Before we prove Theorem 12.15, we show that it implies the optimality of OR-trees. Note that it is very easy to prove a lower bound of $n/2$. The reason is that every input must be fed to a nontrivial gate, and each gate can be fed by at most two inputs.

Corollary 12.16 *Let C_n denote a combinational circuit that implements* OR$_n$. *Then*

$$c(C_n) \geq n - 1.$$

PROOF: Follows directly from Claim 12.12 and Theorem 12.15. ∎

The proof of Theorem 12.15 is based on the following lemma that generalizes Lemma 12.4.

Lemma 12.17 *Let $G = (V, E)$ denote a DAG with a single sink in which the in-degree of each vertex is at most 2. Then*

$$|\{v \in V \mid deg_{in}(v) = 2\}| \geq |\{v \in V \mid deg_{in}(v) = 0\}| - 1. \qquad (12.2)$$

PROOF: If G is a rooted tree, then by Lemma 12.4, Eq. 12.2 holds with equality. To prove the theorem, we first show that there exist subsets $V' \subseteq V$ and $E' \subset E$ such that (i) V' contains all the sources in G as well as the sink of G and (ii) (V', E') is a rooted tree.

The sets V' and E' are constructed as follows. Let r denote the sink of G.

1. Initialize $E' = \varnothing$ and $V' = \varnothing$.
2. For every source v in G do
    (a) Find a path p_v from v to r.
    (b) Let q_v denote the prefix of p_v, the vertices and edges of which are not contained in V' or E'.
    (c) Add the edges of q_v to E', and add the vertices of q_v to V'.

By construction, V' contains all the sources of G and the sink r. In addition, the algorithm for constructing (V', E') maintains the invariant that there is a single path from every vertex in V' to the sink r (see Problem 12.4). Moreover, this invariant implies that (V', E') is a rooted tree (see Problem 12.3).

Let $deg'_{in}(v)$ denote the in-degree of v with respect to E'. Lemma 12.4, applied to (V, E'), implies that

$$|\{v \in V \mid deg'_{in}(v) = 2\}| = |\{v \in V \mid deg'_{in}(v) = 0\}| - 1.$$

Since

$$\{v \in V \mid deg'_{in}(v) = 2\} \subseteq \{v \in V \mid deg_{in}(v) = 2\}$$

$$\{v \in V \mid deg'_{in}(v) = 0\} = \{v \in V \mid deg_{in}(v) = 0\},$$

Eq. 12.2 holds, and the lemma follows. ∎

PROOF OF THEOREM 12.15: Consider a combinational circuit $C = (G, \pi)$ that implements f. Since the range of f is $\{0, 1\}$, the circuit C has a single output gate, and therefore G has a single sink. Since C implements f, it must have an input gate x_i for every $i \in cone(f)$. Thus the number of sources in C is at least $|cone(f)|$. By Lemma 12.17, $|\{v \in V \mid deg_{in}(v) - 2\}|$ is at least the number of sources in G minus 1. If $deg_{in}(v) \geq 2$, then $c(\pi(v)) \geq 1$, and therefore $c(C) \geq |cone(f)| - 1$, as required. ∎

12.3.3 Lower Bound on Delay

We now turn to proving a lower bound on the delay of a combinational circuit that implements OR_n. Again, we use a general technique and rely on all gates in the design having a constant fan-in.

The following theorem shows a lower bound on the delay of combinational circuits that is logarithmic in the size of the cone. We assume that the delay of every nontrivial gate is at least one.

Theorem 12.18 (*Logarithmic Delay Lower Bound Theorem*) *Let $C = (G, \pi)$ denote a combinational circuit that implements a nonconstant Boolean function $f : \{0, 1\}^n \to \{0, 1\}$. If the fan-in of every gate in C is at most k, then*

$$t_{pd}(C) \geq \log_k |\text{cone}(f)|.$$

Before we prove Theorem 12.18, we show that the theorem implies a lower bound on the delay of combinational circuits that implement OR_n.

Corollary 12.19 *Let C_n denote a combinational circuit that implements OR_n. Let k denote the maximum fan-in of a gate in C_n. Then*

$$t_{pd}(C_n) \geq \lceil \log_k n \rceil.$$

PROOF: The corollary follows directly from Claim 12.12 and Theorem 12.18. ∎

The proof of Theorem 12.18 is based on the following definition and lemma.

Definition 12.13 Let $G = (V, E)$ denote a DAG. The *cone* of a vertex $v \in V$ is defined by

$$cone(v) \triangleq \{u \in V : deg_{in}(u) = 0 \text{ and there is a path from } u \text{ to } v\}.$$

Let $t_{pd}(v)$ denote the maximum delay of a path ending in v as computed by Algorithm 11.1. We assume that the propagation delay of input gates and output gates is zero. However, we assume that the propagation delay of every other gate is one (i.e., $t_{pd}(\gamma) = 1$ for every gate $\gamma \in \Gamma$). The lemma obviously holds if $t_{pd}(\gamma) \geq 1$ for every gate $\gamma \in \Gamma$.

Lemma 12.20 *If $G = (V, E)$ is a DAG in which the in-degree of every vertex is at most k, then*

$$t_{pd}(v) \geq \log_k |cone(v)|.$$

PROOF: We first prove the lemma for all the vertices, except sinks. We prove the lemma by complete induction on $t_{pd}(v)$. The induction basis, for $t_{pd}(v) = 0$, is trivial since $t_{pd}(v) = 0$ implies that v is a source. The cone of a source v consists v itself, and $\log_k 1 = 0$.

The induction hypothesis is

$$t_{pd}(v) \leq i \implies t_{pd}(v) \geq \log_k |cone(v)|. \tag{12.3}$$

In the induction step, we wish to prove that the induction hypothesis implies that Eq. 12.3 holds also if $t_{pd}(v) = i + 1$. Consider a vertex v with $t_{pd}(v) = i + 1$ (see

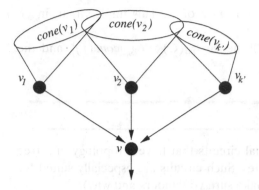

Figure 12.3. The induction step in the proof of Theorem 12.18.

Figure 12.3 for a depiction of the induction step). Denote the vertices that precede v by $v_1, \ldots, v_{k'}$, where $k' \leq k$. Namely, the edges that enter v are $v_1 \to v, \ldots, v_{k'} \to v$, where $k' \leq k$. By the definition of $t_{pd}(v)$ (see Algorithm 11.2), it follows that

$$t_{pd}(v) = \max\{t_{pd}(v_i)\}_{i=1}^{k'} + \delta(v). \tag{12.4}$$

By the definition of $cone(v)$, it follows that

$$cone(v) = \bigcup_{i=1}^{k'} cone(v_i).$$

Hence

$$|cone(v)| \leq \sum_{i=1}^{k'} |cone(v_i)|$$

$$\leq k' \cdot \max\{|cone(v_1)|, \ldots, |cone(v_{k'})|\}. \tag{12.5}$$

Let v' denote a predecessor of v that satisfies $|cone(v')| = \max\{|cone(v_i)|\}_{i=1}^{k'}$. The induction hypothesis implies that

$$t_{pd}(v') \geq \log_k |cone(v')|. \tag{12.6}$$

But

$$t_{pd}(v) \geq \delta(v) + t_{pd}(v'), \qquad \text{by Eq. 12.4}$$

$$\geq \delta(v) + \log_k |cone(v')|, \qquad \text{by Eq. 12.6}$$

$$\geq \delta(v) + \log_k(|cone(v)|/k'). \qquad \text{by Eq. 12.5}$$

Since v is not sink, $\delta(v) \geq 1$. Since $k' \leq k$, it follows that $t_{pd}(v) \geq 1 + \log_k(|cone(v)|/k) = \log_k |cone(v)|$, as required.

To complete the proof, consider a sink v'. Let v denote the vertex such that (v, v') is an arc in G. Note that $cone(v) = cone(v')$ and $t_{pd}(v) = t_{pd}(v')$, and the lemma follows. ∎

PROOF OF THEOREM 12.18: Since the combinational circuit $C = (G, \pi)$ implements f, it must contain an input gate labeled x_i for every $i \in cone(f)$. By Claim 12.14, there must be a path in G from x_i to y, the output gate of C. This implies that, in G, $|cone(y)| \geq |cone(f)|$.

By Lemma 12.20, $t_{pd}(y) \geq \log_k |cone(y)|$, hence $t_{pd}(C) \geq \log_k |cone(f)|$, and the theorem follows. ∎

12.4 SUMMARY

In this chapter, we focused on combinational circuits that have a topology of a tree and are built from instances of identical gates. Such circuits are especially suited for computing associative Boolean functions (make sure you understand why).

We began this chapter by extending associative dyadic functions to n arguments. We argued that there are only four nontrivial associative Boolean functions, and we decided to focus on OR_n. We then defined an OR-tree(n) to be a combinational circuit that implements OR_n using a topology of a tree.

Although it is intuitive that OR-trees are the cheapest designs for implementing OR_n, we had to work a bit to prove it. It is also intuitive that balanced OR-trees are the fastest designs for implementing OR_n, and again, we had to work a bit to prove that, too.

We will be using the lower bounds that we proved in this chapter also in the next chapters. To prove these lower bounds, we introduced the $cone(f)$ of a Boolean function f. The cone of f is the set of inputs on which the function f depends.

If all the gates have a fan-in of at most two and the cost and delay of nontrivial gates is at least one, then the lower bounds are as follows. The first lower bound states that the number of gates of a combinational circuit implementing a Boolean function f must be at least $|cone(f)| - 1$. The second lower bound states that the propagation delay of a circuit implementing a Boolean function f is at least $\log_2 |cone(f)|$.

PROBLEMS

12.1. Design a zero-tester, defined as follows.
Input: $x[n-1:0]$.
Output: y
Functionality:

$$y = 1 \quad \text{iff} \quad x[n-1:0] = 0^n.$$

(a) Suggest a design based on an OR-tree.
(b) Suggest a design based on an AND-tree.
(c) What do you think about a design based on a tree of NOR-gates?

12.2. Prove that each of the following functions $f : \{0,1\}^n \to \{0,1\}$ is associative:

$$f \in \{\text{constant } 0, \text{constant } 1, x_1, x_n, AND_n, OR_n, XOR_n, NXOR_n\}.$$

12.3. Let $G = (V, E)$ be a DAG with a single sink r. Prove the following statement:

$$\forall v \in V \ \exists \text{ a single path from } v \text{ to } r \Rightarrow G \text{ is a rooted tree.}$$

12.4. Recall the algorithm for constructing (V', E') in the proof of Lemma 12.17. Prove that this algorithm maintains the following invariant:

There is a single path from every $v \in V'$ to the sink r.

12.5. Prove that there is only one balanced partition of n if and only if n is a power of 2.

12.6. An *even partition* of n is the partition $a = \lceil n/2 \rceil$ and $b = \lfloor n/2 \rfloor$.
   (a) Give an example of a balanced partition that is not an even partition.
   (b) Prove that every even partition is a balanced partition. Namely, prove that

$$\forall n \geq 2: \quad \lceil \log_2 \lceil n/2 \rceil \rceil = \lceil \log_2 n \rceil - 1. \tag{12.7}$$

   Hint: the proof of Eq. 12.7 is easy if n is even. If n is odd, then $\lceil \log_2 \lceil \frac{n}{2} \rceil \rceil =$
   $\lceil \log_2 (n + 1) \rceil - 1$. *Thus one needs to prove that*

$$\forall n = 2k + 1: \quad \lceil \log_2 (n + 1) \rceil = \lceil \log_2 n \rceil. \tag{12.8}$$

12.7. Prove the second direction in Claim 12.8, that is; prove that if (a, b) is a balanced partition, then $(a, b) \in P$.

12.8. Consider the Boolean function XOR_n.
   (a) What is the cost and delay of a $\text{XOR-tree}(n)$?
   (b) What is the length of the shortest SOP Boolean formula φ^* that represents XOR_n?
   (c) What is the cost and delay of a combinational circuit obtained from φ^*? What is the maximum fan-in and fan-out of this circuit?

12.9. State and prove a generalization of Theorem 12.15 for the case that the fan-in of every gate is bounded by a constant k.

12.10. Let $U \subseteq V$ denote a subset of vertices of a directed graph $G = (V, E)$, and let $r \in V$. Let $dist(u, v)$ denote the length of a shortest path in G from u to v. If there is no such path, then $dist(u, v) = \infty$. Let k denote the maximum in-degree in G.
   Prove that there exists a vertex $u \in U$ such that $dist(u, r) \geq \log_k |U|$.

CHAPTER 13

Decoders and Encoders

Consider the following problem. We need a combinational circuit that controls many devices numbered $0, 1, \ldots, 2^k - 1$. At every moment, the circuit instructs exactly one device to work while the others must be inactive. The input to the circuit is a k-bit string that represents the number i of the device to be active. Now, the circuit has 2^k outputs, one for each device, and only the ith output should equal 1; the other outputs must equal zero. How do we design such a circuit? The circuit described previously is known as a *decoder*. The circuit that implements the inverse Boolean function is called an *encoder*.

In this chapter, we specify and design decoders and encoders. We also prove that the combinational circuit are correct, namely, they satisfy the specification. Moreover, we prove that these designs are asymptotically optimal.

13.1 BUSES

We begin this section by describing what buses are. Consider a circuit that contains an adder and a register (a memory device). The output of the adder should be stored by the register. Suppose that the adder outputs 8 bits. This means that there are eight different wires that emanate from the output of the adder to the input of the register. These eight wires are distinct and must have distinct names. Instead of naming the wires $a, b, c, \ldots$, we often use names such as $a[0], a[1], \ldots, a[7]$.

Definition 13.1 A *bus* is a set of wires that are connected to the same modules. The *width* of a bus is the number of wires in the bus.

Very often buses are used to connect multiple components or modules. For example, a PCI bus is used to connect hardware devices (e.g., network cards, sound cards, USB adapters) to the main memory. In our settings, we consider wires instead of nets.

In VLSI-CAD tools and hardware description languages (such as VHDL), one often uses indexes to represent buses. Indexing of buses is often a cause of confusion. For example, assume that the terminals on one side of a bus are called $a[0:3]$ and the terminals on the other side of the bus are called $b[3:0]$. Does that mean that

$a[0]$ is connected to $b[0]$ or does it mean that $a[0]$ is connected to $b[3]$? Obviously, naming rules are well defined in hardware description languages, but these rules are too strict for our purposes (e.g., negative indexes are not allowed, and connections are not implied).

Our convention regarding indexing of terminals and their connection by buses is as follows:

1. Connection of terminals is done by assignment statements. For example, the terminals $a[0:3]$ are connected to the terminals $b[0:3]$ by the statement $b[0:3] \leftarrow a[0:3]$. This statement is meaningful if $a[0:3]$ are output terminals and $b[0:3]$ are input terminals. The statement $b[0:3] \leftarrow a[0:3]$ means connect $a[i]$ to $b[i]$.
2. "Reversing" of indexes does not take place unless explicitly stated. Hence, unless stated otherwise, assignments of buses in which the index ranges are the same or reversed, such as $b[i:j] \leftarrow a[i:j]$ and $b[i:j] \leftarrow a[j:i]$, have the same meaning, that is, $b[i] \leftarrow a[i], \ldots, b[j] \leftarrow a[j]$.
3. "Shifting" is done by default. For example, will often write $a[0:3] \leftarrow b[4:7]$, meaning that $a[0] \leftarrow b[4], a[1] \leftarrow b[5]$, and so on. Similarly, assignments in which the index ranges are shifted, such as $b[i+5:j+5] \leftarrow a[i:j]$, mean $b[i+5] \leftarrow a[i], \ldots, b[j+5] \leftarrow a[j]$. We refer to such an implied reassignment of indexes as *hardwired shifting*.

Recall that we denote the (digital) signal on a wire N by $N(t)$. This notation is a bit cumbersome in buses, for example, $a[i](t)$ means the signal on the wire $a[i]$. To shorten notation, we will often refer to $a[i](t)$ simply as $a[i]$. Note that $a[i](t)$ is a bit (this is true only after the signal stabilizes). So, according to our shortened notation, we often refer to $a[i]$ as a bit meaning actually "the stable value of the signal $a[i](t)$." This establishes the somewhat confusing convention of attaching several meanings to $a[n-1:0]$; it is a bus, a string, a binary vector, or a binary representation of a number.

We will often use an even shorter abbreviation for signals on buses, namely, vector notation. We often use the shorthand $\bar{a}$ for a binary string $a[n-1:0]$ provided, of course, that the indexes of the string $a[n-1:0]$ are obvious from the context.

Consider a gate G with two input terminals a and b and one output terminal z. The combinational circuit $G(n)$ is simply n instances of the gate G, as depicted in Figure 13.1a. The ith instance of gate G in $G(n)$ is denoted by G_i. The two input terminals of G_i are denoted by a_i and b_i. The output terminal of G_i is denoted by z_i.

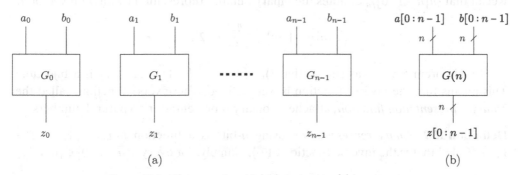

Figure 13.1. Vector notation: Multiple instances of the same gate.

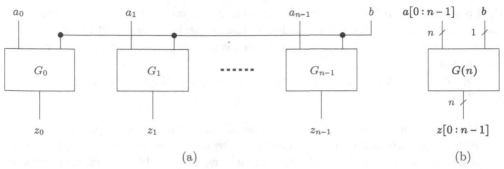

Figure 13.2. Vector notation: b feeds all the gates.

We use shorthand when drawing the schematics of $G(n)$ as depicted in Figure 13.1b. The short segment drawn across a wire indicates that the line represents a bus. The bus width is written next to the short segment.

We often wish to feed all the second input terminals of gates in $G(n)$ with the same signal. Figure 13.2 denotes a circuit $G(n)$ in which the value b is fed to the second input terminal of all the gates.

Note that the fan-out of the net that carries the signal b in Figure 13.2 is n. In practice, the capacity of a net increases linearly with the fan-out, hence large fan-out increases the propagation delay. To keep our delay model simple, we often ignore this important phenomenon in this course.

13.2 DECODERS

In this section, we present a combinational module called a *decoder*. We start by defining decoders. We then suggest an implementation, prove its correctness, and analyze its cost and delay. Finally, we prove that the cost and delay of our implementation is asymptotically optimal.

13.2.1 Division in Binary Representation

Recall that $\langle a[n-1:0]\rangle_n$ denotes the binary number represented by an n-bit vector $\vec{a}$:

$$\langle a[n-1:0]\rangle_n \triangleq \sum_{i=0}^{n-1} a_i \cdot 2^i.$$

In Theorem 5.6, it was shown that $\langle\rangle_n : \{0,1\}^n \to \{0,1,\ldots,2^n-1\}$ is a bijection. This means that the inverse function is well defined. The inverse function, called the *binary representation function*, attaches a binary representation to natural numbers.

Definition 13.2 *Binary representation* using n-bits is a function $bin_n : \{0,1,\ldots,2^n-1\} \to \{0,1\}^n$ that is the inverse function of $\langle\cdot\rangle$. Namely, for every $a[n-1:0] \in \{0,1\}^n$,

$$bin_n(\langle a[n-1:0]\rangle_n) = a[n-1:0].$$

We defined division and modulo in Section 5.1. Recall that division of a by b means finding a quotient q and a remainder r that satisfy

$$a = q \cdot b + r, \text{ where } 0 \le r < b.$$

One advantage of binary representation is that it is trivial to divide by powers of two as well as compute the remainders. We summarize this property in the following claim.

Claim 13.1 *Let $s = \langle x[n-1:0] \rangle_n$, and $0 \le k \le n-1$. Let q and r denote the quotient and remainder obtained by dividing s by 2^k. Define the binary strings $x_R[k-1:0]$ and $x_L[n-1:n-k-1]$, as follows:*

$$x_R[k-1:0] \triangleq x[k-1:0]$$
$$x_L[n-k-1:0] \triangleq x[n-1:k].$$

Then

$$q = \langle x_L[n-k-1:0] \rangle$$
$$r = \langle x_R[k-1:0] \rangle.$$

13.2.2 Definition of Decoder

Definition 13.3 A *decoder with input length n* is a combinational circuit specified as follows:

Input: $x[n-1:0] \in \{0,1\}^n$.
Output: $y[2^n - 1:0] \in \{0,1\}^{2^n}$
Functionality:

$$y[i] \triangleq \begin{cases} 1 & \text{if } \langle \bar{x} \rangle = i \\ 0 & \text{otherwise.} \end{cases}$$

We denote a decoder with input length n by DECODER(n).

Note that the number of outputs of a decoder is exponential in the number of inputs. Note also that exactly one bit of the output $\bar{y}$ is set to one. Such a representation of a number is often termed *one-hot encoding* or *1-out-of-k encoding*.

Example 13.1 Consider a decoder DECODER(3). On input $x = 101$, the output y equals 00100000.

An example of how a decoder is used is in decoding of controller instructions. Suppose that each instruction is coded by a 4-bit string. Our goal is to determine what instruction is to be executed. For this purpose, we feed the 4 bits to a DECODER(4). There are 16 outputs, exactly one of which will equal 1. This output will activate a module that should be activated in this instruction.

13.2.3 Brute Force Design

The simplest way to design a decoder is to build a separate circuit for every output bit $y[i]$. The circuit for $y[i]$ is simply a product of n literals. Let $v \triangleq bin_n(i)$, that is, v is the binary representation of the index i. Using the notation from Definition 9.5, define the minterm p_v to be $p_v \triangleq (\ell_1^v \cdot \ell_2^v \cdots \ell_n^v)$, where

$$\ell_j^v \triangleq \begin{cases} x_j & \text{if } v_j = 1 \\ \bar{x}_j & \text{if } v_j = 0. \end{cases}$$

In the following claim, we refer to p_v as a Boolean function of the input $x[n-1:0]$.

Claim 13.2 *If* $\langle v \rangle = i$, *then* $y[i] = p_v$.

PROOF: By definition, $y[i] = 1$ iff $\langle \bar{x} \rangle = i$. Now $\langle \bar{x} \rangle = i$ iff $\bar{x} = v$. Indeed, p_v attains the value 1 iff $\bar{x} = v$, as required. ∎

The brute force decoder circuit consists of (i) n inverters used to compute $\text{INV}(\bar{x})$ and (ii) computing p_v by a separate $\text{AND}(n)$-tree for every $v \in \{0,1\}^n$. The delay of the brute force design is $t_{pd}(\text{INV}) + t_{pd}(\text{AND}(n)\text{-tree}) = O(\log_2 n)$. The cost of the brute force design is $\Theta(n \cdot 2^n)$, since we have an $\text{AND}(n)$-tree for each of the 2^n outputs.

Intuitively, the brute force design is wasteful because, if the binary representation of i and j differ in a single bit, then the AND-trees of $y[i]$ and $y[j]$ share all but a single input. Hence the product of $n - 1$ bits is computed twice. In the next section, we present a systematic way to share hardware between different outputs.

13.2.4 An Optimal Decoder Design

We design a DECODER(n) using recursion on n. The base case, for $n = 1$, is trivial. We then proceed with the reduction rule by designing a DECODER(n) based on "smaller" decoders.

Base case DECODER(1): The circuit DECODER(1) is simply one inverter where: $y[0] \leftarrow \text{INV}(x[0])$ and $y[1] \leftarrow x[0]$.

Reduction rule DECODER(n): We assume that we know how to design decoders with input length less than n and design a decoder with input length n.

The method we apply for our design is called *divide-and-conquer*. Consider a parameter k, where $0 < k < n$. We partition the input string $x[n-1:0]$ into two strings as follows:

1. The right part (or lower part) is $x_R[k-1:0]$ and is defined by $x_R[k-1:0] = x[k-1:0]$.
2. The left part (or upper part) is $x_L[n-k-1:0]$ and is defined by $x_L[i] \leftarrow x[i+k]$. We write this also by $x_L[n-k-1:0] = x[n-1:k]$, which means that a hardwired shift by k positions is applied.

We will later show that to reduce delay, it is best to choose k as close to $n/2$ as possible. However, at this point, we consider k to be an arbitrary integer such that $0 < k < n$.

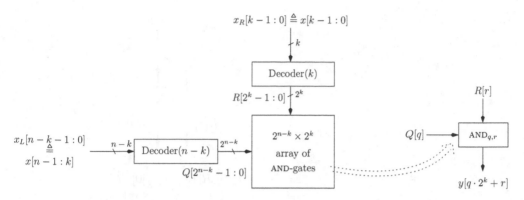

Figure 13.3. A recursive implementation of DECODER(n).

Figure 13.3 depicts a recursive implementation of a DECODER(n). Our recursive design feeds $x_L[n - k - 1 : 0]$ to DECODER($n - k$). We denote the output of the decoder DECODER($n - k$) by $Q[2^{n-k} - 1 : 0]$. (The letter "Q" stands for "quotient.") In a similar manner, our recursive design feeds $x_R[k - 1 : 0]$ to DECODER(k). We denote the output of the decoder DECODER(k) by $R[2^k - 1 : 0]$. (The letter "R" stands for "remainder.")

The decoder outputs $Q[2^{n-k} - 1 : 0]$ and $R[2^k - 1 : 0]$ are fed to a $2^{n-k} \times 2^k$ array of AND-gates. We denote the AND-gate in position (q, r) in the array by AND$_{q,r}$. The rules for connecting the AND-gates in the array are as follows. The inputs of the gate AND$_{q,r}$ are $Q[q]$ and $R[r]$. The output of the gate AND$_{q,r}$ is $y[q \cdot 2^k + r]$.

Note that we have defined a routing rule for connecting the outputs $Q[2^{n-k} - 1 : 0]$ and $R[2^k - 1 : 0]$ to the inputs of the AND-gates in the array. This routing rule (that involves division with remainder by 2^k) is not computed by the circuit; the routing rule defines the circuit and must be followed by the person implementing the design.

In Figure 13.3, we do not draw the connections in the array of AND-gates. Instead, connections are inferred by the names of the wires (e.g., two wires called $R[5]$ belong to the same net).

Example: Implementing DECODER(2). In this example, we unroll the recursive design, DECODER(n), for $n = 2$. The implementation of DECODER(2) is depicted in Figure 13.4.

13.2.5 Correctness

In this section, we prove the correctness of the DECODER(n) design.

Claim 13.3 *The* DECODER(n) *design is a correct implementation of a decoder.*

PROOF: Our goal is to prove that for every n and every $0 \le i < 2^n$, the following holds:

$$y[i] = 1 \iff \langle x[n-1:0] \rangle = i.$$

The proof is by induction on n. The induction basis for $n = 1$ is trivial. We proceed directly to the induction step. Fix an index i and divide i by 2^k to obtain $i = q \cdot 2^k + r$, where $r \in [2^k - 1 : 0]$.

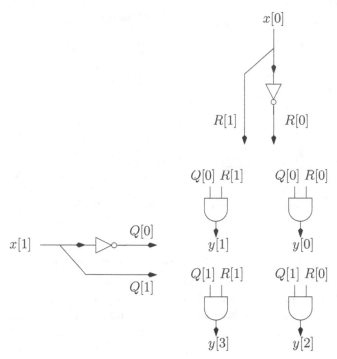

Figure 13.4. An implementation of DECODER(2).

We apply the induction hypothesis to DECODER(k) to conclude that $R[r] = 1$ iff $\langle x_R[k-1:0]\rangle = r$. Similarly, the induction hypothesis when applied to DECODER($n-k$) implies that $Q[q] = 1$ iff $\langle x_L[n-k-1:0]\rangle = q$. Since $i = q \cdot 2^k + r$, this implies that

$$y[i] = 1 \Longleftrightarrow R[r] = 1 \text{ and } Q[q] = 1$$
$$\Longleftrightarrow \langle x_R[k-1:0]\rangle = r \text{ and } \langle x_L[n-k-1:0]\rangle = q$$
$$\Longleftrightarrow \langle x[n-1:0]\rangle = i,$$

where the first line is by the functionality of the AND-gate that outputs $y[i]$. The second line follows from the induction hypothesis. The third line follows from the property of division by 2^k, and the claim follows. ∎

13.2.6 Cost and Delay Analysis

In this section, we analyze the cost and delay of the DECODER(n) design. We denote the cost and delay of DECODER(n) by $c(n)$ and $d(n)$, respectively.

Cost Analysis. The cost $c(n)$ satisfies the following recurrence equation:

$$c(n) = \begin{cases} c(\text{INV}) & \text{if n=1} \\ c(k) + c(n-k) + 2^n \cdot c(\text{AND}) & \text{otherwise.} \end{cases}$$

It follows that, up to constant factors,

$$c(n) = \begin{cases} 1 & \text{if } n = 1 \\ c(k) + c(n-k) + 2^n & \text{if } n > 1. \end{cases} \tag{13.1}$$

Obviously, $c(n) = \Omega(2^n)$ (regardless of the value of k), so the best we can hope for is to find a value of k such that $c(n) = O(2^n)$. In fact, it can be shown that $c(n) = O(2^n)$ for every choice of $1 \le k < n$. The following claim considers the case that $k = \lceil n/2 \rceil$.

Claim 13.4 *The solution of Eq. 13.1 is $c(n) = O(2^n)$ if $k = \lceil n/2 \rceil$.*

PROOF: By Lemma 7.2, it suffices to consider the case that n is a power of 2, namely, $n = 2^\ell$. Define $\gamma(n)$ for $n \ge 1$, as follows,

$$\gamma(n) \triangleq \frac{c(n)}{2^n}.$$

We now prove that $\gamma(n) < 2$, for powers of 2, by induction on n. The induction basis for $n = 1$ is immediate since

$$\gamma(1) = \frac{c(1)}{2^1} = \frac{1}{2}.$$

The induction step is proved as follows:

$$\begin{aligned} \gamma(2n) &= \frac{c(2n)}{2^{2n}} \\ &= \frac{1}{2^{2n}} \cdot (2c(n) + 2^{2n}) \\ &= \frac{2c(n)}{2^{2n}} + 1 \\ &= \frac{2 \cdot 2^n \cdot \gamma(n)}{2^{2n}} + 1 \\ &= \frac{\gamma(n)}{2^{n-1}} + 1 < 2. \end{aligned}$$

The first line follows from the definition of γ. The second line follows from Eq. 13.1. The fourth line uses the identity $c(n) = 2^n \cdot \gamma(n)$. Since $n \ge 2$, it follows that $2^{n-1} \ge 2$. By the induction hypothesis, $\gamma(n) < 2$, hence $\gamma(n)/2^{n-1} < 1$, and the last line holds. Thus $\gamma(2n) < 2$, and the induction step follows. We conclude that $c(n) < 2 \cdot 2^n$, as required. ∎

Delay Analysis. The delay of DECODER(n) satisfies the following recurrence equation:

$$d(n) = \begin{cases} d(\text{INV}) & \text{if } n=1 \\ \max\{d(k), d(n-k)\} + d(\text{AND}) & \text{otherwise.} \end{cases}$$

Set $k = n/2$. By Problem 7.9 it follows that $d(n) = \Theta(\log n)$.

13.2.7 Asymptotic Optimality

Our goal is to prove that the design we presented is optimal. Optimality is not well defined since we are not committed to specific costs and propagation delays of the basic gates. Instead, we resort to asymptotic optimality. Of course, we are also very interested in the constants since they are important from a practical point of view. The analysis presented in the previous section also proves very reasonable constants (i.e., $c(n) \le 2 \cdot 2^n \cdot \max\{c(\text{AND}), c(\text{INV})\}$ and $d(n) \le \log_2 n \cdot \max\{c(\text{AND}), c(\text{INV})\}$).

In the following theorem, we assume that every gate in G has a constant number of input terminals (say, at most two).

Theorem 13.5 *For every decoder G of input length n,*

$$d(G) = \Omega(\log n)$$

$$c(G) = \Omega(2^n).$$

PROOF: We begin by proving that $d(G) = \Omega(\log n)$. The proof is a simple application of the logarithmic delay lower bound (Theorem 12.18). Consider the output $y[0]$. The Boolean function implemented by $y[0]$ is

$$y[0] = \text{NOT}(\text{OR}(x[n-1], \dots, x[0])).$$

The cone of this Boolean function is the set $\{0, \dots, n-1\}$, and the first part of the theorem follows. (In fact, every output bit depends on all the inputs—see Problem 13.3.)

We now prove that $c(G) = \Omega(2^n)$. The proof is based on the following observations: (i) computing each output bit requires at least one nontrivial gate; (ii) no two output bits are identical. Assume, for the sake of contradiction, that the first observation does not hold. Then there exists an index $i \in [0 : 2^n - 1]$ such that $y[i]$ equals one of the input bits, say, $x[j]$. But $y[i] = 1$ only for one unique input vector—a contradiction.

Assume, for the sake of contradiction, that the second observation does not hold. Then there exist two distinct indexes $i, j \in [0 : 2^n - 1]$ such that $y[i] = y[j]$ for every input. However, consider the input vector $\vec{x}$ such that $\langle \vec{x} \rangle = i$. Given this input, we have $y[i] = 1$ and $y[j] = 0$—a contradiction.

These two observations imply that the 2^n output bits are outcomes of distinct nontrivial gates, and the theorem follows. ∎

Note that Theorem 12.15 only implies that for every decoder G of input length n, $c(G) = \Omega(n)$—a very weak result. In Theorem 13.5, we proved a much stronger lower bound.

13.3 ENCODERS

An encoder implements the inverse Boolean function implemented by a decoder. Note however, that the Boolean function implemented by a decoder is not surjective. In fact, the range of the Boolean function implemented by a decoder is the set of binary vectors in which exactly one bit equals 1. It follows that an encoder implements a partial Boolean function (i.e., a function that is not defined for every binary string).

13.3.1 Hamming Distance and Weight

We first define the Hamming weight of binary strings.

Definition 13.4 The *Hamming distance* between two binary strings $u, v \in \{0, 1\}^n$ is defined by

$$dist(u, v) \triangleq \{i \mid u_i \neq v_i\}.$$

Definition 13.5 The *Hamming weight* of a binary string $u \in \{0, 1\}^n$ equals $dist(u, 0^n)$, namely, the number of nonzero symbols in the string.

We denote the Hamming weight of a binary string $\vec{a}$ by $wt(\vec{a})$, namely,

$$wt(a[n - 1 : 0]) \triangleq |\{i : a[i] \neq 0\}|.$$

13.3.2 Concatenation of Strings

Recall that the concatenation of the strings a and b is denoted by $a \circ b$.

Definition 13.6 The binary string obtained by i concatenations of the string a is denoted by a^i.

Consider the following examples of string concatenation:

- If $a = 01$ and $b = 10$, then $a \circ b = 0110$.
- If $a = 1$ and $i = 5$, then $a^i = 11111$.
- If $a = 01$ and $i = 3$, then $a^i = 010101$.
- We denote the zeros string of length n by 0^n (it is hoped that there is no confusion between exponentiation and concatenation of the binary string 0).

13.3.3 Definition of Encoder

We define the encoder partial function as follows.

Definition 13.7 The function $\text{ENCODER}_n : \{\vec{y} \in \{0, 1\}^{2^n} : wt(\vec{y}) = 1\} \to \{0, 1\}^n$ is defined as follows: $\langle \text{ENCODER}_n(\vec{y}) \rangle$ equals the index of the bit of $y[2^n - 1 : 0]$ that equals one. Formally,

$$wt(y) = 1 \implies y[\langle \text{ENCODER}_n(\vec{y}) \rangle] = 1.$$

Examples:

1. $\text{ENCODER}_2(0001) = 00$, $\text{ENCODER}_2(0010) = 01$
    $\text{ENCODER}_2(0100) = 10$, $\text{ENCODER}_2(1000) = 11$.
2. $\text{ENCODER}_n(0^{2^n - k - 1} \circ 1 \circ 0^k) = bin_n(k)$.

Definition 13.8 An *encoder* with input length 2^n and output length n is a combinational circuit that implements the Boolean function ENCODER_n.

We denote an encoder with input length 2^n and output length n by $\text{ENCODER}(n)$. An $\text{ENCODER}(n)$ can be also specified as follows:

Input: $y[2^n - 1 : 0] \in \{0, 1\}^{2^n}$.
Output: $x[n - 1 : 0] \in \{0, 1\}^n$.
Functionality: If $wt(\bar{y}) = 1$, let i denote the index such that $y[i] = 1$. In this case, $\bar{x}$
  should satisfy $\langle \bar{x} \rangle = i$. Formally,

$$wt(\bar{y}) = 1 \implies y[\langle \bar{x} \rangle] = 1.$$

Note that the functionality is not specified for all inputs $\bar{y}$. Functionality is only
specified for inputs whose Hamming weight equals 1. Since an encoder is a combinational circuit, it implements a Boolean function. This means that it outputs a digital
value even if $wt(y) \neq 1$. The specification only requires that two encoders agree with
respect to inputs whose Hamming weight equals 1.

If $\bar{y}$ is output by a decoder, then $wt(\bar{y}) = 1$, and hence an encoder implements the
inverse function of a decoder.

13.3.4 Brute Force Implementation

We begin by describing a brute force implementation. Recall that $bin_n(i)[j]$ denotes
the jth bit in the binary representation of i. Let A_j denote the set of all integers in
$[0 : 2^n - 1]$ whose jth bit in binary representation equals 1. Formally,

$$A_j \triangleq \{i \in [0 : 2^n - 1] \mid bin_n(i)[j] = 1\}.$$

Claim 13.6 *If* $wt(y) = 1$, *then* $x[j] = \bigvee_{i \in A_j} y[i]$ *for every* $j \in [0 : n - 1]$.

PROOF: Assume that the output of an encoder with input y equals x. Let $\ell \in [0 : 2^n - 1]$
denote the position of the one in y, namely, $y[\ell] = 1$. We consider two cases:

1. If $\ell = 0$, then $y = 0^{2^n}$ and $x = 0^n$. Therefore $\bigvee_{i \in A_j} y[i]$ equals 0, for each j, as required.
2. If $\ell > 0$, then $\langle x \rangle = \ell$. By the definition of binary representation, $x[j] = 1$ iff $bin_n(\ell)[j] = 1$, namely, $x[j] = 1$ iff $\ell \in A_j$. But

$$\bigvee_{i \in A_j} y[i] = \begin{cases} 0 & \text{if } \ell \notin A_j \\ 1 & \text{if } \ell \in A_j. \end{cases}$$

Thus $x[j] = \bigvee_{i \in A_j} y[i]$, as required. ∎

Claim 13.6 gives us a recipe for implementing an ENCODER(n). For each output
x_j, use a separate OR-tree whose inputs are $\{y[i] \mid i \in A_j\}$. Each such OR-tree has at
most 2^n inputs (in fact, $|A_j| = 2^{n-1}$ for every j). Therefore the cost of each OR-tree is
$O(2^n)$. There are n outputs, so the total cost is $O(n \cdot 2^n)$. The delay of each OR-tree is
$O(\log 2^n) = O(n)$.

In the following sections, we try to design a better encoder.

13.3.5 Implementation and Correctness

In this section, we present a step-by-step implementation of an encoder. We start with
a rather costly design, which we denote by ENCODER$'(n)$. We then show how to modify
ENCODER$'(n)$ to an asymptotically optimal one.

Implementation. As in the design of a decoder, our design is recursive. The design for $n = 1$ is simply $x[0] \leftarrow y[1]$. Hence, for $n = 1$, the cost and delay of our design are zero. We proceed with the design for $n > 1$.

Again, we use the divide-and-conquer method. We partition the input $\vec{y}$ into two strings of equal length, as follows:

$$y_L[2^{n-1} - 1 : 0] = y[2^n - 1 : 2^{n-1}] \qquad y_R[2^{n-1} - 1 : 0] = y[2^{n-1} - 1 : 0].$$

The idea is to feed these two parts into two encoders $\text{ENCODER}'(n-1)$ (see Figure 13.5). However, there is a problem with this approach. The problem is that even if $\vec{y}$ is a "legal" input (namely, $wt(\vec{y}) = 1$), then one of the strings $\vec{y}_L$ or $\vec{y}_R$ is all zeros, which is not a legal input. An "illegal" input can produce an arbitrary output, which might make the design wrong.

To fix this problem, we augment the definition of the ENCODER_n function so that its domain also includes the all-zeros string 0^{2^n}. We define

$$\text{ENCODER}_n(0^{2^n}) \triangleq 0^n.$$

Note that $\text{ENCODER}'(1)$ also meets this new condition, so the induction basis of the correctness proof holds.

Let $a[n - 2 : 0]$ (respectively, $b[n - 2 : 0]$) denote the output of the $\text{ENCODER}'(n-1)$ circuit that is fed by $\vec{y}_R$ (resp., $\vec{y}_L$). The output is defined by

$$x[i] \leftarrow \text{OR}(b[i], a[i]), \text{ if } 0 \le i \le n - 2 \text{ and}$$

$$x[n - 1] \leftarrow \text{OR}_{2^{n-1}}(\vec{y}_L)$$

Correctness

Claim 13.7 *The circuit* $\text{ENCODER}'(n)$ *depicted in Figure 13.5 implements the Boolean function* ENCODER_n.

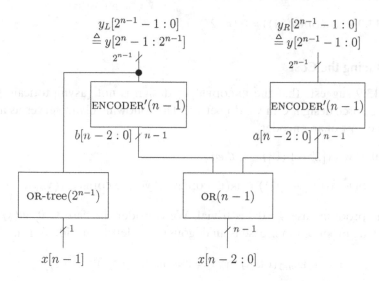

Figure 13.5. A recursive implementation of $\text{ENCODER}'(n)$.

PROOF: The correctness of the encoder design is proved as follows. We distinguish between three cases, depending on which half contains the bit that is lit in $\vec{y}$, if any:

1. If $wt(\vec{y}_L) = 0$ and $wt(\vec{y}_R) = 1$, then the induction hypothesis implies that $\vec{b} = 0^{n-1}$ and $y_R[\langle\vec{a}\rangle] = 1$. It follows that $y[\langle\vec{a}\rangle] = 1$, hence the required output is $\vec{x} = 0 \cdot \vec{a}$. The actual output equals the required output, and correctness holds in this case.
2. If $wt(\vec{y}_L) = 1$ and $wt(\vec{y}_R) = 0$, then the induction hypothesis implies that $y_L[\langle\vec{b}\rangle] = 1$ and $\vec{a} = 0^{n-1}$. It follows that $y[2^{n-1} + \langle\vec{b}\rangle] = 1$, hence the required output is $\vec{x} = 1 \cdot \vec{b}$. The actual output equals the required output, and correctness holds in this case.
3. If $wt(\langle\vec{y}\rangle) = 0$, then the required output is $\vec{x} = 0^n$. The induction hypothesis implies that $\vec{a} = \vec{b} = 0^{n-1}$. The actual output is $\vec{x} = 0^n$, and correctness follows. ∎

13.3.6 Cost Analysis

The problem with the ENCODER$'(n)$ design is that it is too costly. The cost of ENCODER$'(n)$ satisfies the following recurrence:

$$c(\text{ENCODER}'(n)) = \begin{cases} 0 & \text{if } n = 1 \\ 2 \cdot c(\text{ENCODER}'(n-1)) + c(\text{OR-tree}(2^{n-1})) + (n-1) \cdot c(\text{OR}) & \text{if } n > 1. \end{cases}$$

Let $c(n) \triangleq c(\text{ENCODER}'(n))/c(\text{OR})$. Then $c(n)$ satisfies the recurrence

$$c(n) = \begin{cases} 0 & \text{if } n = 1 \\ 2 \cdot c(n-1) + (2^{n-1} - 1 + n - 1) & \text{if } n > 1. \end{cases} \tag{13.2}$$

Claim 13.8 $c(n) = \Theta(n \cdot 2^n)$.

PROOF: Define $a(2^k) \triangleq c(k)$. Then $a(2^k) = 2 \cdot a(2^{k-1}) + \Theta(2^k)$. By Lemma 7.4, it follows that $a(2^k) = \Theta(k \cdot 2^k)$. Hence $c(n) = \Theta(n \cdot 2^n)$, as required. ∎

We conclude with the following corollary.

Corollary 13.9 $c(\text{ENCODER}'(n)) = \Theta(n \cdot 2^n)$.

13.3.7 Reducing the Cost

Corollary 13.9 suggests that the ENCODER$'(n)$ design is not (asymptotically) cheaper than a brute force design. Can we do better? The following claim serves as a basis for reducing the cost of an encoder.

Claim 13.10 If $wt(y[2^n - 1 : 0]) \leq 1$, then

$$\text{ENCODER}_{n-1}(\text{OR}(\vec{y}_L, \vec{y}_R)) = \text{OR}(\text{ENCODER}_{n-1}(\vec{y}_L), \text{ENCODER}_{n-1}(\vec{y}_R)). \tag{13.3}$$

PROOF: The proof in case $\vec{y} = 0^{2^n}$ is trivial. We consider the case that $wt(\vec{y}_L) = 0$ and $wt(\vec{y}_R) = 1$ (the proof of other case is analogous). The left-hand side of Eq. 13.3 equals

$$\text{ENCODER}_{n-1}(\text{OR}(\vec{y}_L, \vec{y}_R)) = \text{ENCODER}_{n-1}(\text{OR}(0^{2^{n-1}}, \vec{y}_R))$$

$$= \text{ENCODER}_{n-1}(\vec{y}_R).$$

However, the right-hand side of Eq. 13.3 equals

$$\mathrm{OR}\big(\mathrm{ENCODER}_{n-1}(\vec{y}_L),\ \mathrm{ENCODER}_{n-1}(\vec{y}_R)\big) = \mathrm{OR}\big(\mathrm{ENCODER}_{n-1}(0^{2^{n-1}}),\ \mathrm{ENCODER}_{n-1}(\vec{y}_R)\big)$$
$$= \mathrm{OR}\big(0^{n-1},\ \mathrm{ENCODER}_{n-1}(\vec{y}_R)\big)$$
$$= \mathrm{ENCODER}_{n-1}(\vec{y}_R),$$

and the claim follows. ∎

Figure 13.6 depicts the design ENCODER$^*(n)$ obtained from ENCODER$'(n)$ after commuting the OR and the ENCODER$(n-1)$ operations. Claim 13.10 implies that ENCODER$'(n)$ and ENCODER$^*(n)$ are functionally equivalent.

Definition 13.9 Two combinational circuits are *functionally equivalent* if they implement the same Boolean function.

In other words, functionally equivalent combinational circuits output the same output when they are input by the same values.

We conclude that we do not need to prove the correctness of the ENCODER$^*(n)$ circuit from scratch, namely, the correctness of ENCODER$'(n)$ implies the correctness of ENCODER$^*(n)$. The following claim is proved by induction on n.

Claim 13.11 *The circuits* ENCODER$'(n)$ *and* ENCODER$^*(n)$ *are functionally equivalent.*

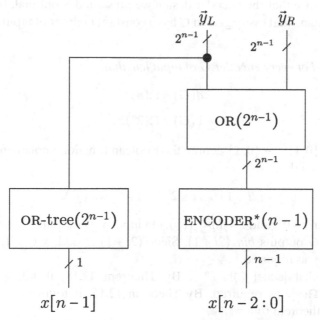

Figure 13.6. A recursive implementation of ENCODER$^*(n)$.

13.3.8 Cost and Delay Analysis

The cost of $\text{ENCODER}^*(n)$ satisfies the following recurrence equation:

$$c(\text{ENCODER}^*(n)) = \begin{cases} 0 & \text{if } n = 1 \\ c(\text{ENCODER}^*(n-1)) + (2^n - 1) \cdot c(\text{OR}) & \text{otherwise.} \end{cases}$$

Let us rewrite the recurrence so that the parameter is the number of inputs. Note that the error term is linear in the number of inputs. In other words, let $C(2^k) \triangleq c(\text{ENCODER}^*(k))/c(\text{OR})$. Then

$$C(2^k) = \begin{cases} 0 & \text{if } k = 0 \\ C(2^{k-1}) + (2^k - 1) & \text{otherwise.} \end{cases}$$

By Lemma 7.1, we conclude that $C(2^k) = \Theta(2^k)$.

Corollary 13.12 $c(\text{ENCODER}^*(n)) = \Theta(2^n)$.

The delay of $\text{ENCODER}^*(n)$ satisfies the following recurrence equation:

$$d(\text{ENCODER}^*(n)) = \begin{cases} 0 & \text{if } n = 1 \\ \max\{d(\text{OR-tree}(2^{n-1})), d(\text{ENCODER}^*(n-1) + d(\text{OR}))\} & \text{otherwise.} \end{cases}$$

Since $d(\text{OR-tree}(2^{n-1})) = (n-1) \cdot d(\text{OR})$, it can be proven by induction that

$$d(\text{ENCODER}^*(n)) = (n-1) \cdot d(\text{OR}).$$

13.3.9 Asymptotic Optimality

Our goal is to prove that the encoder design we presented is optimal. In the following theorem, we assume that every gate in G has a constant number of input terminals (say, at most two).

Theorem 13.13 *For every encoder G of input length n,*

$$d(G) = \Omega(n)$$
$$c(G) = \Omega(2^n).$$

PROOF: Let $f_0 : \{0,1\}^{2^n} \to \{0,1\}$ denote the Boolean function implemented by the output $x[0]$. We claim that

$$\{2i + 1 \mid 0 \leq i \leq 2^{n-1} - 1\} \subseteq cone(f_0).$$

Indeed, consider $y = 0^{2^n}$ and $z \triangleq flip_{2i+1}(y)$. On input y, G outputs 0^{2^n}, and hence $x[0] = 0$. On input z, G outputs $bin_n(2i + 1)$. Since $(2i + 1)$ is odd, $x[0] = 1$, and therefore $2i + 1 \in cone(f_0)$, as required.

It follows that $|cone(f_0)| \geq 2^{n-1}$. By Theorem 12.18, it follows that $d(G) \geq \log|cone(f_0)| = \Omega(n)$, as required. By Theorem 12.15, if follows that $c(G) \geq 2^{n-1} = \Omega(2^n)$, and the theorem follows. ∎

13.4 SUMMARY

In this chapter, we introduced notation for buses that is used to denote indexed signals (e.g., $a[n-1:0]$). We presented designs for decoders and encoders using a design methodology called divide-and-conquer.

The first combinational circuit we described is a decoder. A decoder can be viewed as a circuit that translates a number represented in binary representation to a 1-out-of-2^n encoding. We started by presenting a brute force design in which a separate AND-tree is used for each output bit. The brute force design is simple yet wasteful. We then presented a recursive decoder design with asymptotically optimal cost and delay.

There are many advantages in using recursion. First, we were able to formally define the circuit. The other option would have been to draw small cases (say, $n = 3, 4$) and then argue informally that the circuit is built in a similar fashion for larger values of n. Second, having recursively defined the design, we were able to prove its correctness using induction. Third, writing the recurrence equations for cost and delay is easy. We proved that our decoder design is asymptotically optimal both in cost and in delay.

The second combinational circuit we described is an encoder. An encoder is the inverse circuit of a decoder. We presented a naive design and proved its correctness. We then reduced the cost of the naive design by commuting the order of two operations without changing the functionality. We proved that the final encoder design has asymptotically optimal cost and delay.

Three main techniques were used in this chapter:

- *Divide-and-conquer.* We solve a problem by dividing it into smaller subproblems. The solutions of the smaller subproblems are glued together to solve the big problem. Divide-and-conquer is a design methodology that uses recursion.
- *Extend specification to make problem easier.* We encountered a difficulty in the encoder design due to an all-zeros input. We bypassed this problem by extending the specification of an encoder so that it must output all zeros when input an all zeros. Adding restrictions to the specification made the task easier since we were able to add assumptions in our recursive designs.
- *Evolution.* We started with a naive and correct design. This design turned out to be too costly. We improved the naive design while preserving its functionality to obtain a cheaper design. The correctness of the improved design follows from the correctness of the naive design and the fact that it is functionally equivalent to the naive design.

PROBLEMS

13.1. Answer the following questions.

    1. Implement the DECODER(3) combinational circuit using the Logisim software.

        - First, implement DECODER(1) and DECODER(2). Hint: implement an array of AND gates.

- Verify that the outputs of these decoders are indexed in ascending order, that is, edit the subcircuit's appearance.
- Submit: (i) printouts of DECODER(1),DECODER(2) and DECODER(3), (ii) printouts of the truth tables of each of these decoders, and (iii) simulate the following input vector $\bar{x} = 010$, that is, draw (by hand) the logical values on every wire on your printout of DECODER(3).

2. Implement the ENCODER*(3) combinational circuit using the Logisim software.
   - First, implement ENCODER*(1), ENCODER*(2), and OR-tree(4).
   - Verify that the outputs of these encoders are indexed in ascending order, that is, edit the subcircuit's appearance.
   - Submit: (i) printouts of ENCODER*(1),ENCODER*(2) and ENCODER*(3), (ii) printouts of the truth tables of each of these encoders, and (iii) simulate the following input vector $\bar{y} = 00100000$, that is, draw (by hand) the logical values on every wire on your printout of ENCODER*(3).

3. Connect the output of DECODER(3) to the input of ENCODER*(3). Print the truth table containing the decoder's input, the decoder's output, and the encoder's output.

13.2. Let $c(n)$ and $d(n)$ denote the cost of the decoder with n inputs presented in Section 13.2.4.

1. Prove that $c(n) = O(2^n)$ even if $k = 1$ in all the reduction rules.
2. Analyze $d(n)$ if $k = 1$ in all the reduction rules.
3*. Prove that $c(n) = O(2^n)$, for every choice of $1 \le k < n$.

13.3. Prove that every output bit of a decoder depends on all the inputs.

13.4. Prove that $d(\text{ENCODER}'(n)) = \Theta(n)$.

13.5. Provide a direct correctness proof for the ENCODER*(n) design (i.e., do not rely on the correctness of ENCODER$'(n)$). Does the correctness of ENCODER*(n) require that ENCODER*$(n-1)$ output an all-zeros string when the input is an all-zeros string?

13.6. The following question is based on the following definitions:

Definition 13.10 A binary string $x'[n-1:0]$ *dominates* the binary string $x''[n-1:0]$ if

$$\forall i \in [n-1:0]: \quad x''[i] = 1 \Rightarrow x'[i] = 1.$$

Definition 13.11 A Boolean function f is *monotone* if x' dominates x'' implies that $f(x')$ dominates $f(x'')$:

1. Prove that if a combinational circuit C contains only gates that implement monotone Boolean functions (e.g., only AND-gates and OR-gates, no inverters), then C implements a monotone Boolean function.
2. The designs ENCODER$'(n)$ and ENCODER*(n) lack inverters and hence are monotone circuits. Is the Boolean function ENCODER$_n$ a monotone Boolean function?
3. Suppose that G is an encoder and is a monotone combinational circuit. Suppose that the input y of G has two ones (namely, $wt(y) = 2$). Can you immediately deduce which outputs of G must equal one?

CHAPTER 14

Selectors and Shifters

In this chapter, we present combinational circuits that manipulate the input bits. By manipulation we mean that the bits in the output appear in the input. Why do we need such circuits?

We deal with two settings in which such manipulations take place: selection and shifting.

- In selection, we are given an n-bit string $D[n-1:0]$ and an encoding of an index $0 \leq i < n$ in binary representation. The output is simply $D[i]$. Namely, we want the output to equal the ith bit of the input. The circuit that performs selection is often called a *multiplexer*.
- In shifting, we wish to "move" the input bits around. Most programming languages include shift instructions, so we must design combinational circuits that can execute these instructions.

14.1 MULTIPLEXERS

In this section, we present designs of $(n:1)$-multiplexers. Multiplexers are often also called *selectors*.

We first define a MUX-gate (also known as a $(2:1)$-multiplexer).

Definition 14.1 A MUX-gate is a combinational gate that has three inputs $D[0]$, $D[1]$, and S and one output Y. The functionality is defined by

$$Y = \begin{cases} D[0] & \text{if } S = 0 \\ D[1] & \text{if } S = 1. \end{cases}$$

Note that we could have used the shorter expression $Y = D[S]$ to define the functionality of a MUX-gate.

An (n:1)-MUX is a combinational circuit defined as follows:

Input: $D[n-1:0]$ and $S[k-1:0]$, where $k = \lceil \log_2 n \rceil$.
Output: $Y \in \{0, 1\}$.

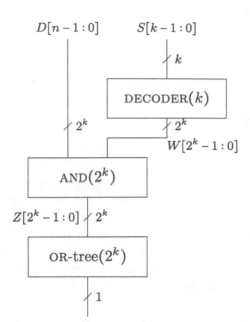

Figure 14.1. An (n:1)-MUX based on a decoder ($n = 2^k$).

Functionality:

$$Y = D[\langle \vec{S} \rangle].$$

We often refer to $\vec{D}$ as the *data input* and to $\vec{S}$ as the *select input*. The select input $\vec{S}$ encodes the index of the bit of the data input $\vec{D}$ that should be output. To simplify the discussion, we will assume in this chapter that n is a power of 2, namely, $n = 2^k$.

Example 14.1 Let $n = 4$ and $D[3:0] = 0101$. If $S[1:0] = 00$, then $Y = D[0] = 1$. If $S[1:0] = 01$, then $Y = D[1] = 0$.

14.1.1 Implementation

We describe two implementations of (n:1)-MUX. The first implementation is based on translating the number $\langle \vec{S} \rangle$ to 1-out-of-n representation (using a decoder). The second implementation is basically a tree.

A Decoder-Based Implementation. Figure 14.1 depicts an implementation of a (n:1)-MUX based on a decoder. The input $S[k-1:0]$ is fed to a DECODER(k). The decoder outputs a 1-out-of-n representation of $\langle \vec{S} \rangle$. Bitwise-AND is applied to the output of the decoder and the input $D[n-1:0]$. The output of the bitwise-AND is then fed to an OR-tree to produce Y.

Claim 14.1 *The (n:1)-MUX design depicted in Figure 14.1 is correct.*

PROOF: Let $s = \langle S[k-1:0] \rangle$. The output $\vec{W}$ of the decoder satisfies

$$W[i] = \begin{cases} 1 & \text{if } i = s \\ 0 & \text{otherwise.} \end{cases}$$

The output $\vec{Z}$ of the bitwise-AND satisfies

$$Z[i] = \begin{cases} D[i] & \text{if } i = s \\ 0 & \text{otherwise.} \end{cases}$$

It follows that $Y = D[s]$, as required. ∎

Claim 14.2 *The cost of the (n:1)-MUX design depicted in Figure 14.1 is $\Theta(n)$.*

PROOF: The cost consists of three parts: (i) $c(\text{DECODER}(k)) = \Theta(2^k)$, (ii) $c(\text{AND}(2^k)) = \Theta(2^k)$ and (iii) $c(\text{OR-tree}(2^k)) = \Theta(2^k)$. It follows that $c((n{:}1)\text{-MUX}) = \Theta(n)$, as required. ∎

Claim 14.3 *The delay of the (n:1)-MUX design depicted in Figure 14.1 is $\Theta(\log n)$.*

PROOF: The delay consists of three parts: (i) $d(\text{DECODER}(k)) = \Theta(\log k)$, (ii) $d(\text{AND}(2^k)) = \Theta(1)$, and (iii) $d(\text{OR-tree}(2^k)) = \Theta(k)$. It follows that $d((n{:}1)\text{-MUX}) = \Theta(k)$, as required. ∎

Claim 14.4 *The cone of the Boolean function implemented by a $(n:1)$-MUX circuit contains at least n elements.*

PROOF: Fix an index $i \in \{0, \ldots, n-1\}$. Let $S[k-1:0]$ satisfy $\langle \vec{S} \rangle = i$. Let $D[n-1:0] = 0^n$. Since $Y = D[\langle \vec{S} \rangle]$, if we flip $D[i]$ from 0 to 1, then the output Y flips from 0 to 1. Thus the cone contains all n indexes that correspond to the input D. ∎

Corollary 14.5 *The cost of the (n:1)-MUX design depicted in Figure 14.1 is asymptotically optimal.*

PROOF: Follows from Theorem 12.15 and Claim 14.4. ∎

Corollary 14.6 *The delay of the (n:1)-MUX design depicted in Figure 14.1 is asymptotically optimal.*

PROOF: Follows from Theorem 12.18 and Claim 14.4. ∎

A Tree-Like Implementation. A second implementation of (n:1)-MUX is a recursive tree-like implementation. The design for $n = 2$ is simply a MUX-gate. The design for $n = 2^k$ is depicted in Figure 14.2. The input $\vec{D}$ is divided into two parts of equal length. Each part is fed to an $(\frac{n}{2}:1)$-MUX controlled by the signal $S[k-2:0]$. The outputs of the $(\frac{n}{2}:1)$-MUXs are Y_L and Y_R. Finally, a MUX selects between Y_L and Y_R according to the value of $S[k-1]$.

Claim 14.7 *The (n:1)-MUX design depicted in Figure 14.2 is correct.*

PROOF: The proof is by induction on k. The induction basis for $k = 1$ follows from the correctness of a MUX-gate. The induction step is proved as follows.

Let $s = \langle S[k-1:0] \rangle$ and $s' = \langle S[k-2:0] \rangle$. By the induction hypothesis, $Y_R = D[s']$ and $Y_L = D[\frac{n}{2} + s']$. The MUX-gate selects

$$Y = \begin{cases} Y_R & \text{if } S[k-1] = 0 \\ Y_L & \text{if } S[k-1] = 1. \end{cases}$$

It follows that $Y = D[s]$, as required. ∎

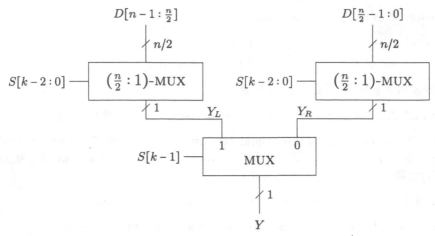

Figure 14.2. A recursive implementation of (n:1)-MUX ($n = 2^k$).

Claim 14.8 *The cost of the (n:1)-MUX design depicted in Figure 14.2 is $\Theta(n)$.*

PROOF: Since we are not interested in the constants, let $c(\text{MUX}) = 1$. The cost satisfies the recurrence

$$c(n) = \begin{cases} 1 & \text{if } n = 2 \\ 2 \cdot c(n/2) + 1 & \text{otherwise.} \end{cases}$$

We claim that $c(n) = n - 1$. The proof is by induction on n. The induction basis for $n = 2$ holds because $c(2) = 1$. The induction step is proved as follows: $c(n) = 2c(n/2) + 1 = 2(n/2 - 1) + 1 = n - 1$, and the claim follows. ∎

The proof of Claim 14.8 shows, in fact, that $c((\text{n:1})\text{-MUX}) = (n - 1) \cdot c(\text{MUX})$, if implemented according to Figure 14.2.

Claim 14.9 *The delay of the (n:1)-MUX design depicted in Figure 14.2 is $\Theta(\log n)$.*

PROOF: Since we are not interested in the constants, let $d(\text{MUX}) = 1$. The delay satisfies the recurrence

$$d(n) = \begin{cases} 1 & \text{if } n = 2 \\ d(n/2) + 1 & \text{otherwise.} \end{cases}$$

We claim that $d(n) = \log_2(n)$. The proof is by induction on n. Indeed, $d(2) = 1$, and $d(n) = d(n/2) + 1 = \log_2(n/2) + 1 = \log_2(n)$, as required. ∎

Comparison. Both implementations suggested in this section are asymptotically optimal with respect to cost and delay. Which design is better? A cost and delay analysis based on the cost and delay of gates listed in Table 11.1 suggests that the tree-like implementation is cheaper and faster. Nevertheless, our model is not refined enough to answer this question sharply. On one hand, the tree-like design is simply a tree of multiplexers. The decoder based design contains, in addition to an OR(n)-tree with n inputs, also a line of AND-gates and a decoder. So one may conclude that the decoder-based design is worse. Conversely, OR-gates are typically cheaper and faster than MUX-gates. Moreover, fast and cheap implementations of MUX-gates in CMOS technology do not restore the signals well; this means that long paths consisting only of MUX-gates are not allowed. We conclude that the model we use cannot be used to deduce conclusively which multiplexer design is better.

14.2 CYCLIC SHIFTERS

We explain what a cyclic shift is by the following example. Consider a binary string $a[1:12]$ and assume that we place the bits of a on a wheel. The position of $a[1]$ is at one o'clock, the position of $a[2]$ is at two o'clock, and so on. We now rotate the wheel and read the bits in clockwise order starting from one o'clock and ending at twelve o'clock. The resulting string is a cyclic shift of $a[1:12]$. Figure 14.3 depicts an example of a cyclic shift.

Notation. In this section, we denote $(a \bmod b)$ by $\mathrm{mod}(a, b)$.

Definition 14.2 The string $b[n-1:0]$ is a *cyclic left shift by i positions* of the string $a[n-1:0]$ if

$$\forall j: \quad b[j] = a[\mathrm{mod}(j-i, n)].$$

Example 14.2 Let $a[3:0] = 0010$. A cyclic left shift by one position of $\vec{a}$ is the string 0100. A cyclic left shift by three positions of $\vec{a}$ is the string 0001.

Definition 14.3 A BARREL-SHIFTER(n) is a combinational circuit defined as follows:

Input: $x[n-1:0] \in \{0,1\}^n$ and $sa[k-1:0] \in \{0,1\}^k$, where $k = \lceil \log_2 n \rceil$.
Output: $y[n-1:0] \in \{0,1\}^n$.
Functionality: $\vec{y}$ is a cyclic left shift of $\vec{x}$ by $\langle \vec{sa} \rangle$ positions. Formally,

$$\forall j \in [n-1:0]: \quad y[j] = x[\mathrm{mod}(j - \langle \vec{sa} \rangle, n)].$$

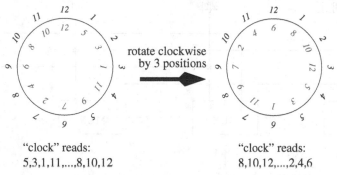

"clock" reads: "clock" reads:
5,3,1,11,...,8,10,12   8,10,12,...,2,4,6

Figure 14.3. An example of a cyclic shift. The clock "reads" the numbers stored in each clock notch in clockwise order starting from the one o'clock notch.

We often refer to the input $\bar{x}$ as the *data input* and to the input $\bar{sa}$ as the *shift amount input*. To simplify the discussion, we will assume in this section that n is a power of 2, namely, $n = 2^k$.

14.2.1 Implementation

We break the task of designing a barrel shifter into smaller subtasks of shifting by powers of 2. We define this subtask formally as follows.

A $\textsc{cls}(n, 2^i)$ is a combinational circuit that implements a cyclic left shift by zero or 2^i positions, depending on the value of its select input.

Definition 14.4 A $\textsc{cls}(n, i)$ is a combinational circuit defined as follows:

Input: $x[n-1:0]$ and $s \in \{0, 1\}$.
Output: $y[n-1:0]$.
Functionality:

$$\forall j \in [n-1:0]: \quad y[j] = x[\mod(j - s \cdot i, n)].$$

A $\textsc{cls}(n, i)$ is quite simple to implement since $y[j]$ is either $x[j]$ or $x[\mod(j - i, n)]$. So all one needs is a $\textsc{mux}$-gate to select between $x[j]$ or $x[\mod(j - i, n)]$. The selection is based on the value of s. It follows that the delay of $\textsc{cls}(n, i)$ is the delay of a $\textsc{mux}$, and the cost is n times the cost of a $\textsc{mux}$. Figure 14.4 depicts an implementation of a $\textsc{cls}(4, 2)$. It is self-evident that the main complication with the design of $\textsc{cls}(n, i)$ is routing (i.e., drawing the wires). However, we do not deal with the area required for routing in this book.

The design of a $\textsc{barrel-shifter}(n)$ is based on $\textsc{cls}(n, 2^i)$ shifters. Figure 14.5 depicts an implementation of a $\textsc{barrel-shifter}(n)$. The implementation is based on k levels of $\textsc{cls}(n, 2^i)$, for $i \in [k-1:0]$, where the ith level is controlled by $sa[i]$.

14.2.2 Correctness and Analysis of Cost and Delay

We now prove the correctness of the design for a barrel shifter depicted in Figure 14.5. The proof uses the following observation.

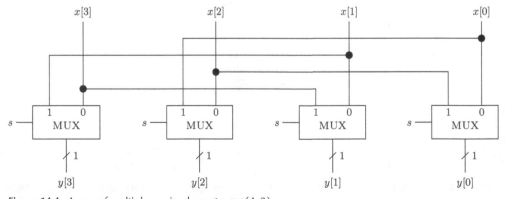

Figure 14.4. A row of multiplexers implement a $\textsc{cls}(4, 2)$.

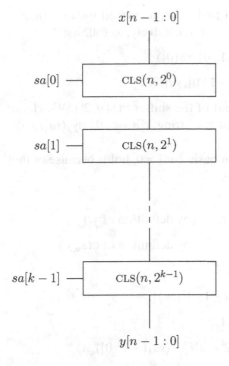

$x[n-1:0]$

$sa[0]$ — CLS$(n, 2^0)$

$sa[1]$ — CLS$(n, 2^1)$

Figure 14.5. A BARREL-SHIFTER(n) built of k levels of CLS$(n, 2^i)$ $(n = 2^k)$.

$sa[k-1]$ — CLS$(n, 2^{k-1})$

$y[n-1:0]$

Observation 14.1 *If* $\alpha = \mathrm{mod}(a, n)$ *and* $\beta = \mathrm{mod}(b, n)$, *then*

$$\mathrm{mod}(a - b, n) = \mathrm{mod}(\alpha - \beta, n).$$

PROOF: Divide a by n to obtain the quotient q_a and the remainder α:

$$a = q_a \cdot n + \alpha.$$

Similarly,

$$b = q_b \cdot n + \beta.$$

Divide $\alpha - \beta$ by n to obtain the quotient q and the remainder r, namely,

$$\alpha - \beta = q \cdot n + r.$$

Then

$$a - b = q_a n + \alpha - (q_b n + \beta)$$
$$= (q_a - q_b) \cdot n + (\alpha - \beta)$$
$$= (q_a - q_b) \cdot n + (qn + r)$$
$$= (q_a - q_b + q) \cdot n + r.$$

Hence $\mathrm{mod}(a - b, n) = r$, as required. ∎

Claim 14.10 *The barrel shifter design depicted in Figure 14.5 is correct.*

PROOF: Let $\text{CLS}_{n,2^i}$ denote the Boolean function that is implemented by a $\text{CLS}(n, 2^i)$ circuit. Define the strings $y_i[n - 1 : 0]$, for $0 \le i \le k - 1$, recursively, as follows:

$$y_0[n - 1 : 0] \leftarrow \text{CLS}_{n,2^0}(x[n - 1 : 0], sa[0])$$

$$y_{i+1}[n - 1 : 0] \leftarrow \text{CLS}_{n,2^{i+1}}(y_i[n - 1 : 0], sa[i + 1]).$$

Note that the vector $y_i[n - 1 : 0]$ equals the output of the shifter $\text{CLS}(n, 2^i)$. We claim that the string $y_i[n - 1 : 0]$ is a cyclic left shift of the string $x[n - 1 : 0]$ by $\langle sa[i : 0] \rangle$ positions.

The proof is by induction on i. The induction basis, for $i = 0$, holds because of the definition of $\text{CLS}(2, 2^0)$.

The induction step is proved as follows:

$$y_i[j] = \text{CLS}_{n,2^i}(y_{i-1}[n - 1 : 0], sa[i])[j] \qquad \text{(by definition of } y_i)$$

$$= y_{i-1}[\text{mod}(j - 2^i \cdot sa[i], n)]. \qquad \text{(by definition of } \text{CLS}_{n,2^i})$$

The induction hypothesis states that, for every j,

$$y_{i-1}[j] = x[\text{mod}(j - \langle sa[i - 1 : 0] \rangle, n)].$$

Let $\ell = \text{mod}(j - 2^i \cdot sa[i], n)$. By Observation 14.1,

$$\text{mod}(\ell - \langle sa[i - 1 : 0] \rangle, n) = \text{mod}(j - 2^i \cdot sa[i] - \langle sa[i - 1 : 0] \rangle, n)$$

$$= \text{mod}(j - \langle sa[i : 0] \rangle, n).$$

Therefore

$$y_i[j] = x[\text{mod}(j - \langle sa[i : 0] \rangle, n)],$$

and the claim follows. ■

Claim 14.11 *The cost and delay of* BARREL-SHIFTER(n) *satisfy:*

$$c(\text{BARREL-SHIFTER}(n)) = n \log_2 n \cdot c(\text{MUX})$$

$$d(\text{BARREL-SHIFTER}(n)) = \log_2 n \cdot d(\text{MUX}).$$

PROOF: Follows from the fact that the design consists of $\log_2 n$ levels of $\text{CLS}(n, 2^i)$ shifters. ■

Consider the output $y[0]$ of BARREL-SHIFTER(n).

Claim 14.12 *The cone of the Boolean function implemented by the output $y[0]$ contains at least n elements.*

PROOF: Fix an index i. Let $sa[k - 1 : 0]$ satisfy $\langle sa[k - 1 : 0] \rangle = i$. Consider the input $x[n - 1 : 0] = 0^n$. If we flip $x[n - i]$ from 0 to 1, then the output $y[0]$ flips from 0 to 1. Hence the index corresponding to the input $x[n - i]$ belongs to the cone. Since this is true for every index $i \in \{0, \ldots, n - 1\}$, we conclude that the cone contains at least n elements. ■

Corollary 14.13 *The delay of* BARREL-SHIFTER(n) *is asymptotically optimal.*

PROOF: The claim follows from Theorem 12.18 and Claim 14.12. ■

14.3 LOGICAL SHIFTERS

Logical shifting is used for shifting binary strings that represent unsigned integers in binary representation. Shifting to the left by s positions corresponds to multiplying by 2^s followed by modulo 2^n. Shifting to the right by s positions corresponds to division by 2^s followed by truncation.

Definition 14.5 The binary string $y[n-1:0]$ is a *logical left shift* by ℓ positions of the binary string $x[n-1:0]$ if

$$y[i] \triangleq \begin{cases} 0 & \text{if } i < \ell \\ x[i-\ell] & \text{if } \ell \le i < n. \end{cases}$$

For example, $y[3:0] = 0100$ is a logical left shift of $x[3:0] = 1001$ by $\ell = 2$ positions. When we apply a logical left shift to $x[n-1:0]$ by ℓ positions, we obtain the string $x[n-1-\ell:0] \circ 0^\ell$.

Definition 14.6 The binary string $y[n-1:0]$ is a *logical right shift* by ℓ positions of the binary string $x[n-1:0]$ if

$$y[i] \triangleq \begin{cases} 0 & \text{if } i \ge n-\ell \\ x[i+\ell] & \text{if } 0 \le i < n-\ell. \end{cases}$$

For example, $y[3:0] = 0010$ is a logical right shift of $x[3:0] = 1001$ by $\ell = 2$ positions. When we apply a logical right shift to $x[n-1:0]$ by ℓ positions, we obtain the string $0^\ell \circ x[n-1:\ell]$.

Notation. Let $\text{LLS}(\bar{x}, i)$ denote the logical left shift of $\bar{x}$ by i positions. Let $\text{LRS}(\bar{x}, i)$ denote the logical right shift of $\bar{x}$ by i positions.

A bidirectional logical shifter is defined as follows.

Definition 14.7 A L-SHIFT(n) is a combinational circuit defined as follows:

Input:

- $x[n-1:0] \in \{0,1\}^n$,
- $sa[k-1:0] \in \{0,1\}^k$, where $k = \lceil \log_2 n \rceil$,
- $\ell \in \{0,1\}$.

Output: $y[n-1:0] \in \{0,1\}^n$.
Functionality: The output $\bar{y}$ satisfies

$$\bar{y} \triangleq \begin{cases} \text{LLS}(\bar{x}, \langle \bar{sa} \rangle) & \text{if } \ell = 1, \\ \text{LRS}(\bar{x}, \langle \bar{sa} \rangle) & \text{if } \ell = 0. \end{cases}$$

For example, let $x[3:0] = 0010$. If $sa[1:0] = 10$ and $\ell = 1$, then L-SHIFT(4) outputs $y[3:0] = 1000$. If $\ell = 0$, then the output equals $y[3:0] = 0000$.

14.3.1 Implementation

As in the case of cyclic shifters, we break the task of designing a logical shifter into subtasks of logical shifts by powers of 2.

Definition 14.8 An LBS(n, i) is a combinational circuit defined as follows:

Input: $x[n - 1 : 0]$ and $s, \ell \in \{0, 1\}$.
Output: $y[n - 1 : 0]$.
Functionality: The output $\vec{y}$ satisfies

$$\vec{y} \triangleq \begin{cases} \vec{x} & \text{if } s = 0, \\ \text{LLS}(\vec{x}, i) & \text{if } s = 1 \text{ and } \ell = 1, \\ \text{LRS}(\vec{x}, i) & \text{if } s = 1 \text{ and } \ell = 0. \end{cases}$$

The role of the input s is to determine if a shift (in either direction) takes place at all. If $s = 0$, then $y[j] = x[j]$, and no shift takes place. If $s = 1$, then the direction of the shift is determined by ℓ.

A bit slice of an implementation of an LBS(n, i) is depicted in Figure 14.6. By the term *bit slice*, we mean that the figure depicts only how a single output bit $y[j]$ is computed. The whole circuit is obtained by combining such circuits for every output bit $y[j]$. We do not depict the whole circuit to avoid a messy figure with lots of wires that are hard to follow. The implementation of LBS(n, i) uses the following notation:

$$x'[i] \triangleq \begin{cases} x[i] & \text{if } 0 \le i \le n - 1 \\ 0 & \text{otherwise.} \end{cases}$$

We leave it to the reader to complete the following details:

1. Show how LBS(n, i) circuits can be cascaded to obtain a L-SHIFT(n). Hint: follow the design of a BARREL-SHIFTER(n).
2. Prove the correctness of your L-SHIFT(n) design.
3. Analyze the cost and delay of the resulting circuit.
4. Can you prove asymptotic optimality of the delay?

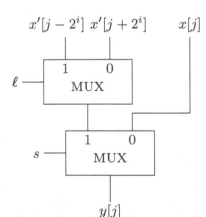

Figure 14.6. A bit slice of an implementation of LBS$(n, 2^i)$.

14.4 ARITHMETIC SHIFTERS

14.4.1 Two's Complement

We briefly deal with the representation of negative integers. This issue is dealt with in detail in Chapter 16.

Definition 14.9 The number represented in *two's complement* representation by $A[n - 1 : 0] \in \{0, 1\}^n$ is

$$-2^{n-1} \cdot A[n - 1] + \langle A[n - 2 : 0] \rangle.$$

We denote the number represented in two's complement representation by $A[n - 1 : 0]$, as follows:

$$[A[n - 1 : 0]] \triangleq -2^{n-1} \cdot A[n - 1] + \langle A[n - 2 : 0] \rangle.$$

14.4.2 Arithmetic Shifter

Arithmetic shifters are used for shifting binary strings that represent signed integers in two's complement representation. Since left shifting is the same in logical shifting and in arithmetic shifting, we discuss only right shifting (i.e., division by a power of 2).

Definition 14.10 The binary string $y[n - 1 : 0]$ is an *arithmetic right shift* by ℓ positions of the binary string $x[n - 1 : 0]$ if the following holds:

$$y[i] \triangleq \begin{cases} x[n - 1] & \text{if } i \geq n - \ell \\ x[i + \ell] & \text{if } 0 \leq i < n - \ell. \end{cases}$$

For example, $y[3 : 0] = 0010$ is an arithmetic shift of $x[3 : 0] = 0101$ by $\ell = -1$ positions.

Conversely, $y[3 : 0] = 1110$ is an arithmetic shift of $x[3 : 0] = 1001$ by $\ell = -2$ positions. When we apply an arithmetic shift by $\ell < 0$ positions to $x[n - 1 : 0]$, we obtain the string $x[n - 1]^\ell \circ x[n - 1 : \ell]$.

Notation. Let $\text{ARS}(\vec{x}, i)$ denote the arithmetic right shift of $\vec{x}$ by i positions.

The following claim shows that an arithmetic right shift by ℓ positions implements division by 2^ℓ with respect to two's complement representation.

Claim 14.14 *Let* $X[n - 1 : 0]$ *and* $Y[n - 1 : 0]$ *satisfy* $\vec{Y} = \text{ARS}(\vec{X}, \ell)$. *Let* $x = [\vec{X}]$ *and* $y = [\vec{Y}]$, *then*

$$y = \left\lfloor \frac{x}{2^\ell} \right\rfloor.$$

PROOF: By definition,

$$y = -2^{n-1} \cdot Y[n-1] + \sum_{j=0}^{n-2} Y[j] \cdot 2^j$$

$$= -2^{n-1} \cdot Y[n-1] + \sum_{j=n-\ell}^{n-2} Y[j] \cdot 2^j + \sum_{j=0}^{n-\ell-1} Y[j] \cdot 2^j. \qquad (14.1)$$

We simplify the first two addends in Eq. 14.1 by noticing that $Y[j] = X[n-1]$ for $j \geq n - \ell$:

$$-2^{n-1} \cdot Y[n-1] + \sum_{j=n-\ell}^{n-2} Y[j] \cdot 2^j = X[n-1] \cdot \left(-2^{n-1} + \sum_{j=n-\ell}^{n-2} 2^j\right)$$

$$= X[n-1] \cdot (-2^{n-\ell}).$$

The last addend in Eq. 14.1 is simplified by noticing that $Y[j] = X[j + \ell]$ for $j < n - \ell$:

$$\sum_{j=0}^{n-\ell-1} Y[j] \cdot 2^j = \sum_{j=0}^{n-\ell-1} X[j+\ell] \cdot 2^j$$

$$= \frac{1}{2^\ell} \cdot \sum_{j=\ell}^{n-1} X[j] \cdot 2^j.$$

We combine these two simplifications to obtain

$$y = \frac{1}{2^\ell} \cdot \left(-X[n-1] \cdot 2^n + \sum_{j=\ell}^{n-1} X[j] \cdot 2^j\right).$$

Hence $y = \lfloor x \cdot 2^{-\ell} \rfloor$, as required. ∎

An arithmetic right shifter is defined as follows.

Definition 14.11 An ARITH-SHIFT(n) is a combinational circuit defined as follows:

Input: $x[n-1:0] \in \{0,1\}^n$ and $sa[k-1:0] \in \{0,1\}^k$, where $k = \lceil \log_2 n \rceil$.
Output: $y[n-1:0] \in \{0,1\}^n$.
Functionality: The output $\vec{y}$ is a (sign-extended) arithmetic right shift of $\vec{x}$ by $\langle \vec{sa} \rangle$ positions. Formally,

$$y[n-1:0] \triangleq \text{ARS}(x[n-1:0], \langle \vec{sa} \rangle).$$

Example 14.3 Let $x[3:0] = 1001$. If $sa[1:0] = 10$, then ARITH-SHIFT(4) outputs $y[3:0] = 1110$.

We leave it to the reader to complete the following details:

1. Suggest a circuit ARS(n, i) that implements an arithmetic right shift by i positions.
2. Show how ARS(n, i) circuits can be cascaded to obtain a ARITH-SHIFT(n). Hint: follow the design of a BARREL-SHIFTER(n).
3. Prove the correctness of your ARITH-SHIFT(n) design.
4. Analyze the cost and delay of the resulting circuit.
5. Can you prove asymptotic optimality of the delay?

14.5 SUMMARY

We began this chapter by defining $(n:1)$-multiplexers. We presented two optimal implementations. One implementations is based on a decoder, and the other implementation is based on a tree of multiplexers.

We continued by defining three types of shifts: cyclic, logical, and arithmetic. The method we propose for designing such shifters is to cascade a logarithmic number of shifters (with parameter i) that either perform a shift by 2^i positions or no shift at all.

PROBLEMS

14.1. Compute the cost and delay of both implementations of (n:1)-MUX based on the data in Table 11.1 for various values of n (e.g., $n = 4, 8, 16, 32$).

14.2. Is the functionality of BARREL-SHIFTER(n) preserved if the order of the levels is changed?

14.3. Recall the definition of the combinational circuit LBS(n, i) (see Definition 14.8). Recall the definition of the combinational circuit L-SHIFT(n) (see Definition 14.7). Complete the following details:
  (a) Show how LBS(n, i) circuits can be cascaded to obtain a L-SHIFT(n). Hint: follow the design of a BARREL-SHIFTER(n).
  (b) Prove the correctness of your L-SHIFT(n) design.
  (c) Analyze the cost and delay of the resulting circuit.
  (d) Can you prove asymptotic optimality of the delay?

14.4. Recall that ARS$(\bar{x}, i)$ denotes the arithmetic shift of $\bar{x}$ by i positions (see Definition 14.10). Recall the definition of the combinational circuit ARITH-SHIFT(n) (see Definition 14.11). Complete the following details:
  (a) Suggest a circuit ARS(n, i) that implements an arithmetic right shift by i positions.
  (b) Show how ARS(n, i) circuits can be cascaded to obtain a ARITH-SHIFT(n). Hint: follow the design of a BARREL-SHIFTER(n).
  (c) Prove the correctness of your ARITH-SHIFT(n) design.
  (d) Analyze the cost and delay of the resulting circuit.
  (e) Can you prove asymptotic optimality of the delay?

14.5. Prove that every Boolean function can be implemented by a combinational circuit containing only $(2:1)$-MUX gates.

14.6. Design a bidirectional cyclic shifter. Such a shifter is like a cyclic left shifter but has an additional input $\ell \in \{0, 1\}$ that indicates the direction of the required shift. Hint: consider reducing a cyclic right shift to a cyclic left shifter. To simplify the reduction you may assume that $n = 2^k - 1$ (hint: use one's complement negation). Suggest a simple reduction in case $n = 2^k$ (hint: avoid explicit subtraction!).

14.7. A *priority encoder* with input length 2^n is defined as follows:
  Input: $y[2^n - 1 : 0] \in \{0, 1\}^{2^n}$.

Output: $x[n-1:0] \in \{0,1\}^n$.

Functionality: If $y \ne 0^{2^n}$, let i denote the smallest index i such that $y[i] = 1$. In this case, $\vec{x}$ should satisfy $\langle \vec{x} \rangle = i$. Formally,

$$wt(\vec{y}) > 0 \implies y[\langle \vec{x} \rangle : 0] = 1 \circ 0^{\langle \vec{x} \rangle - 1}.$$

(a) Design a priority encoder with input length 2^n. Hint: add an output indicating if $y = 0^{2^n}$ and apply divide-and-conquer.

(b) Prove the correctness of your design.

(c) Prove asymptotic lower bounds on the cost and delay of a priority encoder with input length 2^n.

CHAPTER 15

Addition

In this chapter, we define binary adders. An adder is a combinational circuit that implements the function $f(x, y) = x + y$. To be more precise, we want the function f to be a Boolean function, not a function defined over the integers. We therefore use binary representation. This means that the inputs are two n-bit strings, where each string represents a nonnegative integer in binary representation. The output should represent their sum in binary representation.

One complication that we must address if we wish to be precise is that the sum might be too large and cannot be represented using n bits. We solve this problem by adding one bit to the output, called the *carry-out bit*.

We present three different combinational circuits for addition. These designs have an increasing level of sophistication. The first design, called a *ripple carry adder*, implements a binary version of how addition is taught in elementary school. Its correctness proof can be easily modified to finally prove the correctness of the addition algorithm we have been using since elementary school.

15.1 DEFINITION OF A BINARY ADDER

Definition 15.1 A *binary adder* with input length n is a combinational circuit specified as follows:

Input: $A[n-1:0], B[n-1:0] \in \{0, 1\}^n$, and $C[0] \in \{0, 1\}$.
Output: $S[n-1:0] \in \{0, 1\}^n$ and $C[n] \in \{0, 1\}$.
Functionality:

$$\langle \vec{S} \rangle + 2^n \cdot C[n] = \langle \vec{A} \rangle + \langle \vec{B} \rangle + C[0]. \tag{15.1}$$

We denote a binary adder with input length n by ADDER(n). The inputs $\vec{A}$ and $\vec{B}$ are the binary representations of the addends. The input $C[0]$ is often called the *carry-in bit*. The output $\vec{S}$ is the binary representation of the sum (more precisely, $\vec{S}$ is the binary representation of the sum modulo 2^n), and the output $C[n]$ is often called the *carry-out bit*.

215

The following claim shows that the functionality of a binary adder is well defined.

Claim 15.1 *For every* $A[n-1:0], B[n-1:0] \in \{0,1\}^n$, *and* $C[0] \in \{0,1\}$, *there exist* $S[n-1:0] \in \{0,1\}^n$ *and* $C[n] \in \{0,1\}$ *such that*

$$\langle \vec{S} \rangle + 2^n \cdot C[n] = \langle \vec{A} \rangle + \langle \vec{B} \rangle + C[0].$$

PROOF: Since $0 \le \vec{A}, \vec{B} \le 2^n - 1$, it follows that

$$0 \le \langle \vec{A} \rangle + \langle \vec{B} \rangle + C[0] \le 2^{n+1} - 1.$$

By Lemma 5.2, we can represent any integer in the set $\{0, \dots, 2^{n+1} - 1\}$ if we have $n + 1$ bits. Since $\vec{S}$ and $C[n]$ together represent a number in binary representation, the claim follows. ■

There are many ways to implement an ADDER(n). In this chapter, we present a few ADDER(n) designs.

15.2 RIPPLE CARRY ADDER

Ripple carry adders are built by chaining a row of full-adders. We denote a ripple carry adder that implements an ADDER(n) by RCA(n). A full-adder is a combinational circuit that adds three bits and represents their sum in binary representation.

Definition 15.2 (*Full-Adder*) A *full-adder* is a combinational circuit with three inputs $x, y, z \in \{0,1\}$ and two outputs $c, s \in \{0,1\}$ that satisfies

$$2c + s = x + y + z.$$

The output s of a full-adder is often called the *sum output*. The output c of a full-adder is often called the *carry-out output*. We denote a full-adder by FA. The Boolean function corresponding the carry-out output is called the 3-bit carry function (see p. 14). The Boolean formula for the outputs of a full-adder are presented in the following claim. We denote the Boolean functions OR, AND, and XOR by $\vee$, $\cdot$, and $\oplus$, respectively.

Claim 15.2 *The following equations specify the Boolean formulas for c and s in a full-adder:*

$$s = x \oplus y \oplus z$$

$$c = (x \cdot y) \vee (y \cdot z) \vee (x \cdot z).$$

PROOF: The claim can be easily proved using a truth table. Instead, we consider four cases based on the value of the sum $x + y + z$ (this is a regular sum, not an OR).

1. If $x + y + z = 0$, then $x \oplus y \oplus z = 0$ and $(x \cdot y) \vee (y \cdot z) \vee (x \cdot z) = 0$, hence $2c + s = 0$, as required.
2. If $x + y + z = 1$, then exactly one of the inputs equals one. Therefore $x \oplus y \oplus z = 1$ and $(x \cdot y) \vee (y \cdot z) \vee (x \cdot z) = 0$, hence $2c + s = 1$, as required.
3. If $x + y + z = 2$, then exactly two of the inputs equal one. Therefore $x \oplus y \oplus z = 0$ and $(x \cdot y) \vee (y \cdot z) \vee (x \cdot z) = 1$, hence $2c + s = 2$, as required.

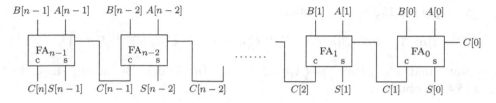

Figure 15.1. A ripple carry adder bf RCA(n).

4. If $x + y + z = 3$, then all the inputs equal one. Therefore $x \oplus y \oplus z = 1$ and $(x \cdot y) \vee (y \cdot z) \vee (x \cdot z) = 1$, hence $2c + s = 3$, as required. ∎

Implementation of RCA(n). A ripple carry adder, RCA(n), is built by chaining a row of n full-adders. An RCA(n) is depicted in Figure 15.1. Note that the carry-out output of the ith full-adder is denoted by $c[i + 1]$. The weight of $c[i + 1]$ is 2^{i+1}. This way, the weight of every signal is two to the power of its index. One can readily notice that an RCA(n) adds numbers using the same addition algorithm that we use for adding numbers by hand.

15.2.1 Correctness Proof

In this section, we prove the correctness of an RCA(n). To facilitate the proof, we use an equivalent recursive definition of RCA(n). The recursive definition is as follows.

The basis, RCA(1), is simply a full-adder. The reduction rule for designing RCA(n), for $n > 1$, is depicted in Figure 15.2.

The following claim deals with the correctness of RCA(n).

Claim 15.3 RCA(n) *is a correct implementation of* ADDER(n).

PROOF: The proof is by induction on n. The induction basis, for $n = 1$, follows directly from the definition of a full-adder. The induction step is proved as follows.

The induction hypothesis, for $n - 1$, is

$$\langle A[n - 2 : 0] \rangle + \langle B[n - 2 : 0] \rangle + C[0] = 2^{n-1} \cdot C[n - 1] + \langle S[n - 2 : 0] \rangle. \quad (15.2)$$

The definition of a full-adder states that

$$A[n - 1] + B[n - 1] + C[n - 1] = 2 \cdot C[n] + S[n - 1]. \quad (15.3)$$

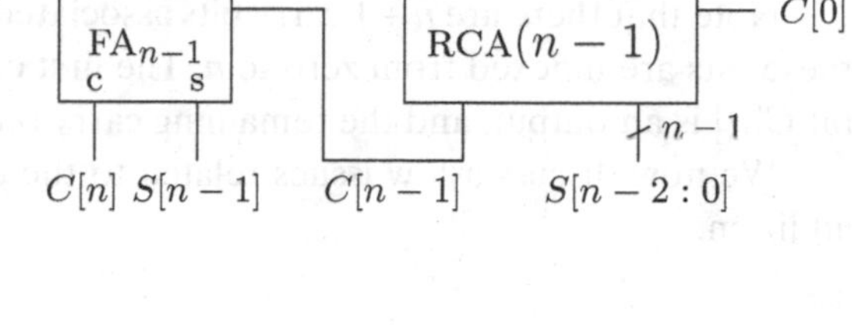

Figure 15.2. A recursive description of RCA(n).

Multiply Eq. 15.3 by 2^{n-1} to obtain

$$2^{n-1} \cdot A[n-1] + 2^{n-1} \cdot B[n-1] + 2^{n-1} \cdot C[n-1] = 2^n \cdot C[n] + 2^{n-1} \cdot S[n-1]. \qquad (15.4)$$

Note that $2^{n-1} \cdot A[n-1] + \langle A[n-2:0] \rangle = \langle A[n-1:0] \rangle$. By adding Eqs. 15.2 and 15.4, we obtain

$$2^{n-1} \cdot C[n-1] + \langle A[n-1:0] \rangle + \langle B[n-1:0] \rangle + C[0]$$
$$= 2^n \cdot C[n] + 2^{n-1} \cdot C[n-1] + \langle S[n-1:0] \rangle.$$

Cancel out $2^{n-1} \cdot C[n-1]$, and the claim follows. ∎

15.2.2 Delay and Cost Analysis

The cost of an RCA(n) satisfies

$$c(\text{RCA}(n)) = n \cdot c(\text{FA}) = \Theta(n).$$

The delay of an RCA(n) satisfies

$$d(\text{RCA}(n)) = n \cdot d(\text{FA}) = \Theta(n).$$

Clock rates in modern microprocessors correspond to the delay of 15–20 gates (in more aggressive designs, the critical paths are even shorter). Most microprocessors easily add 32-bit numbers within one clock cycle (high-end microprocessors even add 100-bit number in a cycle). Obviously, adders in such microprocessors are not ripple carry adders. In the rest of the chapter, we present faster ADDER(n) designs.

15.3 LOWER BOUNDS

15.3.1 Carry Bits

We now define the carry bits associated with the addition

$$\langle A[n-1:0] \rangle + \langle B[n-1:0] \rangle + C[0] = \langle S[n-1:0] \rangle + 2^n \cdot C[n]. \qquad (15.5)$$

Our definition is based on the values of the signals $C[n-1:1]$ of an RCA(n). This definition is well defined in light of the simulation theorem of combinational circuits.

Definition 15.3 The carry bits $C[n:0]$ corresponding to the addition in Eq. 15.5 are defined as the values of the stable signals $C[n:0]$ in an RCA(n).

Note that there are $n + 1$ carry bits associated with the addition defined in Eq. 15.5; these bits are indexed from zero to n. The first carry bit $C[0]$ is an input, the last carry bit $C[n]$ is an output, and the remaining carry bits $C[n-1:0]$ are internal signals.

We now discuss a few issues related to the definition of the carry bits and binary addition.

15.3.2 Cone of Adder Outputs

The correctness proof of RCA(n) implies that, for every $0 \le i \le n-1$,

$$\langle A[i:0] \rangle + \langle B[i:0] \rangle + C[0] = 2^{i+1} \cdot C[i+1] + \langle S[i:0] \rangle. \qquad (15.6)$$

Equation 15.6 implies that, for every $0 \le i \le n-1$,

$$\langle S[i:0] \rangle = \mathrm{mod}(\langle A[i:0] \rangle + \langle B[i:0] \rangle + C[0], 2^{i+1}).$$

These equations imply that the cones of each of the signals $C[i+1]$ and $S[i]$ is the set of inputs corresponding to $A[i:0] \cup B[i:0] \cup C[0]$.

Claim 15.4 *For each $0 \le i \le n-1$, the cone of Boolean functions corresponding to $C[i+1]$ and $S[i]$ consists of $2i+3$ inputs corresponding to $A[i:0]$, $B[i:0]$, and $C[0]$.*

PROOF: To simplify notation, we abuse notation and say that $A[j]$ is in the $cone(C[i])$. Formally, we should say that the index of the input corresponding to the input $A[j]$ belongs to the cone of the Boolean function corresponding to $C[i]$.

Equation 15.6 implies that the bits $S[i]$ and $C[i+1]$ are determined by the bits of $A[i:0]$, $B[i:0]$, and $C[0]$. This implies that the cone is contained in the union of these $2i+3$ input bits.

We need to prove that every bit among these $2i+3$ influences the bits $S[i]$ and $C[i+1]$. For example, consider $A[j]$ for $0 \le j \le i$. Let $A[i:0] = 0^{i+1}$, $B[i:0] = 1^{i-j+1} \circ 0^j$, and $C[0] = 0$. Since

$$\langle A[i:0] \rangle + \langle B[i:0] \rangle + C[0] = 2^{i+1} - 2^j,$$

by Eq. 15.6, it follows that

$$C[i+1] = 0 \text{ and } S[i] = 1.$$

We now flip $A[j]$, namely, set $A[j] = 1$. This increases the sum $\langle A[i:0] \rangle + \langle B[i:0] \rangle + C[0]$ by 2^j. Therefore

$$\langle A[i:0] \rangle + \langle B[i:0] \rangle + C[0] = 2^{i+1}.$$

By Eq. 15.6, it follows that

$$C[i+1] = 1 \text{ and } S[i] = 0.$$

It follows that $A[j]$ belongs to the cones of $S[i]$ and $C[i+1]$. By interchanging the roles of $\vec{A}$ and $\vec{B}$, we obtain that $B[j]$ also belongs to the cones of $S[i]$ and $C[i+1]$. To prove that $C[0]$ also belongs to these cones, consider $\vec{A} = 0^{i+1}$, $\vec{B} = 1^{i+1}$, and the two possible values of $C[0]$. ∎

15.3.3 Lower Bounds

Claim 15.4 implies the following lower bounds.

Claim 15.5 *Let A denote a combinational circuit that implements an* ADDER(n). *If the fan-in in C is at most* 2, *then*

$$c(A) \geq 2n$$

$$d(A) \geq \log_2(2n + 1).$$

PROOF: By Claim 15.4, the cones of $C[n]$ and $S[n - 1]$ contain $2n + 1$ elements. The claim follows from Theorems 12.15 and 12.18. ∎

Hence the cost of the ripple carry adder is asymptotically optimal, but its delay is far from the lower bound.

15.4 CONDITIONAL SUM ADDER

A conditional sum adder is a recursive adder design that is based on divide-and-conquer. One often uses only one level of recursion, namely, three adders with input length $n/2$ are used to construct one adder with input size n.

15.4.1 Motivation

The following story captures the main idea behind a Conditional Sum Adder.

Imagine a situation in which Alice, who is positioned on Earth, holds the strings $A[k - 1 : 0], B[k - 1 : 0], C[0]$. Bob, who is stationed on the Moon, holds the strings $A[n - 1 : k], B[n - 1 : k]$. The goal of Alice and Bob is to jointly compute the sum $\langle A[n - 1 : 0] \rangle + \langle B[n - 1 : 0] \rangle + C[0]$. They don't care who holds the sum bits and $C[n]$, as long as one of them does. Now, sending information from Alice to Bob is costly. The first question we pose is, how many bits must Alice send to Bob? After some thought, Alice figures out that it suffices to send $C[k]$ to Bob. Alice is happy since she only needs to pay for sending a single bit (which is a big savings compared to sending her $2k + 1$ input bits!).

Unfortunately, sending information from Alice to Bob takes time. Even at the speed of light, it takes a second, which is a lot compared to the time it takes to compute the sum. Suppose Bob wants to finish his task as soon as possible after receiving $C[k]$ from Alice. The second question we pose is, what should Bob do during the second it takes $C[k]$ to reach him? Since the message has only two possible values (one or zero), an industrious Bob will compute two sums; one under the assumption that $C[k] = 0$ and one under the assumption that $C[k] = 1$. Finally, when $C[k]$ arrives, Bob only needs to select between the two sums he has precomputed.

15.4.2 Implementation

A conditional sum adder is designed recursively using divide-and-conquer. We denote a conditional sum adder that implements an ADDER(n) by CSA(n). A CSA(1) is simply a full-adder. A CSA(n) for $n > 1$ is depicted in Figure 15.3. The input is partitioned into a lower part consisting of the bits in positions $[k - 1 : 0]$ and an upper part consisting of

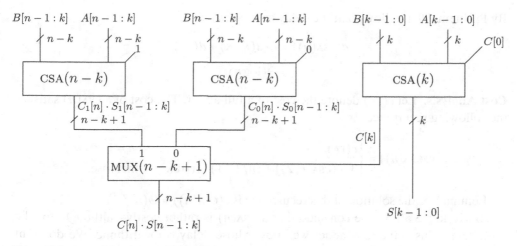

Figure 15.3. A conditional sum adder $\text{CSA}(n)$.

the bits in positions $[n - 1 : k]$. The lower part (handled by Alice in our short tale) is fed to a $\text{CSA}(k)$ to produce the sum bits $S[k - 1 : 0]$ and the carry bit $C[k]$. The upper part (handled by Bob) is fed to two $\text{CSA}(n - k)$ circuits. The first one is given a carry-in of 0 and the second is given a carry-in of 1. These two $\text{CSA}(n - k)$ circuits output $n - k + 1$ bits each. A multiplexer selects one of these outputs according to the value of $C[k]$, which arrives from the lower part.

Claim 15.6 *The $\text{CSA}(n)$ is a correct $\text{ADDER}(n)$ design.*

PROOF: The proof is by complete induction on n. The induction basis for $n = 1$ follows from the correctness of a full-adder. The induction step is proved as follows. By the induction hypothesis and the functionality of a MUX, it follows that

$$C[k] \cdot 2^k + \langle S[k - 1 : 0] \rangle - \langle A[k - 1 : 0] \rangle + \langle B[k - 1 : 0] \rangle + C[0] \qquad (15.7)$$

$$2^{n-k} \cdot C[n] + \langle S[n - 1 : k] \rangle = \langle A[n - 1 : k] \rangle + \langle B[n - 1 : k] \rangle + C[k]. \qquad (15.8)$$

We multiply Eq. 15.8 by 2^k and add it to Eq. 15.7 to obtain

$$2^n \cdot C[n] + \langle S[n - 1 : 0] \rangle = \langle A[n - 1 : 0] \rangle + \langle B[n - 1 : 0] \rangle,$$

and the claim follows. ∎

15.4.3 Delay and Cost Analysis

Simplifying Assumptions. To simplify the analysis, we assume that $n = 2^\ell$. To optimize the delay, we use $k = n/2$.

Delay Analysis. Let $d(\text{FA})$ denote the delay of a full-adder. The delay of a $\text{CSA}(n)$ satisfies the following recurrence:

$$d(\text{CSA}(n)) = \begin{cases} d(\text{FA}) & \text{if } n = 1 \\ d(\text{CSA}(n/2)) + d(\text{MUX}) & \text{otherwise.} \end{cases}$$

By Problem 7.9, it follows that the delay of a $\text{CSA}(n)$ is

$$d(\text{CSA}(n)) = \ell \cdot d(\text{MUX}) + d(\text{FA})$$

$$= \Theta(\log n).$$

Cost Analysis. Let $c(\text{FA})$ denote the cost of a full-adder. The cost of a $\text{CSA}(n)$ satisfies the following recurrence:

$$c(\text{CSA}(n)) = \begin{cases} c(\text{FA}) & \text{if } n = 1 \\ 3 \cdot c(\text{CSA}(n/2)) + (n/2 + 1) \cdot c(\text{MUX}) & \text{otherwise.} \end{cases}$$

By Lemma 7.5, the solution of this recurrence is $c(\text{CSA}(n)) = \Theta(n^{\log_2 3})$.

Since $\log_2 3 \approx 1.58$, we conclude that a $\text{CSA}(n)$ is rather costly—although, for the time being, this is the only adder we know whose delay is logarithmic. We do point out that the $\text{CSA}(n)$ design does allow us to use three half-size adders (i.e., adders with input length $n/2$) to implement a full-size adder (i.e., input length n).

15.5 COMPOUND ADDER

The conditional sum adder is a divide-and-conquer design that uses two adders in the upper part, one with a zero carry-in and one with a one carry-in. This motivates the definition of an adder that computes both the sum and the incremented sum. Surprisingly, this augmented specification leads to an asymptotically cheaper design. We refer to such an adder as a compound adder.

Definition 15.4 A *compound adder* with input length n is a combinational circuit specified as follows:

Input: $A[n-1:0], B[n-1:0] \in \{0,1\}^n$.
Output: $S[n:0], T[n:0] \in \{0,1\}^{n+1}$.
Functionality:

$$\langle \vec{S} \rangle = \langle \vec{A} \rangle + \langle \vec{B} \rangle$$

$$\langle \vec{T} \rangle = \langle \vec{A} \rangle + \langle \vec{B} \rangle + 1.$$

Note that a compound adder does not have carry-in input. To simplify notation, the carry-out bits are denoted by $S[n]$ for the sum and by $T[n]$ for the incremented sum. We denote a compound adder with input length n by $\text{COMP-ADDER}(n)$.

15.5.1 Implementation

We apply divide-and-conquer to design a $\text{COMP-ADDER}(n)$. For $n = 1$, we simply use a full-adder and a half-adder (one could optimize this a bit and combine the half-adder and the full-adder to reduce the constants). The design for $n > 1$ is depicted in Figure 15.4.

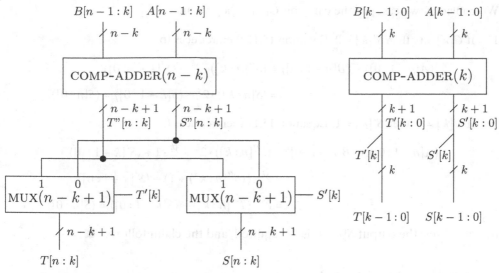

Figure 15.4. A compound adder COMP-ADDER(n).

Example 15.1 Consider a COMP-ADDER(4) with input $A[3:0] = 0110$ and $B[3:0] = 1001$. The lower part computes $S'[2:0] = 011$ and $T'[2:0] = 100$. The two lower bits of the outputs are simply $S[1:0] = S'[1:0] = 11$ and $T[1:0] = T'[1:0] = 00$. The upper part computes $S''[4:2] = 011$ and $T''[4:2] = 100$. The output $S[4:2]$ is selected to be $S''[4:2]$ since $S'[2] = 0$. The output $T[4:2]$ is selected to be $T''[4:2]$ since $T'[2] = 1$. Hence $S[4:0] = 01111$ and $T[4:0] = 10000$.

15.5.2 Correctness

We prove the correctness of COMP-ADDER(n).

Claim 15.7 *The* COMP-ADDER(n) *design depicted in Figure 15.4 is a correct adder.*

PROOF: The proof is by induction on n. The case of $n = 1$ follows from the correctness of a full-adder and a half-adder. We prove the induction step for the output $S[n:0]$; the correctness of $T[n:0]$ can be proved in a similar fashion and is left as an exercise.

The induction hypothesis implies that

$$\langle S'[k:0]\rangle = \langle A[k-1:0]\rangle + \langle B[k-1:0]\rangle. \tag{15.9}$$

Note that (i) the output $S[k-1:0]$ equals $S'[k-1:0]$ and (ii) $S'[k]$ equals the carry bit $C[k]$ corresponding to the addition $\langle A[k-1:0]\rangle + \langle B[k-1:0]\rangle$.

The induction hypothesis implies that

$$\langle S''[n:k]\rangle = \langle A[n-1:k]\rangle + \langle B[n-1:k]\rangle$$
$$\langle T''[n:k]\rangle = \langle A[n-1:k]\rangle + \langle B[n-1:k]\rangle + 1. \tag{15.10}$$

It follows from Eqs. 15.9 and 15.10 that

$$\langle S''[n:k]\rangle \cdot 2^k + \langle S'[k:0]\rangle = \langle A[n-1:0]\rangle + \langle B[n-1:0]\rangle. \tag{15.11}$$

We consider two cases of the carry bit $C[k]$: $C[k] = 0$ and $C[k] = 1$.

1. If $C[k] = 0$, then $S'[k] = 0$. Equation 15.11 then reduces to

$$\langle A[n-1:0]\rangle + \langle B[n-1:0]\rangle = \langle S''[n:k]\rangle \cdot 2^k + \langle S'[k-1:0]\rangle$$
$$= \langle S[n:k]\rangle \cdot 2^k + \langle S[k-1:0]\rangle = \langle S[n:0]\rangle.$$

2. If $C[k] = 1$, then $S'[k] = 1$. Equation 15.11 then reduces to

$$\langle A[n-1:0]\rangle + \langle B[n-1:0]\rangle = \langle S''[n:k]\rangle \cdot 2^k + 2^k \cdot 1 + \langle S'[k-1:0]\rangle$$
$$= 2^k \cdot (\langle S''[n:k]\rangle + 1) + \langle S'[k-1:0]\rangle$$
$$= 2^k \cdot \langle T''[n:k]\rangle + \langle S[k-1:0]\rangle = \langle S[n:0]\rangle.$$

In both cases, the output $S[n:0]$ is as required, and the claim follows. ∎

15.5.3 Delay and Cost Analysis

Simplifying Assumptions. To simplify the analysis, we assume that $n = 2^\ell$. To optimize the delay, we use $k = n/2$.

Delay Analysis. The delay of a COMP-ADDER(n) satisfies the following recurrence:

$$d(\text{COMP-ADDER}(n)) = \begin{cases} d(\text{FA}) & \text{if } n = 1 \\ d(\text{COMP-ADDER}(n/2)) + d(\text{MUX}) & \text{otherwise.} \end{cases}$$

By Problem 7.9, it follows that the delay of a COMP-ADDER(n) is

$$d(\text{COMP-ADDER}(n)) = \ell \cdot d(\text{MUX}) + d(\text{FA})$$
$$= \Theta(\log n).$$

Cost Analysis. The cost of a COMP-ADDER(n) satisfies the following recurrence:

$$c(\text{COMP-ADDER}(n)) = \begin{cases} c(\text{FA}) + c(\text{HA}) & \text{if } n = 1 \\ 2 \cdot c(\text{COMP-ADDER}(n/2)) + 2 \cdot (n/2 + 1) \cdot c(\text{MUX}) & \text{otherwise.} \end{cases}$$

By Lemma 7.4, the solution to this recurrence is $c(\text{COMP-ADDER}) = \Theta(n \log n)$.

15.6 REDUCTIONS BETWEEN SUM AND CARRY BITS

The correctness of RCA(n) implies that for every $0 \le i \le n-1$,

$$S[i] = \text{XOR}(A[i], B[i], C[i]). \tag{15.12}$$

This immediately implies that for every $0 \le i \le n-1$,

$$C[i] = \text{XOR}(A[i], B[i], S[i]). \tag{15.13}$$

Equations 15.12 and 15.13 imply constant-time linear-cost reductions between the problems of computing the sum bits $S[n - 1 : 0]$ and computing the carry bits $C[n - 1 : 0]$. (This reduction uses the addends $\vec{A}$ and $\vec{B}$.) The task of computing the sum bits is the task of an adder. In an RCA(n), the carry bit $C[i]$ is computed first, and then the sum bit $S[i]$ is computed according to Eq. 15.12. We will later design an asymptotically optimal adder that first computes all the carry bits and then obtains the sum bits from the carry bits by applying Eq. 15.12.

15.7 REDUNDANT AND NONREDUNDANT REPRESENTATION

Consider Eq. 15.5 and let $x = \langle \vec{A} \rangle + \langle \vec{B} \rangle + C[0]$. Equation 15.5 means that the sum x admits two representations. The representation of x on the right hand side is the standard binary representation. This representation is *nonredundant*. This means that every number that is representable by $n + 1$ bits has a unique representation. (Note that we need to restrict ourselves to $n + 1$ bits, otherwise leading zeros create multiple representations. For example, 1, 01, and 001 are different representations of the same number.)

One nice characteristic of nonredundant representation is that comparison is easy. Suppose that $X[n - 1 : 0]$ is a binary representation of x and that $Y[n - 1 : 0]$ is a binary representation of y. If we wish to check if $x = y$, all we need to do is check if the binary strings $\vec{X}$ and $\vec{Y}$ are identical.

The left-hand side represents the same value represented by $C[n]$ and $S[n - 1 : 0]$. However, on the left-hand side, we have two binary strings and a carry-in bit. Given x, there are many possible combinations of values of $\langle \vec{A} \rangle$, $\langle \vec{B} \rangle$ and $C[0]$ that represent x. For example, $8 = 4 + 3 + 1$ and also $8 = 5 + 3 + 0$.

We refer to such a representation as *redundant representation*. Comparison of values represented in redundant representation is not as easy as it is with nonredundant representation. For example, assume that

$$x = \vec{A} + \vec{B}$$

$$x' = \vec{A'} + \vec{B'}.$$

It is possible that $x = x'$ even though $A \neq A'$ and $B \neq B'$. Namely, in redundant representation, inequality of the representations does not imply inequality of the represented values.

Some of you might wonder at this point whether redundant representations are useful at all. We just saw that redundant representation makes comparison nontrivial. The answer is that redundant representation is most useful. Probably the most noted application of redundant representation is fast multiplication. In fast multiplication, redundant representation is used for fast (redundant) addition.

We summarize this discussion by noting that an alternative way to interpret an RCA(n) (or an ADDER(n), in general) is to say that it translates a redundant representation to a nonredundant binary representation.

15.8 SUMMARY

We started by defining binary addition. We reviewed the ripple carry adder. We proved its correctness rigorously and used it to define the carry bits associated with addition.

We showed that the problems of computing the sum bits and the carry bits are equivalent modulo a constant-time linear-cost reduction. Since the cost of every adder is $\Omega(n)$ and the delay is $\Omega(\log n)$, we regard the problems of computing the sum bits and the carry bits as equivalently hard.

We presented an adder design called conditional sum adder ($\text{CSA}(n)$). The $\text{CSA}(n)$ design is based on divide-and-conquer. Its delay is asymptotically optimal (if fan-out is not taken into account). However, its cost is rather large—approximately $\Theta(n^{1.58})$.

We then considered the problem of simultaneously computing the sum and incremented sum of two binary numbers. We presented a design called compound adder ($\text{COMP-ADDER}(n)$). This design is also based on divide-and-conquer. The asymptotic delay is also logarithmic, however, the cost is $\Theta(n \cdot \log n)$.

This result is rather surprising: a $\text{COMP-ADDER}(n)$ is much cheaper asymptotically than a $\text{CSA}(n)$! You should make sure that you understand the rational behind this magic. Moreover, by adding a line of multiplexers controlled by the carry-in bit $C[0]$, one can obtain an $\text{ADDER}(n)$ from a $\text{COMP-ADDER}(n)$. So, asymptotically, the design of a $\text{COMP-ADDER}(n)$ is a real improvement over the $\text{CSA}(n)$.

There exists an adder design that is asymptotically optimal both with respect to delay and with respect to cost. Moreover, the asymptotic delay and cost of this asymptotically optimal design is not affected by considering fan-out. This adder is often called a parallel prefix adder (Müller and Paul, 1996; Ercegovac and Lang, 2003).

PROBLEMS

15.1. Manually simulate the following input on CSA(4) and COMP-ADDER(4) with $k = 2$:

$$A[3:0] = 0110,$$

$$B[3:0] = 1001,$$

$$C[0] = 0.$$

15.2. **(Effect of Fan-out on $\text{CSA}(n)$)** Consider the $\text{CSA}(n)$ design. The fan-out of the net fed by the carry bit $C[k]$ is $n/2 + 1$ if $k = n/2$.
  (a) Suppose that we associate a delay of $\log_2(f)$ with a fan-out f. How would taking the fan-out into account change the delay analysis of a $\text{CSA}(n)$?
  (b) Suppose that we associate a cost $O(f)$ with a fan-out f. How would taking the fan-out into account change the cost analysis of a $\text{CSA}(n)$?

15.3. Complete the correctness of $\text{COMP-ADDER}(n)$, that is, prove that $T[n:0]$ satisfies the specification.

15.4. Prove the following claims.

    (a) Consider two binary strings $S[k:0]$ and $T[k:0]$. Prove that if $S[k] > T[k]$, then $\langle \vec{S} \rangle > \langle \vec{T} \rangle$.

    (b)   **(i)** Implement COMP-ADDER(2) by using two COMP-ADDER(1). Print all possible outputs, and show that $T'[1] \geq S'[1]$.

        (ii) Consider $S'[k]$ and $T'[k]$ in the design of COMP-ADDER(n). Prove that $T'[k] \geq S'[k]$.

        Prove that $T'[k] \geq S'[k]$.

    (c.) Present an example for COMP-ADDER(4) in which $T[4:2]$ is selected to be $S''[4:2]$. Is it possible that $S'[k] = 1$ and $T'[k] = 0$? Which combinations of $S'[k]$ and $T'[k]$ are possible?

15.5. **(Effect of Fan-Out on COMP-ADDER(n))** Note that the fan-out of $S'[k]$ and $T'[k]$ is $n/2 + 1$. Prove that if the effect of fan-out on delay is taken into account, then, as in the case of CSA(n), the delay is actually $\Theta(\log^2 n)$. Here we assume that the delay incurred by a fan-out f is $\Theta(\log f)$.

15.6. Prove Eq. 15.13, that is, for every $0 \leq i \leq n-1$,

$$C[i] = \text{XOR}(A[i], B[i], S[i]).$$

15.7. **(Subtraction)** Consider the following definition of a subtractor.

Definition 15.5 A *binary subtractor* with input length n is a combinational circuit specified as follows.

Input: $X[n-1:0], Y[n-1:0] \in \{0,1\}^n$, and $B[0] \in \{0,1\}$.
Output: $S[n-1:0] \in \{0,1\}^n$ and $B[n] \in \{0,1\}$.
Functionality:

$$\langle S[n-1:0] \rangle - 2^n \cdot B[n] = \langle X[n-1:0] \rangle - \langle Y[n-1:0] \rangle - B[0]. \qquad (15.14)$$

    Our goal is to define a *ripple borrow subtractor*, a combinational circuit that is analogous to an RCA(n).

    (a) Define a full-subtractor (analogous to a full-adder).

    (b) Suggest an implementation of a full-subtractor that uses a full-adder and three inverters.

    (c) Build a binary subtractor by chaining together n full-subtractors.

    (d) Implement your circuit for $n = 2$ using Logisim and simulate it for all possible inputs.

    (e) Prove the correctness of your design.

CHAPTER 16

Signed Addition

So far we have dealt with the representation of nonnegative integers by binary strings. We also designed combinational circuits that perform addition for nonnegative numbers represented by binary strings. How are negative integers represented? Can we add and subtract negative integers?

We refer to integers that are either positive, zero, or negative as signed integers. In this chapter, we deal with the representation of signed integers by binary strings. We focus on a representation that is called *two's complement*. We present combinational circuits for adding and subtracting signed numbers that are represented in two's complement representation. Although the designs are obtained by very minor changes of a binary adder designs, the theory behind these changes requires some effort.

16.1 REPRESENTATION OF NEGATIVE INTEGERS

We use binary representation to represent nonnegative integers. We now address the issue of representing positive and negative integers. Following programming languages, we refer to nonnegative integers as *unsigned numbers* and to negative and positive numbers as *signed numbers*.

There are three common methods for representing signed numbers: sign-magnitude, one's complement, and two's complement.

Definition 16.1 The number represented in *sign-magnitude* representation by $A[n-1:0] \in \{0,1\}^n$ and $S \in \{0,1\}$ is

$$(-1)^S \cdot \langle A[n-1:0] \rangle.$$

Definition 16.2 The number represented in *one's complement* representation by $A[n-1:0] \in \{0,1\}^n$ is

$$-(2^{n-1}-1) \cdot A[n-1] + \langle A[n-2:0] \rangle.$$

Table 16.1. Comparison between representation of negative integers. Note that zero has two representations in one's complement and sign-magnitude representations. In sign-magnitude, one may distinguish between +0 and −0.

Binary String $\vec{X}$	$\langle \vec{X} \rangle$	Two's Complement	One's Complement	Sign-Magnitude
000	0	0	0	+0
001	1	1	1	1
010	2	2	2	2
011	3	3	3	3
100	4	−4	−3	−0
101	5	−3	−2	−1
110	6	−2	−1	−2
111	7	−1	0	−3

Definition 16.3 The number represented in *two's complement* representation by $A[n-1:0] \in \{0,1\}^n$ is

$$-2^{n-1} \cdot A[n-1] + \langle A[n-2:0] \rangle.$$

We denote the number represented in two's complement representation by $A[n-1:0]$, as follows:

$$[A[n-1:0]] \triangleq -2^{n-1} \cdot A[n-1] + \langle A[n-2:0] \rangle.$$

We often use the term *a two's complement number $A[n-1:0]$* as an abbreviation of the longer phrase *the number represented by $A[n-1:0]$ in two's complement representation.*

The most common method for representing signed numbers is two's complement representation. The main reason is that adding, subtracting, and multiplying signed numbers represented in two's complement representation is almost as easy as performing these computations on unsigned binary numbers.

Example 16.1 Table 16.1 compares representations of negative integers. Note that the sign bit in the last column is $X[2]$.

16.2 COMPUTING A TWO'S COMPLEMENT REPRESENTATION

We denote the set of signed numbers that are representable in two's complement representation using n-bit binary strings by T_n.

Claim 16.1

$$T_n = \left\{ -2^{n-1}, -2^{n-1} + 1, \dots, 2^{n-1} - 1 \right\}.$$

PROOF: Consider a binary string $A[n-1:0]$. Clearly

$$[A[n-1:0]] \triangleq -2^{n-1} \cdot A[n-1] + \langle A[n-2:0] \rangle$$

$$\leq \langle A[n-2:0] \rangle$$

$$\leq 2^{n-1} - 1.$$

Similarly,

$$[A[n-1:0]] \stackrel{\triangle}{=} -2^{n-1} \cdot A[n-1] + \langle A[n-2:0]\rangle$$

$$\geq -2^{n-1}.$$

This proves that $T_n \subseteq \{-2^{n-1}, -2^{n-1}+1, \ldots, 2^{n-1}-1\}$. To prove the other direction, consider an integer $-2^{n-1} \leq x \leq 2^{n-1}-1$. We prove that $x \in T_n$ by considering the following two cases:

1. If $x \geq 0$, then x can be represented in binary representation by a string $A[n-2:0]$. Hence $x = [0 \circ A[n-2:0]]$, as required.
2. If $x < 0$, let $y \stackrel{\triangle}{=} x + 2^n$. Since $-2^{n-1} \leq x \leq -1$, it follows that $2^{n-1} < y \leq 2^n - 1$. Thus y can be represented in binary representation by $Y[n-1:0]$, where $Y[n-1] = 1$. We know that $y = \langle Y[n-1:0]\rangle$. We now check which value is represented by $Y[n-1:0]$ in two's complement representation:

$$[Y[n-1:0]] = \langle Y[n-2:0]\rangle - 2^{n-1} \cdot Y[n-1]$$

$$= (y - 2^{n-1}) - 2^{n-1} \cdot 1$$

$$= y - 2^n = x.$$

Hence $x \in T_n$, as required. ∎

The proof of Claim 16.1 justifies the following algorithm for computing the two's complement representation of a number $x \in T_n$.

Algorithm 16.1 two-comp(x, n)—an algorithm for computing the two's complement representation of x using n bits.

---

1. If $x \notin T_n$ return (fail).
2. If $x \geq 0$ return $(0 \circ bin_{n-1}(x))$.
3. If $x < 0$ return $(bin_n(x + 2^n))$.

Example 16.2 Claim 16.1 implies that

$$T_4 = \{-2^3, -2^3+1, \ldots, 2^3-1\}.$$

Hence

$$\text{two-comp}(8, 4) = \text{fail},$$

$$\text{two-comp}(5, 4) = (0 \circ bin_3(5)) = 0101,$$

$$\text{two-comp}(-6, 4) = (bin_4(-6+2^4)) = 1010,$$

$$\text{two-comp}(-1, 4) = (bin_4(-1+2^4)) = 1111.$$

16.3 NEGATION IN TWO'S COMPLEMENT REPRESENTATION

The following claim deals with negating a value represented in two's complement representation.

Claim 16.2

$$-[A[n-1:0]] = [\text{INV}(A[n-1:0])] + 1.$$

PROOF: Note that $\text{INV}(A[i]) = 1 - A[i]$. Hence

$$[\text{INV}(A[n-1:0])] = -2^{n-1} \cdot \text{INV}(A[n-1]) + \langle \text{INV}(A[n-2:0]) \rangle$$

$$= -2^{n-1} \cdot (1 - A[n-1]) + \sum_{i=0}^{n-2}(1 - A[i]) \cdot 2^i$$

$$= \underbrace{-2^{n-1} + \sum_{i=0}^{n-2} 2^i}_{=-1} + \underbrace{2^{n-1} \cdot A[n-1] - \sum_{i=0}^{n-2} A[i] \cdot 2^i}_{=-[A[n-1:0]]}$$

$$= -1 - [A[n-1:0]]. \quad \blacksquare$$

Example 16.3 Let $n = 4$ and let $A[3:0] = 1001$; then

$$-[A[3:0]] = 7$$

$$[\text{INV}(A[3:0])] + 1 = [0110] + 1 = 6 + 1 = 7.$$

Hence

$$-[A[3:0]] = [\text{INV}(A[3:0])] + 1.$$

In Figure 16.1, we depict a design for negating numbers based on Claim 16.2. The circuit is input $\vec{A}$ and is supposed to compute the two's complement representation of $-[\vec{A}]$. The bits in the string $\vec{A}$ are first inverted to obtain $\overline{A[n-1:0]}$. An increment circuit outputs $C[n] \cdot B[n-1:0]$ such that

$$\langle C[n] \cdot B[n-1:0] \rangle = \langle \overline{A[n-1:0]} \rangle + 1.$$

Such an increment circuit can be implemented simply by using a binary adder with one addend string fixed to $0^{n-1} \cdot 1$.

We would like to claim that the circuit depicted in Figure 16.1 is correct. Unfortunately, we do not have yet the tools to prove the correctness. Let us try to see the point at which we run into trouble.

Claim 16.2 implies that all we need to do to compute $-[\vec{A}]$ is invert the bits of $\vec{A}$ and increment. The problem is with the meaning of *increment*. The increment circuit computes

$$\langle \overline{A[n-1:0]} \rangle + 1.$$

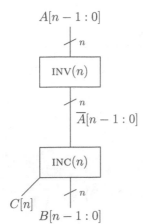

$A[n-1:0]$

n

INV(n)

n

$\overline{A}[n-1:0]$

INC(n)

$C[n]$

n

$B[n-1:0]$

Figure 16.1. A (wrong) circuit for negating a value represented in two's complement representation.

However, Claim 16.2 requires that we compute

$$\left[\overline{A[n-1:0]}\right] + 1.$$

Now, let $C[n] \cdot B[n-1:0]$ denote the output of the incrementor. We know that

$$\langle C[n] \cdot B[n-1:0] \rangle = \langle \overline{A[n-1:0]} \rangle + 1.$$

One may suspect that if $C[n] = 1$, then correctness might fail due to the "lost" carry bit. Assume we are "lucky" and $C[n] = 0$. In this case,

$$\langle B[n-1:0] \rangle = \langle \overline{A[n-1:0]} \rangle + 1.$$

Why should this imply that

$$[B[n-1:0]] = \left[\overline{A[n-1:0]}\right] + 1?$$

At this point, we leave this issue unresolved. We prove a more general result in Theorem 16.7. Note, however, that the circuit errs with the input $A[n-1:0] = 1 \cdot 0^{n-1}$. The value represented by $\vec{A}$ equals -2^{n-1}. Inversion yields $\overline{A[n-1:0]} = 0 \cdot 1^{n-2}$. Increment yields $C[n] = 0$ and $B[n-1:0] = 1 \cdot 0^{n-2} = A[n-1:0]$. This, of course, is not a counterexample to Claim 16.2; it is an example in which an increment with respect to $\langle A[n-1:0] \rangle$ is not an increment with respect to $\left[A[n-1:0]\right]$. This is exactly the point which concerned us. A more careful look at this case shows that every circuit must err with such an input. The reason is that $-\left[\vec{A}\right] \notin T_n$. Hence the negated value cannot be represented using an n-bit string, and negation had to fail.

Interestingly, as opposed to negation in two's complement representation, negation in sign-magnitude and one's complement representation is very easy.

16.4 PROPERTIES OF TWO'S COMPLEMENT REPRESENTATION

Alternative Definition of Two's Complement Representation. The following claim follows immediately from the definition of two's complement representation.

Claim 16.3 *For every* $A[n-1:0] \in \{0,1\}^n$,

$$\mathrm{mod}(\langle \vec{A} \rangle, 2^n) = \mathrm{mod}([\vec{A}], 2^n).$$

PROOF: It suffices to show that $\langle \vec{A} \rangle - [\vec{A}]$ is a multiple of 2^n. Indeed, $\langle \vec{A} \rangle - [\vec{A}] \in \{0, 2^n\}$, and the claim follows. ∎

Example 16.4 Let $n = 4$ and let $A[3:0] = 0110$, $B[3:0] = 1001$; then

$$\langle A[3:0] \rangle = 6, \qquad\qquad [A[3:0]] = 6,$$
$$\langle B[3:0] \rangle = 9, \qquad\qquad [B[3:0]] = -7.$$

Hence

$$\langle \vec{A} \rangle - [\vec{A}] = 6 - 6 = 0 = 0 \pmod{2^4}$$
$$\langle \vec{B} \rangle - [\vec{B}] = 9 - (-7) = 16 = 0 \pmod{2^4}.$$

Claim 16.3 provides an explanation for the term *two's complement representation*. In fact, the precise term is 2^n complement representation. Moreover, one could define two's complement representation based on the claim, namely, represent $x \in [-2^{n-1}, 2^{n-1}-1]$ by $bin_n(x')$, where $x' \in [0, 2^n-1]$ satisfies $x' = \mathrm{mod}(x, 2^n)$.

Sign Bit. The most significant bit $A[n-1]$ of a string $A[n-1:0]$ that represents a two's complement number is often called the *sign bit* of $\vec{A}$. The following claim justifies this term.

Claim 16.4

$$[A[n-1:0]] < 0 \quad\Longleftrightarrow\quad A[n-1] = 1.$$

PROOF: Consider a binary string $A[n-1:0]$. If $A[n-1] = 0$, then $[A[n-1:0]] = \langle A[n-2:0] \rangle \geq 0$. Conversely, if $A[n-1:0] = 1$, then

$$[A[n-1:0]] \triangleq -2^{n-1} \cdot A[n-1] + \langle A[n-2:0] \rangle$$
$$\leq -2^{n-1} + (2^{n-1}-1)$$
$$\leq -1. \qquad\qquad ∎$$

Do not be misled by the term *sign bit*. Two's complement representation is not sign-magnitude representation. In particular, the prefix $A[n-2:0]$ is not a binary representation of the magnitude of $[A[n-1:0]]$. Computing the absolute value of a negative signed number represented in two's complement representation involves inversion of the bits and an increment (as suggested by Claim 16.2).

Sign Extension. The following claim is often referred to as *sign extension*. It basically means that duplicating the most significant bit does not affect the value represented in two's complement representation. This is similar to padding zeros from the left in binary representation.

Claim 16.5 *If* $A[n] = A[n-1]$, *then*

$$[A[n:0]] = [A[n-1:0]] .$$

PROOF:

$$
\begin{aligned}
[A[n:0]] &= -2^n \cdot A[n] + \langle A[n-1:0] \rangle \\
&= -2^n \cdot A[n] + 2^{n-1} \cdot A[n-1] + \langle A[n-2:0] \rangle \\
&= -2^n \cdot A[n-1] + 2^{n-1} \cdot A[n-1] + \langle A[n-2:0] \rangle \\
&= -2^{n-1} \cdot A[n-1] + \langle A[n-2:0] \rangle \\
&= [A[n-1:0]] . \quad \blacksquare
\end{aligned}
$$

We can now apply arbitrarily long sign extension, as summarized in the following corollary (proved by induction on the length of the sign extension).

Corollary 16.6

$$[A[n-1]^* \circ A[n-1:0]] = [A[n-1:0]] ,$$

where $A[n-1]^*$ denotes an arbitrarily long binary string that consists of concatenations of $A[n-1]$.

Example 16.5 Let $n = 2$ and let $A[1:0] = 10$.

$$[A[1:0]] = -2 + 0 = -2$$

$$[A[1] \circ A[1] \circ A[1:0]] = [1110] = -2^3 + 6 = -2 .$$

Also,

$$[1111111111111111110] = [10] = -2$$

$$[1111111111111111111] = [1] = -1 .$$

16.5 REDUCTION: TWO'S COMPLEMENT ADDITION TO BINARY ADDITION

In Section 16.3, we tried (and partly failed) to use a binary incrementor for incrementing a two's complement signed number. In this section, we deal with a more general case, namely, computing the two's complement representation of

$$[\vec{A}] + [\vec{B}] + C[0].$$

The following theorem deals with the following setting. Let

$$A[n-1:0], B[n-1:0], S[n-1:0] \in \{0,1\}^n$$

$$C[0], C[n] \in \{0,1\}$$

satisfy

$$\langle A[n-1:0] \rangle + \langle B[n-1:0] \rangle + C[0] = \langle C[n] \cdot S[n-1:0] \rangle. \qquad (16.1)$$

Namely, $\vec{A}$, $\vec{B}$, and $C[0]$ are fed to a binary adder $\text{ADDER}(n)$ and $\vec{S}$ and $C[n]$ are output by the adder. The theorem addresses the following questions:

- When does the output $S[n-1:0]$ satisfy

$$[\vec{S}] = [A[n-1:0]] + [B[n-1:0]] + C[0]?\tag{16.2}$$

- How can we know that Eq. 16.2 holds?

Theorem 16.7 *Let $C[n-1]$ denote the carry bit in position $[n-1]$ associated with the binary addition described in Eq. 16.1 and let*

$$z \triangleq [A[n-1:0]] + [B[n-1:0]] + C[0].$$

Then

$$C[n] - C[n-1] = 1 \quad\Longrightarrow\quad z < -2^{n-1},\tag{16.3}$$

$$C[n-1] - C[n] = 1 \quad\Longrightarrow\quad z > 2^{n-1} - 1,\tag{16.4}$$

$$z \in T_n \quad\Longleftrightarrow\quad C[n] = C[n-1],\tag{16.5}$$

$$z \in T_n \quad\Longrightarrow\quad z = [S[n-1:0]].\tag{16.6}$$

PROOF: Recall that the definition of the functionality of FA_{n-1} in a ripple carry adder $\text{RCA}(n)$ implies that

$$A[n-1] + B[n-1] + C[n-1] = 2C[n] + S[n-1].$$

Hence

$$A[n-1] + B[n-1] = 2C[n] - C[n-1] + S[n-1].\tag{16.7}$$

We now expand z as follows:

$$z = [A[n-1:0]] + [B[n-1:0]] + C[0]$$
$$= -2^{n-1} \cdot (A[n-1] + B[n-1]) + \langle A[n-2:0]\rangle + \langle B[n-2:0]\rangle + C[0]$$
$$= -2^{n-1} \cdot (2C[n] - C[n-1] + S[n-1]) + \langle C[n-1] \cdot S[n-2:0]\rangle,$$

where the last line is based on Eq. 16.7 and on

$$\langle A[n-2:0]\rangle + \langle B[n-2:0]\rangle + C[0] = \langle C[n-1] \cdot S[n-2:0]\rangle.$$

Commuting $S[n-1]$ and $C[n-1]$ implies that

$$z = -2^{n-1} \cdot (2C[n] - C[n-1] - C[n-1]) + [S[n-1] \cdot S[n-2:0]]$$
$$= -2^n \cdot (C[n] - C[n-1]) + [S[n-1:0]].$$

We distinguish between three cases:

1. If $C[n] - C[n-1] = 1$, then

$$z = -2^n + [S[n-1:0]]$$
$$\leq -2^n + 2^{n-1} - 1 = -2^{n-1} - 1.$$

Hence Eq. 16.3 follows.

2. If $C[n] - C[n-1] = -1$, then

$$z = 2^n + [S[n-1:0]]$$
$$\geq 2^n - 2^{n-1} = 2^{n-1}.$$

Hence Eq. 16.4 follows.

3. If $C[n] = C[n-1]$, then $z = [S[n-1:0]]$, and obviously $z \in T_n$.

The converse direction of Eq. 16.5 follows from the fact that if $C[n] \neq C[n-1]$, then either $C[n] - C[n-1] = 1$ or $C[n-1] - C[n] = 1$. In both these cases, $z \notin T_n$. Equation 16.6 follows from the third case as well, and the theorem follows. ∎

16.5.1 Detecting Overflow

Overflow occurs when the sum of signed numbers is not in T_n. Using the notation of Theorem 16.7, overflow is defined as follows.

Definition 16.4 Let $z \triangleq [A[n-1:0]] + [B[n-1:0]] + C[0]$. The signal OVF is defined as follows:

$$\text{OVF} \triangleq \begin{cases} 1 & \text{if } z \notin T_n \\ 0 & \text{otherwise.} \end{cases}$$

Note that overflow means that the sum is either too large or too small. Perhaps the term *out of range* is more appropriate than *overflow* (which suggests that the sum is too big). We choose to favor tradition here and follow the common term *overflow* rather than introducing a new term.

By Theorem 16.7, overflow occurs iff $C[n-1] \neq C[n]$, namely,

$$\text{OVF} = \text{XOR}(C[n-1], C[n]).$$

Moreover, if overflow does not occur, then Eq. 16.2 holds. Hence we have a simple way to answer both questions raised before the statement of Theorem 16.7. The signal $C[n-1]$ may not be available if one uses a black box binary adder (e.g., a library component in which $C[n-1]$ is an internal signal). In this case, we detect overflow based on the following claim.

Claim 16.8

$$\text{XOR}(C[n-1], C[n]) = \text{XOR}_4(A[n-1], B[n-1], S[n-1], C[n]).$$

PROOF: By Eq. 15.13,

$$C[n-1] = \text{XOR}_3(A[n-1], B[n-1], S[n-1]). \quad \blacksquare$$

16.5.2 Determining the Sign of the Sum

How do we determine the sign of the sum z? Obviously, if $z \in T_n$, then Claim 16.4 implies that $S[n-1]$ indicates whether z is negative. However, if overflow occurs, this is not true.

We would like to be able to know whether z is negative regardless of whether overflow occurs. We define the NEG signal.

Definition 16.5 The signal NEG is defined as follows:

$$\text{NEG} \triangleq \begin{cases} 1 & \text{if } z < 0 \\ 0 & \text{if } z \geq 0. \end{cases}$$

A brute force method based on Theorem 16.7 for computing the NEG signal is as follows:

$$\text{NEG} = \begin{cases} S[n-1] & \text{if no overflow} \\ 1 & \text{if } C[n] - C[n-1] = 1 \\ 0 & \text{if } C[n-1] - C[n] = 1. \end{cases} \tag{16.8}$$

Although this computation obviously signals correctly whether the sum is negative, it requires some further work if we wish to obtain a small circuit for computing NEG that is not given $C[n-1]$ as input.

Instead pursuing this direction, we compute NEG using a more elegant method.

Claim 16.9

$$\text{NEG} = \text{XOR}_3(A[n-1], B[n-1], C[n]).$$

PROOF: The proof is based on playing the following mental game. We extend the computation to $n+1$ bits. We then show that overflow does not occur. This means that the sum bit in position n indicates correctly the sign of the sum z. We then express this sum bit using n-bit addition signals.

Let

$$\tilde{A}[n:0] \triangleq A[n-1] \circ A[n-1:0]$$

$$\tilde{B}[n:0] \triangleq B[n-1] \circ B[n-1:0]$$

$$\langle \tilde{C}[n+1] \circ \tilde{S}[n:0] \rangle \triangleq \langle \tilde{A}[n:0] \rangle + \langle \tilde{B}[n:0] \rangle + C[0].$$

Since sign extension preserves value (see Claim 16.5), it follows that

$$z = [\tilde{A}[n:0]] + [\tilde{B}[n:0]] + C[0].$$

We claim that $z \in T_{n+1}$. This follows from

$$z = [A[n-1:0]] + [B[n-1:0]] + C[0]$$

$$\leq 2^{n-1} - 1 + 2^{n-1} - 1 + 1$$

$$\leq 2^n - 1.$$

Table 16.2. Values of $C[n]$, $C[n-1]$, $[\tilde{S}]$, and z for various values of $[\tilde{A}]$, $[\tilde{B}]$, and $C[0]$.

$[A[3:0]]$	-3	-4	-6	7
$[B[3:0]]$	-5	-5	5	1
$C[0]$	1	0	0	1
$C[n]$	1	1	1	0
$C[n-1]$	1	0	1	1
$[S[n-1:0]]$	-7	6	-1	-7
z	-7	-9	-1	9

Similarly $z \geq 2^{-n}$. Hence $z \in T_{n+1}$, and therefore, by Theorem 16.7,

$$\left[\tilde{S}[n:0]\right] = \left[\tilde{A}[n:0]\right] + \left[\tilde{B}[n:0]\right] + C[0].$$

We conclude that $z = \left[\tilde{S}[n:0]\right]$. It follows that $\text{NEG} = \tilde{S}[n]$. However,

$$\tilde{S}[n] = \text{XOR}_3(\tilde{A}[n], \tilde{B}[n], \tilde{C}[n])$$
$$= \text{XOR}_3(A[n-1], B[n-1], C[n]),$$

and the claim follows. ∎

Example 16.6 Let $n = 4$. Claim 16.1 implies that

$$T_4 = \left\{-2^3, -2^3 + 1, \ldots, 2^3 - 1\right\}.$$

Table 16.2 presents the values of $C[n]$, $C[n-1]$, $[S[n-1:0]]$, and z for various values of A, B, and $C[0]$.

16.6 A TWO'S-COMPLEMENT ADDER

In this section, we define and implement a two's complement adder.

Definition 16.6 A *two's-complement adder* with input length n is a combinational circuit specified as follows.

Input: $A[n-1:0], B[n-1:0] \in \{0,1\}^n$, and $C[0] \in \{0,1\}$.
Output: $S[n-1:0] \in \{0,1\}^n$ and $\text{NEG}, \text{OVF} \in \{0,1\}$.
Functionality: Define z as follows:

$$z \triangleq [A[n-1:0]] + [B[n-1:0]] + C[0].$$

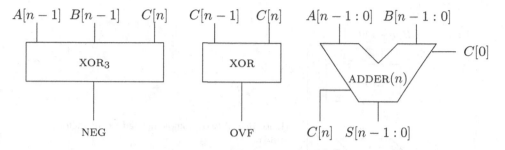

Figure 16.2. A two's complement adder S-ADDER(n).

The functionality is defined as follows:

$$z \in T_n \implies [S[n-1:0]] = z,$$

$$\text{OVF} = \begin{cases} 0 & \text{if } z \in T_n, \\ 1 & \text{if } z \notin T_n, \end{cases}$$

$$\text{NEG} = \begin{cases} 0 & \text{if } z \geq 0, \\ 1 & \text{if } z < 0. \end{cases}$$

Note that no carry-out $C[n]$ is output. We denote a two's-complement adder by S-ADDER(n). The implementation of an S-ADDER(n) is depicted in Figure 16.2 and is as follows:

1. The outputs $C[n]$ and $S[n-1:0]$ are computed by a binary adder ADDER(n) that is fed by $A[n-1:0]$, $B[n-1:0]$, and $C[0]$.
2. The output OVF is simply XOR($C[n-1], C[n]$) if $C[n-1]$ is available. Otherwise, we apply Claim 16.8, namely, OVF = XOR$_4$($A[n-1], B[n-1], S[n-1], C[n]$).
3. The output NEG is computed according to Claim 16.9. Namely, NEG = XOR$_3$($A[n-1], B[n-1], C[n]$).

Note that except for the circuitry that computes the flags OVF and NEG, a two's complement adder is identical to a binary adder. Hence, in an arithmetic logic unit (ALU), one may use the same circuit for signed addition and unsigned addition.

16.7 A TWO'S COMPLEMENT ADDER/SUBTRACTOR

In this section, we define and implement a two's complement adder/subtractor. A two's complement adder/subtractor is used in ALUs to implement addition and subtraction of signed numbers.

Definition 16.7 A *two's-complement adder/subtractor* with input length n is a combinational circuit specified as follows.

Input: $A[n-1:0], B[n-1:0] \in \{0,1\}^n$, and $sub \in \{0,1\}$.
Output: $S[n-1:0] \in \{0,1\}^n$ and NEG, OVF $\in \{0,1\}$.

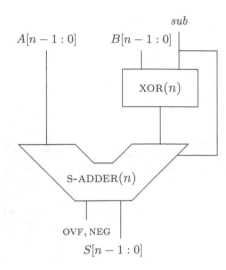

Figure 16.3. A two's complement adder/subtractor ADD-SUB(n).

Functionality: Define z as follows:

$$z \stackrel{\triangle}{=} \begin{cases} [A[n-1:0]] + [B[n-1:0]] & \text{if } sub = 0 \\ [A[n-1:0]] - [B[n-1:0]] & \text{if } sub = 1. \end{cases}$$

The functionality is defined as follows:

$$z \in T_n \implies [S[n-1:0]] = z,$$

$$\text{OVF} = \begin{cases} 0 & \text{if } z \in T_n, \\ 1 & \text{if } z \notin T_n, \end{cases}$$

$$\text{NEG} = \begin{cases} 0 & \text{if } z \geq 0, \\ 1 & \text{if } z < 0. \end{cases}$$

We denote a two's complement adder/subtractor by ADD-SUB(n). Note that the input *sub* indicates if the operation is addition or subtraction. Note also that no carry-in bit $C[0]$ is input and no carry-out $C[n]$ is output.

An implementation of a two's complement adder/subtractor ADD-SUB(n) is depicted in Figure 16.3. The implementation is based on a two's complement adder S-ADDER(n) and Claim 16.2.

Claim 16.10 *The implementation of* ADD-SUB(n) *depicted in Figure 16.3 is correct.*

PROOF: The correctness follows from Claim 16.2 and the correctness of S-ADDER(n). ∎

16.8 SUMMARY

In this chapter, we presented circuits for adding and subtracting two's complement signed numbers. We started by describing three ways for representing negative integers:

sign-magnitude, one's complement, and two's complement. We then focused on two's complement representation.

The first task we consider is negating. We proved that negating in two's complement representation requires inverting the bits and incrementing. The claim that describes negation was insufficient to argue about the correctness of a circuit for negating a two's complement signed number. We also noticed that negating the represented value is harder in two's complement representation than in the other two representations.

In Section 16.4, we discussed a few properties of two's complement representation: (i) we showed that the values represented by the same n-bit string in binary representation and in two's complement representation are congruent modulo 2^n; (ii) we showed that the most significant bit indicates whether the represented value is negative; and (iii) finally, we discussed sign extension. Sign extension enables us to increase the number of bits used to represent a two's complement number while preserving the represented value.

The main result of this chapter is presented in Section 16.5. We reduce the task of two's complement addition to binary addition. Theorem 16.7 also provides a rule that enables us to tell when this reduction fails. The rest of this section deals with (i) the detection of overflow—this is the case in which the sum is out of range—and (ii) determining the sign of the sum even if an overflow occurs.

In Section 16.6, we present an implementation of a circuit that adds two's complement numbers. Finally, in Section 16.7, we present an implementation of a circuit that can add and subtract two's complement numbers. Such a circuit is used in ALUs to implement signed addition and subtraction.

PROBLEMS

16.1. Recall the definition of one's complement representation (see Definition 16.2). We denote the number represented in one's complement representation $A[n - 1 : 0]$ by $\text{ONE'S}(\vec{A})$.

Definition 16.8 A one's complement negating circuit with input length n is a combinational circuit specified as follows:
Input: $A[n - 1 : 0] \in \{0, 1\}^n$.
Output: $B[n - 1 : 0] \in \{0, 1\}^n$.
Functionality:

$$\text{ONE'S}(\vec{A}) - -\text{ONE'S}(\vec{B}).$$

(a) Design a circuit that implements a one's complement negator.
(b) Prove the correctness of your design.

16.2. Prove that

$$\text{OVF} = A[n - 1] \cdot B[n - 1] \cdot \text{INV}(S[n - 1]) + \text{INV}(A[n - 1]) \cdot \text{INV}(B[n - 1]) \cdot S[n - 1].$$

16.3. Provide an example in which the sign of z is not signaled correctly by $S[n - 1]$.

16.4. Prove that $\text{NEG} = \text{XOR}(\text{OVF}, S[n - 1])$.

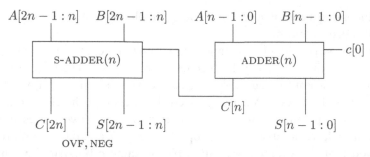

Figure 16.4. Concatenating an s-adder(n) with an adder(n).

16.5. Prove the correctness of the implementation of s-adder(n) depicted in Figure 16.2.

16.6. Is the design depicted in Figure 16.4 a correct s-adder($2n$)?

16.7. (back to the negation circuit) Consider the negation circuit depicted in Figure 16.1.
(a) When is the circuit correct?
(b) Suppose we wish to add a signal that indicates whether the circuit satisfies $[\vec{B}] = -[\vec{A}]$. How should we compute this signal?

16.8. (wrong implementation of add-sub(n)) Find an input for which the circuit depicted in Figure 16.5 errs. Can you list all the inputs for which this circuit outputs a wrong output?

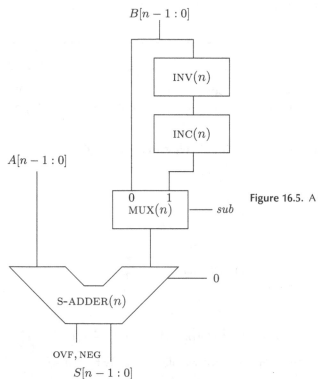

Figure 16.5. A wrong implementation of add-sub(n).

16.9. (OVF and NEG **flags in high-level programming**) High-level programming languages such as C and Java do not enable one to see the value of the OVF and NEG signals (although these signals are computed by adders in all microprocessors).

    (a) Write a short program that deduces the values of these flags. Count how many instructions are needed to recover these lost flags.

    (b) Short segments in a low-level language (Assembly) can be integrated into C programs. Do you know how to see the values of the OVF and NEG flags using a low-level language?

16.10. (**bidirectional cyclic shifting**) The goal in this question is to design a bidirectional barrel shifter.

    Definition 16.9 A bidirectional barrel shifter BI-BARREL-SHIFTER(n) is a combinational circuit defined as follows:

    Input: $x[n-1:0]$, $dir \in \{0,1\}$, and $sa[k-1:0]$, where $k = \lceil \log_2 n \rceil$.

    Output: $y[n-1:0]$.

    Functionality: If $dir = 0$, then $\vec{y}$ is a cyclic right shift of $\vec{x}$ by $\langle \vec{sa} \rangle$ positions. Formally,

$$\forall j \in [n-1:0]: \quad y[j] = x[\mathrm{mod}(j + \langle \vec{sa} \rangle, n)].$$

    If $dir = 1$, then $\vec{y}$ is a cyclic left shift of $\vec{x}$ by $\langle \vec{sa} \rangle$ positions. Formally,

$$\forall j \in [n-1:0]: \quad y[j] = x[\mathrm{mod}(j - \langle \vec{sa} \rangle, n)].$$

    (a) Suggest a reduction of right cyclic shifting to left cyclic shifting for $n = 2^k$. Hint: shift by x to the right is equivalent to shift by $2^k - x$ to the left.

    (b) If your reduction includes an increment, suggest a method that avoids the $\Omega(\log k)$ delay associated with incrementing.

16.11. (**comparison**) Design a combinational circuit COMPARE(n) defined as follows:

    Inputs: $A[n-1:0]$, $B[n-1:0] \in \{0,1\}^n$.

    Output: $LT, EQ, GT \in \{0,1\}$.

    Functionality:

$$(GT, EQ, LT) \triangleq \begin{cases} (1,0,0), & \text{if } [\vec{A}] > [\vec{B}], \\ (0,1,0), & \text{if } [\vec{A}] = [\vec{B}], \\ (0,0,1), & \text{if } [\vec{A}] < [\vec{B}]. \end{cases}$$

    (a) Design a comparator based on a two's complement subtractor and a zero-tester.

    (b) Implement your design in Logisim. Verify *by yourself* that your design is correct. Submit a printout of your implementation.

16.12. (**one's complement adder/subtractor**) Design an adder/subtractor with respect to one's complement representation.

16.13. (**sign-magnitude adder/subtractor**) Design an adder/subtractor with respect to sign-magnitude representation.

SYNCHRONOUS CIRCUITS

CHAPTER 17

Flip-Flops

So far we have focused only on combinational circuits. It is time to deal with circuits that have a memory. Memory, in principle, means that the output depends not only on the input but also on the history. However, if we wish to refer to the history, then we need a notion of time. So before we consider a memory device, we must address the issue of time.

Time in digital logic is defined by a special signal called the *clock*. The clock signal is not a clock in everyday terms; it is simply a periodic signal that alternates between zero and one. The alternations help us partition time into disjoint intervals, called *clock cycles*.

Bits are stored in a special memory device called a *flip-flop*. The definition of flip-flops is rather elaborate and requires that the input be stable during a critical segment. One may wonder why such a complicated definition is required. We prove that flip-flops with empty critical segments do not exist.

17.1 THE CLOCK

Synchronous circuits depend on a special signal called the clock. In practice, the clock is generated by rectifying and amplifying a signal generated by special nondigital devices (e.g., crystal oscillators). Since our course is about digital circuits, we use the following abstraction to describe the clock.

Definition 17.1 A *clock* is a periodic logical signal that oscillates instantaneously between logical one and logical zero. There are two instantaneous transitions in every clock period: (i) in the beginning of the clock period, the clock transitions instantaneously from zero to one; and (ii) at some time in the interior of the clock period, the clock transitions instantaneously from one to zero.

Figure 17.1 depicts a clock signal. We use the convention that the clock rise occurs in the beginning of the clock period. Note that we assume that the transitions of the clock signal are instantaneous; this is obviously impossible in practice. We show later how we get around this unrealistic assumption.

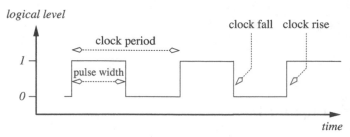

Figure 17.1. A clock signal.

Notation and Terminology. We denote the clock signal by CLK. The *clock pulse* is the period of time within a clock period during which the clock equals one (see Figure 17.1). The duration of the clock pulse is denoted by CLK_{pw}. The clock period is denoted by $\varphi(CLK)$. A clock signal CLK is *symmetric* if $CLK_{pw} = \varphi(CLK)/2$. A clock is said to have *narrow pulses* if $CLK_{pw} < \varphi(CLK)/2$. A clock is said to have *wide pulses* if $CLK_{pw} > \varphi(CLK)/2$. See Figure 17.2 for three examples.

Clock Cycles. A signal clock partitions time into discrete intervals. Throughout this chapter, we denote the starting time of the ith clock periods by t_i. We refer to the

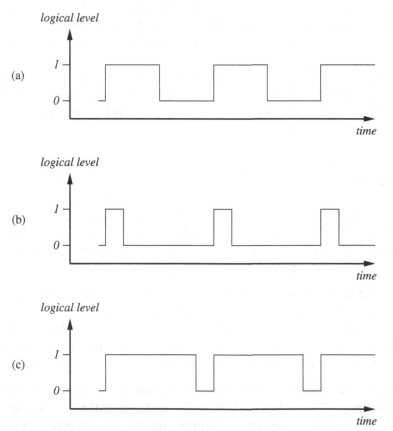

Figure 17.2. (a) A symmetric clock. (b) A clock with narrow pulses. (c) A clock with wide pulses.

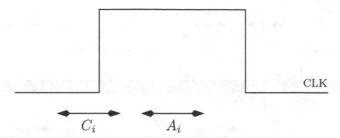

Figure 17.3. The critical segment $C_i = (t_i - t_{su}, t_i + t_{hold})$ and instability segment $A_i = [t_i + t_{cont}, t_i + t_{pd}]$ corresponding the clock period starting at t_i.

half-closed interval $[t_i, t_{i+1})$ as *clock cycle i*. This convention avoids overlaps or gaps between clock periods. From a practical point of view, one could use open or closed intervals instead to define clock cycles.

17.2 EDGE-TRIGGERED FLIP-FLOP

In this section, we define edge-triggered flip-flops.

Definition 17.2 An edge-triggered flip-flop is defined as follows:

Inputs: A digital signal $D(t)$ and a clock CLK.
Output: A digital signal $Q(t)$.
Parameters: Four parameters are used to specify the functionality of a flip-flop:

- *Setup time* denoted by t_{su}.
- *Hold time* denoted by t_{hold}.
- *Contamination delay* denoted by t_{cont}.
- *Propagation delay* denoted by t_{pd}.

These parameters satisfy $-t_{su} < t_{hold} < t_{cont} < t_{pd}$. We refer to the interval $(t_i - t_{su}, t_i + t_{hold})$ as the *critical segment* C_i and to the interval $[t_i + t_{cont}, t_i + t_{pd}]$ as the *instability segment* A_i. See Figure 17.3 for a depiction of these parameters.
Functionality: If $D(t)$ is stable during the critical segment C_i, then $Q(t) = D(t_i)$ during the interval $(t_i + t_{pd}, t_{i+1} + t_{cont})$.

The definition of edge-triggered flip-flops is rather complicated, so we elaborate:

1. The assumption $-t_{su} < t_{hold} < t_{cont} < t_{pd}$ implies that the critical segment C_i and the instability segment A_i are disjoint.
2. If $D(t)$ is stable during the critical segment C_i, then the value of $D(t)$ during the critical segment C_i is well defined and equals $D(t_i)$.
3. The flip-flop *samples* the input signal $D(t)$ during the critical segment C_i. The sampled value $D(t_i)$ is output during the interval $(t_i + t_{pd}, t_{i+1} + t_{cont})$. Sampling is successful only if $D(t)$ is stable while it is sampled. This is why we refer to C_i as a critical segment.
4. If the input $D(t)$ is stable during the critical segments $\{C_i\}_i$, then the output $Q(t)$ is stable in between the instability segments $\{A_i\}_i$.

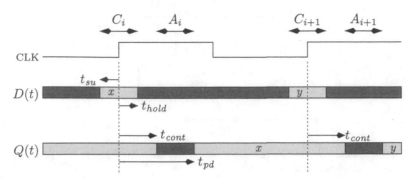

Figure 17.4. A simplified timing diagram of an edge-triggered flip-flop.

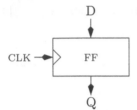

Figure 17.5. A schematic of an edge-triggered flip-flop.

5. The stability of the input $D(t)$ during the critical segments depends on the clock period. We will later see that slowing down the clock (i.e., increasing the clock period) helps in achieving a stable signal $D(t)$ during the critical segments.

Figure 17.4 depicts a simplified timing diagram of a flip-flop. The x-axis corresponds to time. A light gray interval means that the signal is stable during this interval. A dark gray interval means that the signal may be unstable. Note that if $D(t) = x$ during the critical segment C_i, then $Q(t) = x$ during the interval $(t_i + t_{pd}, t_{i+1} + t_{cont})$.

Figure 17.5 depicts a schematic of an edge-triggered flip-flop. Note the special "arrow" that marks the clock port. We refer to an edge-triggered flip-flop, in short, as a flip-flop.

17.3* ARBITRATION

Arbitration in the context of digital design is the problem of deciding which event occurs first. For the sake of simplicity, we focus on the event that the digital interpretation of an analog signal becomes 1. Hence an arbiter is supposed to determine which of two signals first reaches the value one. We formally define arbitration as follows:

Definition 17.3 An *arbiter* is a circuit defined as follows.

Inputs: Nondecreasing analog signals $A_0(t), A_1(t)$ defined for every $t \geq 0$.
Output: An analog signal $Z(t)$.
Functionality: Assume that $A_0(0) = A_1(0) = 0$. Define T_i, for $i = 0, 1$, as follows:

$$T_i \triangleq \inf\{t \mid dig(A_i(t)) = 1\}.$$

Let $t' \triangleq 10 + \max\{T_0, T_1\}$. The output $Z(t)$ must satisfy, for every $t \geq t'$,

$$dig(Z(t)) = \begin{cases} 0 & \text{if } T_0 < T_1 - 1 \\ 1 & \text{if } T_1 < T_0 - 1 \\ 0 \text{ or } 1 & \text{otherwise.} \end{cases}$$

Note that if T_0 or T_1 equals infinity, then t' equals infinity, and there is no requirement on the output $Z(t)$. The idea is that the arbiter circuit is given 10 time units starting from $\max\{T_0, T_1\}$ to determine if $T_0 < T_1$ or $T_1 < T_0$. We refer to the case in which $|T_0 - T_1| \leq 1$ as a *tie*. The arbiter is not required to make a specific decision if a tie occurs. However, even in the case of a tie, the arbiter must make some decision after 10 time units, and its output $Z(t)$ must have a logical value.

Arbiters are very important in many applications since an arbiter determines the order between events. For example, an arbiter can determine which message arrived first in a network switch.

We will show in this chapter that under very reasonable assumptions, arbiters do not exist. Moreover, we will show that a flip-flop with an empty critical segment can be used to implement an arbiter. The lesson is that flip-flops without critical segments do not exist.

17.4* ARBITERS: AN IMPOSSIBILITY RESULT

In this section, we prove that arbiters do not exist.

Claim 17.1 *There does not exist a circuit C that implements an arbiter.*

PROOF: Let C denote an analog circuit with inputs $A_0(t)$, $A_1(t)$ and output $Z(t)$. Define $A_0(t)$ to be the analog signal that rises linearly in the interval $[0, 100]$ from 0 to $V_{in,high}$, and for every $t \geq 100$, $A_0(t) = V_{in,high}$. Let x denote a parameter that defines $A_1(t)$ as follows: $A_1(t)$ rises linearly in the interval $[0, 100 + x]$ from 0 to $V_{in,high}$, and for every $t \geq 100 + x$, $A_1(t) = V_{in,high}$. Let $f(x)$ denote the function that describes the value of $Z(200)$ (i.e., the value of $Z(t)$ at time $t = 200$) when fed by the signals $A_0(t)$ and $A_1(t)$. We study the function $f(x)$ in the interval $x \in [-2, 2]$. We make the following observations:

1. $f(-2) \geq V_{out,high}$. The reason is that if $x = -2$, then $T_0 = 100$ and $T_1 = 98$. Hence $A_1(t)$ *wins*, and by time $t = 200$, the arbiter's output should stabilize on the logical value 1.
2. $f(2) \leq V_{out,low}$. The reason is that if $x = 2$, then $T_0 = 100$ and $T_1 = 102$. Hence $A_0(t)$ *wins*, and $dig(Z(200)) = 0$.
3. $f(x)$ is continuous in the interval $[-2, 2]$. This is not a trivial statement, and its formal proof is not within the scope of this course. We provide an intuitive proof of this fact. The idea of the proof of the continuity of $f(x)$ is that the output $Z(200)$ depends on the following: (i) the initial state of the device C at time $t = 0$—we assume that the device C is in a stable state and that the charge is known everywhere—and (ii) the signal $A_i(t)$ is continuous in the interval $[0, 200]$ for $i = 0, 1$.

An infinitesimal change in x affects only $A_1(t)$ (i.e., the initial state of the circuit and $A_0(t)$ are not affected by x). Moreover, the difference in energy of $A_1(t)$ corresponding to two very close values of x is infinitesimal. Hence the difference in $Z(200)$ for two very close values of x is also infinitesimal. This is the same assumption that we make with respect to noise, namely, since noise is small, its effect on the output is also small.

If this were not the case, then noise would cause uncontrollable changes in $Z(t)$ and the circuit C would not be useful anyhow.

By the mean value theorem, it follows that for every $y \in [V_{out,low}, V_{out,high}]$, there exists an $x \in [-2, 2]$ such that $f(x) = y$. In particular, choose a value y for which $dig(y)$ is not logical. We conclude that circuit C is not a valid arbiter since its output can be forced to be nonlogical way past the time it should be logical. ∎

Claim 17.1 and its proof are very hard to grasp at first. It seems to imply some serious flaw in our perception. Among other things, the claim implies that there does not exist a perfect judge who can determine the winner in a 100-m dash. This statement remains true even in the presence of high-speed cameras located at the finish line and even if the runners run slowly. Moreover, the judge is given several hours to decide, and if the running times of the winner and runner-up are within a second, then the judge may decide arbitrarily! Does this mean that races are pointless? We just proved that, for every judge, there exist two runners whose running times are such that the judge still hangs after an hour.

Our predicament can be clarified by the example depicted in Figure 17.6. Consider a player whose goal is to throw a ball past an obstacle so that it rolls past point P. If the ball is rolled at a speed above v', then it will pass the obstacle and then roll past point P. If the ball is thrown at a speed below v', it will not pass the obstacle. The judge is supposed to announce her decision 24 hours after the player throws the ball. The judge's decision must be either "passed" or "did not pass." This seems like an easy task. However, if the player throws the ball at speed v', then the ball reaches the tip of the obstacle and may remain there indefinitely long! If the ball remains on the obstacle's tip 24 hours past the throw, then the judge cannot announce her decision.

We refer to the state of the ball when resting on the tip of the obstacle as a *metastable* state of equilibrium (see Figure 17.7). Luckily, throwing the ball so that it rests on the tip of the obstacle is a very hard task. Suppose there is some probability distribution for the speed of the ball when thrown. Unless this probability distribution is pathological, the probability of obtaining a metastable state is small. Moreover, the probability of metastability occurring can be reduced by sharpening the tip of the obstacle or giving

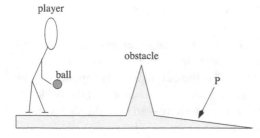

Figure 17.6. A player attempting to roll a ball so that it passes point P.

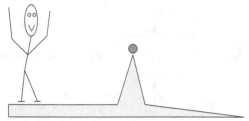

Figure 17.7. The event of metastability.

the arbiter more time to decide. This ability to control the probability of the event that a decision cannot be reached plays a crucial role in real life. In VLSI chips, millions of transistors transition from one state to another millions of times per second. If even one transistor is "stuck" in a metastable state, then the chip might output a wrong value. By reducing the probability of metastability, one can estimate that metastability will not happen during the lifetime of the chip (lightning will hit the chip before metastability happens).

The consequence of this discussion is that Claim 17.1 does not make judges unemployed just as a coin toss is not likely to end up with the coin standing on its perimeter (but bear in mind that it could!). The moral of Claim 17.1 is that (i) certain tasks are not achievable with probability 1. If we consider the random nature of noise, we should not be surprised at all. In fact, noise could be big enough to cause the digital value of a signal to flip from zero to one. If the noise margin is large enough, then such an event is not likely to occur. However, there is always a positive probability that such an error will occur. (ii) Increasing the amount of time during which the arbiter is allowed to reach a decision (significantly) decreases the chances of metastability. As time progresses, even if the ball is resting on the tip of the obstacle, it is likely to fall to one of the sides. Note, however, that increasing the clock rate means that "decisions" must be made faster (i.e., within a clock period) and the chance of metastability increases.

17.5* NECESSITY OF CRITICAL SEGMENTS

In this section, we present a reduction from flip-flops without critical segments to arbiters. Since arbiters do not exist, the implication of this reduction is that flip-flops without critical segments do not exist as well.

We define a flip-flop without a critical segment as a flip-flop in which the setup time and hold time satisfy $t_{su} = t_{hold} = 0$. The functionality is defined as follows: for every i, $Q(t)$ is logical (either zero or one) during the interval $t \in (t_i + t_{pd}, t_{i+1} + t_{cont})$ regardless of whether $D(t_i)$ is logical. If $dig(D(t_i)) \in \{0, 1\}$, then $dig(Q(t)) = dig(D(t_i))$ during the interval $t \in (t_i + t_{pd}, t_{i-1} + t_{cont})$.

The definition of a flip-flop without a critical segment is similar to an arbiter. Just as the arbiter's decision is free if a tie occurs, the flip-flop is allowed to output zero or one if $D(t_i)$ is not logical. However, the output of the flip-flop must be logical once the instability segment ends.

Consider the circuit depicted in Figure 17.8 in which the flip-flop is without a critical segment. Assume that the parameters t_{cont} and t_{pd} are significantly smaller than one time

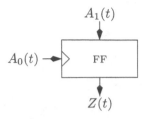

Figure 17.8. An arbiter based on a flip-flop without a critical segment.

unit (e.g., at most 10^{-9} second, where one time unit equals one second). Assume also that the intervals during which the inputs $A_0(t)$ and $A_1(t)$ are nonlogical are also very short (e.g., 10^{-9} second). Let $\varepsilon = 10^{-9}$, and define the signals $A_0(t)$ and $A_1(t)$ as follows:

$$A_0(t) = \begin{cases} 0 & \text{if } t < T_0 - \varepsilon, \\ V_{in,high} & \text{if } t > T_0, \\ \frac{t-(T_0-\varepsilon)}{\varepsilon} \cdot V_{in,high} & \text{if } t \in (T_0 - \varepsilon, T_0), \end{cases}$$

$$A_1(t) = \begin{cases} 0 & \text{if } t < T_1 - \varepsilon, \\ V_{in,high} & \text{if } t > T_1, \\ \frac{t-(T_1-\varepsilon)}{\varepsilon} \cdot V_{in,high} & \text{if } t \in (T_1 - \varepsilon, T_1). \end{cases}$$

Note that the signal $A_0(t)$ is input as a clock to the flip-flop. This is not a standard clock signal; it has one single transition from low to high. This transition occurs at time $t = T_0$. Claim 17.2 uses only one *tick of the clock*, so we may regard $A_0(t)$ as a clock with a very long period.

Claim 17.2 *The circuit depicted in Figure 17.8 is an arbiter.*

PROOF: We need to show that (i) if $T_1 < T_0 - 1$, then $dig(Z(t)) = 1$, for every $t \geq T_0 + t_{pd}$, and (ii) if $T_0 < T_1 - 1$, then $dig(Z(t)) = 0$, for every $t \geq T_0 + t_{pd}$. The case $T_1 - 1 \leq T_0 \leq T_1 + 1$ is solved because the flip-flop's output $Z(t)$ is always logical at time $T_0 + t_{pd}$.

Indeed, the transition of the clock input from zero to one is completed at time T_0. At this time, the flip-flop samples its input $A_1(T_0)$. If $dig(A_1(T_0)) \in \{0, 1\}$, then $dig(Z(t)) = dig(A_1(T_0))$ during the interval $(T_0 + t_{pd}, \infty)$. Note that the signal $A_1(t)$ transitions from zero to one at time T_1.

If $T_1 < T_0 - 1$, then at time T_0, the signal $A_1(t)$ is already high. Thus, $dig(A_1(T_0)) = 1$, and hence $dig(Z(t)) = 1$ for every $t \geq T_0 + t_{pd}$, as required.

If $T_0 < T_1 - 1$, then $dig(A_1(T_0)) = 0$. It follows that $dig(Z(t)) = 0$ for every $t \geq T_0 + t_{pd}$, as required. ∎

Claims 17.1 and 17.2 imply that a flip-flop without a critical segment does not exist. In other words, for every flip-flop, if there is no critical segment requirement, then there exist input signals that can cause it to output a nonlogical value outside of the instability segment.

Corollary 17.3 *There does not exist an edge-triggered flip-flop without a critical segment.*

17.6 A TIMING EXAMPLE

Figure 17.9a depicts a circuit consisting of two identical flip-flops and a combinational circuit C in between. A simplified timing diagram of this circuit is depicted in Figure 17.9b. Instead of drawing the clock signal, only the times t_i and t_{i+1} are marked on the time axis. In addition, the critical segment and instability segment are depicted for each clock period. The digital signals $D_0(t), Q_0(t), D_1(t), Q_1(t)$ are depicted using a simplified timing diagram. In this diagram, intervals during which a digital signal is guaranteed to be stable are marked by a light gray block. Conversely, intervals during which a digital signal is possibly nonlogical are marked by a dark gray block.

In this example, we make the pessimistic assumption that the signal $D_0(t)$ is stable only during the critical segments. As a result, the signal $Q_0(t)$ is stable in the complement of the instability segments A_i and A_{i+1}. The signal $D_1(t)$ is output by the combinational circuit C. We assume that the contamination delay of the combinational circuit is zero, and thus the signal $D_1(t)$ becomes unstable as soon as $Q_0(T)$ (the input of C) becomes unstable. We denote the propagation delay of the combinational circuit C by $d(C)$. The signal $D_1(t)$ stabilizes at most $d(C)$ time units after $Q_0(t)$ stabilizes. The signal $D_1(t)$ is stable during the critical segment C_{i+1}, and therefore $Q_1(t)$ is stable during the complement of the instability segments.

From a functional point of view, stability of $D_0(t)$ during the critical segments implies that $D_0(t_i)$ is logical. We denote $D_0(t_i)$ by $X \in \{0, 1\}$. During the interval $(t_i + t_{pd}, t_{i+1} + t_{cont})$ the flip-flop's output $Q_0(t)$ equals X. The circuit C outputs a logical value $f(X) \in \{0, 1\}$, which is a Boolean function of X. The value $f(X)$ is output by C during the interval $(t_i + t_{pd} + d(C), t_{i+1} + t_{cont})$. It follows that $Q_1(t)$ equals $f(X)$ during the interval $(t_{i+1} + t_{pd}, t_{i+2} + t_{cont})$.

17.6.1 Nonempty Intersection of C_i and A_i

The timing analysis fails if the critical segment C_i and the instability segment intersect, namely,

$$C_i \cap A_i \neq \emptyset.$$

This could happen if $t_{hold} > t_{cont}$ (in contradiction to Definition 17.2).

We now explain why this can cause the circuit to fail (see Figure 17.10). The period during which $D_1(t)$ is guaranteed to be stable is $(t_i + t_{pd} + d(C), t_{i+1} + t_{cont})$. However, if $t_{cont} < t_{hold}$, then $D_1(t)$ is not guaranteed to be stable during the critical segment C_{i+1}. This is a violation of the assumptions we require to guarantee correct functionality. As a result of this violation, the signal $Q_1(t)$ is unspecified outside the instability segments.

In many flip-flop implementations, it so happens that $t_{hold} > t_{cont}$. How are such flip-flops used? The answer is that one needs to rely on the contamination delay of the combinational circuit C. Let $cont(C)$ denote the contamination delay of C. The interval during which $D_1(t)$ is guaranteed to be stable is

$$(t_i + t_{pd} + d(C), t_{i+1} + t_{cont} + cont(C)).$$

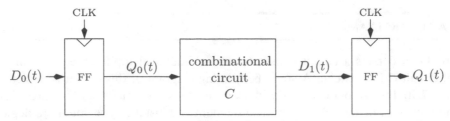

(a) A circuit with two identical flip-flops and a combinational circuit in between

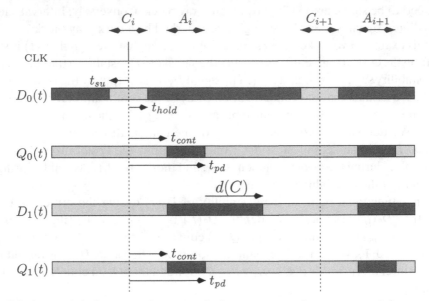

(b) A simplified timing diagram; dark gray areas denote potential instability of asignal, light gray areas denote intervals during which the signal is guaranteed to be stable

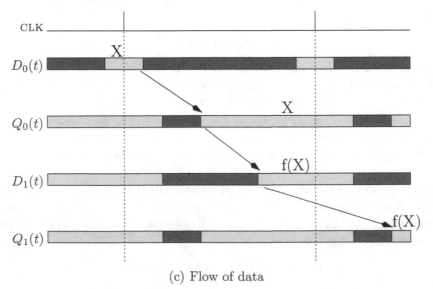

(c) Flow of data

Figure 17.9. A circuit and its simplified timing analysis.

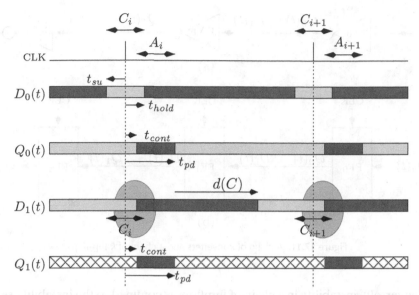

Figure 17.10. The simplified timing diagram in the case that $A_i \cap C_i \neq \varnothing$. Note that $D_1(t)$ is not guaranteed to be stable during the critical segment C_{i+1}. The hatched pattern denotes intervals during which the signal is unspecified.

If $t_{cont} + cont(C) > t_{hold}$, then the signal $D_1(t)$ is stable during the critical segment C_{i+1}, and correct functionality is obtained.

In this book, we simplify by adopting the pessimistic assumption that the contamination delay of every combinational circuit is zero. This means that we need to be more restrictive with respect to flip-flops and require that the critical segment and the instability segments are disjoint. Note, however, that even if the contamination delay of C is positive (although we assumed it is zero), then our analysis is still valid. Hence, assuming zero contamination delay of combinational circuits does not introduce errors even if the contamination delay is positive.

17.7 BOUNDING INSTABILITY

Flip-flops play a crucial role in bounding the segments of time during which signals may be instable. Informally, uncertainty increases as the segments of stability become shorter. In this section, we discuss the role of flip-flops in bounding instability.

Figure 17.11 depicts two circuits: (a) a chain of $k = 3$ inverters and (b) a chain of $k = 3$ flip-flops. We use the same naming convention in both circuits. Namely, we index the k components from 0 to $k - 1$. The input of the ith component is denoted by D_i, and the output is denoted by $Q_i(t)$. Note that $D_{i+1}(t)$ is fed by $Q_i(t)$.

The timing diagrams of the two chains are depicted in Figure 17.12. Figure 17.12a shows the timing analysis for a chain of k inverters. The input $D_0(t)$ is stable for a *long* time. Each inverter along the chain decreases the segment of stability by $t_{pd}(\text{INV})$. Thus uncertainty increases along the chain of inverters.

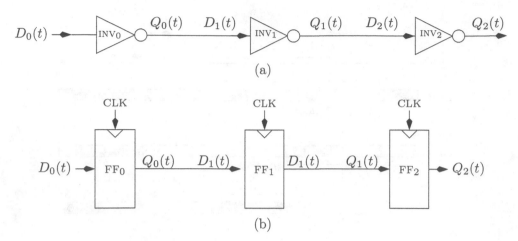

Figure 17.11. A chain of k inverters and a chain of k flip-flops.

Conversely, instability in a chain of flip-flops is confined to the instability segments $\{A_i\}_i$ of the flip-flops. Formally, if $D_j(t)$ is stable during the interval $(t_i - t_{su}, t_i + t_{hold})$, then $Q_j(t)$ is stable during the interval $(t_i + t_{pd}, t_{i+1} + t_{cont})$.

17.8 OTHER TYPES OF MEMORY DEVICES

Edge-triggered flip-flops are not the only memory device that exists. We briefly overview some of these devices.

17.8.1 D-Latch

A D-latch, unlike an edge-triggered flip-flop, is characterized by three parameters t_{su}, t_{hold}, and d. The critical segment is defined with respect to the falling edge of the clock. Let t_i' denote the time of the falling edge of the clock during the ith clock cycle. The critical segment of a D-latch is defined to be $C_i \triangleq (t_i' - t_{su}, t_i' + t_{hold})$. In addition, the D-latch is characterized by a combinational delay d. The functionality of a D-latch is defined as follows (see Figure 17.13).

1.   During the interval $[t_i + d, t_i')$, the output $Q(t)$ satisfies $Q(t) = D(t)$, provided that $D(t)$ is stable during the interval $(t - d, t)$. We say that the D-latch is *transparent* during the interval $[t_i + d, t_i')$.
2.   During the interval $(t_i' + t_{hold}, t_{i+1})$, if $D(t)$ is stable during the critical segment $(t_i' - t_{su}, t_i' + t_{hold})$, then $Q(t) = D(t_i')$. We say that the D-latch is *opaque* during the interval $(t_i' + t_{hold}, t_{i+1})$.

Figure 17.13 depicts a timing diagram of a D-latch. During the pulse (t_i, t_i'), the input $D(t)$ stabilizes on the value x. Since the D-latch is transparent, after a delay of d, the output $Q(t)$ equals x. During the critical segment C_i, the input $D(t)$ is stable and equals y. The D-latch is opaque when the clock is zero. Therefore, during the interval

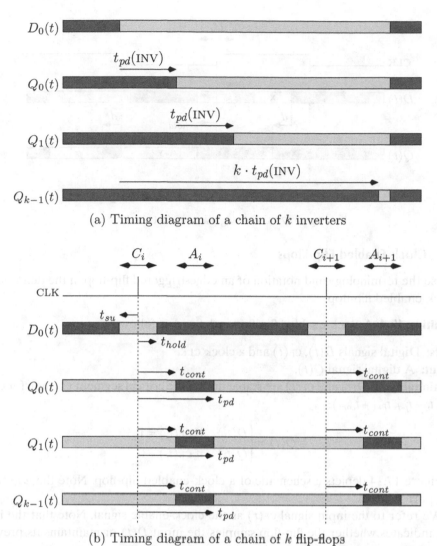

(a) Timing diagram of a chain of k inverters

(b) Timing diagram of a chain of k flip-flops

Figure 17.12. Comparison of segments of instability in two chains.

$(t'_i + d, t_{i+1})$, the output equals y. Note that during the interval $(t'_i + d, t_{i+1})$, the output is not affected by changes in the input. The input stabilizes on z before t_{i+1}. But the value of $D(t)$ during the interval $(t'_i + t_{hold})$ does not affect the output. After the clock rise in t_{i+1}, the D-latch is transparent again. Therefore the output $Q(t)$ equals z after a delay of d.

D-latches are very important devices. In fact, D-latches are the building blocks of flip-flops. A flip-flop can be built from two D-latches and additional inverters (required to restore the signals). Designs based on D-latches lead to faster designs. However, such designs based on D latches require multiple clock phases and are harder to analyze. Although timing with multiple clock phases is an important and interesting topic, we do not deal with it in this book.

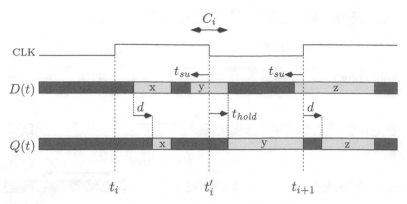

Figure 17.13. A timing diagram of a D-latch.

17.8.2 Clock-Enabled Flip-Flops

We use the terminology and notation of an edge-triggered flip-flop in the definition of a clock-enabled flip-flop.

Definition 17.4 A clock-enabled flip-flop is defined as follows.

Inputs: Digital signals $D(t)$, CE(t) and a clock CLK.
Output: A digital signal $Q(t)$.
Functionality: If $D(t)$ and CE(t) are stable during the critical segment C_i, then for every $t \in (t_i + t_{pd}, t_{i+1} + t_{cont})$,

$$Q(t) = \begin{cases} D(t_i) & \text{if CE}(t_i) = 1 \\ Q(t_i) & \text{if CE}(t_i) = 0. \end{cases}$$

Figure 17.14 depicts a schematic of a clock-enabled flip-flop. Note the additional CE(t) port.

We refer to the input signal CE(t) as the clock-enable signal. Note that the input CE(t) indicates whether the flip-flop samples the input $D(t)$ or maintains its previous value.

Figure 17.15a depicts a successful implementation of a clock-enabled flip-flop. This implementation uses a MUX and an edge-triggered flip-flop. Figure 17.15b depicts a weak implementation of a clock-enabled flip-flop.

The main weakness of the design depicted in Figure 17.15b is that the output of the AND-gate is not a clock signal. For example, the output of the AND-gate is allowed to fluctuate when CE(t) is not logical. Such fluctuations (called *glitches*) can cause the

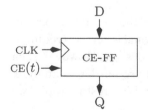

Figure 17.14. A schematic of a clock-enabled flip-flop.

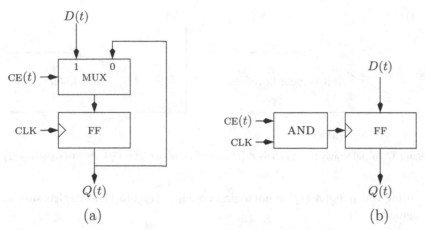

Figure 17.15. (a) A successful implementation of a clock-enabled flip-flop. (b) A wrong design.

flip-flop to sample the input when not needed. In addition, the transitions of the output of the AND-gate might be slow and require increasing the hold time. Moreover, in some technologies, the flip-flop does not retain the stored bit forever. For example, consider the case in which the stored value is retained only for two or three clock cycles. In such a case, if the clock-enabled signal is low for a long period, then the flip-flop's output may become nonlogical.

17.9 SUMMARY

In this chapter, we presented memory devices called *flip-flops*. We consider using flip-flops in the presence of a *clock signal*. The clock signal causes the flip-flop to sample the value of the input toward the end of a clock cycle and output the sampled value during the next clock cycle. Flip-flops play a crucial role in bounding the segments of time during which signals may be unstable.

In a sense, flip-flops and combinational circuits have opposite roles. Combinational circuits compute interesting Boolean functions but increase uncertainty (namely, lengthen segments of time during which signals may be unstable). Flip-flops, conversely, output the same value that is fed as input, but they limit uncertainty.

We considered a task called *arbitration*. We proved that no circuit can implement an arbiter. We then proved that a flip-flop with an empty critical segment can be used to build an arbiter. This proves that a flip-flop must have a nonempty critical segment.

PROBLEMS

17.1. Is an edge-triggered flip-flop a combinational gate?

17.2. Does the proof of Claim 17.1 hold only if the signals $A_i(t)$ rise "slowly"? Prove the claim with respect to nondecreasing signals $A_i(t)$ such that the length of the interval

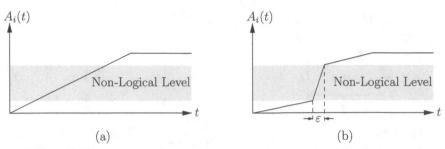

Figure 17.16. (a) Slowly rising signals $A_i(t)$ used in proof of Claim 17.1. (b) Fast signals $A_i(t)$.

during which $dig(A_i(t))$ is nonlogical equals ε. (Figure 17.16 depicts slow and fast signals.)

17.3. Assume that we have an edge-triggered flip-flop FF in which $t_{hold} > t_{cont}$. Suppose that we have an inverter with a contamination delay $cont(\text{INV}) > 0$. Suggest how to design an edge-triggered flip-flop FF$'$ that satisfies $t_{hold}(\text{FF}') < t_{cont}(\text{FF}')$. What are the parameters of FF$'$?

17.4. Compute the parameters of the clock-enabled flip-flop depicted in Figure 17.15a in terms of the parameters of the edge-triggered flip-flop and the MUX.

17.5. Figure 17.17 depicts a schematic of a flip-flop FF$_{new}$. This new flip-flop is composed of a regular flip-flop and two combinational circuits C_1 and C_2. The parameters of the flip-flop FF are $t_{su}, t_{hold}, t_{cont}$, and t_{pd}. The propagation delay and contamination delay of the combinational circuit C_i are $t_{pd}(C_i), cont(C_i)$, respectively, for $i \in \{1, 2\}$.

What are the parameters $t'_{su}, t'_{hold}, t'_{cont}$, and t'_{pd} of the new flip-flop FF$_{new}$?

17.6. Design a circuit that satisfies the following specification:
Input: $\{X(t)\}_{t=0}^{\infty}$, where $X(t) \in \{0, 1\}$ for every clock cycle t, and a clock signal CLK.
Output: $\{Y(t)\}_{t=0}^{\infty}$, where $Y(t) \in \{0, 1\}$ for every clock cycle t. $\{Z(t)\}_{t=0}^{\infty}$, where $Z(t) \in \{0, 1\}$ for every clock cycle t.

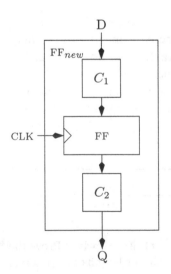

Figure 17.17. A schematic of a "new" flip-flop that is composed of a flip-flop and two additional combinational circuits C_1 and C_2.

Functionality:

$$\forall t \geq 1 : Y(t) = \text{XOR}(X(0), \ldots, X(t-1))$$

$$\forall t \geq 0 : Z(t) = \text{XOR}(X(0), \ldots, X(t)).$$

(a) Implement your design using Logisim. Submit a printout of your design.
(b) Simulate two different inputs of length 5: (i) 01010 and (ii) 11111. Verify by *yourself* that your design is correct (make sure you know how to initialize the flip-flops and to see the values of a signal in each clock cycle).

CHAPTER 18

Memory Modules

In this chapter, we present circuits that serve as memory modules. The first type of circuit, called a *parallel load register*, is simply built of identical copies of clock-enabled flip-flops. The second type, called a *shift register*, remembers the input from k clock cycles ago. Such a shift register is build from k clock-enabled flip-flops connected in chain.

We also consider memory circuits. The first circuit, called a *Random Access Memory* (RAM), is capable of storing and reading values. It is like a blackboard divided into many cells. We can write a value in each cell, and we can read the value written in a cell. When we write in a cell, it erases the previous value so that only the new value is written in the cell. The second memory circuit is called a *Read-Only Memory* (ROM). It is like a blackboard on which a value has been written in each cell with permanent ink. The contents of each cell cannot be erased or written over, and we can only read values stored in the cells.

The functionality of a flip-flop is complicated and following the timing is tedious. Instead, we propose an abstract model called the *zero delay model*. In this simplified model, all transitions are instantaneous. The zero delay model enables us to separate between functionality and timing so that we can focus on functionality.

18.1 THE ZERO DELAY MODEL

In the zero delay model, transitions of all signals are instantaneous. This means that the propagation delay and contamination delay of combinational circuits are zero. In addition, the parameters of flip-flops satisfy

$$t_{su} = t_{i+1} - t_i$$

$$t_{hold} = t_{cont} = t_{pd} = 0.$$

We emphasize that this model is used only as a simplified model for specifying and simulating the functionality of circuits with flip-flops.

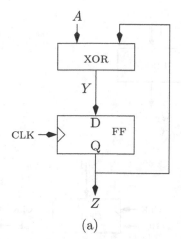

i	A_i	Y_i	Z_i
0	0	0	0
1	0	0	0
2	1	1	0
3	0	1	1
4	0	1	1
5	1	0	1
6	0	0	0
7	1	1	0
8	0	1	1

(a)   (b)

Figure 18.1. A sequential XOR circuit. (a) schematic. (b) logical simulation in the zero delay model. We assume that the flip-flop is initialized to zero. Note that $Z_{i+1} = Y_i$ and $Y_i = \text{XOR}(A_i, Z_i)$.

The clock period in the zero delay model equals 1; that is, $t_{i+1} - t_i = 1$ for every i. Hence the duration of the ith clock cycle is the interval $[t_i, t_{i+1}) = [i, i + 1)$.

Since all transitions are instantaneous, we may assume that each signal is stable during each clock cycle. Let X_i denote the digital value of the signal X during the ith clock cycle.

Under the zero delay model, the functionality of a flip-flop is specified as follows:

$$Q(t) = D(t - 1).$$

Since each signal is stable during each clock cycle, we could also write $Q_i = D_{i-1}$. The meaning of this specification is as follows. The critical segment C_i equals $[t_{i-1}, t_i)$. The value of $D(t)$ is stable during the critical segment $[t_{i-1}, t_i)$. This value, denoted by D_{i-1}, is sampled by the flip-flop during the clock cycle $(i - 1)$. In the next clock cycle $[t_i, t_{i+1})$, the flip-flop's output $Q(t)$ equals the value of the input sampled during the previous cycle.

18.1.1 Example: Sequential XOR

Consider the circuit depicted in Figure 18.1. Let A_i denote the value of the input A during the interval $[t_i, t_{i+1})$.

18.2 REGISTERS

A term *register* is used to define a memory device that stores a bit or more. There are two main types of register, depending on how their contents are loaded.

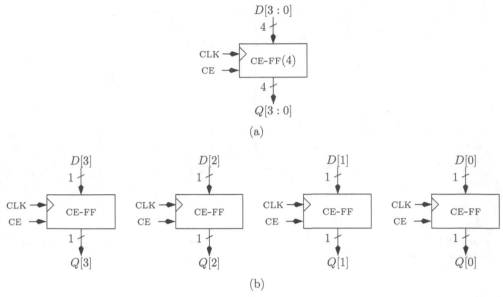

Figure 18.2. A 4-bit parallel load register: (a) a shorthand drawing of the schematics of a 4-bit parallel load register; (b) an elaborated drawing of the schematics of a 4-bit parallel load register.

18.2.1 Parallel Load Register

Definition 18.1 An n-bit *parallel load register* is specified as follows:

Inputs: (i) $D[n-1:0](t)$, (ii) $\text{CE}(t)$, and (iii) a clock CLK.
Output: $Q[n-1:0](t)$.
Functionality:

$$Q[n-1:0](t+1) = \begin{cases} D[n-1:0](t) & \text{if } \text{CE}(t) = 1 \\ Q[n-1:0](t) & \text{if } \text{CE}(t) = 0. \end{cases}$$

An n-bit parallel load register is simply built from n clock-enabled flip-flops. The ith flip-flop is fed by $D[i]$ and CE and outputs $Q[i]$. Figure 18.2 depicts a 4-bit parallel load register.

18.2.2 Shift Register

A shift register is also called a serial load register.

Definition 18.2 A *shift register* of n bits is defined as follows:

Inputs: $D[0](t)$ and a clock CLK.
Output: $Q[n-1](t)$.
Functionality: $Q[n-1](t+n) = D[0](t)$.

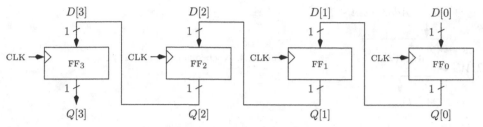

Figure 18.3. A 4-bit shift register.

An n-bit shift register is built from a chain of n flip-flops, indexed from 0 to $n-1$. The ith flip-flop is fed by $D[i]$ and outputs $Q[i]$. Since the flip-flops are chained, $D[i+1] \leftarrow Q[i]$. Figure 18.3 depicts a 4-bit shift register.

18.3 RANDOM ACCESS MEMORY (RAM)

The module called RAM is an array of memory cells. Each memory cell stores a single bit. In each cycle, a single memory cell is accessed. Two operations are supported: read and write. In a read operation, the contents of the accessed memory are output. In a write operation, a new value is stored in the accessed memory.

The number of memory cells is denoted by 2^n. Each cell has a distinct address between 0 and $2^n - 1$. The cell to be accessed is specified by an n-bit string called an address.

The array of memory cells is denoted by $M[2^n - 1 : 0]$. Let $M[i](t)$ denote the value stored in the ith entry of the array M during clock cycle t.

Table 10.1. Comparison of simulations of a parallel load register and a shift register. We assume all flip-flops are initialized to zero

(a) Simulation of parallel load register

i	$D[3:0]$	CE	$Q[3:0]$
0	1010	1	0000
1	0101	1	1010
2	1100	0	0101
3	1100	1	0101
4	0011	1	1100

(b) Simulation of shift register

i	$D[0]$	$Q[3:0]$
0	1	0000
1	1	0001
2	1	0011
3	0	0111
4	1	1110

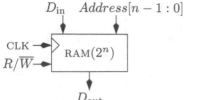

Figure 18.4. A schematic of a RAM(2^n).

The module RAM(2^n) is specified using the zero delay model, as follows (a schematic symbol is depicted in Figure 18.4):

Definition 18.3 A RAM(2^n) is specified as follows:

Inputs: $Address[n-1:0](t) \in \{0,1\}^n$, $D_{in}(t) \in \{0,1\}$, $R/\overline{W}(t) \in \{0,1\}$ and a clock CLK.
Output: $D_{out}(t) \in \{0,1\}$.
Functionality: The functionality of a RAM is specified by the following program:

1. data: array $M[2^n - 1 : 0]$ of bits.
2. initialize: $\forall i : M[i] \leftarrow 0$.
3. For $t = 0$ to ∞ do
   (a) $D_{out}(t) = M[\langle Address \rangle](t)$.
   (b) For all $i \neq \langle Address \rangle$: $M[i](t+1) \leftarrow M[i](t)$.
   (c)

$$M[\langle Address \rangle](t+1) \leftarrow \begin{cases} D_{in}(t) & \text{if } R/\overline{W}(t) = 0 \\ M[\langle Address \rangle](t) & \text{else.} \end{cases}$$

We note that the value of $D_{out}(t)$ in a write cycle (i.e., when $R/\overline{W}(t) = 0$) is not really important. For simplicity, we define it to be the old value of the memory entry, that is, the value before $D_{in}(t)$ is stored in $M[\langle Address \rangle]$.

18.3.1 A Simple Implementation of a RAM

In this section, we present a simple implementation of a RAM(2^n), the schematics of which are depicted in Figure 18.5. The implementation consists of the following three parts:

1. An address decoder
2. An array of 2^n memory cells
3. A $(2^n : 1)$-MUX

Each memory cell is specified as follows:

Definition 18.4 A single-bit *memory cell* is defined as follows:

Inputs: $D_{in}(t)$, $R/\overline{W}(t)$, $sel(t)$, and a clock CLK.
Output: $D_{out}(t)$.
Functionality: Let $S(t) \in \{0,1\}$ denote the state of memory cell in cycle t. Assume that the state is initialized to be $S(0) = 0$. The functionality is defined according to the following cases.

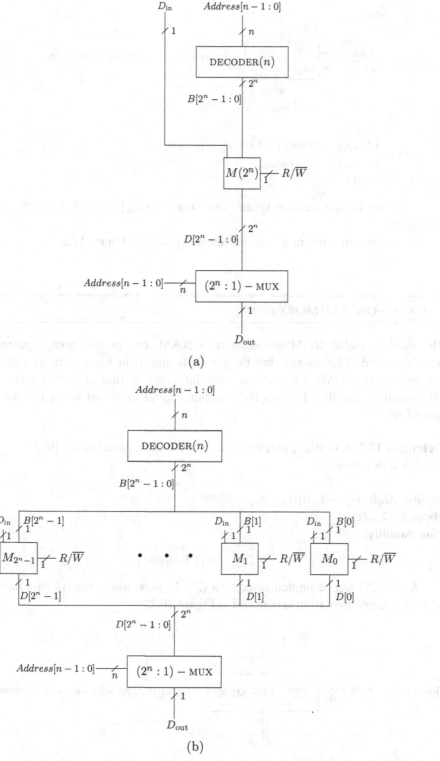

Figure 18.5. A simplified implementation of a RAM(2^n): (a) a shorthand drawing of the schematics of RAM(2^n); (b) an elaborated drawing of the schematics of RAM(2^n).

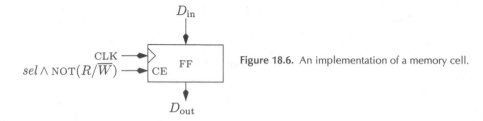

Figure 18.6. An implementation of a memory cell.

1. $S(t) \leftarrow \begin{cases} D_{\text{in}}(t) & \text{if } sel(t) = 1 \text{ and } R/\overline{W}(t) = 0 \\ S(t-1) & \text{otherwise.} \end{cases}$
2. $D_{\text{out}}(t) \leftarrow S(t-1)$.

Note that we do not need to specify the value of $D_{\text{out}}(t)$ if $sel(t) = 0$. We do so for simplicity.

An implementation of a memory cell is depicted in Figure 18.6.

18.4 READ-ONLY MEMORY (ROM)

The module called ROM is similar to a RAM, except that write operations are not supported. This means that the contents stored in each memory cell are pre-set and fixed. ROMs are used to store information that should not be changed. For example, the ROM stores the program that is executed when the computer is turned on.

Definition 18.5 A ROM(2^n) that implements a Boolean function $M : [0..2^n - 1] \rightarrow \{0, 1\}$ is defined as follows:

Inputs: $Address[n - 1 : 0](t)$.
Output: $D_{\text{out}}(t)$.
Functionality:

$$D_{\text{out}} = M[\langle Address \rangle] .$$

A ROM(2^n) can be implemented by a $(2^n : 1)$-MUX, where the ith data input equals $M[i]$. An implementation is depicted in Figure 18.7.

$M[2^n - 1 : 0]$

$Address[n - 1 : 0]$ —/n— $(2^n : 1) - \text{MUX}$ **Figure 18.7.** An implementation of a ROM(2^n).

D_{out}

18.5 SUMMARY

In this chapter, we defined four major memory modules and presented simple implementations for each module. In practice, memory modules such as RAMs are highly optimized circuits that are implemented using analog methods.

PROBLEMS

18.1. Define and implement a shift register with a clock-enable signal CE. When CE = 1, a shift occurs. When CE = 0, the contents of the register remain unchanged.

18.2. A shift register *with a parallel load* is a shift register with additional inputs, as follows. This register has an input $D[n-1:0]$ and an extra input called *load* $\in \{0,1\}$. When *load* = 0, a shift takes place. When *load* = 1, the vector $D[n-1:0]$ is stored in the register. Design a shift register with a parallel load that satisfies this definition.

18.3. Design a RAM with 2^n memory cells, where each cell can store k bits.

18.4. Design a dual-port RAM with 2^n memory cells, where each cell can store 1 bit. In a dual-port memory, there are two address inputs A_1 and A_2 and two data outputs D_1 and D_2. In each cycle, either a write operation takes place to the cell $M[\langle A_1 \rangle]$ or two read operations take place, namely,

$$D_1(t) \leftarrow M[\langle A_1(t) \rangle](t) \qquad\qquad D_2(t) \leftarrow M[\langle A_2(t) \rangle](t).$$

CHAPTER 19

Foundations of Synchronous Circuits

In this chapter, we deal with synchronous circuits. We begin with a formal definition that builds on the definition of combinational circuits. This definition is syntactic, and we must prove that a circuit that satisfies this definition does what we expect it to do. But how do we define what it should do? Namely, how do we specify functionality, and how do we specify timing?

We begin with a simple form of synchronous circuits that we call the *canonic form*. In the canonic form, it is clear what the flip-flops do, where the output is computed, and where we compute the inputs of the flip-flops. We begin by analyzing the timing of a synchronous circuit in canonic form. We show that stability during the critical segments of the flip-flops can be achieved if the clock period is sufficiently long. We also address the painful issue of initialization. The functionality of a synchronous circuit in canonic form is specified using an abstract model called a *finite state machine*.

We then proceed with the timing analysis of synchronous circuits in general. We present two algorithms for timing analysis. The first algorithm, FEAS, tells us if the timing constraints of the circuit are feasible. The second algorithm, Min- $-\Phi$, finds the minimum clock period. We also present an algorithm for simulating a synchronous circuit.

Two tasks are often associated with synchronous circuits. The first task, called *analysis*, is to find the finite state machine that specifies the functionality of a given synchronous circuit. The second task, called *synthesis*, is to design a synchronous circuit, the functionality of which is specified by a given finite state machine.

19.1 DEFINITION

The building blocks of a synchronous circuit are combinational gates, wires, and flip-flops. As in the case of a combinational circuit, a synchronous circuit is a netlist $H = (V, N, \pi)$. However, the requirements are somewhat different. First, the graph $DG(H)$ is directed but may contain cycles. Second, we also use flip-flops, hence Γ includes combinational gates, input–output gates, and flip-flops (FF and CE-FF). Thus a vertex may be labeled as a flip-flip.

Since a flip-flop has two inputs, D and CLK, that play quite different roles, we must make sure that we know the input port of each incoming edge. This task is quite easy since the clock signal must be fed to the CLK input port of each and every flip-flop.

In the following definition, we do not deal with the graph G and the labeling π. Instead, we transform the circuit C to a different circuit C' and require that C' be a combinational circuit.

Definition 19.1 A *synchronous circuit* is a circuit C composed of combinational gates, wires, and flip-flops that satisfies the following conditions:

1. There is an input gate that feeds the clock signal CLK.
2. The set of ports that are fed by the clock CLK equals the set of clock inputs of the flip-flops.
3. Let C' denote a circuit obtained from C by the following changes: (i) delete the input gate that feeds the clock CLK and all the wires carrying the clock signal and (ii) replace each flip-flop with an output gate (instead of the port D) and an input gate (instead of the port Q). We require that the circuit C' be a combinational circuit.

We emphasize again that in a synchronous circuit, the clock signal is connected only to the clock port of the flip-flops; the clock may not feed other inputs (i.e., inputs of combinational gates or the D-port of flip-flops). Moreover, every clock port of a flip-flop is fed by the clock signal.

Part 3 in the definition of a synchronous circuit considers the circuit after the flip-flops are removed. We refer to this transformation as *stripping away the flip-flops*. Figure 19.1 depicts a synchronous circuit C and the corresponding combinational circuit C' obtained from C by stripping away the flip-flops.

An equivalent way to define a synchronous circuit is to start with a combinational circuit C'. Now flip-flips are added as follows. Of course, the clock port of each flip-flip is fed by the clock signal. In addition, for each flip-flop, designate a pair consisting of an output gate and an input gate of C'. We replace this pair by a flip-flop. The D-port of the flip flop is fed by the signal that feeds the output gate, and the Q-port of the flip-flop feeds the signal that is fed by the input gate.

Finally, we point out that it is easy to check if a given circuit C is a synchronous circuit. We simply check if there is a clock signal that is connected to all the clock terminals of the flip-flops, and only to them. Strip the flip-flops away to obtain the circuit C'. Now all we need to do is to check if C' is a combinational circuit—a task we have already discussed in Chapter 11.

Claim 19.1 *Every cycle in a synchronous circuit traverses at least one flip-flop.*

PROOF: Consider a cycle p in a synchronous circuit C. Clearly p cannot contain an edge that carries the clock signal. Indeed, the clock signal emanates from an input gate, which is a source, and a cycle cannot contain a source.

Consider the circuit C' obtained from C by stripping away the flip-flops. Since p does not contain edges that carry the clock signal, all the edges of p are also edges in C'.

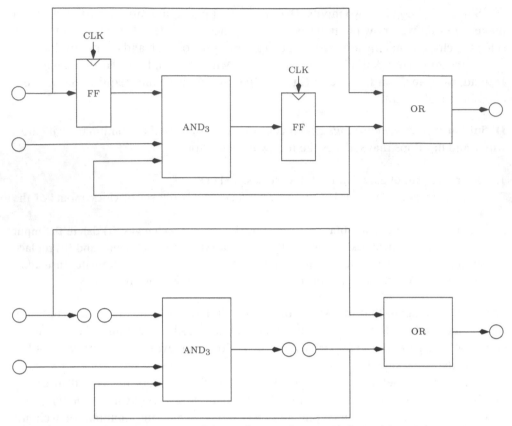

Figure 19.1. A synchronous circuit C and the combinational circuit C' obtained from C by stripping away the flip-flops.

Since C' is acyclic, it follows that one of the vertices in p is split into a sink and a source. This implies that p contains a flip-flop, as required. ∎

19.2 THE CANONIC FORM OF A SYNCHRONOUS CIRCUIT

Consider the synchronous circuit depicted in Figure 19.2. The circuit has an input IN, an output OUT, and internal signals S (for "state") and NS (for "next state"). We abuse notation and refer to the combinational circuits λ and δ by the Boolean functions that they implement. In this example, all the signals in the circuit carry single bits (as normal signals do). However, we could easily deal with the case in which IN, OUT, S, and NS are buses (i.e., multiple-bit signals).

One can transform every synchronous circuit so that it fits the description in Figure 19.2. This is achieved by (i) gathering the flip-flops into one group and (ii) duplicating the combinational circuits (if necessary) so that we can separate between the combinational circuits that produce output signals and combinational circuits that produce signals that are fed back to the flip-flops. This is why we refer to the circuit depicted in Figure 19.2 as a *canonic form* of a synchronous circuit.

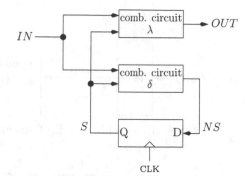

Figure 19.2. A synchronous circuit in canonic form.

19.3 TIMING ANALYSIS: THE CANONIC FORM

In this section, we analyze the timing constraints of a synchronous circuit that is given in canonic form.

Stability Interval. We associate with each signal an interval corresponding to the ith clock cycle during which the signal is supposed to be stable. We refer to this interval as the *stability interval*. We denote the stability interval corresponding to the ith clock cycle of a signal X by $stable(X)_i$. We denote the digital value of X during the interval $stable(X)_i$ by X_i.

The stability interval is part of the specification. When referring to an input X, this means that we are guaranteed that the input will stable during $stable(X)_i$. When referring to an output Y, this means that we must design the circuit so that Y will be stable during $stable(Y)_i$.

19.3.1 An Easy Example

Consider the simple synchronous circuit depicted in Figure 19.3a. A simplified timing diagram of this circuit is depicted in Figure 19.3b. In this example, we *do not* assume that the two flip-flops have the same parameters.

We require that the input $D_0(t)$ to flip-flop FF_1 be stable during the critical segments of FF_1, namely, for every $i \geq 0$:

$$stable(D_0)_i \triangleq C_{i+1}(FF_1) \tag{19.1}$$

$$= (t_{i+1} - t_{su}(FF_1), t_{i+1} + t_{hold}(FF_1)). \tag{19.2}$$

Note that the stability interval corresponding to the ith clock cycle of an input of a flip-flop must contain the critical segment C_{i+1}. Indeed, in the ith clock cycle, the flip-flop samples its input at the end of the cycle at time t_{i+1}.

The stability interval of the output $Q_0(t)$ of flip-flop FF_1 is defined by

$$stable(Q_0)_i \triangleq (t_i + t_{pd}(FF_1), t_{i+1} + t_{cont}(FF_1)). \tag{19.3}$$

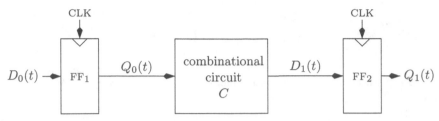

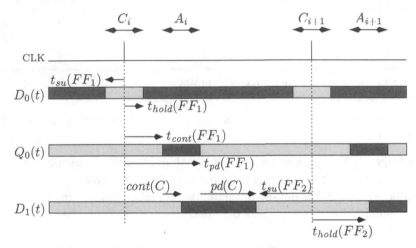

(a) A circuit with two flip-flops and a combinational circuit in between

(b) A simplified timing diagram

Figure 19.3. A simple synchronous circuit. In this example, the two flip-flops have different parameters: $t_{su}(FF_2) > t_{su}(FF_1)$ and $t_{hold}(FF_2) > t_{hold}(FF_1)$.

The rationale behind this definition is that if the input $D_0(t)$ is stable during every critical segment C_i, then the output $Q_0(t)$ of the flip-flop is stable in the preceding interval.

Note that we have a problem with the guarantee for the stability interval of Q_0 during clock cycle zero. This is not a minor technical issue! How can we argue anything about the output of FF_1 during clock cycle zero? To solve this problem, we need an initialization assumption that tells us what the value of the output of the flip-flop is during the first clock cycle and when it is stable. Indeed, the issue of proper initialization has the role of the induction basis in the timing analysis of synchronous circuits. We elaborate on this important issue in Section 19.3.5. In the meantime, assume that Eq. 19.3 holds also for $i = 0$.

To ensure proper functionality, the input $D_1(t)$ must be stable during the critical segments of flip-flop FF_2. Therefore we define the stability interval of $D_1(t)$ as follows:

$$stable(D_1)_i \triangleq C_{i+1}(FF_2). \tag{19.4}$$

$$= (t_{i+1} - t_{su}(FF_2), t_{i+1} + t_{hold}(FF_2)). \tag{19.5}$$

The following claim provides a sufficient condition that guarantees that $D_1(t)$ is indeed stable during the stability intervals $\{stable(D_1)_i\}_{i \geq 0}$.

Claim 19.2 *The signal $D_1(t)$ is stable during the critical segments of flip-flop FF_2 if*

$$\forall i \geq 0: \; t_{\mathrm{pd}}(FF_1) + \mathrm{pd}(C) + t_{\mathrm{su}}(FF_2) \leq t_{i+1} - t_i, \tag{19.6}$$

$$t_{\mathrm{hold}}(FF_2) \leq t_{\mathrm{cont}}(FF_1) + \mathrm{cont}(C). \tag{19.7}$$

PROOF: The signal $D_1(t)$ is output by the combinational circuit C. The circuit C has a contamination delay $cont(C)$ and a propagation delay $pd(C)$. Since $stable(Q_0)_i$ satisfies Eq. 19.3 and since $D_1(t)$ is output by C, the signal $D_1(t)$ is stable during the intervals:

$$(t_i + t_{pd}(FF_1) + pd(C), t_{i+1} + t_{cont}(FF_1) + cont(C)). \tag{19.8}$$

Thus we require that

$$C_{i+1}(FF_2) \subseteq (t_i + t_{pd}(FF_1) + pd(C), t_{i+1} + t_{cont}(FF_1) + cont(C)). \tag{19.9}$$

Note that Eq. 19.9 is in fact two inequalities:

$$t_{i+1} - t_{su}(FF_2) \geq t_i + t_{pd}(FF_1) + pd(C)$$

$$t_{i+1} + t_{hold}(FF_2) \leq t_{i+1} + t_{cont}(FF_1) + cont(C).$$

These two inequalities are equivalent to Eqs. 19.6 and 19.7, respectively, and the claim follows. ∎

Claim 19.2 teaches us two important lessons:

Minimum Clock Period. To ensure proper functionality, the clock period cannot be too short. Namely, the time $t_{i+1} - t_i$ between two consecutive rising clock edges must be longer than $t_{pd}(FF_1) + pd(C) + t_{su}(FF_2)$.

Use Simple Flip-Flops. Inequality 19.7 is satisfied if $t_{cont}(FF_1) \geq t_{hold}(FF_2)$. When we defined a flip-flop, we assumed that $t_{cont} \geq t_{hold}$ so that the critical segment and the segment of instability are disjoint. There are many ways to complicate the task of designing correct synchronous circuits. One possibility for such a complication is to use two or more types of flip-flops FF_1 and FF_2, in which $t_{cont}(FF_1) < t_{hold}(FF_2)$. In such a case, one has to rely on the contamination delay of the combinational logic between the flip-flops.

19.3.2 Input–Output Timing Constraints

The input–output timing constraints formulate the timing interface between the circuit and the external world. The constraint corresponding to the input tells us when the input is guaranteed to be stable, and the constraint corresponding to the output tells us when the circuit's output is required to be stable. Usually the external world is also a synchronous circuit. This means that the signal IN is an output of another synchronous circuit. Similarly, the signal OUT is an input of another synchronous circuit. Hence it is helpful to think of IN as the output of a flip-flop and of OUT as the input of a flip-flop.

1. The timing constraint corresponding to IN is defined by two parameters; $pd(IN) > cont(IN)$, as follows. The stability intervals of signal IN are defined, for every $i \geq 0$, by

$$stable(IN)_i \triangleq (t_i + pd(IN), t_{i+1} + cont(IN)). \tag{19.10}$$

Recall that t_i denotes the starting time of the ith clock period. Note that if $pd(IN) \leq cont(IN)$, then the stability intervals $stable(IN)_i$ and $stable(IN)_{i+1}$ overlap. This means that IN is always stable, and hence constant, which is obviously not an interesting case. Hence we require that $pd(IN) > cont(IN)$.

2. The timing constraint corresponding to OUT is defined by two parameters; $setup(OUT)$ and $hold(OUT)$, as follows. The stability intervals of signal OUT are defined, for every $i \geq 0$, by

$$stable(OUT)_i \triangleq (t_{i+1} - setup(OUT), t_{i+1} + hold(OUT)). \qquad (19.11)$$

Note that, as in Eq. 19.1, the timing constraint of OUT is given relative to the end of the ith cycle (i.e., t_{i+1}).

Note that there is an asymmetry in the terminology regarding IN and OUT. The parameters associated with IN are $pd(IN)$ and $cont(IN)$, whereas the parameters associated with OUT are $setup(OUT)$ and $hold(OUT)$. This is not very aesthetic if OUT is itself an input to another synchronous circuit. The reason for this asymmetric choice is that it is useful to regard IN as an output of a flip-flip and OUT as an input of a flip-flop (even if they are not). Hence there is an analogy between the signals IN and S. Similarly, there is an analogy between the signals OUT and NS.

19.3.3 Sufficient Conditions

In this section, we formulate sufficient conditions for guaranteeing correct functionality and satisfying the timing constraints of the output signal.

Timing Constraints of Internal Signals. The only constraint we have for an internal signal is that the signal NS that feeds a flip-flop is stable during the critical segments. Namely, for every $i \geq 0$,

$$stable(NS)_i \triangleq C_{i+1}. \qquad (19.12)$$

Note that, as in Eq. 19.1, the timing constraint of NS corresponding to clock cycle i is relative to the end of the ith clock cycle (i.e., the critical segment C_{i+1}).

When performing a timing analysis of a synchronous circuit in canonic form, we notice that there are only four maximal paths without flip-flops:

1. The path $IN \to \delta \to NS$
2. The path $S \to \delta \to NS$
3. The path $IN \to \lambda \to OUT$
4. The path $S \to \lambda \to OUT$

If we regard the signal IN to be the output of a flip-flop, and the signal OUT to be an input to a flip-flop, then we have four paths of the type studied in Figure 19.3a.

Consider the two paths that end in NS. By Claim 19.2, the timing constraints of NS are satisfied if

$$\forall i \geq 0: \quad \max\{pd(IN), t_{pd}(FF)\} + pd(\delta) + t_{su}(FF) \leq t_{i+1} - t_i \qquad (19.13)$$

$$\min\{cont(IN), t_{cont}(FF)\} + cont(\delta) \geq t_{hold}(FF). \qquad (19.14)$$

Consider the two paths that end in OUT. By Claim 19.2, the timing constraints of OUT are satisfied if

$$\forall i \geq 0: \quad \max\{pd(IN), t_{pd}(FF)\} + pd(\lambda) + setup(OUT) \leq t_{i+1} - t_i, \quad (19.15)$$

$$\min\{cont(IN), t_{cont}(FF)\} + cont(\lambda) \geq hold(OUT). \quad (19.16)$$

This leads us to the following claim, which is proved by induction on the clock cycle t. (See Claim 19.6 for a proof of a more general claim.)

Claim 19.3 *The timing constraints of the signals OUT and NS (as stated in Eqs. 19.11 and 19.12) are satisfied if Eqs. 19.13–19.16 hold.*

We point out that we are left with the assumption that the flip-flop is properly initialized so that S is stable during $stable(S)_0$. We deal with issue of initialization in Section 19.3.5.

19.3.4 Satisfying the Timing Constraints

What do we need to do to make sure that the timing constraints of a synchronous circuit are satisfied? In this section, we consider the canonic form of a synchronous circuit. Claim 19.3 gives us two types of constraints: a minimum clock period and contamination delay greater than hold time.

The constraints in Eqs. 19.13 and 19.15 are lower bounds on the clock period. All we need to do is to use a clock period $\Phi \triangleq t_{i+1} - t_i$ that is large enough. Clearly the longer the propagation delay of the combinational logic, the longer Φ must be. This is an important reason to be interested in combinational circuits with a short propagation delay.

The constraints in Eqs. 19.14 and 19.16 can be regraded as technological constraints. If we use simple flip-flops in which $t_{cont} \geq t_{hold}$, then these constraints are satisfied without any further requirements. If not, then we may need to add extra combinational circuitry (such as two cascaded inverters) to increase the contamination delay. This extra combinational circuitry also increases the lower bound on the clock period. So we stick to our recommendation: use flip-flops with $t_{cont} \geq t_{hold}$.

We return to the issue of satisfying the timing constraints even when the synchronous circuit is not in canonic form in Section 19.6.

19.3.5 Initialization

Meeting the timing constraints relies on the circuit being properly initialized. Specifically, we require that the output of every flip-flop be defined and stable during the interval $(t_0 + t_{pd}(FF), t_1 + t_{cont}(FF))$.

Consider the flip-flop in the circuit depicted in Figure 19.3a. How is the first clock cycle $[t_0, t_1)$ defined? It is natural to define it as the first clock cycle after power is turned on. In this case, we know nothing about the output of each flip-flop. In fact, the outputs of flip-flops might be metastable, and their output might not even be logical!

The natural solution to the problem of initialization is to introduce a *reset signal*. There are other situations in which resetting the circuit is desirable, for example, a human user presses a reset button or the operating system decides to reset the system. However, the situation after power-up combines all the complications associated with reset.

Here we are confronted with a boot strapping problem: how is a reset signal generated? Why does a reset signal differ from the the output of the flip-flop? After all, the reset signal might be metastable. So we must address the issue of guaranteeing a stability interval for the reset signal.

Not surprisingly, there is no solution to this problem within the digital abstraction becasue a circuit attempting to generate a reset signal might be in a metastable state. All we can try to do is reduce the probability of such an event.

We have already discussed two methods to reduce the probability of metastability: (i) allow slow decisions and (ii) increase the "slope" (i.e., the derivative of the energy). Slowing down the decision is achieved by using a slow clock in the circuit that generates the reset signal. For example, the reset circuitry might use a clock frequency of 1 KHz, while the clock frequency of the synchronous circuit can be a million times larger). Increasing the slope is achieved by cascading (i.e., connecting in series) edge-triggered flip-flops. In practice, a special circuit, often called a *reset controller*, generates a reset signal that is stable during the first clock period with very high probability. In fact, the first clock period of the synchronous circuit is defined by the reset controller.

Assume that the reset signal is output by a flip-flop so that it satisfies two conditions:

$$reset(t) \triangleq \begin{cases} 1 & \text{if } t \in (t_0 + t_{pd}(FF), t_1 + t_{cont}(FF)) \\ 0 & \text{if } t > t_1 + t_{pd}(FF). \end{cases} \tag{19.17}$$

Such a reset signal is employed as depicted in Figure 19.4. We must take into account the possibility that the output Q of each flip-flop is not logical or stable during the first clock cycle. Hence the implementation of the MUX that selects between the initial state (a constant string) and Q should be such that if *reset* = 1, then the MUX outputs the initial state even if the input D is not logical. Again, the details of such an implementation is not within the scope of the digital abstraction.

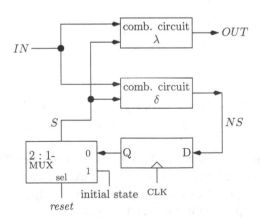

Figure 19.4. A synchronous circuit in canonic form with reset.

Usually the flip-flops with the multiplexer are encapsulated into a single module called an *edge-triggered flip-flop with a reset*. Of course, the propagation delay and the contamination delay of the multiplexer are added to $t_{pd}(FF)$ and $t_{cont}(FF)$. Let FF' denote an edge-triggered flip-flop with a reset; then $t_{pd}(FF') = t_{pd}(FF) + pd(\text{MUX})$ and $t_{cont}(FF') = t_{cont}(FF) + cont(\text{MUX})$. Conversely, $t_{su}(FF') = t_{su}(FF)$ and $t_{hold}(FF') = t_{hold}(FF)$.

We conclude with the following claim, which resolves the issue of the value of the signal S and its stability interval in the first clock cycle.

Claim 19.4 *If the reset signal satisfies Eq. 19.17, then $S(t)$ is stable during the interval*

$$(t_0 + t_{\text{pd}}(FF) + \text{pd}(\text{MUX}), t_1 + t_{\text{cont}}(FF) + \text{cont}(\text{MUX})).$$

Note that the stability interval of S in the first clock cycle does not depend on the stability of the flip-flop's output.

19.4 FUNCTIONALITY: THE CANONIC FORM

In this section, we deal with the functionality of a synchronous circuit in canonic form. Functionality is well defined provided that the following conditions hold:

1. *Initialization.* The signal S satisfies

$$(t_0 + t_{pd}(FF), t_1 + t_{cont}(FF)) \subseteq stable(S)_0. \tag{19.18}$$

2. *Clock period is long enough.* Let Φ denote the clock period (i.e., $\Phi = t_{i+1} - t_i$, for every $i \geq 0$). Then

$$\max\{pd(IN), t_{pd}(FF)\} + pd(\delta) + t_{su}(FF) \leq \Phi \tag{19.19}$$

$$\max\{pd(IN), t_{pd}(FF)\} + pd(\lambda) + setup(OUT) \leq \Phi. \tag{19.20}$$

3. *Hold times are smaller than the contamination delays.* Formally we require that

$$\min\{cont(IN), t_{cont}(FF)\} + cont(\delta) \geq t_{hold}(FF) \tag{19.21}$$

$$\min\{cont(IN), t_{cont}(FF)\} + cont(\lambda) \geq hold(OUT). \tag{19.22}$$

We denote the logical value of a signal X during the stability interval $stable(X)_i$ by X_i.

Claim 19.5 *If Eqs. 19.18–19.22 hold, then the following relations hold for every $i \geq 0$:*

$$NS_i = \delta(IN_i, S_i),$$

$$OUT_i = \lambda(IN_i, S_i),$$

$$S_{i+1} = NS_i.$$

PROOF: The proof is by induction on i. The induction basis for $i = 0$ is proved as follows. Since S_0 is properly initialized (see Eq. 19.18), and since IN is stable during $stable(IN)_0$ (see Eq. 19.10), it follows that they are both stable during the interval

$$(t_0 + \max\{pd(IN), t_{pd}(FF)\}, t_1 + \min\{cont(IN), t_{cont}(FF)\}).$$

This implies that the signal NS is stable during the interval

$$(t_0 + \max\{pd(IN), t_{pd}(FF)\} + pd(\delta), t_1 + \min\{cont(IN), t_{cont}(FF)\} + cont(\delta)).$$

By Eqs. 19.19 and 19.21,

$$(t_1 - t_{su}(FF), t_1 + t_{hold}(FF))$$

$$\subseteq (t_0 + \max\{pd(IN), t_{pd}(FF)\} + pd(\delta), t_1 + \min\{cont(IN), t_{cont}(FF)\} + cont(\delta)).$$

Hence NS is stable during the critical segment C_1 and $NS_0 = \delta(IN_0, S_0)$, as required.

The induction step for $i > 0$ is proved in the same fashion. Simply replace t_0 by t_i and t_1 by t_{i+1}. The only difference is that we do not rely on initialization. To show that S_{i+1} is well defined, note that NS_i is stable during the critical segment C_i. It follows that the flip-flop's output S_{i+1} equals NS_i. We omit the proof for OUT_{i+1} since it follows the same lines. ∎

19.5 FINITE STATE MACHINES

The functionality of a synchronous circuit in the canonic form is so important that it justifies a term called *finite state machines*.

Definition 19.2 A *finite state machine* (FSM) is a 6-tuple $\mathcal{A} = \langle Q, \Sigma, \Delta, \delta, \lambda, q_0 \rangle$, where the following hold:

- Q is a set of *states*.
- Σ is the alphabet of the input.
- Δ is the alphabet of the output.
- $\delta : Q \times \Sigma \to Q$ is a *transition function*.
- $\lambda : Q \times \Sigma \to \Delta$ is an *output function*.
- $q_0 \in Q$ is an *initial state*.

Other terms for a finite state machine are a *finite automaton with outputs* and a *transducer*. In the literature, an FSM according to Definition 19.2 is often called a *Mealy machine*. Another type of machine, called a *Moore machine*, is an FSM in which the domain of output function λ is Q (namely, the output is only a function of the state and does not depend on the input).

An FSM is an abstract machine that operates as follows. The input is a sequence $\{x_i\}_{i=0}^{n-1}$ of symbols over the alphabet Σ. The output is a sequence $\{y_i\}_{i=0}^{n-1}$ of symbols over the alphabet Δ. An FSM transitions through the sequence of states $\{q_i\}_{i=0}^{n}$. The state q_i is defined recursively as follows:

$$q_{i+1} \stackrel{\Delta}{=} \delta(q_i, x_i).$$

The output y_i is defined as follows:

$$y_i \stackrel{\Delta}{=} \lambda(q_i, x_i).$$

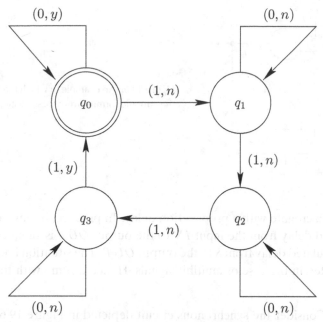

Figure 19.5. A state diagram of an FSM that counts (mod 4).

State Diagrams. FSMs are often depicted using state diagrams.

Definition 19.3 The *state diagram* corresponding to an FSM $\mathcal{A}$ is a directed graph $G = (Q, E)$ with edge input–output labels $(x, y) \in \Sigma \times \Delta$. The edge set E is defined by

$$E \triangleq \{(q, \delta(q, x)) : q \in Q \text{ and } x \in \Sigma\}.$$

Each edge $(q, \delta(q, x))$ is labeled $(x, \lambda(q, x))$.

Consider an edge from vertex q to vertex q' labeled by (x, y). This means that if the input equals x when the FSM is in state q, then the FSM outputs y and transitions to the state $q' \triangleq \delta(q, x)$.

The vertex q_0 corresponding to the initial state of an FSM is usually marked in an FSM by a double circle.

We remark that a state diagram is in fact a *multigraph*, namely, one allows more than one directed edge between two vertices. Such edges are often called *parallel edges*. Note that the out-degree of every vertex in a state diagram equals $|\Delta|$.

Example 19.1 Figure 19.5 depicts a state diagram of an FSM that outputs "y" if the weight of the input so far is divisible by 4, and "n" otherwise.

19.6 TIMING ANALYSIS: THE GENERAL CASE

In this section, we present a timing analysis of a synchronous circuit that is not in canonic form. Indeed, the timing analysis of synchronous circuits in canonic form is overly pessimistic. The problem is that each of the combinational circuits λ and δ is

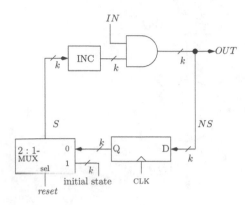

Figure 19.6. An example in which the timing analysis for the canonic form is overly pessimistic.

regarded as a macrogate with a propagation delay. In practice, it may be the case that the accumulated delay from the input IN to the output OUT is significantly different than the accumulated delay from S to the output OUT. The situation is even somewhat more complicated in the case of multibit signals. Hence dealing with the general case is interesting.

Example 19.2 Consider the synchronous circuit depicted in Figure 19.6. Assume that $pd(IN) = 9$ while $t_{pd}(FF) = pd(\text{MUX}) = pd(\text{AND}) = 1$ and $t_{su}(FF) = setup(OUT) = 1$. Moreover, assume that $pd(INC) = 7$. The timing analysis for the canonic form encapsulates the incrementer and the AND-gate into one combinational circuit δ whose propagation delay is 8. The clock period has to be at least

$$t_{i+1} - t_i \geq \max\{t_{pd}(FF) + pd(\text{MUX}), pd(IN)\} + pd(\delta) + t_{su}(FF)$$
$$= 9 + 9 + 1 = 19.$$

However, the output of the incrementer is valid starting $t_i + t_{pd}(FF) + pd(\text{MUX}) + pd(INC) = t_i + 9$. Thus the output of the AND-gate is valid starting $t_i + 10$, and hence the clock period has to be only at least 11.

In this section, we present timing constraints for the signals in a synchronous circuit. We then present an algorithm that decides whether the timing constraints are feasible (i.e., can be satisfied). If the timing constraints are feasible, then the algorithm computes the minimum clock period.

19.6.1 Timing Constraints

Given a synchronous circuit C, we distinguish between four types of signals:

1. Inputs: signals that are fed by input gates
2. Outputs: signals that are fed to output gates
3. Inputs to the D-ports of flip-flops
4. Outputs of flip-flops

The timing constraints of general synchronous circuits are identical to those of the canonic form. For completeness, we list them in the following.

Input constraints: For every input signal IN, it is guaranteed that the stability intervals of IN satisfy, for every $i \geq 0$,

$$stable(IN)_i \triangleq (t_i + pd(IN), t_{i+1} + cont(IN)). \tag{19.23}$$

Output constraints: For every output signal OUT, it is required that the stability intervals of OUT satisfy

$$stable(OUT)_i \triangleq (t_{i+1} - setup(OUT), t_{i+1} + hold(OUT)). \tag{19.24}$$

Critical segments: For every signal NS that feeds a D-port of a flip-flop, it is required that NS be stable during the critical segments, namely,

$$stable(NS)_i \triangleq C_{i+1}. \tag{19.25}$$

We say that a timing constraint of signal X is *satisfied* if the signal X is indeed stable during the intervals $\{stable(X)_i\}_{i \geq 0}$.

Definition 19.4 The timing constraints are *feasible* if there exists a clock period Φ such that all timing constraints are satisfied if $t_{i+1} - t_i = \Phi$.

19.6.2 Algorithms: Feasibility and Minimum Clock Period

We now present two algorithms:

1. Algorithm FEAS(C) decides whether the timing constraints of a synchronous circuit C are feasible.
2. Algorithm Min-Φ(C) computes the minimum clock period of C if the timing constraints are feasible.

The two algorithms are quite similar: FEAS(C) computes a lightest path in a DAG and decides that the timing constraints are feasible if the lightest path is nonnegative. Conversely, Min-Φ(C) computes a longest path in a DAG.

For simplicity, we assume that all the flips-flops in the synchronous circuit C are identical and have the same parameters (i.e., $t_{su}(FF), t_{hold}(FF), t_{cont}(FF), t_{pd}(FF)$).

Algorithm FEAS(C). Algorithm FEAS(C) is listed as Algorithm 19.1. The input of algorithm FEAS(C) consists of

1. A description of the circuit C, namely, a directed graph $G = (V, E)$ and a labeling $\pi : V \to \Gamma \cup IO \cup \{FF\}$
2. $cont(IN)$ for every input signal IN
3. $hold(OUT)$ for every output signal OUT

Algorithm Min-Φ(C). Algorithm Min-Φ(C) is listed as Algorithm 19.2. The input of algorithm Min-Φ(C) consists of

1. A description of the circuit C, namely, a directed graph $G = (V, E)$ and a labeling $\pi : V \to \Gamma \cup IO \cup \{FF\}$
2. $pd(IN)$ for every input signal IN
3. $setup(OUT)$ for every output signal OUT

Algorithm 19.1 FEAS(C)—an algorithm that decides if the timing constraints of a synchronous circuit C are feasible.

---

1. Let C' denote the combinational circuit obtained from C by stripping away the flip-flops (see item 3 in Definition 19.1).
2. Assign weights $w(v)$ to vertices in C' as follows:

$$w(v) \triangleq \begin{cases} cont(IN) & \text{if } v \text{ is an input gate of } C \text{ and } v \text{ feeds the input signal } IN, \\ t_{cont}(FF) & \text{if } v \text{ corresponds to a } Q\text{-port of a flip-flop,} \\ -hold(OUT) & \text{if } v \text{ is an output gate of } C \text{ and } v \text{ is fed by the output signal } OUT, \\ -t_{hold}(FF) & \text{if } v \text{ corresponds to a } D\text{-port of a flip-flop,} \\ cont(\pi(v)) & \text{if } \pi(v) \text{ is a combinational gate.} \end{cases}$$

3. Compute

$$w^* \triangleq \min\{w(p) \mid p \text{ is a path from a source to a sink in } C'\}.$$

4. If $w^* \geq 0$, then return("feasible"), else return("not feasible").

Algorithm 19.2 Min-$\Phi(C)$—an algorithm that computes the minimum clock period of a synchronous circuit C.

---

1. Let C' denote the combinational circuit obtained from C by stripping away the flip-flops (see item 3 in Definition 19.1).
2. Assign delays $d(v)$ to vertices in C' as follows:

$$d(v) \triangleq \begin{cases} pd(IN) & \text{if } v \text{ is an input gate of } C \text{ and } v \text{ feeds the input signal } IN, \\ t_{pd}(FF) & \text{if } v \text{ corresponds to a } Q\text{-port of a flip-flop,} \\ setup(OUT) & \text{if } v \text{ is an output gate of } C \text{ and } v \text{ is fed by the output signal } OUT, \\ t_{su}(FF) & \text{if } v \text{ corresponds to a } D\text{-port of a flip-flop,} \\ pd(\pi(v)) & \text{if } \pi(v) \text{ is a combinational gate.} \end{cases}$$

3. Compute

$$\Phi^* \triangleq \max\{d(p) \mid p \text{ is a path from a source to a sink in } C'\}.$$

4. Return(Φ^*).

Algorithm Min-$\Phi(C)$ reduces the problem of computing the minimum clock period to the problem of computing a longest path in a DAG. Since a longest path in a DAG is computable in linear time, the algorithm runs in linear time as well.

19.6.3 Algorithms: Correctness

In this section, we prove that the algorithms FEAS(C) and Min-$\Phi(C)$ are correct. The idea is that algorithm FEAS(C) checks if the upper limit of each stability interval can be satisfied. Conversely, Min-Φ computes a lower bound on the clock period that guarantees that the lower limit of each stability interval is satisfied.

Notation. Given a vertex $v \in C'$, let $c^*(v)$ denote lightest weight of a path from a source to v. Similarly, let $d^*(v)$ denote the largest delay of a path from a source to v.

Using this notation, we have a simple description of the algorithms: (i) FEAS(C) decides that the timing constraints are feasible if and only if $\min_v c^*(v) \geq 0$ and (ii) Min-$\Phi(C)$ returns $\Phi^* = \max_v d^*(v)$.

Assume that the flip-flops are reset so that their outputs are stable during $(t_0 + t_{pd}(FF), t_1 + t_{cont}(FF))$. Assume also that the inputs satisfy the input constraints in Eq. 19.23.

In the following claim, we abuse notation and mix between the vertices of the synchronous circuit C and the combinational circuit C' obtained by stripping away the flip-flops of C. This notation should not cause any confusion at all. A source in C' is either an input gate or an output of a flip-flop. A sink in C' is either an output gate or an input to a D-port of a flip-flop. Interior vertices are the same in C and in C'.

Claim 19.6 *If $\min_v c^*(v) \geq 0$ and $t_{i+1} - t_i \geq \max_v d^*(v)$, then, for every vertex v, every output of v is stable during the interval*

$$(t_i + d^*(v), t_{i+1} + c^*(v)).$$

Moreover, the inputs to flip-flops are stable during the critical segments and the output constraints are satisfied.

PROOF: The proof uses double induction. The outer induction is on i, and the inner induction is on the topological ordering of the vertices of C'.

Let us begin with the induction basis of the outer induction for $i = 0$. The proof of the induction basis requires applying the inner induction on the topological ordering of the vertices of C'. The induction basis of the inner induction considers the sources. Indeed, suppose v is a source in C'. For simplicity, assume that it is an output of a flip-flop. Since flip-flops are reset properly, the output of v is stable during the interval $(t_0 + t_{pd}(FF), t_1 + t_{cont}(FF))$. Moreover, $d^*(v) = t_{pd}(FF)$ and $c^*(v) = t_{cont}(FF)$. A similar argument holds if v is an input gate. Thus the inner induction basis holds for sources.

The proof of the inner induction step for the case that v is not a source proceeds as follows. If v is not a sink, then it is a combinational gate. The output of v is stable $pd(\pi(v))$ time units after all its inputs are stable. Thus every output of v is stable starting $t_0 + d^*(v)$. Conversely, every output of v remains stable $cont(\pi(v))$ time units after the first input to v becomes unstable. Thus every output of v remains stable until $t_1 + c^*(v)$. Finally, if v is a sink, then it has no outputs, and the claim trivially holds for it. This completes the proof of the outer induction basis for $i = 0$.

The proof of the outer induction step for $i > 0$ is quite similar. The only important difference is the proof of the inner induction basis. Here we cannot rely on the initialization. Instead, we need to show that the input of each flip-flop is stable during the critical segment C_i, and hence the output of the flip-flop is stable during the interval $(t_i + t_{pd}(FF), t_{i+1} + t_{cont}(FF))$.

Consider a node v, the output of which feeds the D-port of a flip-flop u. The outer induction hypothesis states that the output of v is stable during the interval $(t_{i-1} + d^*(v), t_i + c^*(v))$. Hence, it suffices to prove that

$$C_i \subseteq (t_{i-1} + d^*(v), t_i + c^*(v)).$$

Namely, we want to prove that

$$t_i - t_{su}(FF) \geq t_{i-1} + d^*(v) \qquad\qquad (19.26)$$

$$t_i + t_{hold}(FF) \leq t_i + c^*(v). \qquad\qquad (19.27)$$

But $t_i - t_{i-1} \geq d^*(u) = d^*(v) + t_{su}(FF)$, and hence Eq. 19.26 holds. Similarly, $c^*(u) = -t_{hold}(FF) + c^*(v) \geq 0$, and hence Eq. 19.27 holds.

A similar argument proves that the output constraints are satisfied, and the claim follows. ■

We close this section by remarking that the timing analysis is tight. Let p denote a path in C' with a maximum delay. Suppose $t_{i+1} - t_i < d(p)$. If the actual propagation delays along p are maximal, then the signal feeding v is not stable at time $t_{i+1} - d(p)$. If v is a flip-flop, then its input is not stable during the critical segment. If v is an output gate, then its input does not meet the output constraint. We point out that the actual delay along p may indeed be $d(p)$. For example, in a ripple carry adder RCA(n), we might have a ripple of n carries from zeros to ones.

19.7 SIMULATION OF SYNCHRONOUS CIRCUITS

In this section, we present an algorithm for logical simulation of synchronous circuits. The algorithm works under the assumption that the timing constraints are satisfied.

Simulation of a synchronous circuit in the zero delay model during cycles $i = 0, \ldots, n-1$ is listed as Algorithm 19.3. The correctness of the simulation algorithm can be proved by double induction, as in the proof of Claim 19.6.

Let F denote the set of flip-flops in the synchronous circuit. Let $S_i : F \to \{0, 1\}$ denote a function that specifies the values output by each flip-flop in the ith clock cycle. For $i = 0$, the function S_0 specifies the initialization of the flip-flops. Let I denote the set of input gates in the synchronous circuit. Let $IN_i : I \to \{0, 1\}$ denote a function that specifies the input value fed by each input gate in clock cycle i. Let $NS_i : F \to \{0, 1\}$ denote a function that specifies the input to each flip-flop in the (end of the) ith clock cycle. Similarly, let Z denote the set of output gates in the synchronous circuit. Let $OUT_i : Z \to \{0, 1\}$ denote the value fed to each output gate in the ith clock cycle.

Algorithm 19.3 $\mathrm{SIM}(C, S_0, \{IN_i\}_{i=0}^{n-1})$—an algorithm for simulating a synchronous circuit C with respect to an initialization S_0 and a sequence of inputs $\{IN_i\}_{i=0}^{n-1}$.

---

1. Construct the combinational circuit C' obtained from C by stripping away the flip-flops.
2. For $i = 0$ to $n - 1$ do:
   (a) Simulate the combinational circuit C' with input values corresponding to S_i and IN_i. Namely, every input gate in C feeds a value according to IN_i, and every Q-port of a flip-flop feeds a value according to S_i. The outcome of the simulation determines the functions OUT_i and NS_i.
   (a) Define $S_{i+1} \leftarrow NS_i$.

19.8 SYNTHESIS AND ANALYSIS

Two tasks are often associated with synchronous circuits. These tasks are defined as follows:

1. *Analysis*: Given a synchronous circuit C, describe its functionality by an FSM.
2. *Synthesis*: Given an FSM $\mathcal{A}$, design a synchronous circuit C that implements $\mathcal{A}$.

19.8.1 Analysis

The task of analyzing a synchronous circuit C is carried out as follows:

1. Define the FSM $\mathcal{A} = \langle Q, \Sigma, \Delta, \delta, \lambda, q_0 \rangle$ as follows:
   (a) The set of states is $Q \subseteq \{0, 1\}^k$, where k denotes the number of flip-flops in C.
   (b) Define the initial state q_0 to be the initial outputs of the flip-flops.
   (c) $\Sigma = \{0, 1\}^\ell$, where ℓ denotes the number of input gates in C.
   (d) $\Delta = \{0, 1\}^r$, where r denotes the number of output gates in C.
   (e) Transform C to a functionally equivalent synchronous circuit $\tilde{C}$ in canonic form. Compute the truth tables of the combinational circuits λ and δ. Define the Boolean functions according to these truth tables.

19.8.2 Synthesis

Given an FSM $\mathcal{A} = \langle Q, \Sigma, \Delta, \delta, \lambda, q_0 \rangle$, the task of designing a synchronous circuit C that implements $\mathcal{A}$ is carried out as follows:

1. Encode Q, Σ, and Δ by binary strings. Formally, let f, g, h denote one-to-one functions, where

$$f : Q \to \{0, 1\}^k$$

$$g : \Sigma \to \{0, 1\}^\ell$$

$$h : \Delta \to \{0, 1\}^r.$$

2. Design a combinational circuit C_δ that implements the (partial) Boolean function B_δ : $\{0, 1\}^k \times \{0, 1\}^\ell \to \{0, 1\}^k$ defined by

$$B_\delta(f(x), g(y)) \triangleq f(\delta(x, y)), \text{ for every } (x, y) \in Q \times \Sigma.$$

3. Design a combinational circuit C_λ that implements the (partial) Boolean function B_λ : $\{0, 1\}^k \times \{0, 1\}^\ell \to \{0, 1\}^r$ defined by

$$B_\lambda(f(x), g(z)) \triangleq h(\lambda(x, z)), \text{ for every } (x, z) \in Q \times \Sigma.$$

4. Let C denote the synchronous circuit in canonic form constructed from k flip-flops and the combinational circuits C_δ for the next state and C_λ for the output.

The description of the encoding step leaves a great deal of freedom. Since $|\{0, 1\}^k| \geq |Q|$, it follows that $k \geq \log_2 |Q|$, and similar bounds apply to ℓ and r. However, it is not clear that using the smallest lengths is the best idea. Certain encodings lead to more complicated Boolean functions B_δ and B_λ. Thus the question of selecting a "good" encoding is a very complicated task, and there is no simple solution to this problem.

19.9 SUMMARY

This chapter deals with the fundamental issues relating to synchronous circuits. We began by defining synchronous circuits. We first focused on synchronous circuits in canonic form. Timing analysis of synchronous circuits in canonic form is a simple task. However, it requires proper initialization of the flip-flops. Thus we introduced edge-triggered flip-flops with a reset.

The timing analysis leads to a functional specification of synchronous circuit in canonic form. We introduced finite-state machines to describe this functionality.

Since timing analysis in canonic form might be overly pessimistic, we presented algorithms for timing analysis in the general case. Two algorithms are presented: one verifies whether the timing constraints are feasible, and the second algorithm computes the minimum clock period.

We then turned to describing a simulation algorithm. This simulation is based on a reduction to simulating a combinational circuit. We ended this chapter with a description of two tasks: analysis and synthesis of synchronous circuits.

PROBLEMS

19.1. Consider the circuit depicted in Figure 19.7. Is this circuit combinational? Synchronous? Explain your answer.

19.2. Design a synchronous circuit that indicates whether the number of ones in the input so far is divisible by n.
Input: $X(t) \in \{0, 1\}$ and a clock signal CLK.
Output: $Y(t) \in \{0, 1\}$.

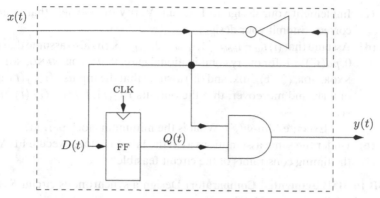

Figure 19.7. A circuit.

Functionality: The output $Y(t)$ should satisfy:

$$Y(t) = \begin{cases} 1 & \text{if } \mathrm{mod}(\sum_{i=0}^{t-1} X(t), n) = 0 \\ 0 & \text{otherwise.} \end{cases}$$

Remarks: (1) You may assume that the flip-flops are initialized to zero. (2) The output in clock cycle 0 is not specified.

(a) Describe an FSM that satisfies the specification.

(b) Synthesize the FSM to obtain an synchronous circuit. Use as few flip-flop as possible.

(c) Compute the minimum clock period of your design.

(d) Suggest another synthesis of the FSM so that the clock period is constant. Hint: use a "cyclic shift register" of n flip-flips.

19.3. **(MSB to LSB Sequential Comparator)** Design a synchronous circuit S that satisfies the following specification:

Input: $x(t), y(t) \in \{0,1\}$, for every clock cycle t.

Output: $EQ(t), LT(t), GT(t) \in \{0,1\}$, for every clock cycle t.

Functionality: • Let

$$X_t \triangleq \sum_{i=0}^{t} x(i) \cdot 2^{t-i}$$

$$Y_t \triangleq \sum_{i=0}^{t} y(i) \cdot 2^{t-i}.$$

• For every clock cycle $t \geq 0$,

$$EQ(t) = \begin{cases} 1, & \text{if } X_t = Y_t, \\ 0, & \text{otherwise,} \end{cases} \quad LT(t) = \begin{cases} 1, & \text{if } X_t < Y_t, \\ 0, & \text{otherwise,} \end{cases} \quad GT(t) = \begin{cases} 1, & \text{if } X_t > Y_t, \\ 0, & \text{otherwise .} \end{cases}$$

Answer the following questions:

(a) Define the finite state machine $FSM(S) = \langle Q, \Sigma, \Delta, \delta, \lambda, q_0 \rangle$ that satisfies the preceding specification.

(b) Implement S by synthesizing $FSM(S)$. Hint: use the canonic form.

(c) Implement your design in Logisim. Verify *by yourself* that your design is correct. Submit your design.

(d) Assume that (i) $t_{su} = t_{hold} = 1$, $t_{cont} = 2$, $t_{pd} = 3$; (ii) also assume that $cont(C) = 0$, $pd(C) = 1$, for every combinational gate, that is, OR, NAND, NOT, AND, XOR, NXOR, NOR, $(2 : 1)$-MUX, and (iii) assume that the inputs $x(t)$, $y(t)$ are outputs of a FF, and moreover, that the outputs $EQ(t)$, $LT(t)$, $GT(t)$ are fed to a FF.

Execute Min-$\Phi(S)$. What is the minimum clock period?

(e) Under the same assumptions as in the last question, execute FEAS(S). Are the timing constraints of the circuit feasible?

19.4. **(LSB to MSB Sequential Comparator)** Design a synchronous circuit S that implements the following specification:

Input: $x, y \in \{0, 1\}$.

Output: $EQ, LT, GT \in \{0, 1\}$.

Functionality: • Let $x_t = \langle x[t : 0] \rangle$,
  • let $y_t = \langle y[t : 0] \rangle$, then
  • for every $t \geq 0$,

$$EQ(t) = \begin{cases} 1, & \text{if } x_t = y_t, \\ 0, & o.w, \end{cases} \qquad LT(t) = \begin{cases} 1, & \text{if } x_t < y_t, \\ 0, & o.w, \end{cases} \qquad GT(t) = \begin{cases} 1, & \text{if } x_t > y_t, \\ 0, & o.w. \end{cases}$$

(a) Define an FSM that models this sequential comparator. Draw its state diagram (write explicitly the set of states, input–output alphabet, transition function, output function, and initial state).

(b) Synthesize your FSM.

(c) Implement your design in Logisim. Verify *by yourself* that your design is correct. Submit a printout of your implementation.

(d) Assume that (i) $t_{su} = t_{hold} = 1$, $t_{cont} = 2$, $t_{pd} = 3$; (ii) also assume that $cont(C) = 0$, $pd(C) = 1$, for every combinational gate, that is, OR, NAND, NOT, AND, XOR, NXOR, NOR, $(2 : 1)$-MUX, and (iii) assume also that the inputs $x(t)$, $y(t)$ are outputs of a FF, and moreover, that the outputs $EQ(t)$, $LT(t)$, $GT(t)$ are fed to a FF.

Execute Min-$\Phi(S)$. What is the minimum clock period?

(e) Under the same assumptions as in the last question, execute FEAS(S). Are the timing constraints of the circuit feasible?

19.5. Let $\sigma \in \{0, 1\}^n$ be a *fixed* binary string. Design a shift register with a *reset* signal that initializes the register to $D[n - 1 : 0] = \sigma$.

19.6. Consider the synchronous circuit depicted in Figure 19.8. This circuit is called a linear feedback shift register (LFSR).

The FFs of the LFSR are initialized at $t = 0$ to $D[3 : 0] = 0001$. The output is $Q[3] \in \{0, 1\}$. Note that $D[0]$ is a function of $Q[3]$, $Q[1]$, and $Q[0]$. Answer the following questions:

(a) Assume that (i) $t_{su} = t_{hold} = 1$, $t_{cont} = 2$, $t_{pd} = 3$; (ii) also assume that $cont(XOR) = 0$, $pd(XOR) = 1$, and (iii) assume that the output $Q[3]$ is fed to a FF.

Execute Min-$\Phi(S)$. What is the minimum clock period?

(b) Under the same assumptions as in the last question, execute FEAS(S). Are the timing constraints of the circuit feasible?

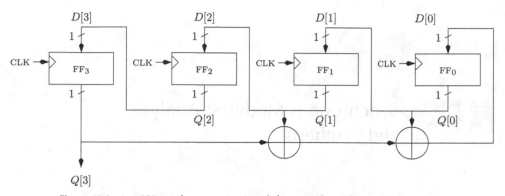

Figure 19.8. An LFSR synchronous circuit with four FFs. The ⊕ denotes a XOR gate.

(c) Present the LFSR in the form of a canonic synchronous circuit.

(d) Analyze the LFSR, that is, define the corresponding FSM $\mathcal{A} = \langle Q, \Sigma, \Delta, \delta, \lambda, q_0 \rangle$. Draw the state diagram of the FSM $\mathcal{A}$.

(e) Implement the LFSR in Logisim. Simulate the circuit with the initial value of 0001 for 10 time steps. How many states has $\mathcal{A}$ visited?

CHAPTER 20

Synchronous Modules: Analysis
and Synthesis

In this chapter, we practice the method of analysis and synthesis of synchronous circuits. We begin with two-state finite state machines. First we synthesize a synchronous circuit, and then we analyze a serial adder. Another simple case is finite state machines (FSMs), the state diagram of which is a simple cycle. These FSMs are called *counters*. We then define, implement, and analyze counters. We also discuss how initialization affects the corresponding FSM.

Finally, we revisit the synchronous circuits described earlier (shift registers and RAM). We analyze these circuits and show that their state diagrams are important graphs.

20.1 EXAMPLE: A TWO-STATE FSM

In this section, we synthesize a two-state FSM. In this example, the encoding of the alphabets and the states are trivial.

Consider the FSM $\mathcal{A} = \langle Q, \Sigma, \Delta, \delta, \lambda, q_0 \rangle$ depicted in Figure 20.1a, where

$$Q = \{q_0, q_1\}$$
$$\Sigma = \Delta = \{0, 1\}.$$

We now apply the synthesis procedure to the FSM $\mathcal{A}$ to obtain an implementation by a synchronous circuit C (see Section 19.8.2 for a description of synthesis):

1. *Encoding.* We need to encode Q, Σ and Δ. In this case, we use the trivial encoding where each state q_i is encoded by the bit i. Similarly, the alphabets Σ and Δ are encoded by the identity functions, namely, $g(\sigma) = h(\sigma) = \sigma$ for $\sigma \in \{0, 1\}$.

   This encoding implies that (i) the state is stored by a single flip-flop and (ii) the input and output are single bits.
2. We need to design a combinational circuit C_δ that computes the next state. Since the transition function $\delta : Q \times \Sigma \to Q$ satisfies

$$\delta(q_i, \sigma) = \text{INV}(\sigma),$$

the Boolean circuit C_δ is simply an inverter.

Table 20.1. The truth table of λ

q_i	σ	$\lambda(q_i, \sigma)$
0	0	1
1	0	1
0	1	0
1	1	1

3. We need to design a combinational circuit C_λ that implements the output function $\lambda : Q \times \Sigma \to \Delta$. The truth table of λ is listed as Table 20.1. It follows that $\lambda(q_i, \sigma) = i \vee \overline{\sigma}$. Hence the circuit C_λ is built from an inverter and an OR-gate.

4. The synchronous circuit in canonic form constructed from one flip-flop and two combinational circuits is depicted in Figure 20.1b.

    We remark that one could share the inverters in C_δ and C_λ to obtain a circuit C that uses only an inverter and an OR-gate.

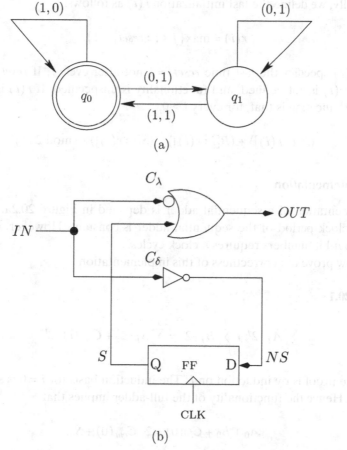

Figure 20.1. (a) A two-state FSM $\mathcal{A}$. (b) An implementation of $\mathcal{A}$ by a synchronous circuit in canonic form.

20.2 SEQUENTIAL ADDER

Definition 20.1 A *sequential adder* is defined as follows.

Inputs: A, B, *reset*, and a clock signal CLK, where A_i, B_i, $reset_i \in \{0, 1\}$.
Output: S, where $S_i \in \{0, 1\}$.
Functionality: The *reset* signal is an initialization signal that satisfies

$$reset_i = \begin{cases} 1 & \text{if } i = 0 \\ 0 & \text{if } i > 0. \end{cases}$$

Then, for every $i \geq 0$, $\langle A[i : 0] \rangle + \langle B[i : 0] \rangle = \langle S[i : 0] \rangle \pmod{2^{i+1}}$.

What happens if the value of the input *reset* equals 1 in more than once cycle? Following the preceding definition, if $reset_i = 1$, then we forget about the past, and we treat clock cycle (t_i, t_{i+1}) as the first clock cycle.

Formally, we define the last initialization $r(i)$ as follows:

$$r(i) \triangleq \max\{j \leq i : reset_j = 1\}.$$

Namely, $r(i)$ specifies the last time $reset_j = 1$ not after cycle i. If $reset_j = 0$ for every $j \leq i$, then $r(i)$ is not defined, and functionality is unspecified. If $r(i)$ is well defined, then the specification is that, for every $i \geq 0$,

$$\langle A[i : r(i)] \rangle + \langle B[i : r(i)] \rangle = \langle S[i : r(i)] \rangle \pmod{2^{i+1}}.$$

20.2.1 Implementation

An implementation of a sequential adder is depicted in Figure 20.2a. Note that the minimum clock period of the sequential adder is constant. However, computing the sum of two n-bit numbers requires n clock cycles.

We now prove the correctness of this implementation.

Theorem 20.1

$$\sum_{j=0}^{i} A_j \cdot 2^j + \sum_{j=0}^{i} B_j \cdot 2^j = \sum_{j=0}^{i} S_j \cdot 2^j + C_{out}(i) \cdot 2^{i+1}.$$

PROOF: The proof is by induction on i. The induction basis for $i = 0$ is simple because $C_{in}(0) = 0$. Hence the functionality of the full-adder implies that

$$A_0 + B_0 + C_{in}(0) = 2 \cdot C_{out}(0) + S_0,$$

and the induction basis follows.

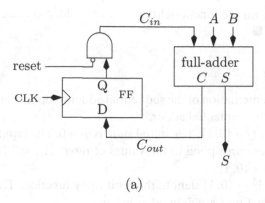

(a)

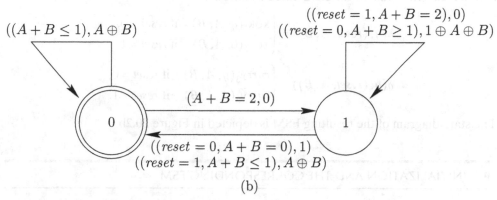

(b)

Figure 20.2. A sequential adder: (a) a synchronous circuit that implements a sequential adder and (b) an FSM of a sequential adder (each transition is labeled by a pair: the condition that the input satisfies and the value of the output).

We now prove the induction step for $i > 0$:

$$\sum_{j=0}^{i} A_j \cdot 2^j + \sum_{j=0}^{i} B_j \cdot 2^j = (A_i + B_i) \cdot 2^i + \sum_{j=0}^{i-1} A_j \cdot 2^j + \sum_{j=0}^{i-1} B_j \cdot 2^j$$

$$= (A_i + B_i) \cdot 2^i + \sum_{j=0}^{i-1} S_j \cdot 2^j + C_{out}(i-1) \cdot 2^i$$

$$= (C_{in}(i) + A_i + B_i) \cdot 2^i + \sum_{j=0}^{i-1} S_j \cdot 2^j$$

$$= (S_i + 2 \cdot C_{out}(i)) \cdot 2^i + \sum_{j=0}^{i-1} S_j \cdot 2^j$$

$$= \sum_{j=0}^{i} S_j \cdot 2^j + C_{out}(i) \cdot 2^{i+1}.$$

The first line is simply a rearrangement, the second line follows from the induction hypothesis, the third line follows from the functionality of a flip-flop in cycle i, the fourth line follows from the functionality of the full-adder in cycle i, and the fifth line is a rearrangement. ∎

20.2.2 Analysis

We analyze the implementation of the sequential adder to obtain an FSM that describes the functionality of the sequential adder.

The set of state is $Q = \{0, 1\}$. The initial state is $q_0 = 0$. The input alphabet is $\{0, 1\}^3$, where the coordinates correspond to the values of $reset_i$, A_i, and B_i, respectively. The output alphabet is $\Delta = \{0, 1\}$.

Let $carry_3 : \{0, 1\}^3 \to \{0, 1\}$ denote the 3-bit carry function. The output function λ and the transition function δ are defined as follows:

$$\lambda(q, (reset, A, B)) \stackrel{\triangle}{=} \begin{cases} \text{XOR}_3(q, A, B) & \text{if } reset = 0, \\ \text{XOR}_3(0, A, B) & \text{if } reset = 1, \end{cases}$$

$$\delta(q, (reset, A, B)) \stackrel{\triangle}{=} \begin{cases} carry_3(q, A, B) & \text{if } reset = 0, \\ carry_3(0, A, B) & \text{if } reset = 1. \end{cases}$$

The state diagram of the resulting FSM is depicted in Figure 20.2b.

20.3 INITIALIZATION AND THE CORRESPONDING FSM

Suppose we have a synchronous circuit C without an initialization signal. Now we introduce an initialization signal $reset$ that initializes the outputs of all flip-flops (namely, it causes the outputs of the flip-flops to equal a value that encodes the initial state). This is done by replacing each edge-triggered D-flop-flop by an edge-triggered D-flip-flop with a reset input. The $reset$ signal is fed to the reset input port of each flip-flop. We denote the new synchronous circuit by $\hat{C}$.

Let $\mathcal{A}$ and $\hat{\mathcal{A}}$ denote the FSMs that model the functionality of C and $\hat{C}$, respectively. What is the relation between $\mathcal{A}$ and $\hat{\mathcal{A}}$?

In the following theorem, we show how the FSM $\hat{\mathcal{A}}$ can be derived from the FSM $\mathcal{A}$.

Theorem 20.2 Let $\mathcal{A} = \langle Q, \Sigma, \Delta, \delta, \lambda, q_0 \rangle$ denote the FSM that models the functionality of the synchronous circuit C. Let $\hat{\mathcal{A}} = \langle Q', \Sigma', \Delta', \delta', \lambda', q_0' \rangle$ denote the FSM that models the synchronous circuit $\hat{C}$. Then

$$Q' \stackrel{\triangle}{=} Q,$$

$$q_0' \stackrel{\triangle}{=} q_0,$$

$$\Sigma' \stackrel{\triangle}{=} \Sigma \times \{0, 1\},$$

$$\Delta' \stackrel{\triangle}{=} \Delta,$$

$$\delta'(q, (\sigma, \text{reset})) \triangleq \begin{cases} \delta(q, \sigma), & if \text{ reset} = 0, \\ \delta(q_0, \sigma), & if \text{ reset} = 1, \end{cases}$$

$$\lambda'(q, (\sigma, \text{reset})) \triangleq \begin{cases} \lambda(q, \sigma), & if \text{ reset} = 0, \\ \lambda(q_0, \sigma), & if \text{ reset} = 1. \end{cases}$$

PROOF: The proof is straightforward. The last bit in the input alphabet Σ is the initialization signal *reset*. Let $(\sigma, reset) \in \Sigma \times \{0, 1\}$ denote the input to the FSM $\hat{\mathcal{A}}$. If *reset* = 0, then the FSM $\hat{\mathcal{A}}$ simulates the FSM $\mathcal{A}$ on the input σ from the current state q. If *reset* = 1, then the FSM $\hat{\mathcal{A}}$ simulates the FSM $\mathcal{A}$ on the input σ from the initial state q_0. ∎

We often ignore initialization or postpone its implementation. The reason is that one can always introduce initialization later. Thus we can focus on the more "interesting" issues first.

20.4 COUNTER

Definition 20.2 An *n-bit counter* is defined as follows.

Inputs: A clock signal CLK.
Output: $N[n - 1 : 0]$.
Functionality: Let $N_i[n - 1 : 0]$ denote the value of $N[n - 1 : 0]$ in clock cycle i. We require that, for every $i \geq 0$,

$$\langle N_i[n - 1 : 0]\rangle = i \ (\text{mod } 2^n).$$

The counter is an unusual synchronous circuit because it does not have any input apart from the clock signal. We are, of course, interested in a counter with initialization. But, as discussed in Section 20.3, this is a modification we prefer to perform after we complete the implementation.

20.4.1 Implementation

In Figure 20.3a, we depict a synchronous circuit that implements a counter with a *reset* signal that initializes all the flip-flops to zero. An incrementer is simply an n-bit binary adder in which (i) one addend is $0^{n-1} \circ 1$ and (ii) there is no carry-out output. Note that the propagation delay of the incrementer is $\Theta(\log n)$, hence the minimum clock period of the counter is also $\Theta(\log n)$.

20.4.2 Analysis

The task of analyzing a synchronous circuit in which the input alphabet Σ is empty needs to be defined. The reason is that we defined analysis only for FSMs in which the input alphabet is not empty. The required modification is quite simple. Simply consider

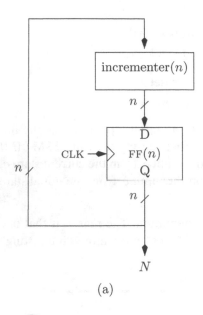

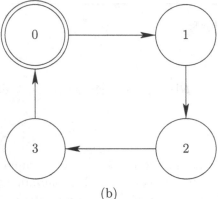

(b)

Figure 20.3. (a) A synchronous circuit that implements an n-bit counter and (b) a state diagram of a counter with $n = 2$. The output always equals the state from which the edge emanates.

the input alphabet Σ as a set with a single input. That means that the input is constant and does not change from one clock cycle to the next.

We now analyze the n-bit counter design to obtain an FSM that models its functionality. Define the FSM $\mathcal{A} = \langle Q, \Sigma, \Delta, \delta, \lambda, q_0 \rangle$ as follows:

1. The set of states is $Q \triangleq \{0, 1\}^n$.
2. Define the initial state q_0 to be $q_0 = 0^n$.
3. $\Sigma = \varnothing$.
4. $\Delta = \{0, 1\}^n$.
5. The output function λ simply outputs the current state, that is, $\lambda(q) = q$. The transition function δ is defined as follows:

$$\delta(q) = bin_n(\langle q \rangle + 1 \ (\mathrm{mod}\ 2^n)).$$

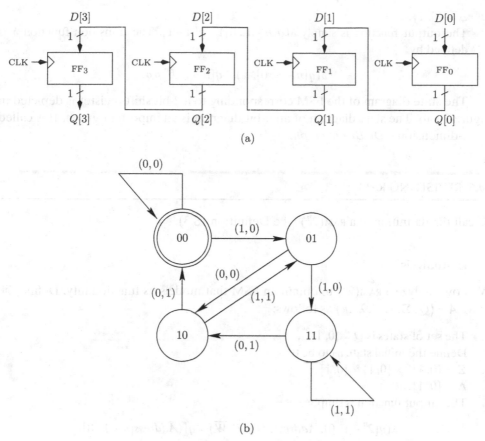

Figure 20.4. (a) A 4-bit shift register and (b) an FSM of a 2-bit shift register.

20.5 REVISITING SHIFT REGISTERS

Recall the definition of an n-bit shift-register (see Definition 18.2), that is; as follows:

Inputs: $D[0](t)$ and a clock CLK.
Output: $Q[n-1](t)$.
Functionality: $Q[n-1](t+n) = D[0](t)$.

An implementation of an 4-bit shift-register is depicted in Figure 20.4a.

20.5.1 Analysis

We now analyze an n-bit shift register to obtain an FSM that models its functionality. Define the FSM $\mathcal{A} = \langle Q, \Sigma, \Delta, \delta, \lambda, q_0 \rangle$ as follows:

1. The set of states is $Q \triangleq \{0,1\}^n$.
2. Define the initial state q_0 to be 0^n.
3. $\Sigma = \{0,1\}$.

4. $\Delta = \{0, 1\}$.
5. The output function is simply $\delta(q[n-1:0]) = q[n-1]$. The transition function δ is defined by

$$\delta(q[n-1:0], \sigma) \triangleq q[n-2:0] \circ \sigma.$$

The state diagram of the FSM corresponding to a 2-bit shift register is depicted in Figure 20.4b. The state diagram of an n-bit diagram is an important graph. It is called the n-dimensional *De Bruijn graph*.

20.6 REVISITING RAM

Recall the definition of a RAM(2^n) (see Definition 18.3).

20.6.1 Analysis

We now analyze a RAM(2^n) to obtain an FSM that models its functionality. Define the FSM $\mathcal{A} = \langle Q, \Sigma, \Delta, \delta, \lambda, q_0 \rangle$ as follows:

1. The set of states is $Q \triangleq \{0, 1\}^{2^n}$.
2. Define the initial state q_0 to be 0^{2^n}.
3. $\Sigma = \{0, 1\}^n \times \{0, 1\} \times \{0, 1\}$.
4. $\Delta = \{0, 1\}$.
5. The output function is simply

$$\lambda(q[2^n - 1:0], Address, D_{in}, R/\overline{W}) = q[\langle Address[n-1:0]\rangle].$$

The transition function δ is defined by

$$\delta(q[2^n - 1:0], Address, D_{in}, R/\overline{W}) \triangleq \begin{cases} q[2^n - 1:0] & \text{if } R/\overline{W} = 1 \\ q'[2^n - 1:0] & \text{if } R/\overline{W} = 0, \end{cases}$$

where $q'[i] = q[i]$, for all i, except $q'[\langle Address[n-1:0]\rangle] = D_{in}$.

The state diagram of the FSM corresponding to a RAM(2^1) is depicted in Figure 20.5b. The state diagram of an n-bit diagram is an important graph. The subgraph corresponding to transitions in which a write operation takes place is called the n-dimensional *hypercube*.

PROBLEMS

20.1. For each of the following specifications, write an FSM that satisfies the specification and synthesize a corresponding synchronous circuit.
  (a) The output is one iff the number of ones in the input so far is even.
  (b) The output is one iff the number of ones in the input so far is odd.
  (c) The output is one iff the the input so far is all ones.
  (d) The output is one iff the the input so far is all zeros.

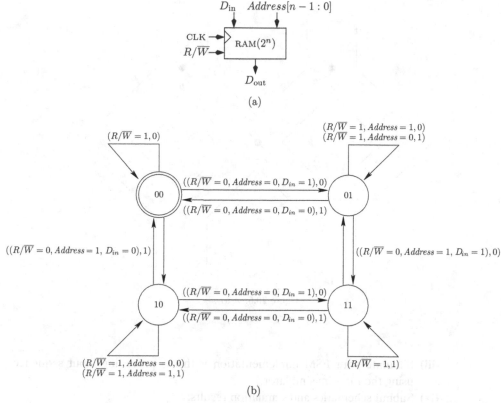

Figure 20.5. (a) A schematic of a RAM(2^n) and (b) an FSM of a RAM(2^1) (transition conditions and the output bit are written next to each edge.

(e) The output is zero iff the every block of zeros in the input so far was followed by a block of ones.

(f) The output is zero iff the number of blocks of zeros in the input so far is even.

(g) The output is zero iff the number of blocks of ones in the input so far is even.

Does one of these specifications match the FSM described in Section 20.1?

20.2. (adopted from [4]) Consider the toy depicted in Figure 20.6. In each cycle, a marble is dropped in A or B (but not both). Levers x, y, z cause the marble to fall either to the left or to the right. If a marble encounters a lever, then it causes the lever to change its state, so that the next marble to encounter the same lever will take the opposite branch.

(a) Define an FSM that models this toy and draw its state diagram (state explicitly the set of states, input–output alphabet, transition function, output function, and initial state). Make sure that (1) your FSM has the minimum number of states, (2) $|\Sigma|$ is minimal, and (3) $|\Delta|$ is minimal.

(b) Synthesis and simulation.

(i) Synthesize your FSM. Use the Logisim schematic entry to implement the synchronous circuit.

(ii) Find an input sequence that causes your FSM to traverse all the states.

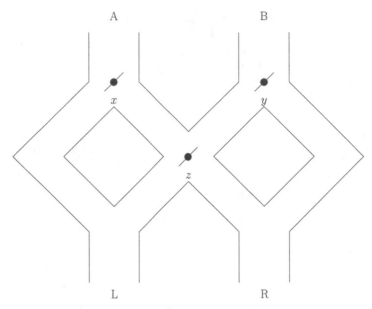

Figure 20.6. A toy.

      (iii) Simulate your FSM implementation with the preceding input sequence, using the Logisim simulator.

      (iv) Submit schematics and simulation results.

  (c) Let C denote the synchronous circuit that implements the toy. Let C' denote the combinational circuit obtained by stripping away the flip-flops. Execute the algorithm FEAS(C) on your circuit. Assume that all the parameters are equal to 1.

  (d) Let C denote the synchronous circuit that implements the toy. let C' denote the combinational circuit obtained by stripping away the flip-flops. Execute the algorithm Min-$\Phi(C)$ on your circuit. Assume that all the parameters are equal to 1.

20.3. The synchronous circuit $C(n)$ is specified as follows. Let $n = 2^k$.

Input: n inputs $\{X_i\}_{i=1}^n$, where each $X_i \in \{0,1\}^k$. Assume that the inputs are valid and stable from clock cycle 0 to clock cycle n.

Output: A single bit Y.

Functionality: The circuit $C(n)$ satisfies the following condition: the output Y should satisfy in every clock cycle $t \geq n$:

$$Y(t) = \begin{cases} 1, & \text{if all } \{X_i\}_{i=1}^n \text{ are distinct} \\ 0, & \text{otherwise.} \end{cases}$$

Note that n strings are distinct if no two are equal.

  (a) How many states does the corresponding FSM have?

  (b) Conclude that you cannot design $C(n)$ by synthesizing an FSM, hence an ad hoc design is required.

(c) Design $C(n)$ so that it meets the following goals:
  (i) Number of flip-flops should be at most $n \cdot k + 1$
  (ii) The minimum clock period should be $O(k) = O(\log n)$
(d) Implement your design for $k = 2$ in Logisim. Verify *by yourself* that your design is correct. Submit a printout of your implementation.

PART IV

A SIMPLIFIED DLX

CHAPTER 21

The ISA of a Simplified DLX

In this chapter we describe a specification of a simple microprocessor called the simplified DLX. The specification of the microprocessor is done by an *instruction set architecture* (ISA). The ISA is a simple programming language, called machine language, that defines manipulations of data as well as control of the program.

The simplified DLX is a *stored-program computer*. This term means that both the data and the instructions are stored in the same memory. In 1945, John von Neumann proposed how to build such a computer. This proposal was influenced by the concept of a universal Turing machine. Modern computers are based on the same principles but include many techniques for speeding up the execution of programs. These techniques include cache memories, pipelining, running instructions in parallel and even out of order, predicting branches, and so on. These topics are discussed in books on computer architecture.

21.1 WHY USE ABSTRACTIONS?

The term *architecture*, according to the Collins Dictionary, means *the art of planning, designing, and constructing buildings*. Computer architecture refers to computers instead of buildings. Computers are rather complicated; even a very simple microprocessor is built from tens of thousands of gates and an operating system spans thousands of lines of instructions. To simplify things, people focus at a given time on certain aspects of computers and ignore other aspects. For example, the hardware designer ignores questions such as which programs will be executed by the computer. The programmer, on the other hand, often does not even know exactly which type of computer will be executing the program she is writing. It is the task of the architect to be aware of different aspects so that the designed system meets the required price and performance goals.

To facilitate focusing on certain aspects, abstractions are used. Several abstractions are used in computer systems. For example, the C programmer uses the abstraction of a computer that runs C programs, owns a private memory, and has access to various peripheral devices (such as a printer, a monitor, and a keyboard). Supporting this abstraction requires software tools (e.g., editor, compiler, linker, loader, debugger). The user, who runs various applications, uses the abstraction of a computer that is capable of running several applications concurrently, supports a file system, and responds to mouse movements and typing on the keyboard. Supporting the user's abstraction requires an operating system (to coordinate between several programs running at the same time and to manage the file system) and hardware (that executes programs, but not in C). The hardware designer is given a specification called the Instruction set architecture (ISA). Her goal is to design a circuit that implements this specification while minimizing cost and delay.

The architect is supposed to be aware of these different viewpoints. The architect's main goal is to suggest an ISA. On one hand, this ISA should provide support for the users of the ISA (these are the programmer, the end user, and even the operating system). On the other hand, the ISA should be simple enough so that the hardware designer can come up with an implementation that is not too expensive or slow.

What exactly is the ISA? The ISA is a specification of the microprocessor from the programmer's point of view. However, this is not a C programmer or a programmer that is programming in a high-level language. Instead, this is a programmer programming in machine language. Since it is not common anymore for people to program in machine language, the machine language programmer is actually a program!

Programs in machine language are output by a program called an *assembler*. The input of an assembler is a program in assembly language. Most assembly programs are also written by programs called *compilers*. Compilers input a program in a high-level language and output assembly programs. Hence a C program undergoes the following sequence of translations: (i) the compiler translates it to an assembly program and (ii) the assembler translates it to a machine language program.

This two-stage sequence of translations starting from a C program and ending with a machine language program has several advantages:

1. The microprocessor executes programs written in a very simple language (machine language). This facilitates the design of the microprocessor.
2. The C programmer need not think about the actual platform that executes the program.
3. Only one compiler is required. For each platform, there is an assembler that translates the assembly programs to the machine language of the platform.
4. Every stage of the translation works in a certain abstraction. The amount of detail increases as one descends to lower level abstractions. In each translation step, decisions can be made that are optimal with respect to the current abstraction.

One can see that all these advantages have to do with good engineering practice. Namely, a task is partitioned in smaller subtasks that are simpler and easier. Clear and precise borderlines between the subtasks guarantee correctness when the subtasks are "glued" together.

21.2 INSTRUCTION SET ARCHITECTURE

We now describe the ISA of the simplified DLX. The term *instruction set architecture* refers to the specification of the computer from the point of view of the machine language programmer. This abstraction consists of two main components:

- The objects that are manipulated; the objects are words (i.e., binary strings) stored in registers or in memory
- The instructions (or commands) that tell the computer what to do to the objects.

21.2.1 Architectural Registers and Memory

Both the registers and the memory store words. In the DLX ISA, a word is a 32-bit string. The memory is often also called the main memory.

The Memory. The memory is used to store both the program itself (i.e., instructions) and the data (i.e., constant and variables used by the program). We regard the memory as an array $M[0 : 2^{32} - 1]$ of words. Each element $M[i]$ in the array holds one word. The memory is organized like a Random Access Memory (RAM). This means that the processor can access the memory in one of two ways:

- *Read or load $M[i]$*. Request to copy the contents of $M[i]$ to a register called MDR (Memory Data Register)
- *Write or store in $M[i]$*. Request to store the contents of a register called MDR in $M[i]$

Note that writing to the memory requires two operands, namely, we need to specify the value we would like to store and we need to specify where we wish to store it. As mentioned earlier, a special register, called the MDR, stores the word that we wish to write to the memory. The index or address i in which we would like to store the contents of the MDR is output by a register called the *MAR* (Memory Address Register).

Hence the (partial) semantics of a write operation are

$$M[\langle MAR \rangle] \leftarrow MDR.$$

Note the angular brackets around the MAR; they signify that we interpret the binary string stored in the MAR as a binary number.

Similarly, the (partial) semantics of a read operation are

$$MDR \leftarrow M[\langle MAR \rangle].$$

The reason that we refer to this description as a partial semantics is that an actual read or write operation involves additional computations. For example, in a read operation, we need to (i) compute the address and store it in the MAR, (ii) copy the contents of the accessed word in the memory to the MDR, and (iii) copy the contents of the MDR to a general purpose register. However, from the point of view of the memory, the interaction with the microprocessor is via the MAR and MDR.

This relatively neat description is incorrect when we consider the task of reading an instruction from the memory. As we will see later, the address of an instruction is stored in a register called PC, and $M[\text{PC}]$, is stored in a register called IR.

Registers. The registers serve as the working space of the microprocessor. They have three main purposes: (i) to control the microprocessor (e.g., the PC and IR), (ii) to serve as the scratch pad for data (e.g., the GPRs), or (iii) to serve as an interface with the main memory (e.g., MAR and MDR). The architectural registers of the simplified DLX are all 32 bits wide and listed in the following:

- Thirty-two General Purpose Registers (GPRs) index from 0 to 31. Informally, we refer to these registers as R0 to R31. Loosely speaking, the general purpose registers are the objects that the program directly manipulates. Register R0 is an exception, as its contents always equal 0^{32}, and cannot be modified.
- Program Counter (PC). The PC stores the address (i.e., index in memory) of the instruction that is currently being executed.
- Instruction Register (IR). The IR stores the current instruction (i.e., IR = $M[PC]$).
- Special Registers MAR, MDR. As mentioned earlier, these registers serve as the interface between the microprocessor and the memory when data are written and read.

Example 21.1 Consider a high-level instruction $z := x + y$. Such an instruction is implemented by the following sequence of instructions. Suppose that x is stored in $M[1]$, y is stored in $M[2]$, and z is stored in $M[3]$. We first need to copy x and y to the GPRs. Namely, we first need to perform two read operations that copy $M[1]$ to R1 and $M[2]$ to R2. We then perform the actual addition: R3 ← R1 + R2. Finally, we copy R3 using a write operation to the memory location $M[3]$.

21.2.2 Instruction Set

The machine language of a processor is often called an instruction set. In general, a machine language has very few rules and a very simple syntax. In the case of the simplified DLX, every sequence of instructions constitutes a legal program (is this the case in C or in Java?). This explains why the machine language is referred to simply as a set of instructions.

Instruction Formats. Every instruction in the instruction set of the simplified DLX is represented by a single word. There are two instruction formats: I-type and R-type. The partitioning of each format into fields is depicted in Figure 21.1. The opcode field encodes the instruction (e.g., load, store, add, jump). The *RS1, RS2, RD* fields encode (in binary representation) the indexes of general purpose registers. Since there are 32 general purpose registers, their indexes are encoded using 5-bit strings. The immediate field encodes (in two's complement representation) a constant. The function field (in an R-type instruction format) is used to encode the instruction.

Assembly Language. Reading and writing instructions as 32-bit binary strings is not a task for humans. The solution is to write instructions using text and numbers. This form of writing instructions is called *assembly language*.

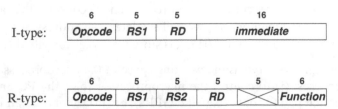

Figure 21.1. Instruction formats of the simplified DLX. (Bits are ordered in descending order, namely, the left-most bit is in position [31] and the rightmost bit is in position [0].)

Each instruction in assembly starts with a text that describes the operation (e.g., add, shift, jump). This text is an abbreviation that consists of two to four letters and is called a *mnemonic*. For example, the mnemonic for "load word" is lw. A full list of the mnemonics appears in Tables 21.1 and 21.2.

The remaining part of an assembly instruction consists of operands in decimal or hexadecimal representation. These operands correspond to the contents of the fields *RS1*, *RS2*, *RD* and the immediate constant. Namely, the operands are either indexes of general purpose registers or the immediate constant. To ease the task of reading assembly instructions, we add the prefix "R" to an index of a register.

The order of the fields in an assembly instruction is not the same order of the fields in the machine code instruction. The order of fields in an assembly instruction is as follows: (i) a mnemonic that represents the operation, (ii) the index of the register where the result should be stored, and (iii) the operands. An operand is either a register or constant. A constant is represented in decimal or hexadecimal notation. If an operand is a register, then the index of the register appears as the operand.

Example 21.2 The assembly instruction addi R4 R8 -10 means add (−10) to the contents of register R8 and store the sum in register R4. Note that in this example, the constant is negative.

List of instructions. We list subsequently the instruction set of the simplified DLX. In this list, $imm \in \{0,1\}^{16}$ denotes the immediate field in an I-type instruction and $sext(imm) \in \{0,1\}^{32}$ denotes a two's complement sign extension of imm to 32 bits. The semantics of each instruction are informally abbreviated and are formally explained after each group of instructions.

Note that every instruction (except for jump instructions and halt) has the side effect of incrementing the PC. Namely, apart from doing whatever the instructions say, the microprocessor also performs the operation

$$PC \leftarrow bin(\mathrm{mod}(\langle PC \rangle + 1, 2^{32})). \tag{21.1}$$

Informally, Eq. 21.1 simply means add one to the binary number represented by the PC. To be precise, the sum is computed modulo 2^{32}, namely, if the sum equals 2^{32}, then replace the sum by zero. Note that (unsigned) binary representation is used for storing the address of the current instruction in the PC.

Load/Store Instructions (I-Type). Load and store instructions deal with copying words between the memory and the GPRs. Subsequently we write the assembly instructions for load and store instructions. We also write an informal and abbreviated interpretation of the load and store instructions next to each instruction.

Load/Store	Semantics
lw RD RS1 imm	RD := M[sext(imm)+RS1]
sw RD RS1 imm	M[sext(imm)+RS1] := RD

The precise semantics of load and store instructions are rather complicated. We first define the effective address; informally, the effective address is the index of the memory word that is accessed in a load or store instruction.

Definition 21.1 The *effective address* in a load or store instruction is defined as follows. Let $j = \langle RS1 \rangle$, namely, the binary number represented by the 5-bit field RS1 in the instruction. Let Rj denote the word stored in the register of the GPR whose index is j. Let $\langle Rj \rangle$ denote the binary number represented by Rj. Recall that $[imm]$ denotes the two's complement number represented by the 16-bit field *imm*. We denote the effective address by *ea*. Then

$$ea \triangleq \mathrm{mod}(\langle Rj \rangle + [imm], 2^{32}).$$

We point out that the event that $\langle Rj \rangle + [imm] \notin \{0, \ldots, 2^{32} - 1\}$ is (most likely) an indication of a programming error. In certain architectures, such an event creates a *segmentation fault*. In the simplified DLX, we do not consider this event to be an error, and the modulo operation is a side effect of using a simple adder for computing the effective address (see Questions 21.4–21.6).

The semantics of load and store instructions are as follows.

Definition 21.2 Let $i = \langle RD \rangle$, namely, i is the number represented in binary representation by the 5-bit field RD in the instruction. Let Ri denote the word stored in the ith register in the GPR.

1. A load instruction has the following meaning:

$$Ri \leftarrow M[ea].$$

   This means that the word stored in $M[ea]$ is copied to register Ri. Of course, $M[ea]$ retains its value.
2. A store instruction has the following meaning:

$$M[ea] \leftarrow Ri.$$

   This means that the word stored in Ri is copied to $M[ea]$. Of course, Ri retains its value.

Note that an implementation of load and store instructions uses the MAR and MDR. In particular, (i) the effective address is stored in the MAR and (ii) copying a word from Ri to $M[ea]$ (or vice versa) is done indirectly via the MDR.

Notation. Following the notation used for load and store instructions, we use the following notation:

- Ri denotes the word stored in the register of the GPR whose index is $\langle RD \rangle$.
- Rj_1 denotes the word stored in the register of the GPR whose index is $\langle RS1 \rangle$.
- Rj_2 denotes the word stored in the register of the GPR whose index is $\langle RS2 \rangle$.

Obviously, $\langle Rj_1 \rangle$ denotes the binary number represented by the word Rj_1. Similarly, $[Rj_2]$ denotes the two's complement number represented by the word Rj_2.

Example 21.3 The assembly instruction `lw R7 R0 15` means copy the word stored in the memory in address ⟨R0⟩ + 15 to R7. Note that "0" stands for R0, which, as we shall see later, always stores the value 0. The assembly instruction `sw R7 R4 0` means copy the word stored in register R7 to the memory in address ⟨R4⟩ + 0.

Add Instruction (I-Type). There are two add instructions in the ISA. We describe the add instruction that belongs to the I-type format. The assembly instruction for addition appears in the table with an informal description.

Instruction	Semantics
`addi   RD RS1 imm`	RD := RS1 + sext(imm)

The precise semantics of an add-immediate instruction are as follows:

$$\mathrm{R}i \leftarrow bin(\mathrm{mod}([\mathrm{R}j_1] + [imm], 2^{32})). \tag{21.2}$$

Equation 21.2 is rather terse; we clarify it now. The goal is to add two numbers. The first addend is the two's complement number represented by the word stored in the register whose index is ⟨RS1⟩. The second addend is the two's complement number represented by the string stored in the immediate field of the instruction. The addition is modulo 2^{32}. The binary representation of the sum is stored in the register whose index is ⟨RD⟩.

This definition is a bit confusing. One might ask, why not encode the sum as a two's complement number? Namely, why not simply use the definition $[\mathrm{R}i] = [\mathrm{R}j_1] + [imm]$? The problem with this so-called simple specification is what happens if the result overflows.

Question 21.7 shows that if no overflow occurs, then Eq. 21.2 is identical to ordinary two's complement addition.

We remark that if interrupts are considered, then one must define two additional side effects of addition instructions, namely, the setting of the overflow flag and negative flag. This is beyond the scope of this chapter.

Example 21.4 The assembly instruction `addi R5 R5 1` means increment the contents of register R5 by 1.

Shift Instructions (R-Type). The shift instructions perform a logical shift by one position either to the left or to the right. The input is word $\mathrm{R}j_1$ and the shifted word is stored in $\mathrm{R}i$. The assembly instructions for logical shift left and logical shift right are listed in the table.

Instruction	Semantics
`sll   RD RS1`	RD := RS1 << 1
`srl   RD RS1`	RD := RS1 >> 1

Example 21.5 The assembly instruction `sll R4 R8` means logically shift the contents of register R8 by one position to the left and store the shifted word in register R4.

The assembly instruction `srl R4 R8` means logically shift the contents of register R8 by one position to the right and store the shifted word in register R4.

ALU Instructions (R-Type). The R-type arithmetic and logical unit (ALU) instructions are add, subtract, and logical bitwise operations (e.g., OR, AND, XOR). The assembly instructions for ALU instructions are listed with an informal description.

Instruction	Semantics
add RD RS1 RS2	RD := RS1 + RS2
sub RD RS1 RS2	RD := RS1 − RS2
and RD RS1 RS2	RD := AND(RS1, RS2)
or RD RS1 RS2	RD := OR(RS1, RS2)
xor RD RS1 RS2	RD := XOR(RS1, RS2)

Formally, the semantics of the add and subtract instructions are

$$R i \leftarrow bin(\mathrm{mod}([R j_1] + [R j_2], 2^{32}))$$

$$R i \leftarrow bin(\mathrm{mod}([R j_1] - [R j_2], 2^{32})).$$

The semantics of the bitwise logical instructions are simple. For example, in an AND instruction, $R i[\ell] = \mathrm{AND}(R j_1[\ell], R j_2[\ell])$.

Example 21.6 The assembly instruction add R4 R8 R12 means store in R4 the sum of the contents of registers R8 and R12. The assembly instruction or R1 R2 R3 means store in R1 the bitwise OR the contents of registers R2 and R3. Hence, if R2 = $(01)^{16}$ and R3 = $(10)^{16}$, then R1 $\leftarrow 1^{32}$.

Test Instructions (I-Type). The test instructions compare the two's complement numbers $[R j_1]$ and $[imm]$. The result of the comparison is stored in $R i$.

For example, consider the slti instruction. The semantics of the slti instruction are

$$R i = \begin{cases} 1 & \text{if } [R j_1] < [imm] \\ 0 & \text{otherwise.} \end{cases}$$

There are six different test instructions: slti, seqi, sgti, slei, sgei, and snei. We summarize their functionality.

Instruction	Semantics
s*rel*i RD RS1 imm	RD := 1, if condition is satisfied,
	RD := 0 otherwise
if *rel* =lt	test if RS1 < sext(imm)
if *rel* =eq	test if RS1 = sext(imm)
if *rel* =gt	test if RS1 > sext(imm)
if *rel* =le	test if RS1 ≤ sext(imm)
if *rel* =ge	test if RS1 ≥ sext(imm)
if *rel* =ne	test if RS1 ≠ sext(imm)

Example 21.7 The assembly instruction slti R4 R8 -12 means store in R4 the value 1 if [R8] < −12; otherwise, store in R4 the value 0. The assembly instruction

snei R1 R8 9 means store in R1 the value 1 if [R8] ≠ 9; otherwise store in R1 the value 0.

Branch/Jump Instructions (I-Type). Branch and jump instructions modify the value stored in the the PC. Recall that during the execution of every instruction, the PC is incremented. In a branch or jump instruction, an additional change is made to the PC.

The simplest instruction in this set is the jump register (jr) instruction. It simply changes the PC so that $PC \leftarrow R j_1$. Hence the next instruction to be executed is the instruction stored in $M[R j_1]$.

A somewhat more evolved instruction is the jump and link register (jalr) instruction. This instruction saves the incremented PC in R31. The idea is that this instruction is used for calling a procedure, and the return address is stored in R31. Formally, the semantics of jalr are

$$R31 \leftarrow bin(\mod(\langle PC \rangle + 1, 2^{32}))$$

$$PC \leftarrow R j_1.$$

We also have two branch instructions: "branch if zero" (beqz) and "branch if not zero" (bnez). In a beqz instruction, if $R j_1 = 0^{32}$, then a branch takes place and the address of the next instruction is $PC + 1 + [imm]$. If $R j_1 \neq 0^{32}$, then the branch is not taken and the address of the next instruction is $PC + 1$. In a bnez instruction, the conditions are reversed.

We summarize these four instructions in the following.

Instruction	Semantics
beqz RS1 imm	PC = PC + 1 + sext(imm), if RS1 = 0
	PC = PC + 1, if RS1 ≠ 0
bnez RS1 imm	PC = PC + 1, if RS1 = 0
	PC = PC + 1 + sext(imm), if RS1 ≠ 0
jr RS1	PC = RS1
jalr RS1	R31 = PC+1; PC = RS1

See Section 21.3 for examples of branch instructions.

Miscellaneous Instructions (I-Type). There are a few special instructions in the I-type format. The first special instruction is the no operation (special-nop) instruction. This instruction has a null effect, and the only thing that happens during its execution is that the PC is incremented.

The second special instruction is the halt (halt) instruction. This instruction causes the microprocessor to freeze and stop the execution of the program. Halting is implemented simply by not updating the PC.

21.2.3 Encoding of the Instruction Set

Tables 21.1 and 21.2 suggest binary encoding of the instructions.

Table 21.1. I-type instructions

IR[31 : 26]	Mnemonic	Semantics
Data Transfer		
100 011	lw	RD = M[sext(imm)+RS1]
101 011	sw	M[sext(imm)+RS1] = RD
Arithmetic, Logical Operation		
001 011	addi	RD = RS1 + sext(imm)
Test Set Operation		
011 rel	s rel i	RD = (RS1 rel sext(imm))
011 001	sgti	RD = (RS1 > sext(imm))
011 010	seqi	RD = (RS1 = sext(imm))
011 011	sgei	RD = (RS1 ≥ sext(imm))
011 100	slti	RD = (RS1 < sext(imm))
011 101	snei	RD = (RS1 ≠ sext(imm))
011 110	slei	RD = (RS1 ≤ sext(imm))
Control Operation		
000 100	beqz	PC = PC + 1 + (RS1 = 0 ? sext(imm): 0)
000 101	bnez	PC = PC + 1 + (RS1 ≠ 0 ? sext(imm): 0)
010 110	jr	PC = RS1
010 111	jalr	R31 = PC + 1; PC = RS1
Miscellaneous Instructions		
110 000	special NOP	no operation
111 111	halt	stop program

Table 21.2. R-type instructions (in R-type instructions IR[31 : 26] = 0^6)

IR[5 : 0]	Mnemonic	Semantics
Shift Operation		
000 000	sll	RD = RS1 ≪ 1
000 010	srl	RD = RS1 ≫ 1
Arithmetic, Logical Operation		
100 011	add	RD = RS1 + RS2
100 010	sub	RD = RS1 − RS2
100 110	and	RD = RS1 ∧ RS2
100 101	or	RD = RS1 ∨ RS2
100 100	xor	RD = RS1 ⊕ RS2

21.3 EXAMPLES OF PROGRAM SEGMENTS

Example 21.8 Convert the following C code segment to a simplified DLX's machine code:

```
    if (i==j)
        goto L1;
    f=g+h;
L1: f=f-i;
```

Table 21.3. Register assignment for
Example 21.8

Variable	Register
f	R1
g	R2
h	R3
i	R4
j	R5

Table 21.4. Conversion of the program
segment in Example 21.8 to the instruction
set of the DLX

C code	DLX assembly
if (i==j)	xor R6 R4 R5
goto L1;	beqz R6 1
f=g+h;	add R1 R2 R3
L1: f=f-i;	sub R1 R1 R4

First, we assign a register to each of the variables in program segment. The register assignment appears in Table 21.3.

Now we convert the C code to a DLX's machine code. The conversion is depicted in Table 21.4.

In Example 21.8, every C instruction is mapped to a single machine code instruction. This is not always the case, as we are about to see in the following example.

Example 21.9 Convert the following C code segment to a simplified DLX's machine code:

```
LOOP: g=g+A[i];
      i=i+j;
      if (i!=h) goto LOOP;
```

Again, we assign a register to each of the variables in program segment. The register assignment appears in Table 21.5.

The evaluation of the program segment requires temporarily storing some values in the registers. We assume that these registers are free. In particular, the address of A[0] (i.e., the address of the first entry of the array A) is held in register R5. We later refer to this address simply by A. Register R6 is used as a temporary placeholder for storing the value of $A + i$. This is the address of $A[i]$. Register R7 is used as a temporary placeholder for $A[i]$. Finally, register R8 stores the outcome of the comparison $i \neq h$.

Now we convert the C code to a DLX's machine code. The conversion is depicted in Table 21.6.

Table 21.5. Register assignment. The variables below the line are temporary registers used for evaluating the program segment in Example 21.9

Variable	Register
g	R1
h	R2
i	R3
j	R4
A	R5
A+i	R6
A[i]	R7
i!=h	R8

Table 21.6. Conversion of the program segment in Example 21.9 to the instruction set of the DLX

C Code	DLX Assembly
`LOOP: g=g+A[i];`	`add R6 R5 R3`
	`lw R7 R6 0`
	`add R1 R1 R7`
`i=i+j;`	`add R3 R3 R4`
`if (i!=h) goto LOOP;`	`xor R8 R3 R2`
	`bnez R8 -6`

21.4 SUMMARY

In this chapter, we described the ISA of the simplified DLX. Even though the ISA is rather simple, C instructions and programs can be translated into the DLX machine language. Missing in this description are issues such as supporting systems calls, distinguishing between protected mode and user mode, and so on. These important issues are beyond the scope of this chapter.

PROBLEMS

21.1. Explain why it is not common anymore for people to program in assembly or machine code. Consider issues such as cost of programming in a high-level language compared to assembly or machine code, ease of debugging programs, protections provided by high-level programming, and length and efficiency of final machine code program.

21.2. Parts of the main memory in many computers are nonvolatile and even Read-Only Memory. Nonvolatile means that the contents are kept even when power is turned off. *Read-only* means that the contents cannot be changed. Can you explain why such read-only nonvolatile memory is required?

21.3. We said that the same memory is used to store operating system programs and data as well as the user's program and data. How can we make sure that the user program does not write to areas in the memory that belong to the operating system?

21.4. If we ignore the issue of overflow, then the effective address is simply $\langle Rj \rangle + [imm]$. Recall that in two's complement representation, the largest representable number is roughly half the largest representable number in binary representation. Since we have only 16 bits for the immediate constant, is it better to define the effective address by $\langle Rj \rangle + \langle imm \rangle$? Do we need negative immediate constants?

21.5. This question deals with how a binary adder is used to compute the effective address.
   (a) Prove that addition modulo 2^{32} is not sensitive to binary or two's complement representation. Namely, let $X[31:0]$ and $Y[31:0]$ be two binary strings; then

$$\text{mod}\left(\langle \vec{X} \rangle + \langle \vec{Y} \rangle, 2^{32}\right) = \text{mod}\left([\vec{X}] + \langle \vec{Y} \rangle, 2^{32}\right) = \text{mod}\left([\vec{X}] + [\vec{Y}], 2^{32}\right).$$

   (b) Prove that $ea = \text{mod}([imm] + [Rj], 2^{32})] = \text{mod}(\langle sext(imm) \rangle + \langle Rj \rangle, 2^{32})]$.
   (c) Suggest a way to compute the effective address. Hint: the immediate constant must be sign-extended before being added with $\langle Rj \rangle$.

21.6. Consider the computation of the effective address. Suppose that we wish to detect the event that the computation overflows. Formally,

$$\langle Rj \rangle + [imm] \geq 2^{32} \quad \text{or} \quad \langle Rj \rangle + [imm] < 0.$$

Suggest how to compute the effective address and how to detect overflow.

21.7. Let $\vec{A}$ and $\vec{C}$ denote 32-bit binary strings. Let $\vec{B}$ denote a binary string of any length. Think of A as the 32-bit two's complement representation of $[X] + [Y]$ if no overflow occurs. Think of B as the representation of $[X] + [Y]$ in two's complement (using as many bits as required). Suppose that $[\vec{A}] = [\vec{B}]$ and that $\langle \vec{C} \rangle = \text{mod}([\vec{B}], 2^{32})$. Prove that $\vec{A} = \vec{C}$.

21.8. How is the condition $[Rj_1] < [imm]$ computed? Let us return to the negative flag of the signed adder/subtractor. Is it crucial that the negative flag indicate correctly whether the sum/difference is negative even in case of an overflow?

21.9. Why is the address of the next instruction defined as $PC + 1 + [imm]$ instead of $PC + [imm]$ when a branch is taken? Does this definition simplify or complicate the implementation of a branch instruction?

21.10. Can you suggest reasons for using the no-operation and halt instructions?

21.11. Convert the following program segments to equivalent program segments in the DLX instruction set:
   • In each example, specify the assignment of registers.
   • Use the DLX assembly editor and compiler to implement and compile your program.

- Use the DLX assembly simulator to verify *by yourself* that your program is correct.
- Submit your annotated program.

1. `A[4]:= A[8];`

2. `A:= B[7];`
   `A:=A+8;`
   `if (A==B[2]) then C:=A+1;`
   `else C:=2*A;`

3. `for i:=1 to K do`
   `   begin`
   `     S:=S+A[i];`
   `   end`

4. `A:=A[A];`

5. `A:=0;`
   `for i:=1 to 13 do`
   `   begin`
   `     A:=A+B;`
   `   end`

6. `if (A[2]==3) then`
   `     C:=1;`
   `else`
   `     C:=2;`

7. `if (A[2]==A[4]) then`
   `     A[2]:=A[2]+A[4];`
   `else`
   `     A[4]:=A[4]-5;`
   `halt;`

CHAPTER 22 A Simplified DLX: Implementation

In this chapter, we show how to implement the simplified DLX. The implementation consists of two parts: a finite state machine, called the *control*, and a circuit containing registers and functional modules, called the *datapath*. The separation of the design into a controller and a datapath greatly simplifies the task of designing the simplified DLX.

The datapath contains all the modules needed to execute instructions. These modules include registers, a shifter, and an arithmetic logic unit. The control is the brain that uses the datapath to execute the instructions.

22.1 DATAPATH

In this section, we outline an implementation of the datapath of a simplified DLX, as depicted in Figure 22.1. We outline the implementation by specifying the inputs, outputs, and functionality of every module in the datapath. The implementation of every module is done by using the memory modules and the combinational circuits that we have implemented throughout this book. Note that Figure 22.1 is not complete: (i) inputs and outputs of the control FSM are not presented and (ii) some of the input–output ports, and their corresponding wires, are not presented. In fact, only wires that are 32-bit wide are presented in Figure 22.1.

22.1.1 The Outside World: The Memory Controller

We begin with the outside world, that is, the (external) memory. Recall that both the executed program and the data are stored in the memory.

The *memory controller* is a circuit that is positioned between the DLX and the main memory. It is a synchronous circuit that receives memory access requests from the DLX. The main problem related to memory access is that it requires an unpredictable number of cycles to complete. Accessing a register always takes a single clock cycle, however, loading or storing in the external memory typically requires several cycles. The reason that memory accesses are not executed in a fixed number of clock cycles has to do with the organization of the memory, also called the *memory hierarchy*. This organization

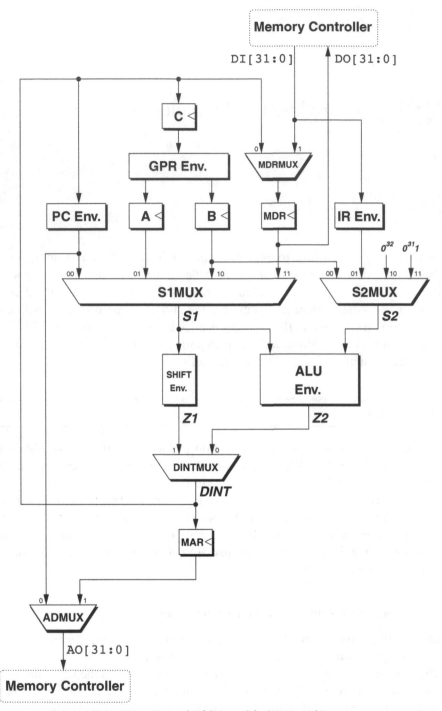

Figure 22.1. Datapath of the simplified DLX machine.

involves caches, cache misses, page faults, and other issues that are beyond the scope of this book.

The fact that the number of clock cycles required to complete a memory is not fixed requires a special signal, called the *busy signal*. The busy signal is an output of the memory controller that tells the DLX whether the memory is still executing the previous memory access. The DLX may issue a new memory access request only if the busy signal is low.

Recall that $M[2^{32} - 1 : 0]$ denotes the memory array. Each memory cell $M[i]$ is 32 bits wide.

Definition 22.1 The *memory controller* is a synchronous circuit specified as follows:

Input: $IN[31 : 0]$, $Address[31 : 0] \in \{0, 1\}^{32}$, MR, MW $\in \{0, 1\}$, and a clock CLK.
Output: $OUT[31 : 0] \in \{0, 1\}^{32}$, busy $\in \{0, 1\}$.
Functionality:

1. The input may change in cycle t only if $\text{busy}(t) = 0$.
2. If $\text{busy}(t) = 0$ and $\text{busy}(t - 1) = 1$, then the output must satisfy the following conditions:
   (a) If $MR(t - 1) = 1$, then

   $$OUT(t) \leftarrow M[\langle Address(t - 1)\rangle](t - 1).$$

   (b) If $MW(t - 1) = 1$, then

   $$M[\langle Address(t - 1)\rangle](t) \leftarrow IN(t - 1).$$

Note that the functionality only refers to the clock cycles in which a memory access has just completed. These clock cycles are characterized by the condition $\text{busy}(t) = 0$ and $\text{busy}(t - 1) = 1$.

The memory controller is depicted in Figure 22.2.

The busses depicted in Figure 22.1 are connected to the memory controller as follows:

- The bus $AO[31 : 0]$ is connected to the $Address[31 : 0]$ input of the memory controller.
- The bus $DO[31 : 0]$ is connected to the $IN[31 : 0]$ input of the memory controller.
- The bus $DI[31 : 0]$ is connected to the $OUT[31 : 0]$ input of the memory controller.

The signals MR, MW and busy are connected to the FSM that is called the DLX control. These signals are discussed in detail in Section 22.2.2.

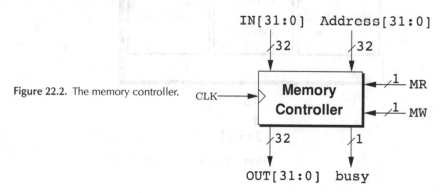

Figure 22.2. The memory controller.

22.1.2 Registers

All the registers of the simplified DLX datapath are 32 bits wide and are as follows:

1. There are 32 *General Purpose Registers* (GPR): R0 to R31. The GPR module is discussed in Section 22.1.7.
2. The *Instruction Register* (IR) is also a clock-enabled parallel load register. This register is part of the *IR environment*. The IR environment is discussed in Section 22.1.5.
3. The remaining registers, *Program Counter* (PC), *Memory Address Register* (MAR), *Memory Data Register* (MDR), and registers *A*, *B*, and *C* are all clock-enabled parallel load registers. Each of these registers has a distinct clock-enabled signal that is computed by an FSM called the DLX control (see Section 22.2). The clock-enabled signals are called `PCCE`, `MARCE`, `MDRCE`, `ACE`, `BCE`, and `CCE`.

22.1.3 ALU Environment

The ALU is a combinational circuit that supports addition and subtraction, bitwise logical instructions, and comparison instructions. A sketch of the ALU is depicted in Figure 22.3. The main three subcircuits of the ALU are (i) 32-bit adder/subtractor, ADD-SUB(32), (ii) bitwise logical operations, XOR, OR, AND, and (iii) a comparator, COMP(32). Note that the comparator is fed by the outputs of the adder/subtractor circuit.

Definition 22.2 An *ALU environment* is a combinational circuit specified as follows:

Input: $x[31:0], y[31:0] \in \{0,1\}^{32}, type \in \{0,1\}^5$.
Output: $z[31:0] \in \{0,1\}^{32}$.
Functionality:

$$\vec{z} \stackrel{\triangle}{=} f_{type}(\vec{x}, \vec{y}),$$

Table 22.1 lists the functions in the set $\{ f_{type} : type \in \{0,1\}^5 \}$.

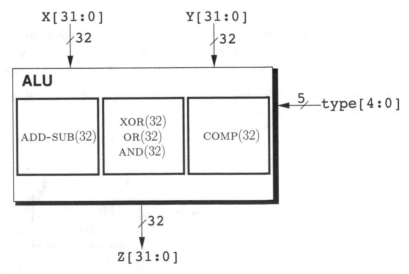

Figure 22.3. A sketch of the ALU.

Table 22.1. The *type* input is partitioned into three fields, i.e., *type*[4 : 2], *type*[1], and *type*[0]. The values of each of these fields are listed in the left three columns. The asterisk symbol denotes a "don't care," that is, the corresponding entry can be either 0 or 1.

$type[4:2]$	$type[1]$	$type[0]$	$f_{type}(\vec{x}, \vec{y})$
001	1	0	$[\vec{x}] > [\vec{y}]$
010	0	0	$[\vec{x}] - [\vec{y}]$ (mod 2^{32})
010	1	0	$[\vec{x}] = [\vec{y}]$
011	0	0	$[\vec{x}] + [\vec{y}]$ (mod 2^{32})
011	1	0	$[\vec{x}] \geq [\vec{y}]$
100	0	0	$\text{XOR}(\vec{x}, \vec{y})$
100	1	0	$[\vec{x}] < [\vec{y}]$
101	0	0	$\text{OR}(\vec{x}, \vec{y})$
101	1	0	$[\vec{x}] \neq [\vec{y}]$
110	0	0	$\text{AND}(\vec{x}, \vec{y})$
110	1	0	$[\vec{x}] \leq [\vec{y}]$
***	*	1	$[\vec{x}] + [\vec{y}]$ (mod 2^{32})

We note the following regarding the functionality of the ALU:

1. The outcome of a comparison is one or zero, depending on whether the expression is true.
2. The logical operations are bitwise.
3. The comparison operations return either 0^{32} or $0^{31} \circ 1$.
4. The input *type*[0] indicates if the function is addition. It is used, for example, to increment the program counter.
5. The input *type*[1] indicates if the function is comparison.

The busses depicted in Figure 22.1 are connected to the ALU as follows:

- The bus $S1[31:0]$ is connected to the $x[31:0]$ input of the ALU.
- The bus $S2[31:0]$ is connected to the $y[31:0]$ input of the ALU.
- The bus $Z2[31:0]$ is connected to the $z[31:0]$ output of the ALU.

The signals *type*[4 : 0] are outputs of the FSM called the DLX control. These signals are discussed in detail in Section 22.2.2.

22.1.4 Shifter Environment

The shifter is a 32-bit bidirectional logical shifter by one position. Formally, recall that $\text{LLS}(\vec{x}, i)$ denotes the logical left shift of $\vec{x}$ by i positions and that $\text{LRS}(\vec{x}, i)$ denotes the logical right shift of $\vec{x}$ by i positions (see Section 14.3 in page 209).

Definition 22.3 The *shifter environment* is a combinational circuit defined as follows:

Input:

- $x[31:0] \in \{0, 1\}^{32}$,
- shift $\in \{0, 1\}$,
- right $\in \{0, 1\}$.

Output: $y[n-1:0] \in \{0,1\}^{32}$.
Functionality: The output $\vec{y}$ satisfies

$$\vec{y} \stackrel{\Delta}{=} \begin{cases} \vec{x}, & \text{if shift} = 0, \\ \text{LLS}(\vec{x}, 1), & \text{if shift} = 1, \text{Right} = 0, \\ \text{LRS}(\vec{x}, 1), & \text{if shift} = 1, \text{Right} = 1. \end{cases}$$

The shifter environment also implements the identity function (i.e., no shift at all). This possibility is used to route a word through the shifter in the execution of some instructions.

The busses depicted in Figure 22.1 are connected to the shifter as follows:

- The bus $S1[31:0]$ is connected to the $x[31:0]$ input of the shifter.
- The bus $Z1[31:0]$ is connected to the $y[31:0]$ output of the shifter.

The signals shift and right are outputs of the FSM that is called the DLX control. These signals are discussed in detail in Section 22.2.2.

22.1.5 The IR Environment

The *IR environment* holds the 32 bits of the current instruction. Recall that there are two instruction formats, that is, I-type and R-type. When executing an I-type instruction, the IR environment outputs the sign extension of the immediate field and the indices of $RS1$ and RD. Conversely, when executing an R-type instruction, the IR environment outputs the indices of $RS1$, $RS2$, and RD. Note that the RD field is positioned in different places. Selecting the right bits requires a circuit that computes whether the instruction is an I-type instruction. We delegate this computation to the DLX control and denote the outcome of this computation as the Itype signal.

Formally, the IR environment is a synchronous circuit defined as follows.

Definition 22.4 The *IR environment* is a synchronous circuit defined as follows:

Input: $DI[31:0] \in \{0,1\}^{32}$, IRce, JLINK, Itype $\in \{0,1\}$, and a clock signal CLK.
Output: An instruction Inst[31:0], sign extension of the immediate constant Imm[31:0], and the GPR addresses Aadr[4:0], Badr[4:0], Cadr[4:0] $\in \{0,1\}^5$.
Functionality:

$$\text{Inst}(t+1) = \begin{cases} \text{Inst}(t) & \text{if IRce}(t) = 0, \\ DI(t) & \text{if IRce}(t) = 1, \end{cases}$$

$$\text{Imm}[31:0](t) = \text{sign extension of Inst}[15:0](t) \text{ to 32 bits,}$$

$$\text{Aadr}[4:0](t) = \text{Inst}[25:21](t),$$

$$\text{Badr}[4:0](t) = \text{Inst}[20:16](t),$$

$$\text{Cadr}[4:0](t) = \begin{cases} 11111 & \text{if JLINK}(t) = 1, \\ \text{Inst}[20:16](t), & \text{if Itype}(t) = 1 \text{ and JLINK}(t) = 0, \\ \text{Inst}[15:11](t), & \text{otherwise.} \end{cases}$$

The IR environment is implemented by a parallel load clock-enabled register and a $3:1$-mux to select the value of Cadr.

Inputs and outputs of IR environment are connected as follows:

- The datapath bus $DI[31:0]$ is connected to the $DI[31:0]$ input of the IR environment.
- The Imm$[31:0]$ output of the IR environment is connected to the S2MUX.
- The outputs Aadr, Badr, and Cadr are input to the GPR environment, as discussed in detail in Section 22.1.7.
- The output Inst$[31:0]$ is input to the FSM, called the DLX control.
- The inputs Itype, JLINK, and IRce are outputs of the DLX control.

22.1.6 The PC Environment

The PC environment is simply a 32-bit clock-enabled parallel load register. The PC is initialized to the value 0^{32}.

22.1.7 The GPR Environment

The GPR environment is sometimes called the register file. There are 32 registers in the GPR environment, called R0, R1, ..., R31. The GPR environment (or GPR) can support one of two operations in each clock cycle:

1. Write the value of input C in Ri, where $i = \langle$Cadr$\rangle$.
2. Read the contents of the registers Ri and Rj, where $i = \langle$Aadr$\rangle$ and $j = \langle$Badr$\rangle$.

Formally, the GPR is specified as follows.

Definition 22.5 A GPR is a synchronous circuit, specified as follows.

Inputs: GPR addresses (output by the IR environment) Aadr$[4:0]$, Badr$[4:0]$, Cadr$[4:0] \in \{0,1\}^5$, a data input $C[31:0] \in \{0,1\}^{32}$, a write-enable signal GPR_WE $\in \{0,1\}$, and a clock signal CLK.

Output: $A[31:0]$, $B[31:0] \in \{0,1\}^{32}$, and a flag AEQZ $\in \{0,1\}$.

Functionality: Let R$[i]$ denote the ith register in the GPR. The functionality of a GPR is specified by the following program:

1. data: array R$[31:0]$ of 32-bit wide registers.
2. initialize: $\forall i : R[i] \leftarrow 0^{32}$.
3. For $t = 0$ to ∞ do
   (a) If GPR_WE -1 and $\langle$Cadr$\rangle \neq 0$, then

$$\text{R}[\langle\text{Cadr}\rangle](t+1) \leftarrow \vec{C}(t).$$

   (b) If GPR_WE $= 0$ then

$$\vec{A}(t) \leftarrow \text{R}[\langle\text{Aadr}\rangle](t),$$

$$\vec{B}(t) \leftarrow \text{R}[\langle\text{Badr}\rangle](t),$$

$$\text{AEQZ}(t) \leftarrow \begin{cases} 1 & \text{if } \vec{A}(t) = 0^{32}, \\ 0 & \text{otherwise.} \end{cases}$$

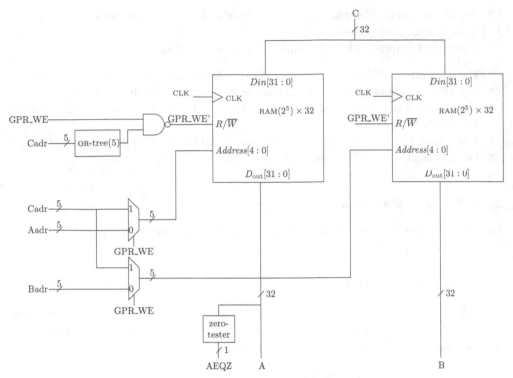

Figure 22.4. An implementation of the GPR environment.

An implementation of the GPR environment is depicted in Figure 22.4. In essence, it is a dual-port RAM (see Question 18.4) that is implemented somewhat inefficiently by two parallel RAMs.

The GPR input C and two outputs A and B are connected to the datapath registers with the same names (see Figure 22.1). The output AEQZ is input to the DLX control. The input GPR_WE is an output of the DLX control.

22.2 CONTROL

The control is an FSM that helps execute a DLX program. Loosely speaking, it tells the datapath what to do in every clock cycle. We begin in Section 22.2.1 with a high-level view of how instructions are executed. We continue in Section 22.2.2 with a detailed description of the FSM. We then continue in Section 22.3 with a description of how the control governs the datapath. We conclude in Section 22.4 with examples of instruction execution.

22.2.1 A High-Level View of the Execution Cycle

An execution of a DLX instruction requires multiple clock cycles. It is common to consider the following steps in the execution of an instruction:

1. *Instruction fetch.* In this step, the instruction to be executed is copied from the main memory to the instruction register (IR). Formally, in this step, the following operation takes place:

$$IR \leftarrow M[\langle PC \rangle].$$

2. *Instruction decode.* In this step, the instruction stored in the IR is decoded. Decoding means that the control decides what actions should take place.
3. *Execute.* In this step, the instruction is executed. For example, in an add instruction, the addition takes place in this step.
4. *Memory access.* In this step, load and store instructions access the main memory.
5. *Write-back.* In this step, the result of an instruction that computes a value is stored, if needed, in the GPR.

22.2.2 The Control FSM

In this section, we present a formal description of the FSM that constitutes the control of the DLX.

States. The FSM has 19 states. We first list the states that correspond to steps in the execution cycle:

1. *Instruction fetch.* The Fetch state is the only state that deals with instruction fetch.
2. *Instruction decode.* The Decode state is the only state that deals with instruction decode.
3. *Execute.* The states Alu, TestI, AluI, and Shift deal with the execute step.
4. *Memory access.* The states Load and Store deal with memory access.
5. *Write-back.* The states WBR and WBI deal with writing back the result in the GPR.

There are additional states that do not belong to the standard execution steps. These include the following states:

1. *States that deal with the execution of branch and jump instructions.* These are the states Branch, Btaken, JR, Save PC, and JALR.
2. *States that deal with load and store instructions.* These are the states Address-Computation, CopyMDR2C, and CopyGPR2MDR.
3. *A sink state.* Halt, for stopping the execution.

FSM Inputs. Each bit of the input alphabet of the FSM is called a *control input*. We list the control inputs as follows:

1. The current instruction Inst[31 : 0] that is an output of the IR environment.
2. The AEQZ flag that indicates if A equals zero. This flag is an output of the GPR environment.
3. The busy flag that is output by the memory controller.

FSM Outputs. Each bit of the output alphabet of the FSM is called a *control output*. Table 22.2 summarizes the control outputs of the simplified DLX and their effect. We elaborate on the control outputs in the following list:

Table 22.2. Summary of the control outputs

Signal	Value	Semantics
ALUf[2:0]		Controls the functionality of ALU
Rce		Register clock enable
S1sel[1:0]	00	PC
	01	A
	10	B
	11	MDR
S2sel[1:0]	00	B
	01	IR
	10	0
	11	1
DINTsel	0	ALU
	1	Shifter
MDRsel	0	DINT
	1	DI
ADsel	0	PC
	1	MAR
shift		explicit Shift-Instruction
right		Shift to the right
add		Forces an addition
test		Forces a test (in the ALU)
MR		Memory Read
MW		Memory Write
GPR_WE		GPR write enable
itype		Itype-Instruction
jlink		jump and link

1. IRCE, PCCE, ACE, BCE, CCE, MARCE, MDRCE: clock-enable signals of the corresponding registers.
2. S1SEL[1:0], S2SEL[1:0], DINTSEL, MDRSEL, ADSEL: select signals of the S1MUX, S2MUX, DINTMUX, MDRMUX, and ADMUX selectors in the datapath.
3. ALUF[2:0], ADD, TEST: signals that are input to the ALU environment, as follows: $type[4:2] \leftarrow$ ALUF[2:0], $type[1] \leftarrow$ test, and $type[0] \leftarrow$ add. The value of ALUF[2:0] is computed by

$$\text{ALUF}[2:0] \leftarrow \begin{cases} opcode[2:0] & \text{if Inst is an I-type instruction} \\ function[2:0] & \text{if Inst is an R-type instruction.} \end{cases} \quad (22.1)$$

Note that the opcode and function strings are fields in the instruction, as described in Figure 21.1.

4. SHIFT, RIGHT: signals that are input to the Shifter environment.
5. Itype: indicates whether the current instruction is an I-type instruction. The Itype signal is input to the IR environment.
6. JLINK: This signal is input to the IR environment. The signal equals one if and only if the current instruction is a jalr instruction.
7. The signals MR, MW are input to the memory controller. These signals indicate whether a read or write access is performed by the memory controller.
8. The signal GPR_WE is the write enable signal of the GPR environment.

Table 22.3. The output function of the DLX control. The leftmost column lists the states of the control. The RTL instructions that are executed in each state are listed in the middle column. The active control outputs in each state are listed in the rightmost column

Name	RTL Instruction	Active Control Outputs
Fetch	$IR = M[PC]$	MR, IRce
Decode	$A = RS1,$ $B = RS2$ $PC = PC + 1$	Ace, Bce, S2sel[1], S2sel[0], add, PCce
Alu	$C = A$ op B	S1sel[0], Cce, active bits in ALUF[2:0]
TestI	$C = (A$ rel $imm)$	S1sel[0], S2sel[0], Cce, test, Itype, active bits in ALUF[2:0]
AluI(add)	$C = A + imm$	S1sel[0], S2sel[0], Cce, add, Itype
Shift	$C = A$ shift sa $sa = 1, (-1)$	S1sel[0], Cce DINTsel, shift (,right)
Adr.Comp	$MAR = A + imm$	S1sel[0], S2sel[0], MARce, add
Load	$MDR = M[MAR]$	MDRce, ADsel, MR, MDRsel
Store	$M[MAR] = MDR$	ADsel, MW
CopyMDR2C	$C = MDR(\gg 0)$	S1sel[0], S1sel[1], S2sel[1], DINTsel, Cce
CopyGPR2MDR	$MDR = B(\ll 0)$	S1sel[1], S2sel[1], DINTsel, MDRce
WBR	$RD = C$ (R-type)	GPR_WE
WBI	$RD = C$ (I-type)	GPR_WE, Itype
Branch	branch taken?	
Btaken	$PC = PC + imm$	S2sel[0], add, PCce
JR	$PC = A$	S1sel[0], S2sel[1], add, PCce
Save PC	$C = PC$	S2sel[1], add, Cce
JALR	$PC = A$ $R31 = C$	S1sel[0], S2sel[1], add, PCce, GPR_WE, jlink

Output Function. Table 22.3 lists the control outputs that equal one in each state. The other control outputs equal zero. One often refers to a control output that equals one as an *active* signal. Note that in states Alu and TestI, the control output *ALUF* is computed according to Eq. 22.1.

State Diagram. Figure 22.5 depicts a sketch of the state diagram of the control of the simplified DLX. Note that the contents of the datapath registers is not part of the state of the FSM of the control. Figure 22.5 does not depict the reset signal. Reset is added to the FSM using the transformation described in Section 20.3. The reset signal causes a transition in the control of the DLX to the Fetch state.

Transition Function. In Figure 22.5, one can easily see that the out-degree of most control states is one. This means that the FSM transitions to the only "next state" independent of the input to the FSM. Only six states have an out-degree greater than one. We elaborate on the transitions from these six states:

1. The Fetch, Load, and Store states have a self-loop labeled by busy. This means, that if the input busy equals one, then the FSM stays in the same state.
2. The Branch state has two possible transitions. The transition to state BTaken is labeled bt, and the transition back to Fetch is labeled NOT(bt). The value of bt is computed

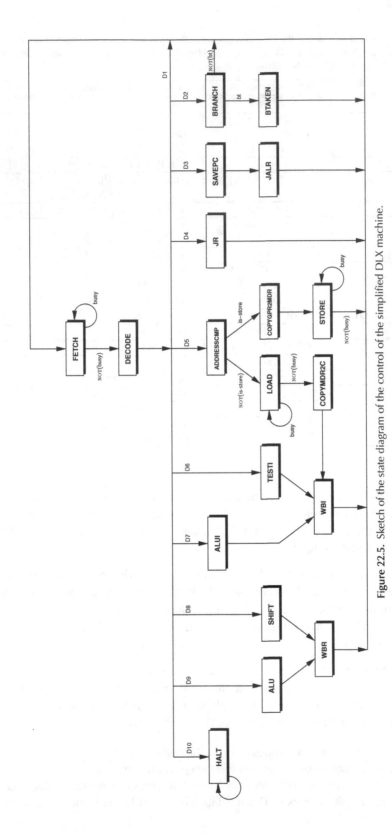

Figure 22.5. Sketch of the state diagram of the control of the simplified DLX machine.

Table 22.4. Determining the transition from the Decode state

Condition	When Does It Equal 1?
D1	special NOP
D2	beqz, bnez
D3	jalr
D4	jr
D5	lw, sw
D6	sgti, seqi, sgei, slti, snei, slei
D7	addi
D8	sll, srl
D9	add, sub, and, or, xor
D10	halt

by the control and equals one if the condition of a conditional branch is satisfied. It is computed by

$$bt = AEQZ \oplus Inst[26].$$

3. The Address-Computation state has two possible transitions. The transition to Copy-GPR2MDR is labeled $is - store$, and transition to Load is labeled NOT($is - store$). The value of $is - store$ is computed by the control and equals one if the current instruction is a store-word (sw) instruction.
4. The Decode state has 10 possible transitions. These transitions are labeled $D1 - D10$. Exactly one of these signals equals one, so that the transition is well defined. Table 22.4 describes how the values of $D1 - D10$ are determined.

22.3 RTL INSTRUCTIONS

The control governs the behavior of the datapath by its outputs, called *control outputs*. The simplest control signal is a clock-enabled signal of a register in the datapath. In each state, the control tells which registers should store new values. We specify this action by a *register transfer language* (RTL) instruction. The operands of an RTL instruction are the datapath registers, and the calculations are performed by the combinational circuits in the datapath.

We list the RTL instructions in each state of the control in Table 22.3. In this table, we refer to a control signal, the value of which is 1, as an *active* control signal.

For example, the RTL in the Fetch state is

$$IR = M[PC];$$

that is, copy the contents of $M[PC]$ to the IR. Reading from the value stored in $M[PC]$ is performed by setting a control signal MR to be high. Once the result of the read is ready, the value is stored in the IR register since the clock enable of the IR register is set to high. We denote this clock-enabled signal by $IRCE$.

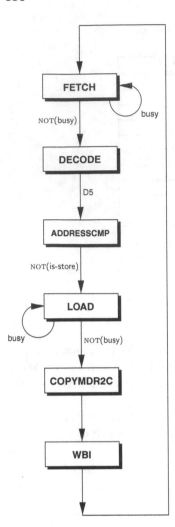

Figure 22.6. The sequence of control states that are traversed in the execution of the `lw` instruction.

22.4 EXAMPLES OF INSTRUCTION EXECUTION

In this section, we present the execution of two instructions, load-word (`lw`) and branch-equal-zero (`beqz`). Executing the rest of the instructions in the ISA is done similarly.

Executing the Load-Word Instruction. In this example, we follow the execution of the `lw` instruction step by step.

We begin by finding out the path of states that are traversed during the execution of the load-word instruction (see Figure 22.6 for a depiction of this path). This path begins with a Fetch state and ends when the control reenters the Fetch state. After the Fetch state, the control always transitions to the Decode state. The current instruction is stored in the IR. The binary representation of the instruction determines which of the internal signals D1–D10 equals one. The active internal signal in the case of a load-word instruction is D5 (see Table 22.4). Thus the control transitions from the Decode state to the AddressCMP. Since the internal signal is-store equals zero, the next transition is to the Load state. Once the busy signal is low, the control transitions to the CopyMDR2C state. The next state is the WBI state, and from there the control transitions back to the Fetch state, and the execution of the load-word instruction is finished.

For each state traversed in the execution of the load-word instruction, we execute the corresponding RTL instructions (as listed in Table 22.4). Figures 22.7 and 22.8 depict the execution of every RTL instruction in every control state in this sequence. For every state in this sequence, Figures 22.7 and 22.8 depict the active modules and the wires along which data are transferred to execute the RTL instruction. For example, in the Fetch state, the RTL instruction $IR = M[PC]$ is executed as follows:

1. Send the output of the PC to the memory controller.
2. Send the data-in signal DI to the IR environment.

This is implemented by the active control outputs MR and IRCE (see Table 22.3). The MR is input to the memory controller and the IRCE is input to the IR register. While the busy signal is high, the FSM stays in the Fetch state. When busy is low, the FSM moves to the next state in the sequence. Note that the IRCE is high during all that time, and hence, eventually, the IR samples and stores the correct value $M[PC]$, as required.

Executing the beqz Instruction. The control states that are traversed while executing the beqz instruction are depicted in Figure 22.9. Indeed, the control's internal signal bt is high iff $AEQZ \oplus IR[26] = 1$. The encoding of beqz (see Table 21.1) implies that $IR[26] = 0$, hence branch is taken iff $AEQZ = 1$. The contents of register RS1 are stored in register A, hence the decision whether or not to branch is correct. Recall that the signal AEQZ is output by the GPR (see Section 22.1.7).

22.5 SUMMARY

We described every module in the datapath by specifying its inputs, outputs, and functionality. We described the control of the DLX by its state machine. We glued all these components by describing which RTL instruction is executed in every step. We conclude the discussion by following the execution of two DLX instructions step by step.

In this chapter, we described all the details of an implementation of the simplified DLX. There is no need to learn this implementation by heart. It is merely a suggestion for an implementation. If this is the first time you have seen such an implementation, try to understand the underlying principles. The best way to see how the design works is to execute all the instructions step by step.

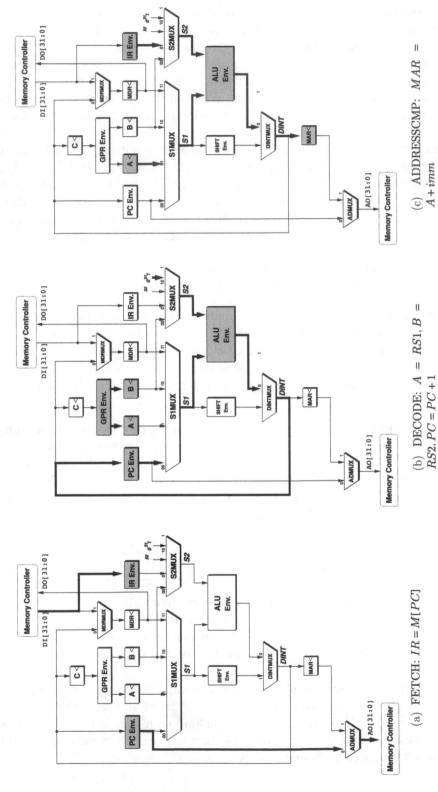

(a) FETCH: $IR = M[PC]$

(b) DECODE: $A = RS1, B = RS2, PC = PC + 1$

(c) ADDRESSCMP: $MAR = A + imm$

Figure 22.7. Execution of the RTL instructions in the FETCH, DECODE, and ADDRESSCMP control states. The active modules in the datapath in each control state are shaded, and the active 32-bit wide buses are in bold.

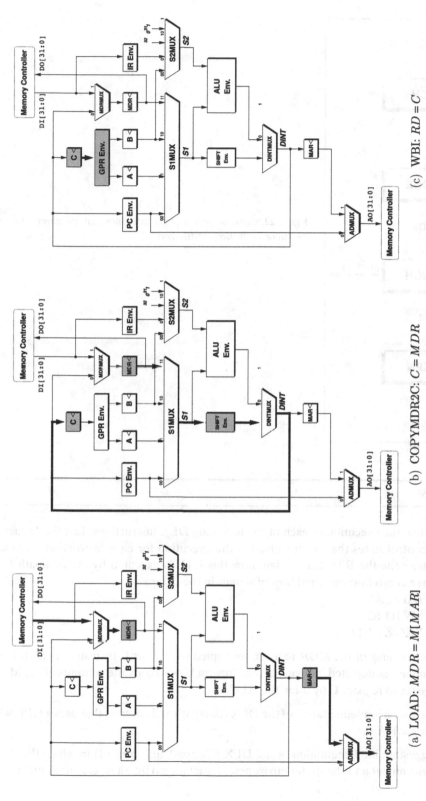

(a) LOAD: $MDR = M[MAR]$ (b) COPYMDR2C: $C = MDR$

(c) WBI: $RD = C$

Figure 22.8. Execution of the $R^{\sim}L$ instructions in the LOAD, COPYMDR2C, and WBI control states. The active modules in the datapath in each control state are shaded, and the active 32-bit wide buses are in bold.

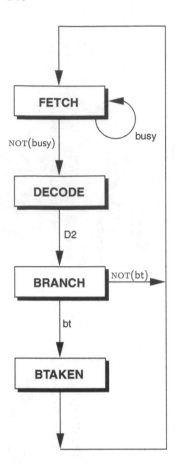

Figure 22.9. The sequence of control states that are traversed in the execution of the beqz instruction.

PROBLEMS

22.1. Follow the execution of each of the following DLX instructions. List the sequence of control states that are traversed in the execution for each instruction. For each state, write the RTL and explain how this RTL is executed by the datapath (i.e., active control outputs, and flow of signals in the datapath):
(a) JALR R2
(b) SW R1 R2 -5
(c) BEQZ R1 12

22.2. The contents of the MDR register are copied to register C by using the Shift environment, as depicted in Figure 22.8b. Suggest how to copy the contents of the MDR register to register C by using the ALU.

22.3. Suggest an implementation of the DLX (datapath and control) that uses a GPR with a single RAM.

22.4. Suggest an implementation of the DLX (datapath and control) in which the ALU environment and the shifter environment are merged into a single environment.

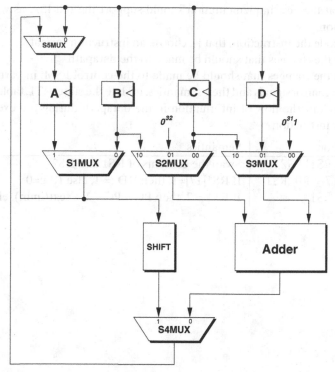

Figure 22.10. A simple data path.

22.5. Suggest an implementation of the DLX (datapath and control) in which the WBI and the WBR states in the DLX control are unified into a single state WB.

22.6. Figure 22.10 depicts a simple datapath that contains clock-enabled registers, muxes, a logical left shifter by one position, and a binary adder (without a carry-out).

Suggest how to execute the following RTL segments using as few clock cycles as possible:

(a)

$$A \leftarrow shift(A)$$

(b)

$$D \leftarrow B + C.$$

$$D \leftarrow shift(D)$$

(c)

$$A \leftarrow B + C.$$

$$A \leftarrow B$$

$$B \leftarrow A.$$

22.7. We would like to extend the DLX ISA. Suggest an implementation of the DLX (datapath and control) that supports the execution of the following new instructions.

Note that the new implementation should support the old ISA as well. For every instruction,

- Encode the instruction, that is, choose an instruction format
- List the changes that should be made to the datapath
- List the changes that should be made to the control FSM; in particular, list the new control signals and their semantics, update the state-RTL table (Table 22.3), and draw the flow of information in the datapath during the execution of the new instruction

Instruction	Semantics
swap RS1 RS2	Swap the contents of RS1 and RS2
check17 RD RS1	If RS1[17]=1, then RD := 1, else RD:=0
beq2 RS1 imm	If RS1 = 2, then PC = PC + 1 + sext(imm), else PC:=PC+1

Bibliography

Cohen, D. On holy wars and a plea for peace. *Computer*, 14(10):48–54, 1981.

Ercegovac, M.D., and T. Lang. *Digital arithmetic*. Morgan Kaufmann, 2003.

Ercegovac, M.D., J.H. Moreno, and T. Lang. *Introduction to digital systems*. John Wiley, New York, 1998.

Hopcroft, J.E., R. Motwani, and J.D. Ullman. *Introduction to automata theory, languages, and computation*. Vol. 3. Addison-Wesley, Reading, MA, 1979.

Howson, C. *Logic with trees: Introduction to symbolic logic*. Routledge, 1997.

Karnaugh, M. The map method for synthesis of combinational logic circuits. *Transactions of the AIEE. I*, 72(9):593–599, 1953.

Litman, A. Lecture notes in digital design (in Hebrew). Faculty of Computer Science, Technion, 2003.

Mattson, H.F. *Discrete mathematics with applications*. John Wiley, New York, 1993.

McCluskey, E.J. Minimization of Boolean functions. *Bell Systems Technical Journal*, 35(5):1417–1444, 1956.

McEliece, R.J., C. Ash, and R.B. Ash. *Introduction to discrete mathematics*. Random House, New York, 1989.

Müller, S.M., and W.J. Paul. *The complexity of simple computer architectures*. Springer Lecture Notes in Computer Science, Vol. 995. Springer, New York, 1996.

Patterson, D.A., and J.L. Hennessy. *Computer organization and design: The hardware/software interface*. Morgan Kaufmann, 1994.

Quine, W.V. The problem of simplifying truth functions. *American Mathematical Monthly*, 59(8):521–531, 1952.

Quine, W.V. A way to simplify truth functions. *American Mathematical Monthly*, 62(9):627–631, 1955.

Savage, J.E. *Models of computation: Exploring the power of computing*. Addison-Wesley Longman, Boston, 1997.

Ward, S.A., and R.H. Halstead. *Computation structures*. MIT Press, Cambridge, MA, 1990.

Index

Printed in the United States
By Bookmasters